Mismanagement, "Jumpers," and Morality

T0331417

"Management is taught as a discipline, which can be applied in any organization, including those in which the employees are highly skilled and highly trained. In this context the 'in-experienced' manager's tendency is to conceal his ignorance or to assume she has all the answers. This ethnography illustrates this all too frequent behavior but also shows how this difficult situation can be managed with ethics and aplomb. While the context of this study is a kibbutz in Israel, the situation applies around the world in many different types of organization, from universities, to information technology, to health care and professional service firms like lawyers and accountants. This book is a must read for any human resources manager filling such a position or any manager taking up such a role and perhaps even more importantly, for any professional managed by someone without your professional expertise."
—Roxanne Zolin, Queensland University of Technology, Australia

Executives' morality and ethics became major research topics following recent business scandals, but the research missed a major explanation of executives' immorality: career advancement by "jumping" between firms that causes ignorance of job-pertinent tacit local knowledge, tempting "jumpers" to covertly conceal this ignorance. Generating distrust, ignorance cycles and mismanagement, this choice bars performance-based career advancement and encourages immoral careerism, advancing by immoral subterfuges. Such careerism is a known managerial malady, but explaining its emergence proved challenging as managerial ignorance is covertly concealed as a dark secret on organizations' dark side by conspiracies of silence.

Managerially educated and experienced, Dr. Shapira achieved a breakthrough through a five-year semi-native anthropological study of five "jumper"-managed automatic processing plants and their parent firms. The book untangles common ignorance and immoral careerism, concealed as dark secrets by executives who "rode" on the successes of mid-level "jumpers" who high-morally risked their authority and power by admitting ignorance and trustfully learned local tacit knowledge. The opposite choice tendencies accorded power, authority, and status rankings, which made practicing immorality easier the higher one's position, suggesting that the common "jumping" between managerial careers nurtures immoral executives similar to those exposed in the recent business scandals.

Reuven Shapira is a Senior Lecturer (Emeritus) of Social Anthropology and Sociology in The Western Galilee Academic College in Acre, Israel.

Routledge Studies in Business Ethics

For a full list of titles in this series, please visit www.routledge.com

Originating from both normative and descriptive philosophical backgrounds, business ethics implicitly regulates areas of behavior which influence decision-making, judgment, behavior and objectives of the leadership and employees of an organization. This series seeks to analyze current and leading-edge issues in business ethics, and the titles within it examine and reflect on the philosophy of business, corporations and organizations pertaining to all aspects of business conduct. They are relevant to the conduct of both individuals and organizations as a whole.

Based in academic theory but relevant to current organizational policy, the series welcomes contributions addressing topics including: ethical strategy; sustainable policies and practices; finance and accountability; CSR; employee relations and workers' rights; law and regulation; economic and taxation systems.

Mismanagement, "Jumpers," and Morality

Covertly Concealed Managerial Ignorance and Immoral Careerism in Industrial Organizations

Reuven Shapira

Routledge
Taylor & Francis Group

LONDON AND NEW YORK

First published 2017
by Routledge

2 Park Square, Milton Park, Abingdon, Oxfordshire OX14 4RN
52 Vanderbilt Avenue, New York, NY 10017

Routledge is an imprint of the Taylor & Francis Group, an informa business

First issued in paperback 2019

Library of Congress Cataloging-in-Publication Data
Names: Shapira, Reuven (Sociologist), author.
Title: Mismanagement, "jumpers," and morality : covertly concealed
    managerial ignorance and immoral careerism in industrial
    organizations / by Reuven Shapira.
Description: New York : Routledge, 2017. | Series: Routledge studies
    in business ethics ; 10 | Includes bibliographical references and index.
Identifiers: LCCN 2016047500 | ISBN 9781138636378 (hardback :
    alk. paper) | ISBN 9781351795777 (ebook)
Subjects: LCSH: Management—Moral and ethical aspects. | Career
    development—Moral and ethical aspects. | Organizational sociology. |
    Industrial organization.
Classification: LCC HF5387 .S466 2017 | DDC 174/.4—dc23
LC record available at https://lccn.loc.gov/2016047500

ISBN: 978-1-138-63637-8 (hbk)
ISBN: 978-0-367-24286-2 (pbk)

Typeset in Sabon
by Apex CoVantage, LLC

To the committed ginners Uri Mor and Naif

Contents

Foreword

Mismanagement, "Jumpers," and Morality by Dr. Reuven Shapira makes for extraordinarily rewarding reading. This book gets at the root causes behind the immorality and incompetence of corporate executives, traits now exposed regularly in financial crises, bankruptcies, fraud investigations, and books on the evils of "casino capitalism." This rich anthropological study is relevant to scholars and organizational actors in management, leadership, organizational studies.

Generalization and case studies:

In an era of "big data" and quantitative social science dominance, readers may be tempted to wonder how can they learn anything from long-term studies of the management practices in a few Israeli kibbutz-owned cotton gin plants. After all, these unique organizations, based on putative democratic/ethical principles developed in an unusual and young country, represent only a tiny fraction of the industrial organizations of the world. Though the book contains wonderfully vivid, extremely long-term ethnographic case studies of inter-kibbutz cotton gins, the question remains why readers should care about inter-kibbutz organizations management if they are not interested in Israel. I experienced an analogous phenomenon when studying the Mondragón industrial cooperatives in Spain. These organizations and the general lessons to be learned from them are largely and incorrectly dismissed as irrelevant to the rest of the world. They are treated as exceptions and therefore the challenges and the support they offer for various analytical frameworks are dismissed.

In fact, the very exceptionality of such cases often tells us much more about social phenomena than studies of "typical" organizations. It is a rule of science that what happens in the world must be possible. Thus kibbutz, cooperatives, and other less common organizational forms tell us much about the boundaries of the possible in organizations. They often teach us great lessons about possibilities forgone in more conventional organizations. But they can also teach us much about processes found within them that are also found in more conventional organizations but may be seen in sharper relief in these less common venues.

This is the case in Shapira's book. The disastrous ignorance and immoral behavior of fly-in managers who are "parachuted" in by various means (patronage among powerful people, executive headhunters, and various kinds of boards of governors and trustees) has rarely been more effectively and descriptively portrayed than in Shapira's study. Based on long-term ethnographic research and on being a member of the kibbutz, which is one of the owners of the organizations he analyzes, this study documents in remarkable detail the negative impacts of importing managers and placing them at the pinnacle of a hierarchical work organization.

Logic alone would counsel against such practices because the best practices in industrial organization are based on matrix organization, flattened hierarchies, team-based organization, and the collaborative posing and resolution of organizational problems. Creating authoritarian, hierarchical organizations with Tayloristic structures reporting only to the organizational apex is a recipe for organizational failure. The hierarchy itself encourages isolation of the manager, even well-intentioned ones, from the value creation process in the organization and means that she/he will have little real-time knowledge of the context in which management decisions will have to operate. That is bad enough, but when the now popular practice of hiring in managers from outside the organization is put into such a structure, a perfect storm is created. Not only does the hierarchy isolate the leader from knowing anything meaningful about the organization but the outsider does not in fact know nearly anything relevant about the organization, its technologies, its processes, etc. Faced with changes, turbulence, and needed decisions, many such managers conceal their ignorance by detachment and/or imposing their authority and blaming others in the organizations when their plans fail. This is a recipe for predictable disaster. We have seen these processes at work in the financial firms, banks, political systems, and publically held corporations whose bosses made their only goal increasing the profits to the external shareholders and cost us all a world economic crisis. This mode of organization and concealment has undermined or demolished many organizations in the private and public sectors including manufacturing and service companies and educational institutions.

So what Shapira portrays in the inter-kibbutz cooperative environment is a vivid close-up view of why these management practices are a disaster. The book shows very clearly that it is precisely such a set of practices make it impossible for organizations operating in a turbulent, competitive environment to be learning organizations. When the boss knows next to nothing and has to cover it up, the organization cannot adapt in any meaningful way. And the rest of the stakeholders are aware of it and often disgruntled and even hostile, making for an unproductive and morally repugnant work environment.

This seemingly localized set of stories actually link directly to the leading-edge literatures in socio-technical systems design, lean production, and team-based management. Shapira's work bridges into the significant community of industrial democracy researchers starting with Trist, Herbst, Emery, and Thorsrud and continues the work of many Scandinavian work researchers, for collaborative, team-based organization is the only viable and sustainable form of industrial work organization.

In the end, Shapira's cases show that it is not merely the lack of ethics of these fly-in managers that is the core problem. Rather, their behavior and positioning prevents their organization from learning and making good decisions. Hiring practices that bring in such people and place them at the apex of a hierarchical work organization are also to blame, as are those who implement such hiring systems.

Moral commitment in social research as an analytical strength:

Finally, Shapira's book arises out of his frustrated commitments to open, competent organizational structures run on a solidary basis. Moral commitment in research is generally punished by armchair positivist social science as being "biased" and therefore not "objective." This red herring is an excuse for the moral nihilism of much social science, nihilism that is every bit as destructive as immoral mismanagement of companies. It is precisely Shapira's commitment to good, competent, and sustainable organizational systems and behavior that fueled this work and that brought the destructive effects of "fly-in" management to the fore. In this case, righteous anger and powerful ethnography coalesce to bring home the central analytical lessons in a way that cannot be ignored.

Davydd J. Greenwood
Goldwin Smith Professor of Anthropology Emeritus
Cornell University, USA

Acknowledgements

This book is the outcome of a very long intellectual journey commenced four decades ago when I became a graduate student at Tel Aviv University and took the late Dafna N. Izraeli's course on organizational power and influence, and Erik Cohen's seminar on social ecology. My previous managerial education and experience encouraged my interest in managers' role in the fast growth of the inter-kibbutz regional industry, which led to its longitudinal study for my MA and PhD theses, in which Emanuel Marx has been my prime teacher, reader, and mentor, a role in which he persevered long afterwards, while Dafna Izraeli read some drafts and gave helpful criticism. The late Israel Shepher helped much by careful reading and commenting on drafts of my book manuscript *Anatomy of Mismanagement* (Hebrew) and Gideon M. Kressel helped by his critique of papers through which the ideas of my second book, *Transforming Kibbutz Research* (2008), were cemented into a coherent structure (at least in my mind). Thanks go also to many other Israeli and international colleagues who aided these projects and enriched my thinking.

In 2006 I commenced drafting the present book, for which many scholars assisted in clearing up my many misunderstandings and provided me with crucial supportive critique, commenting on drafts, papers and parts of the book. Helpful critique of the first partial draft was given by Maxim Voronov, and dialogue with Sharon Stevens about the role of public intellectuals helped direct my efforts. Guido Möllering, Roxanne Zolin, and Antoinette Weibel furthered my knowledge of trust research, which was crucial for the analyses, and I was further assisted by dialogue with Rajiv Vashist and Sara Hernandez. Shay Tzafrir helped by reviewing my 2008 book, which was essential for contextualizing the studied plants, and very helpful were comments on my papers received from students of cooperatives, Yohanan Stryjan, Holger Blisse, Benedicte Brogger, Jerker Nilsson, Paul Jones, Virajlal Sapovadia, Roger Spear, Iiro Jussila, Silvia Gherardi, and Ryszard Stocki, whose book (with others, not published in English) *Total Participation Management* encouraged suggesting solutions to the problems analyzed. Both Martin Parker and Gary A. Fine helped considerably by repeatedly pointing out weaknesses in my ethnographic proof, while encouraging submission of articles that helped clarify my ideas. Also helpful were comments on papers by Paul Sanders, Brigid Carroll, John Weeks, Dennis Tourish, and Joseph Bower. When I attempted to analyze the lack of managerial leadership, my papers were improved by the comments of David Collinson, James O'Toole, Jennifer Jones, Yeliz Eseryel, and especially Bryan Poulin, who also hosted me for lecturing on my findings at Lakehead University (Canada). Of special importance were comments by Harry Collins and Robert Evans, whose studies of science enhanced my understanding of how "jumpers" cope with ignorance, while Tom D. Wilson helped by his critique of the early formulation of covertly concealed managerial ignorance and Robert Whipple concerning trust. My analysis of managerial morality benefitted much from dialogue with John Thoms, Joanne Ciulla, and especially Davydd J. Greenwood, who for years reviewed my papers and was helpful and encouraging in other ways. Halvor Holtskog, who reviewed the entire manuscript and Joe Raelin provided much help with the later stages of the writing. Of some help was the candid critique by journal editors Gayle Baugh, Andrew Delios, Andy Adcroft, and Paul Adler that came with article rejections.

Special thanks go to Martin Kett, Barbara Doron, and especially to Rachel Kessel whose questions while making my English readable cleared up much confusion and, revealed many unclear paragraphs. However, any mistakes contained in this book are my own.

I am also grateful for the financial help I received from Kibbutz Gan Shmuel along the years, which has helped my research in many other ways as well. Last but not least is the support of my family, which has made this lengthy journey possible.

Glossary

CCMI—Covertly Concealed Managerial Ignorance.

I-KOs—Inter-Kibbutz Organizations of which I-KRCs are one type.

I-KRCs—Inter-Kibbutz Regional Cooperatives called "Regional Enterprises"; each is owned by and serves tens of kibbutzim of a certain region.

"Jumping"—Career advancement through alternating managerial jobs among organizations (e.g., Downs 1966).

Kibbutzim (singular: Kibbutz)—Communal egalitarian agro-industrial settlements which, *inter alia*, grow cotton.

LLCT—Leadership Life Cycle Theory (e.g., Hambrick 2007).

Im-C—Immoral Careerism; advancing one's career by non-performance, immoral means.

OPM—Other People's Money; the executive tendency to waste public money.

"Parachuting"—An Israeli term for the import of an outside "jumper" called "parachuted manager" to an executive office.

Pe'ilim (singular: *Pa'il*)—Kibbutz member managers and administrators of inter-kibbutz organizations whose kibbutz received for their work either no salary or a uniform one.

PM—Plant Manager; mostly a *pa'il* from one of the kibbutzim that owned the gin plant.

Rotatzia (rotation)—A kibbutz-declared norm of limiting managerial office for a few years, formally aimed at preventing oligarchy but enhancing it in practice.

S&GH—Stripper & Ground Harvester, a gin plant's first cleaning machine of raw cotton (e.g., www.lummus.com).

TM—Technical manager in charge of both ginning and equipment maintenance.

Preface

Extremes can identify the phenomenon as no other means. According to Hanna Arendt's 1963 book, the vice that promoted Eichmann to a high Nazi position from which he organized the industrialized extermination of millions of Jews and others, i.e. immoral careerism (Im-C for short), is a common vice of mass society. In view of the business scandals in the last decade, managerial ethics and morality has become a major topic of organizational research; this is not true of Im-C. For example, the 58 Sage journals of management and organization studies have 966 article abstracts that contain the word "career," but only five that contain either "careerism" or "careerist," though already Riesman's 1950 book decried American managers' transition from high-moral serving of the social good to pursuing private ends at others' expense. Likewise, ethnographers found Im-C prevalent among corporate managers, but they missed a major explanation of executives' immorality: career advancement by "jumping" between firms that causes ignorance of job-pertinent tacit know-how and *phronesis* (Greek for practical wisdom), tempting "jumpers" to defend authority and status by covertly concealed managerial ignorance (hereafter: CCMI). CCMI causes distrust and ignorance cycles, which generate mismanagement that bars performance-based career advancement and encourages Im-C, advancing by bluffs, power abuses, scapegoating, and other self-serving subterfuges. Though Im-C is a known malady of large organizations, its explanation missed the tendency of "jumpers" to use CCMI, probably because this use remained on organizations' dark side, kept as a dark secret; that is, its very existence was a secret.

"Jumpers" are common: one study found that 58% of US executives were "jumpers" and another found this true of 33% of CEOs in the 500 S&P firms, but the ample organizational knowledge and management learning research missed a crucial question in this regard: Which practices do "jumpers" use as they face inevitable ignorance of job-essential local tacit know-how and *phronesis* of their new job that subordinates have due to specialized education, practicing jobs, and learning within communities of practitioners?

Learning local know-how and *phronesis* requires vulnerable involvement that exposes one's ignorance and gains locals' trust and will to share tacit knowledge. However, ignorance exposure diminishes authority, which may be regained only if learning succeeds. Due to large knowledge gaps, "jumpers" often see little prospect for successful learning, avoid admitting their ignorance, use their powers for CCMI, generate distrust and ignorance cycles, as well as mismanagement that bars performance-based career advancement and encourages Im-C. But exposing the emergence of Im-C proved challenging both due to CCMI and because anthropologists did not study how managers handle their own ignorance as they could not be participant observers as managers. Managerial education and experience plus anthropological education enabled me to achieve a breakthrough in a five-year semi-native anthropological study of five "jumper"-managed automatic processing plants and their parent firms. The book untangles Im-C emergence, how CCMI user executives became immoral and "rode" on the successes of mid-level managers, who high-morally risked their authority and power by admitting ignorance and trustfully learning local tacit knowledge. The opposite morality accorded inverted power, authority, and status rankings, which made practicing Im-C easier the higher one's position, suggesting that the common "jumping" careers nurtures immoral executives, similar to those exposed in the recent business scandals.

1   Practicing Covertly Concealed
Managerial Ignorance

This is a study of immoral mismanagement by intelligent, educated, and experienced but mostly job-ignorant managers and executives, who advanced careers by "jumping" between organizations. The books teach that effective management requires managers to learn and know a lot, hence much research and countless writings have been devoted to the study of organizational knowledge and management learning. However, one crucial question was missed: Which practices do managers use when they are promoted and face inevitable ignorance of job-essential local know-how and *phronesis* (Greek for practical wisdom; Flyvbjerg 2001), which some subordinates know well due to specialized education and/or practicing jobs and learning in communities of practitioners (Orr 1996)? In order to learn from the knowledgeable it is necessary to admit one's own ignorance, but such admission is problematic, degrading one's managerial authority. Ethnographer Blau (1955) found that senior professionals in a US enforcement agency defended their professional authority by consulting only with juniors rather than with senior peers when facing the need for more knowledge to cope with especially problematic tasks, avoiding exposure of their ignorance to the latter, who decided one's professional authority in the department. Ignorance exposure is even harder for an executive: Intel CEO Grove (1996: 144) hesitated much before admitting his ignorance of computer programming to Intel's programmers when he wanted to learn their job secrets prior to leading a corporate transformation that required such know-how.

Many executives avoid such admissions, using their power to conceal and/or camouflage their ignorance by means of bluffs, abuses, double talk, shirking problematic tasks, and other subterfuges, scapegoating others for resulting own mistakes and failures and concealing these immoral deeds as dark secrets, i.e., their very existence is secret, veiled on organizations' dark side by conspiracies of silence.[1] Only few studied managerial ignorance, but these few found it common.[2] Studies of managerial effectiveness concur: Ineffective managers advanced careers more than effective ones (Luthans 1988); among Gallup-studied 80,000 managers only a few were effective (Buckingham and Coffman 1999), as found by others as well.[3] Many ethnographers, from Collins et al. (1946) to Mehri (2005), uncovered managerial ignorance of employees' know-how and *phronesis* as admitted corporate CEOs,[4] while an executive at a large US industrial corporation explained executives' incompetence thus:

> "In the 1960s we thought we were really terrific. We petted ourselves on the back a lot because every decision was so successful. Then came the recession, and we couldn't do anything to stop it. . . . it became clear that we don't know the first thing about how to make this enterprise work"
> (Kanter 1993[1977]: 53).

However, neither Kanter nor other ethnographers studied executives' handling of their own ignorance (Roberts 2012). Ethnographers' findings concerning managers' bluffs, power abuses, scapegoating, and other such subterfuges, suggest that by these immoral means they defended authority and jobs, concealing mistakes, ignorance, and incompetence.[5] However, managers' morality was not grasped as a personal strategic choice (e.g., Mintzberg 1987) that affected ignorance handling, and the finding that managers used immoral means was rarely related to covertly concealed managerial ignorance (CCMI for short). Such means are kept as a dark secret, seemingly explaining how the research missed CCMI as a common strategic personal choice. Also stupidity research missed CCMI and explained mismanagement just by psychological dysfunction (Sternberg 2002), although ignorance escorts promotion: one takes charge of at least some unfamiliar units/functions, lacking their "[p]ractical wisdom . . . [which is] emerging developmentally within an unceasing flow of activities, in which practitioners are inextricably immersed" (Shotter and Tsoukas 2014b: 377). However, her/his authority and power enable avoidance of immersion and, as cited, many found that managers often use immoral means to veil CCMI and resulting incompetence because

> ". . . it is not the generalized knowledge of science that is required in prudently leading people and handling human affairs, but a special sensitivity to the unique contours of the circumstances in which leaders happen to operate each time"
> (Shotter and Tsoukas 2014a: 240).

A review of managerial stupidity studies concurs: "academic and practical intelligence are not highly correlated," managers develop practical intelligence (*phronesis*) by sharpening their abilities, while simultaneously increasing and narrowing them (Wagner 2002: 60). "*Phronesis* [is] knowing what to do and how to do it, at the right time and with the right people, with the right mix of persuasion and challenge and the right sense of what to leave unsaid and undone. . . . the crucial knowledge . . . is knowing which facts and theories matter, when to use which skills, and who should perform actions" (Schweigert 2007: 339–340). *Phronesis* develops by learning local tacit know-how through ignorance-exposing authority-risking vulnerable immersion in practitioners' deliberations that engenders trust, knowledge sharing, and problem-solving.[6] Managers' mistakes, failures, and incompetence are explicable by CCMI through using immoral means which are kept dark secrets, veiled on organizations' dark side, and by employees' avoidance of sharing knowledge with distrusted managers who use immoral means, secrecy, and information and knowledge as control means.[7]

Managerial morality and ethics became a major research topic after Enron, Worldcom, and other such scandals,[8] but research missed the possibility that executives' amorality stemmed from opting for CCMI that led to immoral careerism (hereafter Im-C) because CCMI barred moral career advancement through performance. According to Arendt (1963) the common vice of mass society that promoted Eichmann to a high Nazi position from which he organized the industrialized extermination of millions of Jews and others, was Im-C. Dalton's (1959: 152–157) mid-levelers asserted that their bosses advanced by immoral, non-performance means and many authors, from Riesman (1950) to Wilson (2011), found that managerial Im-C was all too common.[9] However, the etiological connection between Im-C, CCMI, incompetence, and mismanagement, were missed probably because mostly managers were not aware of their own ignorance (Kruger and Dunning 1999) and because they used status, authority, and power to conceal their ignorance as a dark secret.

This begs major unanswered questions: Was CCMI largely missed as a dark secret that explains the common vice of Im-C? Does managerial career advancement by "jumping" between firms (Downs 1966) as is common these days[10] encourage CCMI and Im-C that result in mismanagement? Do mid-levelers further mismanagement by emulating a "jumper" boss's CCMI and Im-C or does contrary choice by some of them amend her/his mismanagement and help its continuity?[11] Does such an ignorant boss advance career by "riding" on mid-levelers' successes, which encourages her/his CCMI and Im-C? Do prospects of career advancement by the auspices of patrons rather than by performance encourage CCMI and Im-C? To what degree are the two encouraged by contextual factors such as an oligarchic field in which sponsored mobility is dominant?[12]

It is not incidental that organizational anthropologists rarely studied executives (Welker et al. 2011), heeding the advice given by sages of old: "Don't judge others until you have stood in their shoes." They faced a major barrier: they could not be executives and "stand in their shoes"; their participant observations as workers did not uncover higher-ups' dark secrets. For example, Mehri (2005: 199), an engineer at Toyota's R&D department, found that its new manager was "incompetent and spineless" and that the previous manager put "his puppet in [his] place so he [could] keep pulling the strings from another department," but untangled nothing about higher-ups' role in the fiasco, for instance whether they disengaged it to conceal their own ignorance of the expertise required of this "puppet" to manage effectively.

Semi-Native Longitudinal Anthropology Exposed Executives' Dark Secrets

In order to untangle the dark secrets of executives' and managers' ignorance concealment anthropologists must become insider-outsiders (Gioia et al. 2010) among them, while in order to assess their expertise levels (Flyvbjerg 2001: 10–16) and how these impacted behaviors such as CCMI an ethnographer needs managerial education, referred expertise, i.e., expertise in other action domains that facilitates the learning of local practices, their language, and interactional expertise—that is, expertise that does not make one a full expert but enables fruitful communication with experts.[13] This enables fruitful interviewing of the executives, subordinate managers, employees, ex-employees free to criticize higher-ups, and trade experts to untangle executives' personal strategies and functioning. Then an anthropologist "enters executives' shoes" and explain them as if s/he is one of them who witness their dark secrets such as bluffs, power abuses, and other subterfuges that conceal ignorance, incompetence, and a lack of experience-based learning (Morgan 2015). Lengthy fieldwork is also required in order to gain full trust, openness, and managers' genuine rapport unattainable by a temporary employee, the organizational anthropologist's usual status. Moreover, when managers practice CCMI, secrecy prevails since even speaking of one's knowledge may have negative effects by generating pressure to reveal knowledge, which superiors can use against one's interests (Mehri 2005). Hence, an anthropologist may need years to become trusted enough to gain access to local secrets.

I overcame these barriers by a unique semi-native longitudinal anthropology: A native anthropologist studies his/her own people and being too close to them s/he may adopt their particularistic views (Narayan 1993), while outsider ethnographers often miss locals' sincere views and/or other decisive insiders' knowledge (Gioia et al. 2013: 19). I have avoided both by studying five cotton gin plants and their parent inter-kibbutz regional cooperatives (hereafter I-KRCs), each owned by dozens of kibbutzim and managed by their members called *pe'ilim* (singular: *pa'il*), which emulated Israeli capitalist firm managers. Like them I was a kibbutz member, had a similar managerial education, and had experienced management at my kibbutz's automatic processing plant that its problems resembled those of plants studied; unlike other ethnographers I knew some managers long before the study and the high-moral kibbutz context that socialized them.[14] I approached *pe'ilim* as their peer and interviews often turned into openly discussed common problems, and I gained access to their documents. I entered the field to explain its culture like other anthropologists, without choosing a research design in advance. I aimed at thick description (Geertz 1973) based on variegated data collected while participating in local life and sensing subjects' feelings, building much mutual trust with informants and achieving openness so that full, reliable, accurate, and sincere information led to my analysis.[15]

However, the present book utilizes much more extensive knowledge of mismanagement, since after studying gin plants for five years I studied it in other inter-kibbutz organizations (hereafter I-KOs) and in kibbutzim, as will be explained below. However, I use the analytic strategy of developing case description (Yin 1988: 107) to ground my theory.

The Main Theory

Ample literature has been devoted to educating executives by management science theories and findings, but Shotter and Tsoukas (2014a: 240) suggest that something else is required:

> "... it is not the generalized knowledge of science that is required in prudently leading people. . . but a special sensitivity to the unique contours of the circumstances . . . an ability to be guided . . . by contingent sensing as each new step brings us into new circumstances, where pre-established rules or recipes cannot . . . apply."

However, executives who conceal ignorance to maintain an authoritative image may not try to acquire "a special sensitivity to the unique contours of the circumstances" and "an ability to be guided . . . by contingent sensing . . . [of] new circumstances" since in order to be motivated for such learning one must know why "pre-established rules or recipes cannot, in principle, apply" to these circumstances and be aware of the need to acquire "practical wisdom and judgment . . . emerging developmentally within an unceasing flow of activities" (Shotter and Tsoukas 2014b: 377). These authors and many others emphasize the decisiveness of tacit local know-how and *phronesis* acquired by practicing jobs, as Flyvbjerg (2006: 362) emphasized: "*phronesis* requires *experience*." According to Schön (1983: 49) "our knowing is ordinarily tacit, implicit in our patterns of action and our feel for the stuff with which we are dealing," and similarly Orlikowski (2002: 249): know-how and *phronesis* are "constituted and reconstituted as actors engaged in the world of practice."[16]

However, executives often do not know how lower ranks "engage the world of practice," cope with work problems, and solve them through "constituting and reconstituting" know-how and *phronesis*; as shown by ethnographers, executives' job routines rarely encourage engaging such coping and feeling "the stuff with which" employees are dealing;[17] they can defend knowledgeable images, authority, and power by avoiding ignorance-exposing engaging employees' problem-solving. Ignorance of at least some of employees' know-how and *phronesis* is unavoidable as with promotion one takes charge of unfamiliar units/functions which s/he did not experience, have no feel of their stuff, do not know their staffs' expertises, and have little if any of their tacit know-how and *phronesis*. Research did not allude to such managerial ignorance, alluding only to problems of acquiring skills with promotion from the ranks. The new executives may learn the processes by which the products or services are produced, but might not learn how these processes function and the tacit know-how and *phronesis* of operators, technicians, and foremen who practice these processes.[18] To learn these executives must indwell and assimilate in employees' problem-solving,[19] but to do this they need to cognize their own ignorance, which is rare (Kruger and Dunning 1999) and to cognize that managerial problems are often incorrectly formulated and/or ill-defined, lacking essential information, and have no single correct answer; only sincere cooperative efforts with knowledgeable locals generate correct formulations and solutions.[20]

However, like others I have found that locals' sincere cooperation with and help for the executive's learning requires her/his practicing ignorance-exposing trust-creating vulnerable involvement.[21] Managers' trustful relations with employees are essential for knowledge sharing, learning, problem-solving, decision-making, and innovating.[22] But as explained, trust-creating ignorance exposure diminishes one's authority, hence it is often avoided unless encouraged by circumstances (Grove 1996: 144) and/or by one's habitus (Bourdieu 1990), past successes (Shapira 1995b, 2013), and prospects of learning due to pertinent expertise or referred expertise (Collins and Sanders 2007). Ignorance-exposing vulnerable involvement leads to virtuous trust and learning cycles, while ignorance-concealing detachment or seductive-coercive autocracy engenders distrust and ignorance cycles, summarized thus (Shapira 2015):

Table 1.1 Ignorance-Exposing Vulnerable Involvement versus CCMI

Virtuous Trust and Learning Cycles versus	*Vicious Distrust and Ignorance Cycles*
Managers' opting for ignorance-exposing vulnerable involvement and avoiding use of information as a means of control creates trust relationships with employees	Managers' choice of either detachment or coercive-seductive autocracy conceals ignorance; they use information to control employees and engender their distrust
↓	↓
Trusting relationships engender openness and knowledge sharing that enhance managers' learning, correct decisions employees' motivation and successes	Distrust causes employees' secrecy that inhibits managers' learning, causing mistaken decisions, indecision, failures, destructive conflicts, and use of subterfuges
↓	↓
Successes further the above process; managers gain interactional expertise and job-competence, enhancing innovation	Immorality furthers secrecy and learning inhibition; managers' incompetence adds mistakes and failures enhances conservatism
↓	↓
The resulting innovation-prone, high-trust culture enhances learning from innovation mistakes, furthers managers' knowledge and the virtuous trust and learning cycle	Conservatism spares some mistakes but causes others' brain drain, furthering the negative effects of a low-trust culture and the vicious distrust and ignorance cycle

Managers' habituses, expertises, perceived vulnerability, psychological safety, efficacy, prospects of career advancement, and other reasons impact their alternative choices.[23] Burns and Stalker (1961) called high-trust, innovation-prone cultures "organic" as against "mechanic," low-trust, conservative-prone cultures. The former are rarer, as suggested by cited bureaucracy ethnographies and cited literatures on trust/distrust, on the rarity of effective managers, on managerial ignorance, on organizations' dark side, and managerial careerism literature. The above model helps explain this rarity by managers' use of information and knowledge as means of control while defending their authority and power by practicing CCMI. With the "practice turn" organization studies rediscovered the concept of practice. A major advantage of the "practice lens" is its critical power,[24] but organizational ethnography has not used this "lens" to analyze the impact of executives' ignorance and rarely studied executives (Welker et al. 2011), while formal studies failed to untangle their dark secrets, including their own ignorance, which they often missed, and hence could not inform students of it (Harvey et al. 2001; Kruger and Dunning 1999).

The Focal Plant and the Case Studies

Israeli kibbutzim, which owned the researched plants, were intended as high-trust high-moral democratic communities: their abstemious officers did not receive extra remuneration, had only few status symbols, and used scanty weak sanctions (Rosner 1993). *Pe'ilim* executives and managers of I-KRCs (inter-kibbutz regional cooperatives) were ex-kibbutz officers; thus one would expect to see high-moral democratic management, but the opposite was found. For five years I intermittently visited the focal Merkaz high-capacity automatic cotton gin plant (a pseudonym, as are all names hereafter) and its I-KRC's well-kept industrial park, during which I held both many casual talks and lengthy open interviews of up to an hour and a half with 168 current and former plant managers (hereafter PMs) and staff, both *pe'ilim* and hired employees, plus 24 executives of its parent I-KRC, as well as cotton growers, some of them more than once (interviews recorded in writing; many were home interviews with a transcript of 565 folio pages). Intensive participant observation was made as a shift worker along the focal plant's 3.5-month high season when it operated non-stop 24/7 and included visits to the other shifts. My registrar job enabled me some writing during the shift and further details were added after it, resulting in a 791-page observation journal. Then I toured four other gin plants, observed their premises, and interviewed 63 present and past executives and managers (331-page transcript). The longitudinal ethnographying, with free access to focal plant documents and 255 interviewees of all echelons both past and present, plus many informal talks with others, made it possible to thoroughly check all major information and assertions, avoiding outsiders' naivety. It enabled experiencing managers' experiences, understanding them from within, and having thick descriptions, judging them as if I stood in their shoes.[25] Moreover, I analyzed and re-analyzed my data several times over the last 30 years, repeatedly returning from aggregate dimensions to first-order concepts (Gioia et al. 2013).

Merkaz had two processing units in some 2,000- and 2,500-square meter halls full of large noisy machines connected by huge pipes, and the larger unit in which I worked was operated by some 240 electric motors of approximately 3000 horsepower. The two together processed 650–700 tons of raw cotton daily during the high season, September–December. Raw cotton was brought to the yard and then to processing units in compressed stacks of eight tons on 6 x 2.5 meter metal stretches which stood on six one-meter-long iron legs transported by specially built tractor-pulled hydraulic carriages (Figure 1.3). The main product, bales of quarter-ton cotton fibers, were stored in three stores, some 2,000 square meters each, until shipped to spinning mills, mostly abroad, while the cotton seeds were lorry-transported to oil extraction plants.

Merkaz's permanent staff included 10 *pe'ilim* and 17 hired employees, supplemented by some 70 hired workers in the high season, when operations continued 24/7. Seven *pe'ilim* managed the plant: the PM, his deputy, the technical manager (hereafter TM), his deputy, the stores manager, garage manager, and office manager. The plant was a part of Merkaz Regional Enterprises I-KRC owned by some 40 kibbutzim with some 12,000 inhabitants and handling much of their agricultural input and output in six plants with some $US350 million sales (e.g., Niv and Bar-On 1992). It was administered by some 200 *pe'ilim* and operated by some 650 hired employees (see Merkaz I-KRC and the gin plant organizations charts below). Kibbutzim received uniform salaries for *pe'ilim*'s work whose formal term of office was five years, in accord with the supposedly egalitarian *rotatzia* (rotation; e.g., Gabriel and Savage 1981) norm at kibbutzim, but senior *pe'ilim* violated it, retaining jobs for decades or moving from one I-KO executive job to another (Shapira 1995a, 2005).

I commenced my research by interviewing the Merkaz CEO and 23 executives who portrayed themselves as servants of the kibbutzim, repeating the mantra: "The Regional Cooperatives are the extended arm of the kibbutzim." However, I discerned obliviousness to inefficiencies and ineffectiveness, preference of growth and technological virtuosity to obtain power, prestige, privileges, and tenure (Galbraith 1971). While the executives of 20 local kibbutz plants, studied by me earlier, sought effectiveness, efficiency, and innovation to succeed in competitive markets, Merkaz plants had no direct competition, marketing their produce through national marketers, some of which were partly owned by kibbutzim and managed by *pe'ilim*. Such was the national Cotton Production and Marketing Council, which assessed cotton fiber quality and marketed cotton in Israel and abroad. All 10 Israeli cotton gin plants belonged to I-KRCs, owner-kibbutzim obliged to use the services of their specific I-KRC, and paid using a "cost plus" system known for the inefficiency it encouraged.

I studied Merkaz cotton gin plant intensively and four other gin plants less, as depicted. Early interviews and intermittent observations raised the suspicion that managers were mostly ignorant of the plant's uncertainty domains (Crozier 1964) of technical, technological, operational, and skilled manpower problems, while the efficient cotton growing by kibbutzim ensured plants' viability despite mismanagement with the "cost plus" system. Coping with the problems of plants' uncertainty domains was learned exclusively on the job; hence I held mini-seminars with nationally renowned ginning experts, learned plants' problems, and acquired "know-that" before learning "know-how" (Brown 2001) by participant observation as bales registrar.

Then I was so knowledgeable that technicians and foremen asked me why I would not succeed their intelligent and educated but ignorant of ginning PM, a *pa'il* whom I called Shavit. I used this knowledge for the less intensive study of the four other gin plants and found that only five of 32 outsider executives studied, three PMs and two CEOs, were effectively and knowledgeably job-competent. These findings corresponded with observations by Arbiv, a past TM of Northern Gin Plant and top ginning expert who became an R&D engineer at the US labs of the world's largest ginning equipment producer (hereafter: WLGEP).

> "The manager of the Coastal Gin Plant who also headed the national Gin Plant Association reached the conclusion that a good technical manager is just a good mechanic and did a bad service to the entire industry. Take Gornitzki from the Coastal Gin Plant—he's an excellent mechanic but during his first five years as technical manager he had no idea about cotton. Fortunately for him, he had two senior shift foremen who did know something about it and saved him . . . And do you think he knows anything about it today? Did you see the automatic sampler he designed? Did you see how he failed with the sampler he wanted to construct by himself to save US $20,000 by avoiding purchasing it from an experienced manufacturer?"

Observing this failure and a few others when visiting other plants, including the failed Gornitzki's sampler, clarified the large gap between a good mechanic and a professional TM of a high-capacity automatic cotton gin plant. This gap was indicated by another top-level expert based on his 20 years of experience as the head of national cotton fiber grading laboratory, a graduate of a major professional school in Mississippi whose lab's grading decided Israeli cotton fiber bales' market value:

> "Only very few people knew the [ginning] trade . . . At each gin plant there was the administrative [plant] manager who did not last long, a *pa'il* whose circulation decided continuity rather than the gin plant [needs], this was the worst defect, because until one learns the subject [of ginning] . . . a plant manager needs at least 5–6 years. The

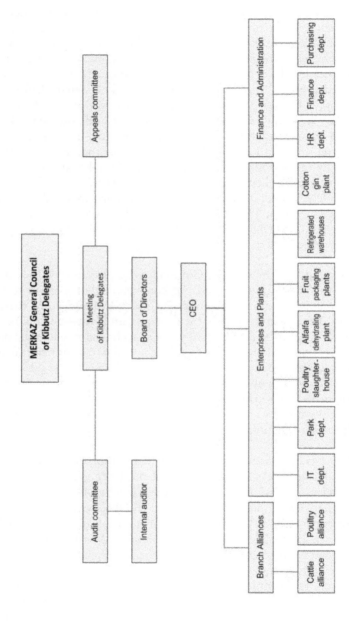

Figure 1.1 Organization Chart of Merkaz I-KRC

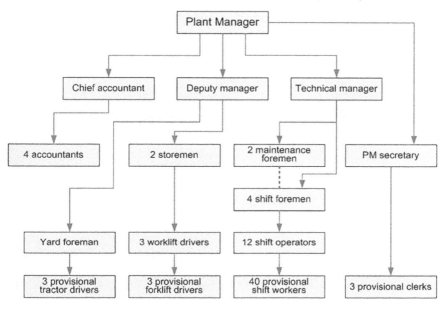

Figure 1.2 Organization Chart of the Merkaz Gin Plant during the High Season

professionals who did the ginning, its changes and innovations were hired mechanics, often good mechanics who knew nothing about cotton— there was a huge gap between [knowing] the technical side and understanding cotton. The Gin Plant Association provided some training which was minimal, some [professional] Americans were invited to train these technicians, but often the latter did not have enough know-how to overcome the complex problems."

Job-Ignorance and Managerial Conservatism and Stupidity

My data corroborated these portrayals of gin PMs and TMs as mostly job-ignorant and stupidly conservative but my explanation of the etiology of common ignorance and incompetence differs meaningfully. Before presenting it, here is one example of stupid conservatism: in the late 1960s some US gin plants developed a mechanized transportation system of raw cotton from the fields by a specially equipped lorry called Mover, which self-loads an eight-ton compressed stack of raw cotton, and then transports and unloads it into an automatic feeder, which feeds the cotton gradually into the ginning process. Some Israeli cotton growers and gin plant managers saw this transportation system at work in 1971, but the first Mover and an automatic feeder were only installed in Israel in 1978. During this period the booming Israeli cotton industry ignored the US innovation and heavily invested in expanding the locally built tractor-pulled carriage transportation system. Merkaz's farmers used some 100 such carriages and some 2,000 steel stretches to transport cotton from as far as 50 kilometers, meaning a two-hour drive instead of a lorry's 45–50 minutes (Figure 1.3). In the early 1980s Merkaz's Movers and automatic feeders spared some 85 drivers plus 12 workers at the two processing units.

Three Generations of Raw Cotton Transport Technology

Tractor-pulled

Cages (1960s)

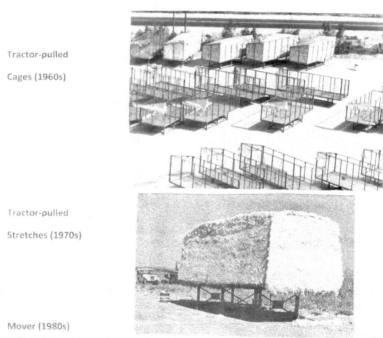

Tractor-pulled

Stretches (1970s)

Mover (1980s)

Figure 1.3 Three Generations of Raw Cotton Transport Technology

Cost could not explain the Mover system's delay for a decade; enlarging the less efficient transportation system to suit needs was no less costly, while sparing its extra operation costs would have repaid the investment in Movers and automatic feeders within a short period. Thus, the only plausible explanation was executives' ignorance and authority-defending stupid conservatism, as asserted by Merkaz Deputy PM Danton, an ex-cotton growing manager who proposed the adoption of Movers four years earlier.

The prime cause of the job-ignorance and stupid conservatism of almost all CEOs studied, most PMs and a third of TMs, was their practice of CCMI and Im-C, due to the dominance of I-KRCs' management by "jumper" CEOs: all 10 CEOs in the five I-KRCs I studied or about whom I have information were outsider *pe'ilim* "parachuted" to their jobs, a term used in Israel for the direct import of high-status outsiders to executive offices; only two of them from Northern I-KRC chose ignorance-exposing vulnerably involved management of its plants and encouraged similar involvement and virtuous trust and learning cycles of its PMs and TMs, leading to excelling in both efficiency and effectiveness (see Chapter 4). The other eight CEOs were mostly detached and ignorant of gin plants' uncertainty domains (e.g., Crozier 1964): technical, technological, operational, and skilled manpower problems, much like the avoidance of such domains by British executives (Armstrong 1987), avoidance which research of high-involvement work practices missed (e.g., Pohler and Luchak 2014). Similar to laypeople, CEOs mostly preferred to deal with well-known and understood domains of action, avoiding unacquainted domains and problems for which their know-how and *phronesis* might have proved insufficient/impertinent, requiring them to endanger their authority and job by exposing their ignorance in order to learn and function effectively. But unlike laypeople, managers had the power, leeway, and means of concealing low morality and stupid ignorance by avoidance, secrecy, power abuses, and camouflages. For instance, not once throughout the 3.5-month high season of my participant observation did Merkaz CEO Zelikovich visit the processing unit in which the new S&GH machine failed, causing heavy damages for both the plant and cotton growers. This fiasco (detailed below) led to the late replacement of PM Shavit and TM Avi a year later, but not when the two ignorant *pe'ilim* should have been replaced, when they failed to solve the S&GH problem.

In addition to the detached CCMI that defended their authority, CEOs dominated I-KRCs through their formal powers enhanced by using information control and the kibbutz field's institutionalized norms of *rotatzia* and "parachutings." Contrary to formal aims, *rotatzia* enhanced oligarchic rule since the short terms of managers weakened them against CEOs, whose power often obtained unlimited continuity and/or enabled circulation to new executive jobs (Shapira 2005). Premature successions of failed *pe'ilim* managers were presented as "normal *rotatzia*," sparing CEOs the need to admit failed nominations according to loyalty rather than competence; likewise, *rotatzia* served to camouflage the suppression and ousting of critical success-empowered innovative mid-managers and the "parachuting" of loyalist *pe'ilim* instead (e.g., Gouldner 1954; see the case of Thomas below).

Rotatzia stipulated fixed job terms of several years, presumably to prevent oligarchization of *pe'ilim*, while the "parachuting" of ginning-ignorant *pe'ilim* rather than promoting knowledgeable hired ginning practitioners was officially aimed at keeping I-KRCs tuned to the interests of kibbutzim. Both norms were created in the 1930s–1940s: *pe'ilim* established and managed I-KRCs and their *rotatzia* was implemented in the name of egalitarianism but enhanced the hegemony of tenured prime leaders of the four kibbutz federations called "The Movements" considered irreplaceable, similar to spiritual leaders such as Jewish rabbis, while beneath them the more powerful I-KO CEOs, including I-KRC CEOs, prevented their own *rotatzia*.[26] The short terms of *pe'ilim* discouraged them from acquiring local know-how and *phronesis*, as the ex-head of the fiber-grading laboratory pointed out (p. 9), hampering trust (Norman et al. 2010), cooperation (Axelrod 1984), and creativity (Jaques 1990).

Combining *rotatzia* with "parachutings" was not unique, nor was its negative impact: US and Israeli armed forces use them despite experts' critique;[27] Imperial China used them for centuries with disastrous effects; ancient Athens suffered grave consequences as a result of the annual *rotatzia* of civil servants; and Latin American states suffered from president terms of office limited to single 4–6-year term while the main power was held by tenured senators, congressmen, and other senior oligarchic politicians.[28] Similarly, Japan's bi-yearly *rotatzia* of prime ministers was controlled in the 1970s and early 1980s by former Prime Minister Kaku'ai Tanaka, and then until 1992, by Shin Kanemru, when the corruption that enabled this control was exposed; *rotatzia* prevented prime ministers from accumulating enough power to overcome the corrupt political machines of the two. Tanaka and Kanemru's rule was supported by and, in turn, enhanced low-trust, coercive, and autocratic public officials.[29]

Kibbutz *rotatzia* and "parachuting" were institutionalized decades ago and their similar use by the Israel Defense Forces furthered their legitimization; no one questioned the logic of many I-KO CEOs continuing for dozens of years, deep into dysfunction phases (e.g., Hambrick 2007), while lesser echelons such as PMs and TMs, whose jobs required years of specialization to achieve proficiency, were frequently rotated. This *rotatzia* served the power needs of ignorant and incompetent immoral careerist executives rather than egalitarianism, while having many negative effects on kibbutzim (Shapira 1990, 2001, 2005, 2008).

Serving superiors' power needs meant that CEOs "parachuted" *pe'ilim* to managerial jobs according to their loyalty or prospective loyalty mostly with minimal pertinent know-how and/or referred expertise unless the "parachuted" "jumper" was brought in to rescue a failing plant. This situation encouraged either detachment or seduction-coercion by "jumpers," engendering vicious distrust and ignorance cycles of secrecy, subterfuges, mistakes, and failures. But total failures, which might have deterred such harmful practices, prevented the import of *pe'ilim* rescuers who due to pertinent expertises and habituses chose vulnerable involvement, created high-trust local cultures through virtuous trust and learning cycles, and rescued failing plants. Successes empowered them (Klein 1998), so that ignorant superiors who felt threatened, suppressed them, and they left. New *pe'ilim* were imported, opted for ignorance concealment, failed, and were replaced by rescuer *pe'ilim* who succeeded as depicted, were empowered and suppressed, and so on; this seesaw prolonged rule by dysfunctional, ignorant CEOs and PMs.

However, as mentioned, higher-ups' power enabled them to conceal their ignorance by detachment and/or autocratic involvement, something that a mid-leveler such as a TM could barely do when closely observed by foremen and technicians. Since concealment of ignorance and incompetence is my prime explanation of the prolonged job survival and career advancement of job-stupid executives, I will now focus on Merkaz plant's and I-KRC's dark side by depicting the job survival of a detached, ignorant TM, the collapse of his authority despite six years of experience without vulnerable involvement, his informal replacement, and his termination due to terrible failures that occurred before my eyes.

Practical Engineer Avi's "Parachuting" and Promotion to the Job of TM

Avi was a certified practical engineer *pa'il* who joined the Merkaz gin plant at the age of 30 as a deputy TM, and after a year and a half succeeded the departing veteran TM Muli. His managerial authority collapsed five years later due to ignorance and failures, a seemingly inexplicable event for an intelligent, educated, and experienced manager. This collapse will be explained by the ignorance caused by the detachment he practiced throughout his previous years at the plant, by the habitus he acquired in his previous 10-year kibbutz managerial career, by the practices of the plant's and I-KRC's executives and by the impact of the prime context, i.e., the kibbutz field.[30]

In the kibbutz field *pe'ilim* almost always "jumped" to I-KRC jobs, supposedly to care for kibbutz interests better than inside promoted hired managers when serving kibbutz agriculture. But the reality was different: "jumper" *pe'ilim* managers were ignorant of the local know-how and *phronesis* of sophisticated plants, and mostly they preferred using CCMI, remaining weak as against locals empowered by know-how and *phronesis*, hence they mostly sought their own empowerment by importing their kind to subordinate managerial jobs and using CCMI to defend and advance their careers.

First, I will present Avi's mismanagement, which caused major failures, and then I will depict the collapse of his authority at the height of ginning

Table 1.2 Merkaz Gin Plant's 19-Year Timeline

Year[31]	Events
1	*Pe'ilim* PM Moav and Deputy PMs Yaakov and Aharon establish the plant; Muli is hired TM, a former technician of another gin plant.
5	A second, more advanced processing unit is added; ex-installation contractor Levi joins, learns ginning, and becomes foreman and Muli's informal heir apparent.
6	Aharon leaves, frustrated by Moav's continuing beyond formal term and retirement age; technician Amram joins and becomes foreman.
8	"Natural successor" Yaakov leaves frustrated and "burned" by overburden; Amram becomes Muli's informal heir apparent as Levi suffers serious work accident.
9	Ex-cotton branch manager *pa'il* Yuval is "parachuted" as Deputy PM.
10	Yuval replaces retiring Moav; another *pa'il* Karmi is "parachuted" as Deputy PM.
11	Yuval "parachutes" Avi as Deputy TM; Avi opts to detached CCMI.
13	Job-ignorant Avi replaces Muli and fails miserably; Thomas comes to the rescue as "a second TM."
14	Shavit replaces Yuval; Levi leaves frustrated and Amram follows; I commence I-KRC fieldwork.
15	Danton replaces Karmi; Thomas proposes building an automatic cotton feeder; Avi leaves to be his kibbutz secretary; my fieldwork concentrates on the cotton gin plant.
17	Avi returns as "Second TM."
18	The Board approves purchase of an S&GH cleaner and building of an automatic cotton feeder.
19	The automatic cotton feeder is successfully tested and inaugurated; Avi replaces leaving Thomas and fails once more; my 3.5-month participant observation.

season when the plant was working three shifts 24/7 to minimize the costly storage of picked raw cotton in the fields. I knew Avi from five years of repeated meetings at the plant and from an interview conducted there before I began my participant observation. He came to Merkaz after 10 years of a successful kibbutz managerial career in educational, social, and political jobs since the age of 20. He earned a practical engineering certificate and for two years managed the kibbutz locksmith workshop with two employees. Then, with no experience in mechanics or industrial management, he was nominated deputy of the veteran TM Muli, who was in charge of ginning operations and maintenance, as well as overhauling plant during the rest of the year.

Avi asserted that he was ready to learn ginning but unsure of his competence, so at first he came to check whether the job suited him. However, he remained detached and used CCMI by avoiding ignorance-exposing involvement in staff's coping with technical and operational problems. As a result, he did not learn essential tacit know-how and *phronesis*; employees distrusted his detachment, did not teach him ginning and he remained ignorant, as "no amount of intellectual preparation and understanding can replace the sweat and effort of action" (McLagan and Nel 1997: 227) and without action he missed others' essential knowledge and intuition (Klein 2004). In accord with Leader-Member Exchange theory (LMX), Avi's detachment prevented positive relationships with employees (Moss et al. 2009), and he remained unable to hone broad abilities such as practical engineering know-how acquired in college into sharper ones required for effective management (Wagner 2002). Although he learned about ginning in other ways, his promotion to replace retiring Muli after a year and a half of supposed grooming exposed incompetence through a series of miserable failures. Then deputy, PM Karmi called to the rescue his kibbutz garage manager Thomas (aged 35), a proficient mechanic of agricultural machinery for whom professional competence was a way of being (Sandberg and Pinnington 2009). Karmi depicted the difference between the two:

> "Avi is not made of the right stuff that we [PM Yuval and I] were looking for; he is not that [a truly TM]. Thomas learned the problems much quicker and although he has only been on the job for four months, he has proved that he is made of the right stuff."

Thomas was officially nominated second TM concurrent with Avi on the pretext of a prospective plant enlargement, but in reality he replaced Avi, who retained his formal status although just assisting Thomas with office chores. After five successful years, on the eve of my participant observation, Thomas left, fed up by conflicts with the ignorant boss PM Shavit and after successfully testing his original automatic feeder and Avi replaced him. Ignorant Avi caused awful failures and his authority collapsed, but he nevertheless remained for another year as did Shavit. They were both replaced, seemingly as normal *rotatzia* sparing them and their nominator CEO Zelikovich the stigma of job failure, enabling them successful careers elsewhere, in accord with Luthans (1988) and others who cited that mostly less effective managers succeeded in their careers more than effective ones.

One reason for Avi's detached CCMI was his habitus: he previously developed a kibbutz-based managerial career by minimal coping with difficult social and political problems and/or camouflaging solutions, letting others cope and fail as did many kibbutz managers (Shapira 2001, 2008). He knew this could not work with problematic machines, but for reasons explained below this was the career strategy he chose. Employees distrusted his detached CCMI and their avoidance kept him ignorant, which was known to expert employees but not to his importer, "jumper" PM Yuval. Unfortunately, Yuval was also job-ignorant due to seductive-coercive autocratic involvement and empowerment efforts: importing of two prospective loyalist *pe'ilim* lieutenants as did Gouldner's (1954) outsider. Similar to the latter, both Yuval and his importees were detested by locals who denied them information and kept them ignorant of local know-how and *phronesis*. When Muli left, Yuval promoted Avi to TM, missing his ignorance of ginning despite the year and a half of presumed grooming. Yuval was ignorant of his own ignorance and missed his own incapacity to discern Avi's ignorance.

Employees Knew of Avi's Distrustful Ignorance; Only Bosses Missed It

Employees distrusted Avi since his initiation as Muli's deputy as he remained detached and did not help them with his preferred education; they were aware of his incompetence as asserted by Melkman, a veteran expert in gears and speed reducers:

> "Avi is a good guy but from the point of view of professional know-how he's weak and has no real know-how. You can feel he's never really worked with such machines. A good professional knows how to respond [to questions] but not so Avi. He's not the right man . . . If you have a problem and take it to him and he never has a real solution for it, he is as much in trouble as you are, what's the point of asking him?"
> (e.g., Milliken et al. 2003)

Expert employees discerned Avi's detached CCMI when he stood silently by while a machine was being repaired, neither helping nor asking any professional question or suggesting a solution—they knew he could not learn their trade this way, another reason to avoid communicating with him. Dromi, a mechanic at the time who then studied and became a practical engineer, remembered:

> "Avi used to walk many kilometers between the (two) production halls.[32] He used to stand by silently, watching what we were doing for a long time without uttering a word. Maybe he was trying to learn that way. He never helped dismantle or reassemble a machine. He would have learned much more by doing so. If he really wanted to succeed—that's what he should have done"
> (e.g., Orr 1996).

Avi refrained from active involvement that could have exposed his ignorance, resembling retarded youngsters leaving their shelter and concealing their incompetence by detachment (Edgerton 1967). When Avi became TM for the first time, veteran professional ginner Levi, who was the shop steward and had acquired a 2.5-year practical engineering college education at an advanced age,[33] tried at first to listen to his decisions and orders but concluded that it was pointless:

> "Avi was so unsure of himself that you simply couldn't understand his orders. So you would start asking him questions and he would start

stammering. He didn't understand anything [about ginning]. Thomas understood it in a quarter of the time. I don't remember ever receiving from Avi any good idea about how to solve a problem in all those years; he's incapable of being number one [in the technical domain] at Merkaz under any circumstances, only second driver." Levi's wife, who was present at the interview, commented: "Not everyone needs to know so much." Levi retorted: "But he needed to know a lot and he didn't know, nor did he contribute anything to the plant."

Avi's appearance distinguished him from Thomas: Thomas's dirty blue overalls signaled a TM who managed machinery operation and repairs and constantly learned their problems by reflection-in-action (Schön 1983), through dismantling, repairing, and reassembling machines to get closer to the hard facts and prevent "the corruption of information by the hierarchy, the incurable disease of big organizations" (Boulding 1968: IX). Involvement enabled him to inspect subordinates' reports, which might ignore, conceal, or misconstrue mistakes and ignorance that have to be learned to dialogically enhance their and his own expertise and professional competence.[34] Versus Thomas's dirty overalls, Avi's clothes were always clean since he never dismantled or reassembled a dirty, oiled machine himself and remained a "half-baked manager" (Dore 1973: 54) lacking genuine professional skills, as depicted by Dinitz, a turner and a veteran mechanic with 15 years of experience:

"Avi demonstrated a lack of real know-how in the professional field, a real ability required of a professional. Take for example this wheel [points to it] turned yesterday according to his orders; it's an absolute failure. This hardly ever happened to Thomas. Theoretically speaking, maybe Avi is quite good, but not when it comes to real coping [with machines] and implementing solutions. Then he's really weak, too weak."

Interviewees reported that Avi never admitted such mistakes, as was in the case of the mistaken contour of the S&GH feeding pipe (below). He clearly survived in his job through detached CCMI, trying to conceal his incompetence, which was nevertheless exposed time and again to knowledgeable staff when they contacted him as Thomas's aide despite their distrust in him, while taking care to leave him uninformed. Without their information, and also uninformed due to his own detachment from coping with technical problems, he was unable to make decisions and to act intelligently.

PM Shavit Used Detached CCMI and Mistakenly Promoted Avi Like Yuval

While Thomas rescued the plant from a technical standpoint, Yuval was replaced earlier than stipulated, after four years, due to covert moral failure to be detailed below. His successor Shavit was nominated due to his loyalty to CEO Zelikovich, created when Shavit was the kibbutz economic manager and Zelikovich headed the regional municipality. As a municipality councilor Shavit helped Zelikovich considerably, hence the latter owed him a favor and nominated him as PM although he had no industrial management experience, nor any cotton industry know-how. Having minimal referred expertise (Collins and Sanders 2007) Shavit opted for detached CCMI, and ignorant like Yuval he repeated the mistake of nominating ignorant Avi as TM when frustrated Thomas departed. Thomas's leaving surprised Shavit but Avi seemed the right successor: he was called TM like Thomas; as a management member he proved intelligent and loyal to Shavit, and Shavit supposed that he had been groomed for the job over his years of assisting Thomas.[35] Unfortunately, Avi's detached CCMI kept him job-incompetent, incapable of solving ginning problems. As he took charge he failed to cope with each major technical problem he attempted. Soon he stopped trying, the remains of trust in him vanished, and his authority collapsed; in mid-season he was de facto replaced by two subordinates whom plant manager Shavit accepted informally as de facto joint TMs.

Avi's major failure was unsolving the malfunction of a major new machine, the S&GH cleaner, which was one of the cleaning stages of raw cotton before separating the fibers from the seeds. The machine was new but its work principle of cleaning by rows of round saws circulating against static rods had been known for decades and quite similar machines had been used in Merkaz from its inception. The machine was added for two main reasons:

1   The raw cotton had become dirtier due to the introduction of higher-yield species with stronger vegetation that left more leaf remains in the mechanically picked cotton. Since cotton fiber purity impacted selling prices, the S&GH was added to get a better price.
2   The processing capacity of the plant had increased to suit the needs of the booming cotton growing industry, as it had become the most profitable crop of kibbutzim.

After the replacement of other equipment to a higher capacity in previous years, raising it from 22–24 bales per hour to 35 bales per hour,[36] still more cleaning machines were required. The S&GH producer was WLGEP (world largest ginning equipment producer), with a record of decades of successful machines, including all the new Merkaz equipment. But WLGEP nevertheless made some major mistakes in the machine's propulsion system and it failed when run at full planned capacity of 25 tons of raw cotton per hour. However, it soon became evident to experienced operators that Avi had also severely erred in planning the 30-inch pipe that fed the S&GH: the mistaken contour of this pipe caused unequal dispersion of the intake of cotton, causing an overload on the saws on the left end while most other saws rotated empty. Both errors caused recurring clogging, which halted the ginning process for 30–35 minutes every two-three hours when running at full speed. Avi insisted that his design of this contour was not mistaken and, in any case, "it was a marginal reason for clogging," but top ginner and foreman Nekhas, who was the first to point out Avi's mistake, disproved this by noting the unequal dispersion of the cotton intake. I never saw Avi or PM Shavit or Deputy PM Danton climb the hot (75–80⁰ Celsius) four-meter tall machine to check operators' critique of the feeding pipe contour. Shavit believed Avi's bluff or ignorant view, dispensed with the minor involvement which could have detected the bluff or ignorance, i.e., climbing and watching the one side clog, and the repair of Avi's mistake was delayed for six weeks of needless hardships for us operators and considerable losses for both the plant and cotton growers, although requiring only 10 hours downtime, which equaled production time loss of two to three days due to clogging. The repair after six weeks curbed clogging but even then falsified Avi did not admit his mistake. The mistaken propulsion system was not repaired until the season ended. Its repair required halting ginning for 48–72 hours, but since even a 72-hour stop equaled only a prospective downtime of some 20 days while the season was planned to last some 90 days,[37] it was economically justified, particularly because it would have spared many expenses (below).

The machine's two major problems were neither new nor exclusive; every ginner soon learns that the flow of cotton through the giant pipes and large machines causes frequent unexpected clogging due to machine dysfunction when worn-out driving belts heat up, overload controls stop heated electric motors, and more, or due to operator errors and other problems such as excessively wet cotton, wet weather that caused humid air or the opposite situations. A skilled staff could cope with and solve problems using experience-acquired ginning know-how and *phronesis*, provided managers appreciated this knowledge, and engendered trust and learning cycles by granting them discretion as Thomas did (below). Avi did not do so, discouraged voicing critique of his mistakes (Fast et al. 2014; Milliken et al. 2003), avoided coping with the S&GH's problems and prevented anyone else from doing so for as long as he could. He obstinately placed all responsibility on the manufacturer and denied his own major mistake. The S&GH's repeated clogging became a debacle that caused his de facto demotion. Avi also took a similar course with another new problematic machine, the automatic sampler, of which I, as a registrar, was its operator; hence the etiology of his failure is clearer while the similarity of the two failures ensured my deciphering of the S&GH debacle.

Avi's Failure with the Automatic Sampler

Avi himself had chosen the automatic sampler after touring US manufacturers. He installed it in the plant but it never achieved smooth functioning, although it was proper mechanically. The sampler was an air-piston-operated press, some 180 x 80 x 100 centimeters in height, width, and length, respectively. Such machines succeeded in other Israeli gin plants, sparing a worker on each shift. It was supposed to sample two cotton packs of some 100–150 grams from each bale coming out of the automatic hydraulic press. Since its inauguration it occasionally became blocked and often produced underweight samples, mainly due to mistaken piping and wrong timing of its pistons.

The repeated clogging and irregular samples were a major headache for us registrars, as well as the foremen and technicians. Every time the machine clogged or failed to sample properly—and this often happened after half an hour of operation—the registrar in charge of sampling had to organize manual sampling, namely obtaining from the foreman a temporary employee to sample bales manually. Lacking any communication device, the foreman had to be summoned to the registrar's cabin from wherever he happened to be in the some 2,500 square meter production hall full of tens of large noisy machines, huge pipes, fans, and motors. The foreman had to be convinced that the sampler had failed, then find and install a temporary worker and often also explain to him the job. In the meantime, a good few bales would have passed by on the conveyor with no sampling or registering. Overcoming this backlog while bales continued to come out of the press every 1.75 minutes required half an hour of strenuous work even for an experienced registrar since idle time in the short job cycle was only 20–30 seconds: he had to register the details of each bale on its certificate, attach it to the bale, and repeat this process with each sample. Worse still, quite often due to the time pressures created by hurrying to overcome a backlog, mistakes were made and the registrar was blamed.

If we registrars had felt that the difficulty was temporary and that a real effort was being made to solve the problem as soon as possible, we would have been motivated to make an effort and suffer the extra hardships without doing anything that would interfere with finding a solution. But Avi's attitude soon taught us that the sampler was no more than a nuisance for him. In the first week he was half-involved in efforts at solving the sampler's problem, half since he watched the machine until it clogged, never clearing and tuning it although this required only minor physical effort, rather emphasizing his superiority by calling a technician who did the work as Avi instructed him. Soon, after a few failures, Avi almost stopped, said he was too busy with other problems, but he was bluffing: from time to time he would came and repeated the above except for standing idle also when a technician worked on the machine, as the latter knew what to do and Avi was superfluous. When the S&GH clogged and we cleared it, his bluffing was exposed once more: he often stood by idly for the half-hour necessary until it could run again. His facade (Goffman 1959) of being busy angered my fellow registrars who secretly helped the sampler clog when it suited them to spare the tiring sudden transfer to manual sampling. Soon I found the sampler blocked whenever I came to my shift and noticed that technicians avoided it more and more. The registrars secretly used their power to cope with Avi's failure in solving the sampler's problems, adding a hurdle to the technician who tried to repair the sampler; their faked report of "natural" clogging misled him and technicians soon sensed the bluff and reacted by avoiding the sampler.

Then one day managers of another plant at which the sampler worked smoothly visited our plant, saw the sampler stand blocked, and offered to help solving the problem. They invited Avi or a technician to their plant 70 kilometers away to receive information on their solutions, which required a minimal cost. I too begged Avi to do this, but he retorted, "I didn't even have time to get their advice during their visit," another bluff disproved by observations, while Avi also forbade technicians to drive to the visitors' plant and get their advice, which could have exposed his ignorance and damaged his authority if successful (Fast et al. 2014). When one day the plant was paralyzed as a major shaft broke in the S&GH and repair work prevented bypassing it, a solution used for minor repairs,[38] I travelled to the other plant, learned its solutions to the sampler problem and submitted written findings to Avi and Shavit, who turned me down angrily and ignored my report (e.g., Yanow 2004a).

My action had broken Avi and Shavit's facade of being responsible managers, proving the plausibility of an alternative to Avi's failed coping and his lack of integrity[39] and causing angry reactions rather than productively using my findings. The sampler remained blocked for the rest of the season, while the case raises questions: What explained Avi's initial half-hearted involvement in coping with the sampler contrary to his later avoidance? Why had he not gone to learn solutions at another gin plant or sent a technician to do so? Why did Shavit ignore Avi's ineptness despite the added cost of three sampling workers daily?

Explaining Shavit is relatively simple: the cost of these temporary workers was minor, some 1.5% of the S&GH debacle, and was OPM (other people's money); he ignored the sampler problem, left it to Avi, and never mentioned it even when visiting the registrar's cabin and seeing it standing inactive. The explanation for Avi's conduct is different, commencing with his miserable failure five years earlier.

Thomas rescued the failing plant by opting for vulnerable involvement that engendered virtuous trust and learning cycles due to his experience with mechanics since the age of 14 and then honing his expertise as a highly involved garage manager. He was certain that he would learn ginning as he found its machinery "quite simple," did not fear ignorance exposure, and together with veteran technicians and three other involved *pe'ilim* he solved major problems and shaped a local high-trust culture by servant transformational leadership,[40] as will be explained. Avi kept the title of TM and its insignia when remaining as Thomas's assistant, performing office chores. This spared his bosses the unpleasant task of demoting him while empowering them: Avi remained a loyalist of his bosses, was totally dependent on their will, and hence helped tame Thomas, who was empowered by his successes.

When Thomas left five years later and Avi replaced him, he was helped by a new Deputy TM "parachuted" *pa'il*, certified practical engineer Yehu (30), ignorant of ginning like Avi seven years before. Avi was under great pressure to prove that trusting him to fulfill the role of TM was justified and to regain authority among veteran foremen and technicians, who knew of his incompetence and remembered his awful failure five years earlier, as well as to prove his competence and gain authority over Yehu. At first Avi tried to cope with the sampler, which seemed a simpler task than the S&GH, promising an early win; the sampler was his "baby" in the plant. Thomas had chosen and managed the installation of almost all the other new machines, including choosing the S&GH; he allowed Avi's trip abroad to choose the sampler and install it as an auxiliary machine that did not impact cotton processing. But as Avi's early efforts were unsuccessful and while the S&GH clogging proved a major problem, he retreated to habituated detachment. This explained why he avoided learning from the other plant: learning there required ignorance-exposing involvement in the presence of colleagues who were networked in the industry, hence the negative information could have reached Merkaz to his detriment. Nor did he allow a technician to do this since if a technician had learned, returned with solutions, and succeeded, this would have undermined Avi's authority.

There is no other way to explain Avi's sampler failure. Lack of time was a bluff, and Avi was not indifferent to his "baby," as proven by his early personal attempts to cope with it. There was also the saving incentive: the sampler could have spared three workers at a daily cost of $US 70–80, that is $US 7,500–8,500 per season, [41] a prospect that induced its purchase for some US $20,000. Thus, the only major reason that could explain Avi's forsaking the sampler and limiting others' coping with it was to defend his shaky authority, which was declining daily as the S&GH malfunction continued.

The S&GH Cleaner Debacle: Avi's Terrible Failure

The S&GH's continued malfunction became a debacle as its stoppages of processing for 30–35 minutes every two to three hours curbed production by up to 30%, since in addition to the downtime the processing rate as well was often reduced by 20% to prevent the S&GH from clogging. This was done mostly at night by the shift foreman, tired of waking up operators who often fell asleep when no trouble needed their intervention, urging them to mount the machine and clear its blocking. I have no statistics of processing rate reductions, but during that season Merkaz recorded 32% downtime versus averages of 10–12% in previous seasons and of other gin plants, and less than 3% at the excelling Northern Gin Plant when managed by proficient Gabi (Chapter 4). The stoppages and reduced processing rate prolonged the ginning season from the planned 85–90 days to 105 days; the cost of extra working days of some 25 temporary workers amounted to some US

$10,600; the cost of extra evening and night shifts of foremen and perma-nent operators and technicians amounted to some US $14,000;[42] and even greater were other extra expenses such as energy,[43] machine amortization, worker transportation and services, and others, totaling some US $15,000. In addition, a great deal of money and work were invested in repairs on the spot and at external workshops; on spare parts, some of which were flown from the US and others brought from other gin plants; on inviting numerous costly experts to suggest solutions; and on a rebuilt propulsion system. Alto-gether, plant losses amounted to some US $60,000–70,000 (US $180,000–210,000 in current prices). The lower production rate compelled growers to store an extra 3,000 tons of raw cotton in the fields for months during the rainy season, entailing costs involved in both extra work and materials as well as extra transport costs as cranes were required to load this cotton on trucks, while also degrading fiber quality to an unknown degree although all interviewees agreed it was not negligible. One should bear in mind that these 3,000 tons were worth some US $1.3 million; even a quality damage of 1% would have meant a loss of US $40,000 (current prices), while the quality loss might have been much more than 1%. Worse still, every time the propulsion system was repaired and the machine was bypassed, the cost for cotton growers resulting from degradation of fiber quality was estimated by Avi at US $800–1,000 per hour. There were some 60 such hours; hence this situation added US $150,000–180,000 in today's prices to growers' losses. The total losses for both Merkaz and cotton growers was estimated at US $450,000–500,000 (current prices).

The S&GH manufacturer agreed to pay damages of US $55,000 (US $165,000 in current prices) while the rest of the losses accrued by Merkaz and cotton growers were not prohibitive, as the region's cotton industry prof-ited several times this amount. But had Avi dared risk his authority by clear-ing blockings, listened to foremen and technicians, admitted his mistaken feeding pipe contour and repaired it as soon as Nekhas exposed his mistake, losses would have amounted to only a small fraction of this amount, since this repair would have clarified the need to rebuild the propulsion system, which with manufacturer advice and that of other experts could have been planned, arranged, and implemented within less than two weeks, including a plant stoppage of 48–72 hours. Thus, in three to three-and-a-half weeks Avi could have had a well-working machine much as he indeed had after the season ended. Of course it was easier after the season to carefully build a new propulsion system, check it with raw cotton specially stored for the task, and repair that proven wrong, with advice given throughout the last months, with no time pressure. If Avi had dared become involved he could have received the experts' and manufacturer's advice early, made the repair, and within two-three weeks enhanced production that would have regained the 48–72 hours of downtime. The estimated cost of a rebuilt propulsion system was some US$10,000, and even if the manufacturer would not have paid for it, simply saving 12 hours of bypassing of the S&GH for repairs would have been worth this amount. No one could have predicted the some 60 such hours, nor that after three weeks and tens of blockings a breakdown of the propulsion system would require a 16-hour repair, further indicating the need for its rebuilding.

However, nothing fundamental was done; many repairs and minor modifications were made throughout the months, but the original defective system largely remained although Avi largely knew how it had to be rebuilt and with experts' help there was no reason why he would not have succeeded. But he even delayed consulting experts for almost three weeks after the above mentioned shaft breakdown, an inexplicable delay if not explained as an effort at ignorance concealment.

Further Explanation of Avi's Ignorance and Failures

Avi lacked both Thomas's top-level expertise and his committed readiness to cope with any hard-to-solve, recalcitrant and/or complex problem that technicians couldn't solve; hence he was distrusted and given minimal information while also uninformed due to his detachment. One of the top experts invited said while we stood beside his luxurious American car: "Avi has already consulted enough, he knows what has to be done he simply lacks the guts to do it." But in reality Avi's prime obstacle was not a lack of guts but ignorance and shortage of information due to detached CCMI and distrust of expert employees (e.g., Norman et al. 2010; Obembe 2012). Their distrust deprived him of vital information so he was unsure what was going on and could not decide to act. Distrust maintained his detached CCMI as an aide to Thomas. This was a sinecure; Dalton (1959: 172) pointed to jobs that were sinecures "with pay but few if any fixed duties," but without explaining executives' interest in sinecures. In Avi's case, his ignorant bosses' interest was to tame the rising star, empowered Thomas, by the old Roman strategy of *divide-et-impera*, using loyalist Avi whose sinecure was dependent on them. Keeping Avi's managerial title and insignia with the humble salary of a *pa'il* was a small price to pay to ensure that they could tame Thomas.

Avi's sinecure kept him detached and ignorant throughout Thomas's years, but reading journals, assisting Thomas, touring other plants in Israel and abroad, and listening to experts on various occasions enhanced his self-assurance of ginning expertise and left him unaware of his own ignorance (Kruger and Dunning 1999) since he did not handle pertinent problems. This unawareness explains both his readiness to succeed Thomas and his week or so of failed involved coping with the sampler, from which he returned to his habituated detached CCMI. Regrettably, without learning how the sampler problems were solved by the other plants' technicians, he remained ignorant.

An additional reason for Avi's opting for a detached CCMI was his "parachuting" into the new office of deputy TM, an office which plant manager

Yuval created especially for him. Neither locals nor Avi knew his function and jurisdiction, helping Avi, who suffered lack of pertinent knowledge for technical management, to remain undecided about accepting the job—hence his wait-and-see posture. Yuval secretly promised that he would succeed Muli, who informed Yuval of his intention to leave within one to two years. But Muli preferred to retain the option of staying and suspected that Avi would succeed him even if he would have chosen to remain. Moreover, Muli preferred that his successful informal deputy and heir apparent Amram would succeed him; Avi's "parachuting" was suspected to have been aimed at preventing this. Muli, Amram, and their loyalists closed ranks against Avi, and Avi on his part saw little chance of learning ginning in this situation, another reason for his detached CCMI that engendered a vicious distrust and ignorance cycle.

Avi returned to detached CCMI after failed involvement for a week with the sampler, since beyond habituating it this failure meant he did not know what was going on inside machines, lacking the "unshakeable facts" required for intelligent decision-making, not knowing whether he was getting from employees "apparent facts" or "assumed facts" or "reported facts" or "hoped-for facts" (Geneen 1984: 101). He was in a Kafkaesque situation, seemingly strolling the corridors of a huge building without knowing what hid behind the many closed doors and which of them he should open to find the required knowledge, while knowing that if he asked the employees he would often encounter either an unhelpful, insincere, and distrusted expert from among the staff or someone with better intentions but ignorant, e.g., a seasonal worker. Worse still, ignorance prevented discerning whose advice was helpful and whose was mistaken/wrong, given by an impostor/fool/ignorant bootlicker. Avi, for instance, might have suspected the registrars of secretly thwarting efforts to solve the sampler problem, but as they acted only when alone by the machine inside their cabin, no one could catch them; only trust relations with them could have helped him, but his uncaring for their plight, detachment after early failures and bluffs, prevented such relations.

In short, Avi grasped his expertise world as one inhabited by untrustworthy people suspected of dishonesty, Machiavellianism, and/or incompetence, since staffs indeed used such means against his and other ignorant bosses' mistaken, arbitrary, and amateurish decisions and orders. When facing a hard and seemingly unsolvable problem Avi had no one he trusted in the plant to consult with, while seeking outside help was costly and risked ignorance exposure to influential industry figures, which could have had a negative impact on his authority and job. The same was true of consulting visiting colleagues, while the high cost of paid consultants prevented their use to solve minor problems such as that of the sampler. In addition, outsiders could cause his failure by mistaken advice due to ignorance of the specifics of local problems and solutions and may not have enough motivation to learn them and get the "unshakeable facts" for offering valid advice.[44]

One wise consultant gained such facts and other local knowledge prior to visiting the plant by meeting with the top ginner and shift foreman Nekhas in his nearby Arab village. There he learned facts, explanations, and plausible solutions for the S&GH debacle and then came and "sold" this knowledge and suggestions to Avi as his own.[45] Nekhas did not try to advise Avi, who never listened to him due to his low social status, an uneducated Arab who had learned ginning by 19 years of work, advancing from being an 11-year-old helper of his janitor father to Merkaz's best ginner (see pp. 169–170).

The Collapse of Avi's Authority

Avi's detachment concealed his ignorance and incompetence from his superiors and from some employees but not from experts. Avi's hesitations and inaction when faced with hard-to-solve problems, plus his immoral abuses and bluffs ruined his authority; contravention of his orders proliferated and toward the season's end he could not be considered a manager. Signs of the collapse of his authority became evident to everyone in the production hall. I noticed it on the morning following the day on which the S&GH's broken shafts were repaired, in the season's eighth week. The repair took about 30 hours, and after the machine operated for several hours the usual practice was to examine all the changes made when processing and then stop for final adjustments and screw tightening.

At 10:30 AM, after several hours of smooth ginning, a sudden quiet indicated a stoppage. Two minutes later Avi came and shouted: "Hey, what happened? Who told you to stop? Why couldn't you wait until finishing a grower?" "Finishing a grower" means that the raw cotton of one farmer is finished, and for two to three minutes the machines are emptied of his cotton to enable exact weighing of his fibers and then start the processing of another's cotton. Machine repairs were often made after finishing a grower by not feeding another's cotton and stopping machines when empty since it was safer—there was no danger that the sparks of a repair would ignite the cotton. Atad, a technician, ex-shift foreman, and shop steward who performed the S&GH's final adjustments, explained that since it would still take several hours to finish the cotton of the current grower it was dangerous to continue for so long without tightening the screws. Avi burst out: "But why couldn't you say anything before you stopped? I'm still in charge here. I haven't left this plant yet and you can still tell me before you stop the plant!"

A threatening silence ensued. Atad did not answer and neither did his assistant, the shift foreman, and the three operators who gathered around Avi. Avi looked at them, expecting some answer, but Atad, joined by Yehu, returned to adjusting and tightening screws, while all the others who knew that Atad had ordered the stoppage uttered not a word. After a long moment of silence Avi turned around and went back to the office building. In my notes I wrote that since Atad and Yehu had the relevant knowledge, they had rightly decided to stop operation rather than waiting to finish a grower. Their resolve to continue working without answering Avi signaled his authority collapse. A short while afterward, additional signs of this appeared:

1   Avi's direct reports, Deputy Yehu, technician Atad, and the three shift foremen ignored him more and more often. The first sign was when Atad abandoned the sampler, leaving it unused despite Avi's demands to continue attempting to operate it. Then repairs were carried out without reporting to Avi or reporting only very briefly without asking for his opinion or permission. His vetoes were only partially honored, if at all, while his production hall visits went almost unnoticed. Hence, he appeared there less and less.

2   General discipline waned on all levels, down to the temporary Arab workers (the plant's lowest rank). They were supposed to clean machines whenever there was a stoppage but they often disappeared ("dived" in the jargon of shift foremen) the moment the processing stopped and the foremen had difficulty finding them. However, they just followed permanent staff behavior. One of the worst instances was when fire broke out one night at 1 AM. At 6 AM, when I came for the morning shift, it had already been extinguished, but processing had not yet resumed, since burned remains had to be removed from some of the machines, pipes, and conveyors. I joined the night shift who was working on it, but neither Atad, nor Yehu, or my shift foreman and operators came to help with this urgent work, rather fooling around with trifles such as the weekly handing out of clean work clothes to permanent staff.

3   Atad and Yehu started behaving as if they were the bosses. One day Atad ordered press operators to stop an old custom confirmed by Avi of automatic operation of the piston that pushed out the finished bale from the hydraulic press. From that point on, Atad ordered and operators obeyed; the piston would be operated manually, adding a major inconvenience as they had to do it exactly on time every 1.75 minutes.

4   Atad spoke as if he was the plant manager: "Next year we're going to arrange . . .", "We're going to do . . .", "We'll place this here . . .", and so on. He also started accompanying visitors as if he was the manager, alone or with Yehu, and used expressions such as "I've decided that it's okay this way . . .", "I told him to do this . . .", and similar ones.

5   Employees who abided by Avi's orders were severely reprimanded when Atad and Yehu thought otherwise, and were obliged to obey the latter. For instance, Yiftach, a technician and shift foreman, complained that he was summoned for work on Saturday although Avi had promised him that he would be free to celebrate his son's birthday party, to which he had invited many relatives and friends. Atad retorted: "Avi's promises are no longer valid at Merkaz since he no longer manages here."

When Yiftach finally freed himself from Saturday work it was not due to Avi's promise but to a friend who volunteered to take his place.

6   Avi's orders were no longer regarded as reliable enough for technical decisions so that, for instance, when a repair job was begun according to his instructions, Yehu would suddenly appear and demand a change of repair method. When an argument ensued against his insistence, no one would mention that Avi instructed doing it this way, only arguing that this was the traditional method. Even though it was clear to everyone that Yehu's authority was dubious and that he had not yet been appointed to replace Avi, no one who objected to his orders cited Avi's instructions. It was evident that Avi no longer maintained any real authority.

7   Threats such as "If you don't do as I tell you, you'll go home [be fired]" were made by both Atad and Yehu. Employee reactions made it clear that they were intimidated by these threats even though it was unclear who authorized Atad and Yehu to use them.

On one occasion, a month and a half before the season ended, I heard plant manager Shavit saying that at the end of the season Yehu would replace Avi, but he left unanswered the question whose authority was currently valid. As mentioned, Avi was not replaced at the end of the season; rather he remained for an additional year. Atad explained the situation thus:

"Yehu was only considered a foreman while Avi was called 'TM'. Avi fought for his position. He would not give it up so easily."

In these words one can discern an unconcealed tone whereby "Avi was permitted to bear the title to allow him to leave the plant honorably." This definition of the situation suits Shavit's evasion of the question of authority; he did not interfere and enabled Atad and Yehu to usurp Avi's authority after his incompetence was definitely exposed by the change of the S&GH's feeding pipe on the sixth week, calling Avi's bluff/ignorance. Until then, Avi lost power by his ineptness and by his coercive limiting of others' discretion, which thwarted their problem-solving efforts (Fox 1974), as with the sampler problem, and then his ruined authority collapsed. Shavit's detachment, which permitted Avi's de facto demotion, spared his prestige the negative impact of firing Avi, which would have been a public admission that the nomination had been a mistake. However, the lack of a trusted TM with legitimate authority, convincing competence, and transparent positivity (Norman et al. 2010) prevented a solution to the plant's prime problem, the S&GH's faulty propulsion system. Neither Atad nor Yehu were authorized to stop the plant for 48–72 hours for its repair; even ignorant Shavit discerned that the two were unqualified for the job, hence he continued with Avi's "calming sessions" (below), hoping to no avail that he would do the job.

Executives' Contributions to Avi's Failures
and Authority Collapse

During the months of the S&GH fiasco Avi repeatedly offered his resignation to Shavit and Deputy Danton, but they turned him down and pressured him to decide to rebuild the faulty system, but to no avail. Regrettably, Danton too was ignorant of ginning like Shavit, was detached from the production halls; hence, he believed Avi's bluff or ignorant view about the feeding pipe, which enabled him to postpone its repair for six weeks until demanded by outside consultants. Danton depicted their many sessions with Avi as "calming sessions": "We tried to calm Avi down and to convince him that he would succeed and promised him support for any solution he chose and to pay any expert he asked for." These failed "calming sessions" showed how they ignorantly trusted Avi, missing his professional stupidity due to practicing detached CCMI that denied him experience-based tacit know-how and *phronesis*. Their trust meant the success of his detached CCMI strategy, encouraging his use of more bluffs and power abuses as he did with the sampler, and ignoring bosses' expectations of him to solve problems requiring engaged ignorance exposure. The two bosses' ignorance of ginning resulted in misguided trust in the untrustworthy subordinate manager.

The best Israeli ginning experts came and went except for one, well known to the three and to the Israeli ginning community and also the closest: at a kibbutz 15 kilometers away previous TM Thomas testified that he had been ready to help Avi, even without the generous fees paid to other consultants. But he was disregarded: the prime reasons were Shavit and Avi's envy of his successes and their fear that he would be further empowered by successfully solving the S&GH problem (Klein 1998), as well as Danton's estrangement from Thomas, his friend of some years, due to a major conflict. Thomas overcame the three and convinced the Board to buy the S&GH rather than adding fiber cleaners that the three and some experts suggested installing similar to some gin plants. Thomas objected, pointing out the drawbacks of such machines, as substantiated by a comparative study (Northern Ginning Season Report 1972), and the Board was convinced, largely because of his top expertise. Proof of this was an invitation by WLGEP to join its R&D labs in the US as a senior engineer when he began talking about leaving. He was only waiting for the completion of his innovative automatic feeder (see next chapter) and then left.[46]

Ignorant Shavit nominated ignorant Avi as TM and when he failed avoided firing him. One major reason was to defend his own prestige and authority as Avi's nominator (Levenson 1961: 373) and another was Danton's support. Danton supported Shavit although he disliked both him and Avi; he was Thomas's friend until the last year and supported his innovative automatic cotton feeder for three years up to its success, but in his opinion the S&GH purchase meant surrendering to an unjustified caprice of expert Thomas, who ignored others' arguments to the contrary and contrasting choices of other gin plants. Danton was highly trusted by subordinates as the involved, effective, and transparent manager of his jurisdiction (Norman et al. 2010), which included all operations outside the production halls and seasonal manpower supply, but he rarely visited these halls and was never heard talking knowingly about ginning. His belief in Avi's expertise and continuing the unproductive "calming sessions" also indicated his ignorance of ginning and missing Avi's ignorance. Authors who criticized the persevering with failed strategies did not mention ignorance,[47] which was valid in Shavit and Danton's case not only concerning Avi's present dysfunction but also his past: detached from ginners' problem-solving, the two were not told about Avi's early failure as a TM in Yuval's time. When joining the plant Shavit found two parallel TMs and retained this strange state of affairs as it functioned well, while due to his ignorance of ginning he missed Thomas's pivotal role as a highly trusted transformational leader who created local high-trust culture that resulted in the plant's successful functioning. Danton as a friend knew more about Thomas's role, but as detached and ignorant of ginning he missed why Thomas was highly effective. Both managers were unqualified to probe Avi's (in)competence, while expert employees saw no point in telling them as, for instance, they witnessed Shavit believing Avi's bluff/ignorant view concerning the feeding pipe contour without even trying to check out their contrary argument (e.g., Milliken et al. 2003).

Shavit's superior was I-KRC CEO Zelikovich, who was also detached and ignorant of ginning; I never saw him at the plant throughout the long months of the S&GH debacle. He could have intervened to replace the failing PM and TM with available competent, experienced, and committed insiders: Danton could have replaced Shavit temporarily at least as he competently managed his domain by vulnerable involvement, and Thomas could have replaced Avi. Moreover, Thomas and Danton cooperated successfully until last year in promoting the automatic feeder; hence they could have been a good TMT (top management team) which could practice successful distributed leadership and rescue the plant from inept managers' failed leadership (e.g., Chreim 2015). Zelikovich had nominated Shavit and could have fired him as he did with Yuval, and replacing Avi was even easier by reinstalling Thomas as a natural legitimate reaction to Avi's failure. Why didn't Zelikovich act thus?

The full explanation for his inaction will be spelled out in the next chapters, but a major reason has already been mentioned: firing a manager testifies to the incompetence of the nominating executive and damages her/his authority, thus it is deferred as much as possible. Second major reason was Zelikovich's detached CCMI: the decision to implement such sensitive successions, which would have stigmatized the fired managers as failures and might have angered their loyalists among both employees and cotton growers, required more knowledge than he had. He had to decipher Avi's passivity and Shavit and Danton's failure to convince him to act in order to decide which succession was the right solution. Thomas for sure was competent, but might it be that he was too empowered by successes and mistakenly led to buy the problematic S&GH as all other managers asserted, and hence would not reinstalling him cause more mistakes? Danton as well was not ensured to be a guaranteed bet: he did not exhibit knowledge of ginning, or of plant finances in Board meetings; would he engage these domains successfully? Zelikovich could have found experienced plant managers in the kibbutzim to succeed Shavit, but Shavit was his loyalist on the I-KRC's Board, hence, a successor has to be at least a prospective loyalist. In addition, finding a successor who would be better than Shavit required learning Shavit's failure from knowledgeable plant staff from which he was detached and by which he was distrusted, as he only participated in some Board meetings and visited the plant only to show high-level visitors the successful cotton industry. Employees never saw him as an executive interested in their problems, as one who oversees the functioning of managers reporting to him and acting when discerning their dysfunction.

Summary: Managerial Survival and Failure by CCMI

Observations exposed serious mismanagement due to managers' and executives' use of CCMI, emphasizing the literature's neglect of this harmful phenomenon even when exposing managerial ego defensiveness (Fast et al. 2014), which caused considerable losses for both the gin plant and cotton growers in the studied season. While destructive leadership research depicted such negative managerial behaviors, it missed their detached CCMI explanation; depictions of leaders' destructiveness never explained it by use of CCMI.[48] By pivoting the dysfunction of TM Avi and analyzing his and others' failing practices which discouraged employees from helping his decision-making (Milliken et al. 2003), psychological explanations for stupidity were proven to be marginal and Avi's job dysfunction was fully explained by his choice of detached CCMI to defend his authority, job, and career, largely due to perceived vulnerability and lack of psychological safety as he lacked Thomas's lengthy experience as a mechanic.[49] This choice was probably encouraged by practicing Im-C in previous kibbutz managerial jobs; ethnographies of kibbutzim found many immoral leaders (Chapter 6), but the prime reason was opting for detached CCMI, which left Im-C as the only career advancement option. Other contributing contextual reasons, such as bosses' use of CCMI, have as yet been only partially untangled (see next chapters).

The findings strongly support the theoretical model of choice, either practicing CCMI and using managerial knowledge as means of control that engenders vicious distrust and ignorance cycles, resulting in a low-trust culture of conservatism, ignorance, and mismanagement, or practicing vulnerable involvement that engenders trust and learning cycles without use of managerial knowledge for control of subordinates, leading to an effective innovation-prone high-trust culture. Stupidity research missed incompetence caused by distrust and ignorance cycles due to authority- and job-defensive practices that retained ignorance of local know-how and *phronesis* and caused stupid failures of previously successful intelligent managers. The findings explained the job survival of outsider executives and managers by use of CCMI despite consequent dysfunction and failures, which included failed selection, promotion, and retention of managers and senior staff, missing or ignoring their wrongs and mistakes, concealed or camouflaged by immoral self-serving information abuses. However, a failed CCMI user boss can survive failures if he imports rescuers who opt for vulnerable involvement and use know-how and *phronesis* acquired by virtuous trust and learning cycles, shaping high-trust effective cultures within their jurisdictions. But as such bosses miss how ignorant they are, miss their own lack of interactional expertise, ignorance of local practices' languages and of pertinent experience required to acquire tacit know-how and *phronesis*,[50] they also miss their own incapacity to discern the negative job survival strategies of mid-levelers by CCMI, their mistakes, wrongs, and neglect, trusting them at their own peril.

The findings support research emphasizing the decisiveness of local knowledge[51] and the critique of managerial knowledge portability,[52] as well as the decisiveness of mutual trust between and within echelons for managerial knowledge, as explained by a manager:

> "[p]eople are the only way I get information that matters for me . . . Learning how to use the constellation of people around you requires understanding what they can and will do . . . knowing what they are good at and be relied on for . . . knowing to what degree you can trust someone . . ."
>
> (Cross and Borgatti 2004: 137).

Well-trained and educated managers but "parachuted" with largely irrelevant prior experience and/or habitus of detachment and/or irrelevant expertise chose CCMI, survived in their jobs for years, and advanced careers despite major mistakes, wrong decisions, or indecision and dismal failures. Ignorant bosses ruled by importing their kind and retaining loyalists, rather than promoting talented expert insiders deemed too powerful, while some well-functioning mid-levelers prevented total failure, seemingly facilitating executives' belief that CCMI was inconsequential. While the ignorant executive hardly knew how ignorant importees would remain due to opting for CCMI, he could safely rely on their loyal servility, being powerless, and dependent on his backing unlike empowered knowledgeable insiders. Advancement by ingratiation (Stern and Westphal 2010) and loyal servility based on various subterfuges rather than performance encouraged CCMI, as did the kibbutz *rotatzia* norm that shortened terms, making learning local knowledge less worthwhile.

The next chapter contextualizes Avi's choice of CCMI and his job survival for seven years by depicting and explaining consecutive mismanagement by the three "parachuted" Pms throughout the Merkaz gin plant's 19 years, proving that their detrimental leadership was not incidental but rather systematic and explicable, by using CCMI due to preference for Im-C rather than career advancement by performance. Subsequent chapters will compare them to other PMs and present a full contextualization that explains CCMI and Im-C of most PMs, 16 of the 22 studied, by emulating CEOs whose choices of these practices were encouraged by the kibbutz field context.

Notes

1 See (Boddy et al. 2010; Dalton 1959; Griffin and O'Leary-Kelly 2004; Hase et al. 2006; Hughes 1958; Jackall 1988; Linstead et al. 2014; Mehri 2005; Shapira 1995b). Dark secrets: Costas and Grey (2014); Goffman (1959).
2 Gannon (1983); Hogan and Hogan (2001); Shapira (1987); Smithson (1989); Zbaracki (1998).
3 Baldoni (2008); Curphy et al. (2008); Dalton (1959); Hogan et al. (1990); Hollander (1998: 50); Izraeli (1977).
4 Burawoy (1979); Collinson (2005a); Dalton (1959); Orr (1996). Admitting CEOs: Grove (1996: 144); Robison (2010).
5 Boddy et al. (2010); Dalton (1959); Hughes (1958); Levenson (1961); Mehri (2005: 199); Webb and Cleary (1994).
6 Beer et al. (2011); Edmondson (2008); Orlikowski (2002); Orr (1996); Shapira (1995b); Wilson (2011); Zand (1972).
7 Boddy (2006); Fast et al. (2014); Johnson (2009); Mehri (2005); Parker (2016); Sykes (2006); Wexler (2006).
8 Ailon (2015); Hill (2006); Johnson (2008); Keltner et al. (2006); Pullen and Rhodes (2015); Sendjaya (2005); Villette and Vuillermot (2009); earlier works see: Ciulla (1998b); Jackall (1988); Parker (2000); Scharfstein (1995).
9 Bratton and Kacmar (2004); Chiaburu et al. (2013); Dougherty et al. (1993); Feldman and Weitz (1991); Ficarrotta (1988); Gabriel and Savage (1981); Jackall (1988); Mosier (1988); Shapira (1987); Starbuck (2007); Weissberg (2002).
10 Campbell et al. (1995); Groysberg et al. (2006); Khurana (2002); Townley (2002).
11 Deputy jobs' impact: Bigley and Wiersema (2002). Mid-levelers' emulation: Liu et al. (2012).
12 Contextual factors: Huen (2009); Morita (2014); Sergeeva and Andreeva (2015); Strathern (2004); on oligarchic field see: Kets De Vries (1993); Levenson (1961); Michels (1959[1915]); Shapira (2005, 2008, 2015); Ch. 6 below.
13 Respectively: Yanow (2004a); Collins and Sanders (2007); Klein (1998); Collins (2011); Collins and Evans (2007).
14 Ethnographers: Yanow (2004b); context: Shapira (2005, 2008, 2012); socialization: Fondas and Wiersema (1997).
15 E.g., Fine (2012); Marx (1985); Mehri (2005); Orr (1996). Mutual trust: Fox (1974); Siebert et al. (2015).
16 Also: Bower (2007); Flyvbjerg (2001); Khurana (2002); Klein, G. (1998); Klein, J. (2004); Morgan (2015); Orr (1996); Ribeiro (2013); Schweigert (2007); Shapira (1995b, 2013); Shotter (2006); Townley (2002).
17 Crozier (1964); Dalton (1959); Mehri (2005); Mintzberg (1973); Orr (1996); Robison (2010); Roy (1952); Shapira (1987).

18 Brown (2001); Collins (2011); Grove (1996); Orr (1996); Ribiero (2013); Shapira (2013, 2015).
19 Fine (2012); Gobillot (2007); Meyer (2010); Tsoukas (2005: 149).
20 Bennis (1989: 17); Hargadon and Bechky (2006); Ingvaldsen et al. (2013); Shapira (1995b); Wagner (2002: 50).
21 Guest (1962: Ch. 4); Kanter (1993[1977]: 33); Nienaber et al. (2015b); Norman et al. (2010); Shapira (2013); Zand (1972).
22 Deutsch (1962); Dore (1973); Heskett (2011); Lee et al. (2010); Shapira (1987); Snell (2001); Wang and Clegg (2007).
23 Alvesson and Sandberg (2014); Bourdieu (1990); Collins and Evans (2007); Dalton (1959); Fast et al. (2014); Levenson (1961); Nienaber et al. (2015a); Tsui-Auch and Möllering (2010); other reasons see below.
24 Carroll et al. (2008); Gherardi (2009); Rennstam and Ashcraft (2014); Schatzki et al. (2001).
25 Geertz (1973); Morgan (2015); Shotter (2006, 2015).
26 The "Four Movements" owned many of the I-KOs and impacted nominations of I-KRC CEOs (see Chapter 6).
27 On the US see: Henderson (1990); Gabriel and Savage (1981); Segal (1981). On Israel see: Vald (1987).
28 On China see: Chang (1955); Chow (1966); Folsom (1968); Watt (1972). On Athens: Bowra (1971); Burn (1964); Fuks (1976). On Latin America: Linz (1990); Mainwaring (1990); Sanders (1989); Smith (1986).
29 Kovner (1993); *Newsweek* (1993); Van Wolferen (1989: Ch. 5).
30 On this field: Near (1997); Niv and Bar-On (1992); Shapira (1990, 1995a, 2001, 2005, 2008, 2011) and Ch. 6.
31 For ethical reasons real years are concealed; they were from the 1960s to the 1980s.
32 The second, smaller hall contained a processing system for Pima cotton. I did not observe it and interviewees reported that its mismanagement was quite the same; hence I do not refer to it.
33 A serious work accident crippled his right hand and he was nominated manager of the small mechanical workshop.
34 Baralou and Tsoukas (2015); Bennis (1989: 17); Ingvaldsen et al. (2013); Sandberg and Pinnington (2009).
35 He assisted Thomas only three years, as he left for two years to serve as the general secretary of his kibbutz, but his Merkaz resume also included one and a half earlier years as a deputy TM and almost a year as TM.
36 The gin plant's cotton fiber produce was packed and shipped by compacting it with a 1,500-ton press into jute and eight steel hoop-wrapped bales weighing a quarter of a ton.
37 Due to the S&GH debacle it took 3.5 months to gin the entire year's cotton yield.
38 However, this solution was costly as it degraded fiber quality since the fibers remained dirty.
39 On facades see: Ciulla (1998b); on alternatives: Hawthorn (1991); on integrity: Graham (1995); Simons (2002).
40 Barbuto (1997); Beyer (1999); Burns (1978); Graham (1991); Greenleaf (1977); Sendjaya et al. (2008); see pp. 79–83.
41 Use of US$ terms for transactions made in Israeli shekels was common at the time due to extra high inflation. Due to US inflation one US$ at the time of study (1975–1982) was worth some three US$ in 2017. Numbers are inexact as season length depended on production rate and temporary workers' wages differed somewhat.
42 Israeli law required a 25% wage increase for evening shifts and a 50% increase for night shifts.

43 The ginning process was energy-intensive, required both 3000-horsepower motors and heating large quantities of air from 15–17° to 75–80° Centigrade to dry the raw cotton.
44 Bennis (1989); Fine (2012); Geertz (1983); Hedgecoe (2012); Rouse (1987); Yanow (2000).
45 Nekhas testified and I confirmed with other foremen that he had indeed spoken of these solutions from the early days of the debacle. On importance of such informal collaboration: Kreiner and Schultz (1993).
46 Thomas turned down this invitation, citing a serious health problem in the family, which even the munificent salary offered could hardly have paid for treatment in the US, while the Israeli public health system covered it.
47 E.g., Amason and Mooney (2008); Kolakowski (1964); Miller (1992).
48 E.g., Aasland et al. (2010); Fraher (2016); Krasikova et al. (2013); Lipman-Blumen (2005); Padilla et al. (2007); Thoroughgood et al. (2012).
49 Stupidity psychological explanations: Chiaburu et al. (2013); Wagner (2002); psychological safety: Nienaber et al. (2015a); perceived vulnerability: Fast et al. (2014); Tsui-Auch and Möllering (2010).
50 Respectively: Kruger and Dunning (1999); Collins and Evans (2007); Collins (2011); D'Eredita and Barreto (2006).
51 Collinson (2005b); Fine (2012); Geertz (1983); Shapira (1995b, 2015); Shotter and Tsoukas (2014a, 2014b).
52 Groysberg et al. (2006); Khurana (2002); Kotter (1982); Townley (2002).

References

Aasland, Merethe S., A. Skogstad, et al. 2010. The prevalence of destructive leadership behaviour. *British Journal of Management* 21(4): 438–452.

Ailon, Galit. 2015. From superstars to devils: The ethical discourse on managerial figures involved in a corporate scandal. *Organization* 22(1): 78–99.

Alvesson, Mats, and Jorgen Sandberg. 2014. Habitat and habitus: Boxed-in versus box-breaking research. *Organization Studies* 35(7): 967–987.

Amason, Allen C., and Ann C. Mooney. 2008. The Icarus paradox revisited: How strong performance sows the seeds of dysfunction in future strategic decision-making. *Strategic Organization* 6(4):407–434.

Arendt, Hanna. 1963. *Eichmann in Jerusalem*. New York: Viking Press.

Armstrong, Peter. 1987. Engineers, management and trust. *Work, Employment and Society* 1(4): 421–440.

Axelrod, Robert. 1984. *The Evolution of Cooperation*. New York: Basic Books.

Baldoni, John. 2008. How to fight managerial incompetence. *HBR Blog Network*, April 3.

Baralou, Evangelia, and Haridimos Tsoukas. 2015. How is new organizational knowledge created in a virtual context? An ethnographic study. *Organization Studies* 36(5): 593–620.

Barbuto, John E., Jr. 1997. Taking the charisma out of transformational leadership. *Journal of Social Behaviour and Personality* 12(3): 689–697.

Beer, Michael, R. Eisenstat, et al. 2011. *High-Ambition Ledaership*. Boston: Harvard Business School Press.

Bennis, Warren. 1989. *Why Leaders Can't Lead*. San Francisco: Jossey-Bass.

Beyer, Janice M. 1999. Taming and promoting charisma to change organizations. *Leadership Quarterly* 10(2): 307–330.

Bigley, Gregory A., and Margarethe F. Wiersema. 2002. New CEOs and corporate strategic refocusing: How experience as heir apparent influences the use of power. *Administrative Science Quarterly* 47(4): 707–727.

Blau, Peter M. 1955. *The Dynamics of Bureaucracy*. Chicago: University of Chicago Press.

Boddy, Clive R. P. 2006. The dark side of management decisions: Organisational psychopaths. *Management Decision* 44(9/10): 1461–1475.

Boddy, Clive R. P., R. Ladyshewsky, and P. Galvin. 2010. Leaders without ethics in global business: Corporate psychopaths. *Journal of Public Affairs* 10(1): 121–138.

Boulding, Kenneth E. 1968. *The Organizational Revolution*. Chicago: Quadrangle.

Bourdieu, Pierre. 1990. *The Logic of Practice*. Cambridge: Polity.

Bower, Joseph L. 2007. *The CEO Within*. Boston: Harvard Business School Press.

Bowra, Cecil M. 1971. *Periclean Athens*. London: Weidenfeld and Nicolson.

Bratton, Virginia K., and K. Michele Kacmar. 2004. Extreme careerism: The dark side of impression management. In: R. Griffin and A. O'Leary-Kelly (Eds.), *The Dark Side of Organizational Behaviour*. San Francisco: Jossey-Bass, 291–308.

Brown, John S. 2001. Knowledge and organization: A social-practice perspective. *Organization Science* 12(2): 198–213.

Buckingham, Marcus, and Curt Coffman. 1999. *First Break All the Rules*. New York: Simon and Schuster.

Burawoy, Michael. 1979. *Manufacturing Consent*. Chicago: University of Chicago Press.

Burn, Andrew R. 1964. *Pericles and Athens*. New York: Collier.

Burns, James M. 1978. *Leadership*. New York: Harper.

Burns, Tom, and Gerald M. Stalker. 1961. *The Management of Innovation*. London: Tavistock.

Campbell, Richard J., V. I. Sessa, and J. Taylor. 1995. Choosing top leaders: Learning to do better. *Issues & Observations* 15(4): 1–5.

Carroll, Brigid, L. Levy, and D. Richmond. 2008. Leadership as practice: Challenging the competency paradigm. *Leadership* 4(4): 363–379.

Chang, Chu L. 1955. *The Chinese Gentry*. Washington: University of Washington Press.

Chiaburu, Daniel S., G. J. Munoz, and R. G. Gardner. 2013. How to spot a careerist early on: Psychopathy and exchange ideology as predictors of careerism. *Journal of Business Ethics* 118(3): 473–486.

Chow, Yang T. 1966. *Social Mobility in China*. New York: Atherton.

Chreim, Samia. 2015. The (non)distribution of leadership roles: Considering leadership practices and configurations. *Human Relations* 68(4): 517–543.

Ciulla, Joanne B. 1998b. Leadership and the problem of bogus empowerment. In: J. B. Ciulla (Ed.), *Ethics, the Heart of Leadership*. Westport (CN): Praeger, 63–86.

Collins, Harry M. 2011. Language and practice. *Social Studies of Science* 41(3): 271–300.

Collins, Harry M., and Robert Evans. 2007. *Rethinking Expertise*. Chicago: University of Chicago Press.

Collins, Harry M., and Garry Sanders. 2007. They give you the keys and say 'drive it!'. Managers, referred expertise, and other expertises. *Studies in History and Philosophy of Science* 38(4): 621–641.

Collins, Orvis, M. Dalton, and D. Roy. 1946. Restriction of output and social cleavage in industry. *Applied Anthropology* 5(Summer): 1–14.

Collinson, David. 2005a. Questions of distance. *Leadership* 1(2): 235–250.

Collinson, David. 2005b. Dialectics of leadership. *Human Relations* 58(11): 1419–1442.

Costas, Jana, and Christopher Grey. 2014. Bringing secrecy into the open: Towards a theorization of the social processes of organizational secrecy. *Organization Studies* 35(10): 1423–1447.

Cross, Rob, and Stephen P. Borgatti. 2004. The ties that share: Characteristics that facilitate information seeking. In: M. Huysman and V. Wulf (Eds.), *Social Capital and Information Technology*. Cambridge (MA): MIT Press, 137–161.

Crozier, Michel. 1964. *The Bureaucratic Phenomenon*. Chicago: University of Chicago Press.

Curphy, Gordy, R. Hogan, and J. Hogan. 2008. Managerial incompetence: Is there a dead skunk on the table? Retrieved 30.8.2013: www.leadershipketnote. net_articles_index_a4.htm

Dalton, Melville. 1959. *Man Who Manage*. New York: Wiley.

D'Eredita, Michael A., and Charmaine Barreto. 2006. How does tacit knowledge proliferate? An episode-based perspective. *Organization Studies* 27(12): 1821–1841.

Deutsch, Morton. 1962. Cooperation and trust: Some theoretical notes. In: M. R. Jones (Ed.), *Nebraska Symposium on Motivation*. Lincoln: University of Nebraska Press, 275–319.

Dore, Ronald. 1973. *British Factory—Japanese Factory*. Berkeley (CA): University of California Press.

Dougherty, Thomas W., G. F. Dreher, and W. Whitely. 1993. The MBA as careerist: An analysis of early-career job change. *Journal of Management* 19(3): 535–548.

Downs, Anthony. 1966. *Inside Bureaucracy*. Boston: Little, Brown.

Edgerton, Robert B. 1967. *The Cloak of Competence*. Berkeley (CA): University of California Press.

Edmondson, Amy C. 2008. The competitive imperative of learning. *Harvard Business Review*. July–August. Retrieved 5.7.2011: www.hbr.com

Fast, Nathanel J., Ethan R. Burris, and Caroline A. Bartel. 2014. Managing to stay in the dark: Managerial self-efficacy, ego-defensiveness, and the aversion to employee voice. *Academy of Management Journal* 57(4): 1013–1034.

Feldman, Daniel C., and Barton A. Weitz. 1991. From the invisible hand to the gladhand: Understanding the careerist orientation to work. *Human Resource Management* 30(2): 237–257.

Ficarrotta, Joseph C. 1988. Careerism: A moral analysis of its nature, types, and contributing causes in the military services. Retrieved 14.2.2013: www.isme. tamu.eduJSCOPE88Ficarrotta88

Fine, Gary A. 2012. *Tiny Publics: Idiocultures and the Power of the Local*. New York: Russell Sage.

Flyvbjerg, Bent. 2001. *Making Social Science Matter*. Cambridge: Cambridge University Press.

Flyvbjerg, Bent. 2006. Making organization research matter: Power, values and *phronesis*. In: S. R. Clegg et al. (Eds.), *Sage Handbook of Organization Studies*. Thousand Oaks (CA): Sage, 357–381.

Folsom, Kenneth E. 1968. *Friends, Guests, and Colleagues*. Berkeley (CA): University of California Press.

Fondas, Nanette, and Margaret Wiersema. 1997. Changing of the guard: The influence of CEO socialization on strategic change. *Journal of Management Studies* 34(4): 562–584.

Fox, Alan. 1974. *Beyond Contract*. London: Faber.

Fraher, Amy L. 2016. A toxic triangle of destructive leadership at Bristol Royal Infirmary: A study of organizational Munchausen Syndrome by proxy. *Leadership* 12(1): 34–52.

Fuks, Alexander. 1976. *Studies in Politics and Society in Ancient Greece*. Jerusalem: Bialik (Hebrew).

Gabriel, Richard A., and Paul L. Savage. 1981. *Crisis in Command*. New Delhi: Himalayan.

Galbraith, John K. 1971. *The New Industrial State*. Boston: Houghton Mifflin.

Gannon, Martin J. 1983. Managerial ignorance. *Business Horizons* 26(1): 26–32.

Geertz, Clifford. 1973. *The Interpretation of Cultures*. New York: Basic Books.

Geertz, Clifford. 1983. *Local Knowledge*. New York: Basic Books.

Geneen, Herold. 1984. *Managing*. New York: Avon.

Gherardi, Silvia. 2009. Introduction: The critical power of the 'practice lens'. *Management Learning* 40(2): 115–128.

Gioia, Dennis A., K. G. Korley, and A. L. Hamilton. 2013. Seeking qualitative rigor in inductive research: Notes on the Gioia methodology. *Organizational Research Methods* 16(1): 15–31.

Gioia, Dennis A., K. N. Price, et al. 2010. Forging an identity: An insider-outsider study of processes involved in the formation of organizational identity. *Administrative Science Quarterly* 55(1): 1–46.

Gobillot, Emmanuel. 2007. *The Connected Leader*. London: Kogan Page.

Goffman, Erving. 1959. *The Presentation of Self in Everyday Life*. Garden City (NY): Doubleday.

Gouldner, Alvin W. 1954. *Patterns of Industrial Bureaucracy*. New York: Free Press.

Graham, Jill W. 1991. Servant-leadership in organizations: Inspirational and moral. *Leadership Quarterly* 2(2): 105–119.

Graham, Laurie. 1995. *On the Line at Subaru-Isuzu*. Ithaca (NY): Cornell University Press.

Greenleaf, Robert K. 1977. *Servant Leadership*. New York: Paulist Press.

Griffin, Riki, and Anne O'Leary-Kelly (Eds.). 2004. *The Dark Side of Organizational Behaviour*. San Francisco: Jossey-Bass.

Grove, Andrew S. 1996. *Only the Paranoid Survive*. New York: Doubleday.

Groysberg, Boris, A. N. McLean, and N. Nohria. 2006. Are leaders portable? *Harvard Business Review*, May, reprint R0605E, Retrieved 11.1.2013: www.hbr.org

Guest, Robert H. 1962. *Organizational Change*. London: Tavistock.

Hambrick, Donald C. 2007. Upper echelons theory: An update. *Academy of Management Review* 32(2): 334–343.

Hargadon, Andrew B., and Beth A. Bechky. 2006. When collections of creatives become creative collectives: A field study of problem solving at work. *Organization Science* 17(4): 484–500.

Harvey, Michael G., M. M. Novicevic, et al. 2001. A historic perspective on organizational ignorance. *Journal of Managerial Psychology* 16(5/6): 449–468.

Hase, Stewart, S. Sankaran, and A. Davies. 2006. Overcoming barriers to knowledge management: Visiting the dark side of organisations. *Online Journal of Knowledge Management* 3(1). Retrieved 28.11.2007: www.actcom.org

Hawthorn, Geoffrey. 1991. *Plausible Worlds*. Cambridge: Cambridge University Press.

Hedgecoe, Adam M. 2012. Trust and regulatory organisations: The role of local knowledge and facework in research ethics review. *Social Studies of Science* 42(3): 662–683.

Henderson, Wiliam D. 1990. *The Hollow Army*. New York: Greenwood.

Heskett, John. 2011. *The Culture Cycle*. Upper Saddle River (NJ): FT Press.

Hill, Linda A. 2006. Exercising moral courage: A developmental agenda. In: D. L. Rhode (Ed.), *Moral Leadership*. San Francisco: Jossey-Bass, 267–300.

Hogan, Robert, and Joyce Hogan. 2001. Assessing leadership: A view from the dark side. *International Journal of Selection and Assessment* 9(1/2): 40–51.

Hogan, Robert, R. Raskin, and D. Fazzini. 1990. The dark side of charisma. In: K. E. Clark and M. B. Clark (Eds.), *Measures of Leadership*. Greensboro (NC): Center for Creative Leadership, 343–354.

Hollander, Edwin P. 1998. Ethical challenges in leader-follower relationships. In: J. B. Ciulla (Ed.), *Ethics, the Heart of Leadership*. Westport (CN): Praeger, 49–62.

Huen, Chi W. 2009. What is context? An ethnophilosophical account. *Anthropological Theory* 9(2): 149–169.

Hughes, Everett C. 1958. *Man and Their Work*. Glenco (IL): Free Press.

Ingvaldsen, Jonas A., H. Holtskog, and G. Ringen. 2013. Unlocking work standards through systematic work observation: Implications for team supervision. *Team Performance Management* 19(5/6): 279–291.

Izraeli, Daphna N. 1977. 'Settling-in': An interactionist perspective on the entry of the new manager. *Pacific Sociological Review* 20(1): 135–160.

Jackall, Robert. 1988. *Moral Mazes*. New York: Oxford.

Jaques, Elliot. 1990. *Creativity and Work*. Madison (CN): International Universities.

Johnson, Craig E. 2008. The rise and fall of Carly Fiorina. *Journal of Leadership & Organizational Studies* 15(2): 188–196.

Johnson, Craig E. 2009. *Meeting the Ethical Challenges of Leadership*. Los Angeles: Sage.

Kanter, Rosabeth M. 1993[1977]. *Men and Women of the Corporation*. New York: Basic Books.

Keltner, Dacher, C. A. Langer, and M. L. Allison. 2006. Power and moral leadership. In: D. L. Rhode (Ed.), *Moral Leadership*. San Francisco: Jossey-Bass, 177–194.

Kets De Vries, Manfred F. R. 1993. *Leaders, Fools, and Impostors*. San Francisco: Jossey-Bass.

Khurana, Rakesh. 2002. *Searching for a Corporate Savior*. Princeton (NJ): Princeton University Press.

Klein, Gary. 1998. *Sources of Power*. Cambridge (MA): MIT Press.

Klein, Jane A. 2004. *True Change*. San Francisco: Jossey-Bass.

Kolakowski, Leszek. 1964. In praise of inconsistency. *Dissent* (Spring): 201–209.

Kotter, John P. 1982. *The General Managers*. New York: Free Press.

Kovner, Rotem. 1993. The rise and fall of the man who crowned kings. *Haaretz*, April 9 (Hebrew).

Krasikova, Dina V., S. G. Green, and J. M. LeBreton. 2013. Destructive leadership: A theoretical review, integration, and future research agenda. *Journal of Management* 39(5): 1308–1338.

Kreiner, Kristian, and Majken Schultz. 1993. Informal collaboration in R&D: The formation of networks across organizations. *Organization Studies* 14(2): 189–209.

Kruger, Justin, and David Dunning. 1999. Unskilled and unaware of it: How difficulties in recognizing one's own incompetence lead to inflated self-assessments. *Journal of Personal and Social Psychology* 77(6): 1121–1134.

Lee, Paulin, N. Gillespie, et al. 2010. Leadership and trust: Their effect on knowledge sharing and team performance. *Management Learning* 41(4): 473–491.

Levenson, Bernard. 1961. Bureaucratic succession. In: A. Etzioni (Ed.), *Complex Organizations*. New York: Holt, 362–375.

Linstead, Stephen, G. Marechal, and R. W. Griffin. 2014. Theorizing and researching the dark side of organization. *Organization Studies* 35(2): 165–188.

Linz, Joan J. 1990. The perils of presidentialism. *Journal of Democracy* 1(1): 51–70.

Lipman-Blumen, Jean. 2005. *The Allure of Toxic Leaders*. New York: Oxford University Press.

Liu, Dong, H. Liao, and R. Loi. 2012. The dark side of leadership: A three-level investigation of the cascading effect of abusive supervision on employee creativity. *Academy of Management Journal* 55(5): 1187–1212.

Luthans, Fred. 1988. Successful versus effective managers. *Academy of Management Executive* 2: 127–132.

Mainwaring, Scott. 1990. Presidentialism in Latin America. *Latin America Research Review* 25: 157–179.

Marx, Emanuel. 1985. Social-anthropological research and knowing Arab society. In: Aluf Har'even (Ed.), *To Know Neighboring People*. Jerusalem: Van Lear, 137–152 (Hebrew).

McLagan, Patricia, and Christo Nel. 1997. *The Age of Participation*. San Francisco: Berret-Koehler.

Mehri, Darius. 2005. *Notes from Toyota-Land*. Ithaca (NY): ILR Press.

Meyer, David R. 2010. *The Engaged Manager*. Larkspur (CO): ECI Learning Systems.

Michels, Robert. 1959[1915]. *Political Parties*. New York: Dover.

Miller, Danny. 1992. The Icarus paradox: How exceptional companies bring about their own downfall. *Business Horizons* 35(1): 24–35.

Milliken, Frances J., Elizabeth W. Morrison, and Patricia F. Hewlin. 2003. An exploratory study of employee silence: Issues that employees don't communicate upward and why. *Journal of Management Studies* 40(6): 1453–1476.

Mintzberg, Henry. 1973. *The Nature of Managerial Work*. New York: Harper and Row.

Mintzberg, Henry. 1987. The strategy concept 1: 5 Ps for strategy. *California Management Review* 30(1): 11–21.

Morgan, David L. 2015. Pragmatism as a paradigm for social research. *Qualitative Inquiry* 20(8): 1045–1053.

Morita, Atsuro. 2014. The ethnographic machine: Experimenting with context and comparison in Strathernian Ethnography. *Science, Technology & Human Values* 39(2): 214–235.

Mosier, Michael L. 1988. Getting a grip on careerism. *Airpower Journal* 2(2): 52–60.

Moss, Sherry E., J. I. Sanchez, et al. 2009. The mediating role of feedback avoidance behavior in the LMX—performance relationship. *Group & Organization Management* 34(6): 645–664.

Narayan, Kirin. 1993. How native is a "native" anthropologist? *American Anthropologist* 95(3): 671–686.

Near, Henry. 1992–1997. *The Kibbutz Movement: A History*. Vol. I—New York: Oxford University Press; Vol. II—London: Littman Library.

Newsweek (unsigned). 1993. Building and corruption. October 4.

Nienaber, Ann-Marie, V. Holtorf, et al. 2015a. A climate of psychological safety enhances the success of front end teams. *International Journal of Innovation Management* 19(2). DOI: 10.1142/S1363919615500279.

Nienaber, Ann-Marie, M. Hofeditz, and P. D. Romeike. 2015b. Vulnerability and trust in leader-follower relationships. *Personnel Review* 44(4): 567–591.

Niv, Amitai, and Dan Bar-On. 1992. *The Dilemma of Size from a System Learning Perspective: The Case of the Kibbutz*. Greenwich (CN): JAI.

Norman, Steven M., Bruce J. Avolio, and Fred Luthans. 2010. The impact of positivity and transparency on trust in leaders and their perceived effectiveness. *The Leadership Quarterly* 21(3): 350–364.

Obembe, Demola. 2012. Knowledge sharing, sustained relationships and the habitus. *Management Learning* 44(4): 355–372.

Orlikowski, Wanda J. 2002. Knowing in practice: Enacting a collective capability in distributed organizing. *Organization Science* 13(3): 249–273.

Orr, Julian. 1996. *Talking about Machines*. Ithaca (NY): Cornell University Press.

Padilla, Art, R. Hogan, and R. B. Kaiser. 2007. The toxic triangle: Destructive leaders, susceptible followers, and conducive environments. *Leadership Quarterly* 18(2): 176–194.

Parker, Martin. 2000. *Organizational Culture and Identity*. London: Sage.

Parker, Martin. 2016. Secret societies: Intimations of organization. *Organization Studies* 37(1): 99–113.

Pohler, Dionne M., and Andrew Luchak. 2014. Balancing efficiency, equity, and voice: The impact of unions and high-involvement work practices on work outcomes. *ILR Review* 67(4): 1063–1094.

Pullen, Alison, and Carl Rhodes. 2015. Ethics, embodiment and organizations. *Organization* 22(2): 159–165.

Rennstam, Jens, and Karen L. Ashcraft. 2014. Knowing work: Cultivating a practice-based epistemology of knowledge in organization studies. *Human Relations* 67(1): 3–25.

Ribeiro, Rodrigo. 2013. Tacit knowledge management. *Phenomenology and Cognitive Sciences* 12(2): 337–366.

Riesman, D. 1950. *The Lonely Crowd*. New Haven: Yale University Press.

Roberts, Joan. 2012. Organizational ignorance: Towards a managerial perspective on the unknown. *Management Learning* 44(2): 215–236.

Robison, Jennifer. 2010. Leading engagement from the top. *Gallup Management Journal Online*. Retrieved: 27.7.2011: http://findarticles.com/p/articles/mi_6770

Rosner, Menachem. 1993. Organizations between community and market: The case of the kibbutz. *Economic and Industrial Democracy* 14(4): 369–397.

Rouse, Joseph. 1987. *Knowledge and Power*. Ithaca (NY): Cornell University Press.

Roy, Donald F. 1952. Quota restriction and goldbricking in a machine shop. *American Journal of Sociology* 57(4): 427–442.

Sandberg, Jörgen, and Ashly H. Pinnington. 2009. Professional competence as ways of being: An existential ontological perspective. *Journal of Management Studies* 46(7): 1138–1170.

Sanders, Sol. 1989. *Mexico: Chaos on Our Doorstep.* New York: Madison.

Scharfstein, Ben-Ami. 1995. *Amoral Politics.* Albany (NY): SUNY Press.

Schatzki, Theodore R., K. K. Cetina, and E. V. Savigny (Eds.). 2001. *The Practice Turn in Contemporary Theory.* London: Routledge.

Schön, Donald A. 1983. *The Reflective Practitioner.* New York: Basic Books.

Schweigert, Francis J. 2007. Learning to lead: Strengthening the practice of community leadership. *Leadership* 3(3): 325–342.

Segal, David R. 1981. Leadership and management: Organizations theory. In: J. H. Buck and L. J. Korb (Eds.), *Military Leadership.* Beverly Hills (CA): Sage, 41–69.

Sendjaya, Sen. 2005. Morality and leadership: Examining the ethics of transformational leadership. *Journal of Academic Ethics* 3(1): 75–86.

Sendjaya, Sen, J. C. Sarros, and J. C. Santora. 2008. Defining and measuring servant leadership behaviour. *Journal of Management Studies* 45(2): 402–423.

Sergeeva, Anastasia, and Tatiana Andreeva. 2015. Knowledge sharing research: Bringing context back in. *Journal of Management Inquiry.* DOI: 10.1177/1056492615618271.

Shapira, Reuven. 1987. *Anatomy of Mismanagement.* Tel Aviv: Am Oved (Hebrew).

Shapira, Reuven. 1990. Leadership, rotation and the kibbutz crisis. *Journal of Rural Cooperation* 18(1): 55–66.

Shapira, Reuven. 1995a. The voluntary resignation of outsider managers: Interkibbutz Rotation and Michels's 'Iron Law'. *Israel Social Science Research* 10(1): 59–84.

Shapira, Reuven. 1995b. 'Fresh blood' innovation and the dilemma of personal involvement. *Creativity and Innovation Management* 4(2): 86–99.

Shapira, Reuven. 2001. Communal decline: The vanishing of high-moral leaders and the decay of democratic, high-trust kibbutz cultures. *Sociological Inquiry* 71(1): 13–38.

Shapira, Reuven. 2005. Academic capital or scientific progress? A critique of the studies of kibbutz stratification. *Journal of Anthropological Research* 61(3): 357–380.

Shapira, Reuven. 2008. *Transforming Kibbutz Research.* Cleveland: New World Publishing.

Shapira, Reuven. 2011. Institutional combination for cooperative development: How trustful cultures and transformational mid-levelers overcame old guard conservatism. In: J. Blanc and D. Colongo (Eds.), *Co-operatives Contributions to a Plural Economy.* Paris: L'Harmattan, 75–90.

Shapira, Reuven. 2012. High-trust culture, the decisive but elusive context of shared co-operative leaderships. In: J. Heiskanen et al. (Eds.), *New Opportunities for Co-Operatives: New Opportunities for People.* Mikkeli, Finland: University of Helsinki Press, 154–167.

Shapira, Reuven. 2013. Leaders' vulnerable involvement: Essential for trust, learning, effectiveness and innovation in inter-co-operatives. *Journal of Co-operative Organization and Management* 1(1): 15–26. http://dx.doi.org/10.1016/j.jcom. 2013.06.003

Shapira, Reuven. 2015. Prevalent concealed ignorance of low-moral careerist managers: Contextualization by a semi-native multi-site Strathernian ethnography. *Management Decision* 53(7): 1504–1526. http://dx.doi.org/10.1108/md-10-2014-0620

Shotter, John. 2006. Understanding process from within: An argument for 'withness'-thinking. *Organization Studies* 27(4): 585–604.

Shotter, John. 2015. Reconsidering language use in our talk of expertise—are we missing something? Paper presented at the 7th Symposium on Process Organization Studies, Kos, Greece, June.

Shotter, John, and Haridimos Tsoukas. 2014a. In search of phronesis: Leadership and the art of judgment. *Academy of Management Learning & Education* 13(2): 224–243.

Shotter, John, and Haridimos Tsoukas. 2014b. Performing phronesis: On the way to engaged judgment. *Management Learning* 45(4): 377–396.

Siebert, Sabina, G. Martin, et al. 2015. Looking 'beyond the factory gates': Towards more pluralist and radical approaches to intraorganizational trust research. *Organization Studies* 36(8): 1033–1062.

Simons, Tony. 2002. Behavioural integrity: The perceived alignment between managers' words and deeds as a research focus. *Organization Science* 13(1): 18–35.

Smith, Peter H. 1986. Leadership and change, intellectuals and technocrats in Mexico. In: A Robert Camp (Ed.), *Mexico Political Stability*. Boulder (CO): Westview, 101–117.

Smithson, M. 1989. *Ignorance and Uncertainty*. New York: Springer-Verlag.

Snell, Robin S. 2001. Moral foundations of the learning organization. *Human Relations* 54(3): 319–342.

Starbuck, William A. 2007. Living in mythical spaces. *Organization Studies* 28(1): 21–25.

Stern, Ithai, and James D. Westphal. 2010. Stealthy footsteps to the boardroom: Executives' backgrounds, sophisticated interpersonal influence behaviour, and board appointments. *Administrative Science Quarterly* 55(2): 278–319.

Sternberg, Robert J. (Ed.). 2002. *Why Smart People Can Be So Stupid*. New Haven: Yale University Press.

Strathern, Marilyn. 2004. *Partial Connections: Updated Edition*. Savage (MD): Rowman & Littlefield.

Sykes, Chris. 2006. *Efficient Management/Wasted Knowledge? A Critical Investigation of Organisational Knowledge in Community Service Organisations*. PhD thesis, University of Sydney.

Thoroughgood, Christian N., W. T. Brian, et al. 2012. Bad to the bone: Empirically defining and measuring destructive leader behaviour. *Journal of Management and Organizational Studies* 19(2): 230–255.

Townley, Barbara. 2002. Managing with modernity. *Organization* 9(4): 549–573.

Tsoukas, Haridimos (Ed.). 2005. *Complex Knowledge*. Oxford: Oxford University Press.

Tsui-Auch, L. Si, and Guido Möllering. 2010. Wary managers: Unfavorable environments, perceived vulnerability, and the development of trust in foreign enterprises in China. *Journal of International Business* 41(6): 1016–1015.

Vald, Emanuel. 1987. *The Curse of the Broken Tools*. Jerusalem: Schocken (Hebrew).

Van Wolferen, Karel. 1989. *The Enigma of Japanese Power*. New York: Random House.

Villette, Michel, and Catherine Vuillermot. 2009. *From Predators to Icons*. Ithaca: ILR Press.

Wagner, Richard K. 2002. Smart people doing dumb things: The case of managerial incompetence. In: R. J. Sternberg (Ed.), *Why Smart People Can Be So Stupid*. New Haven: Yale University Press, 42–63.

Wang, Karen Y., and Stewart Clegg. 2007. Managing to lead in private enterprise in China: Work values, demography and the development of trust. *Leadership* 3(2): 149–172.

Watt, John R. 1972. *The District Magistrate in Late Imperial China*. New York: Columbia University Press.

Webb, Janette, and David Cleary. 1994. *Organizational Change and the Management of Expertise*. London: Routledge.

Weissberg, Robert. 2002. Administrative careerism and PC. *Academic Questions* 15(2): 58–68.

Welker, Marina, D. J. Partridge, and R. Hardin. 2011. Corporate lives: New perspectives on the social life of the corporate form. *Current Anthropology* 52(S3): S3–15.

Wexler, Mark N. 2006. Successful resume fraud: Conjectures on the origins of amorality in the workplace. *Journal of Human Values* 12(2): 137–152.

Wilson, George C. 2011. Careerism. In: W. T. Wheeler (Ed.), *The Pentagon Labyrinth*. Washington (DC): Center for Defense Information, 43–59.

Yanow, Dvora. 2000. Seeing organizational learning: A 'cultural' view. *Organization* 7(2): 247–268.

Yanow, Dvora. 2004a. Translating local knowledge at organizational peripheries. *British Journal of Management* 15: S15–S25.

Yanow, Dvora. 2004b. Academic anthropologists in the organizational studies workplace. *Management Learning* 35(2): 225–238.

Yin, Robert K. 1988. *Case Study Research*. Newbury Park (CA): Sage.

Zand, Dale E. 1972. Trust and managerial problem solving. *Administrative Science Quarterly* 17(2): 229–239.

Zbaracki, Mark J. 1998. The rhetoric and reality of total quality management. *Administrative Science Quarterly* 43(4): 602–633.

2 The Dark Secret of Immoral Careerism of "Jumper" Rotational CCMI-User Executives

"A few vices, in Arendt's mind, were more vicious than careerism"

(Robin 2007: 19).

Chapter 1 suggests that a major explanation of managerial incompetence is the use of CCMI by either detachment (CEOs, Moav, Shavit, Avi, Karmi) or seductive-coercive autocracy (Yuval). The decisive avoidance of vulnerable involvement, the use of CCMI, and the use of managerial knowledge and information advantages to defend one's own status, authority, and career, required low morality: bluffs, knowledge abuses, scapegoating, and other subterfuges found ubiquitous by cited ethnographies and by the literature on managerial ignorance, stupidity, incompetence, and organizations' dark side. Ignorance-exposing trust-enhancing vulnerable involvement is high-moral, preferring the common good: one endangers one's authority, status, and career prospects in order to learn, improve job functioning, and prevent mistaken and harmful decisions and actions. A major cause of managers' Im-C seems to be incompetence due to CCMI but, as cited, only few studied managerial ignorance; these few found it pervasive but did not explain it as an effort to defend managers' authority and power and to advance their careers through immoral practices. Similarly, destructive leadership often caused by ignorance and Im-C was found to be pervasive; one recent study estimates its incidence at between 33.5% and 61% and others corroborate this.[1]

Regrettably, ubiquitous Im-C has rarely been studied, apparently because it is a dark secret. Keeping it a dark secret requires immoral power abuses and subterfuges which an immoral careerist never admits publicly, at least not in real time, and rarely admits to oneself, rendering its study problematic, much as with CCMI. In view of the business scandals of the last decade managerial ethics has become a major topic of research and teaching[2] but not so Im-C, a major root of unethical practices. For example, the 58 Sage management and organization studies journals have 966 article abstracts that contain the word "career" but only five contain either "careerism" or "careerist" though, as cited, all authors who alluded to managers' Im-C found it common. Luthans's (1988) finding that ineffective managers managed to advance their careers more than effective ones implied common

Im-C among the formers, as did the finding whereby a larger percentage of psychopaths occupied higher ranks than lower ones, i.e., psychopaths who used immoral means advanced more than high-moral counterparts (Boddy et al. 2010). Feldman and Weitz (1991) found that careerism increased among a US university's business administration alumni from 1970s graduates to 1980s graduates, and others supported Bratton and Kacmar's (2004) conclusion that careerists who promote themselves at the expense of others are all too common.[3]

Curtis (2009: 505) concluded that careerism is "seldom conducive to clear thinking or original thought," and in addition to the above literature US military scholars extensively studied careerism critically.[4] Luttwak (1984: 200) even warned that "If careerism becomes the general attitude, the very basis of [military] leadership is destroyed," but neither this warning nor others' critiques seem to have made any change; recently ex-Marine Corps colonel Wilson (2011: 46) asserted that

> ". . . many senior officers think that the military is all about getting promoted and accumulating as many signs of rank and status as possible, completed with a host of perks . . . [These careerists] are so prevalent because bureaucracies are in effect designed by and for careerists . . . [which] are promoted because of a zero defect record of playing it safe, making no controversial decisions and requiring others to do the same."

Behaviorists explain careerism by careerists' traits, beliefs, and ideologies (e.g., Chiaburu et al. 2013), but Wilson explains it structurally: immoral careerists' hegemony shapes bureaucracies conducive to Im-C. A major route for rapid career advance is frequent changing firms with a façade (Goffman 1959) of successful functioning in previous jobs by concealing, camouflaging, and scapegoating others for one's mistakes, wrongs, and failures while appropriating to oneself others' successes.[5] However, where "parachuting" and *rotatzia* are normative one may advance her/his career even without a zero-defect record in previous jobs and with only minimal concealing and camouflaging of misdeeds and failures. Shavit's and Avi's firings were deferred for a year and presented as normal *rotatzia* to defend the prestige of their boss (Levenson 1961: 373), and sparing them stigmatization enabled further managerial careers. Moreover, Avi became TM twice without proving his capacity for the job due to the two bosses' CCMI, each in turn missing his incompetence due to own ignorance, and when he failed his managerial career was rescued twice as it served bosses' interests. Both bosses' choice of CCMI prevented open and trustful relationships with senior staff, who were fully aware of Avi's incompetence as shown by the citations. The instituted practice of "parachuted" outsiders monopolizing the I-KRC management, combined with the succession-encouraging *rotatzia*, enhanced managers' Im-C and use of CCMI. A similar combination in the US armed forces also enhanced Im-C and explains why many of their students alluded to Im-C, unlike minimal regard of organizational research.

Rotatzia and "parachutings" tend to be concomitant and suit Wilson's (2011) thesis that immoral careerists' hegemony shapes bureaucracies conducive to Im-C: all I-KRC CEOs interviewed supported the *rotatzia* norm, which many of them and their protégés such as PM Moav violated (below), while it shortened kibbutz officers' terms and weakened them by creating a pool of ex-officers seeking further managerial careers by "parachuting" into lucrative I-KO jobs.[6] I-KRC CEOs' control of such jobs pressed kibbutz officers to be submissive as representatives to I-KRCs' Boards to prove loyalty to I-KRC executives. *Rotatzia* norm encouraged "parachuting" of ex-kibbutz officers to mid-level I-KRC jobs, but it was not taken for granted. Only a minority of importees had job-pertinent experience and expertise; they were mostly imported despite their ignorance of I-KRC jobs, and as in Avi's case they were often promoted despite failing in jobs (also Yuval's case below). Thus, why import *pe'ilim* and pay the price of their learning such as mistakes, wrongs, and failures rather than promote knowledgeable competent insiders?

A new king is known to nominate his loyalists as deputies and ministers, but many "parachuted" nominees were only prospective loyalists who might not turn out to be loyal and might fail in their jobs, lacking pertinent expertises and choosing CCMI. Students from Gouldner (1954) onward pointed out how executives elevated/imported their own kind to mid-level jobs, a practice that Moore called (1962: 109) "homosexual reproduction" and that Kanter (1993[1977]: 48) explained as a result of the built-in uncertainty in managerial jobs.[7] By elevating/importing one's kind the executive expects that promoted/imported managers will think, decide, and act as s/he would have done in these offices and will support his policies and decisions, hence they will curb one's uncertainty and enhance one's power, an additional certainty.[8] That all I-KRC executives were "parachuted" *pe'ilim* their importing their own kind to mid-level offices could be explained as attempting to curb uncertainty, although Avi's case proved twice how illusive it was when the importee chooses CCMI.

However, an additional explanation was power advantage through importing rather than elevating: an importee is weak, especially a young one as were many I-KRC importees, unlike an experienced older insider empowered by local knowledge and record of successes (Klein 1998) who may threaten the boss's authority and power, as Thomas defeated his bosses in both the S&GH and the automatic feeder cases (below). *Rotatzia* legitimized the early firing of unwanted importees with minimal damage to the boss's prestige, contrary to Levenson's (1961: 373) findings, and encouraged "parachuting" of *pe'ilim* replacements, while if the latter failed rescuers were called in. Together with other reasons presented below, "parachuted" *pe'ilim* almost monopolized I-KRCs' management. The exceptions were hired TMs such as Muli, whom Merkaz gin plant founding *pa'il* Moav promoted from technician in an older plant due to his precious ginning knowledge needed by greenhorn staff. When a new generation of technically educated young members such as Avi seemed of their kind to young PMs such as Yuval appeared in kibbutzim, they were "parachuted" to TM jobs, creating an unofficial norm of no hired TMs. This norm was legitimized as defending the interests of kibbutzim in I-KRCs by supposedly sparing agency problems of hired managers (Arthurs and Busenitz 2003). But as Chapter 1 has depicted and as further untangled below, "parachutings" encouraged *pe'ilim*'s choice of CCMI that engendered distrust and ignorance cycles which stimulated Im-C, detrimental to the interests of kibbutzim in effective cotton gin plants.

Some Signs of Self-Serving Merkaz *Pe'ilim* Practicing Im-C

Any journalist visiting the Merkaz industrial park and interviewing executives would probably have portrayed them as dynamic industrialists who established several modern advanced processing plants that helped develop kibbutz agriculture to match that of most advanced countries by enabling new and more profitable crops, mostly for export, extracting kibbutz agriculture from the bounds of local markets. I however, following Diefenbach's (2013: 150) critique of "overtly positive and undifferentiated, unrealistically flattering and naive pictures of leaders," soon untangled clear signs of a self-serving, careerist power elite, contrary to *pe'ilim*'s assertions that their prime aim was to advance plants' effectiveness and efficiency to best serve kibbutzim. Contrary to these, I rarely found on plant shop floors signs of genuine interest in these aims (e.g., Alvesson and Kärreman 2013). For example, as against *pe'ilim*'s brand-new company, car forklifts were cheap, old, sluggish models that frequently break down. Another contrast: most plants were enlarged recently far beyond kibbutz agricultural requirements while exhibiting technological virtuosity, signaling the accumulation of power by the managerial elite interested in prestige, status, privileges, and lengthy tenures, as Galbraith (1971) explained corporate "technostructure" (Shapira 1978/9). *Pe'ilim* enjoyed lavish amenities: air-conditioned offices and a dining hall serving high-standard meals, new-model company cars rare in kibbutzim at the time, and privileges such as pocket money for refreshment on *pe'ilim*'s short way to work or back, and their learning trips abroad, which were undeclared bonuses as their itinerary often violated their declared aims.

Kibbutzim had abstemious egalitarian cultures, while *pe'ilim*'s standard of living especially that of senior ones, was well beyond kibbutzim standard. *Pe'ilim* mostly held company cars for their free use, while the kibbutz's hundreds of other members shared 10–15 cars and paid considerable amounts of their small monthly allowances for their use. *Pe'ilim*'s cars were prime status symbols as salaries were uniform, while company cars were graded carefully according to rank. This symbolizing function also reflected *pe'ilim*' interest in company car models: when I came to CEO Zelikovich's office for a scheduled interview, I had to wait some 20 minutes until he and his deputy concluded a long and quite heated debate about the experience of driving the deputy's new model car. Another sign of this role was furnishing junior clerk *pe'ilim* with a humbler car model, a two-door mini Autobianchi A112 with 900 cc engines; senior clerks got 1100 cc engine cars; mid-managers (Avi, Danton) 1300 cc engine cars; while plant manager Shavit drove an automatic 1600 cc engine car, at the time considered a prestigious "executives' car" in Israel. One car did not fit this hierarchy and signaled opposite to Im-C, Thomas's dirty old 3500 cc station wagon with which he remained despite offers to replace it with a new family car like those of other *pe'ilim*. "Most decisive for me" he said, "is that I can load everything I must repair in an outside shop, so that I can shorten the gin's downtime."[9] In view of the decisiveness of minimizing downtime, this insistence leaves little question that he sought to advance his career by performance rather than by Im-C, as did Zelikovich, Shavit, Avi, and most other *pe'ilim*: gaining a high-status job by nurturing ties with higher-ups, its defense by CCMI, exhibiting status symbols, and using politics, which also advances career (see below).

Pe'ilim's little interest in plants' effectiveness was demonstrated by the inefficiency of the Merkaz fodder mix mill's new production unit: before adding this highly computerized unit to the older one, the annual mix production per employee was 1,291 tons, while subsequently instead of the promised enhanced productivity it fell to 1,123 tons. This unit's construction was a mega project-type OPM waste by incompetent, excessively ambitious executives (Flyvbjerg et al. 2003): its planned cost was US$8 million, while the actual cost was US$20 million (fixed prices) with same production capacity. Executives either bent the numbers to legitimize building the largest unit in the country (for which the Swiss producer custom-built its new largest presses) and/or due to ignorance they missed planners' bending them. Soon after construction began, the true cost became known, while updated fodder mix consumption projections showed that only half the planned capacity would be required in the next decade. Board members representing kibbutzim demanded a reduction of the scale of the project, but executive *pe'ilim* stubbornly objected. Such a reduction at this advanced stage was a very complex task requiring much expertise, which *pe'ilim* presumably lacked, beside their prospective loss of the prestige of managing Israel's largest mill. After repeated discussions, *pe'ilim* won: they waived kibbutzim's additional direct investments, but kibbutzim paid for the OPM scandal in years of extra fodder mix prices and moreover, less profitable customers were added to enhance utilization of the plant. Kibbutz representatives agreed because this retained their image as kibbutz interest servers and because their prospects for advancing their careers depended on *pe'ilim*, especially on CEO Zelikovich who led the OPM.[10] Both representatives and the plant's mid-level *pe'ilim* interviewed agreed that the prime reason for executives' stubbornness was self-aggrandizement (Galbraith 1971).

Quite similar excesses and seeking of prestige-enhancing technological virtuosity were also found in other Merkaz plant enlargements, suggesting self-aggrandizing amoral *pe'ilim* (Shapira 1978/9). When joined by *pe'ilim* ignorance, this caused fiascos: PM Yuval decided to replace the gin plant electricity system at the cost of some US $300,000 (US $900,000 at current prices) with an imported system presented by the importer and a colluding consultancy engineer as state-of-the-art. Soon after starting operations, it failed and was replaced, doubling the cost. The former plant's chief electrician, who had left due to his objections to this system, becoming a successful electricity installer contractor, testified that he had warned Yuval that it could be presented as novel because there were no such systems in Israel since they had failed and were replaced. But Yuval, as an ex-cotton branch manager, lacked any experience of industrial electricity and preferred CCMI by autocratic seduction-coercion; he did not check out the warning given by the credential-lacking electrician with experts. He ordered the seemingly "state-of-the-art system" and failed, while also losing a knowledgeable expert electrician whose successor took years to acquire a similar level of local knowledge and competency.

I asked the veteran ex-gin plant manager Moav (see below) whether kibbutzim as owners could prevent the above fiascos and similar others and he answered:

> "The I-KRC is structured so that everything is controlled from the top, its management decides everything. All the kibbutz representatives' assemblies became futile, kibbutzim show no interest in Merkaz problems . . . when establishing an apparatus it then run by itself deciding patterns, deciding actions . . . ."

However, Merkaz did not really "run by itself"; executives run it without allowing owner kibbutzim a real say in its management, as they followed the oligarchic autocracy of prime kibbutz leaders and other I-KO CEOs (to be analyzed in Chapter 6). Kibbutz representatives reacted to the mock Merkaz democracy by avoidance: less than half of them participated in annual plant owners' assemblies,[11] and many participants told me they would not come next year as it was a waste of time: *pe'ilim* pushed through every motion they wished, as with plant enlargements. Owner kibbutzim failed to control *pe'ilim* also because of the prestige and power they accumulated due to plants' large scale and technological virtuosity (Galbraith 1971), and due to senior veteran *pe'ilim*'s domination of their home kibbutzim; they nominated young loyalists to manage them rotationally and then as their patrons decided which of them would be promoted to lucrative I-KO jobs according to loyalty (Shapira 2008). As kibbutz representatives on I-KRC Boards, such kibbutz managers rarely dared object to senior *pe'ilim* on whom their advancement to I-KO jobs might depend. I found such objections only in the fodder mix mill enlargement case in which they failed, not in four other excessive plant enlargement cases, seemingly because their OPM waste was less conspicuous: they were less expensive, their estimated cost was closer to the actual cost, and kibbutzim financed only a small portion of the investment (Shapira 1978/9).

Im-C of First PM Moav

The above findings point to the kibbutzim's lack of control over *pe'ilim*, who used this leeway for self-serving actions and practices. I shall now briefly present the three Merkaz's gin PMs from my data, suggesting that all three throughout the plant's 19-year history studied suffered large gaps of essential local knowledge, lacking interactional and contributory expertises, and deficient of referred expertise. Thus, none of them risked authority by vulnerable involvement in practitioners' problem-solving deliberations in order to learn. Practicing Im-C, they used CCMI to defend their jobs and to maintain their power, authority, and prestige, causing distrust and negatively impacting knowledge sharing, learning, problem-solving, and the plant's functioning.

Cotton growing was introduced in Israel in the early 1950s and as it rapidly proliferated in kibbutzim in 1960 the Merkaz Board decided to establish a gin plant. The veteran CEO suggested Moav, his 61-year-old brother-in-law, as manager although Moav had no cotton or industrial management experience; as a *pa'il* he had some 35 years' experience in bookkeeping and as treasurer of a national commercial I-KC (some 1,500 employees) and seemingly did not fail. His clean record assisted the Board's approval of his nomination despite the nepotism involved and his minimal job-relevant knowledge, while Moav accepted it due to his advanced age and having no better offer. He found two enthusiastic mid-age deputies, Yaakov and Aharon, both ex-managers of kibbutz cotton branches who experienced the problems inherent in raw cotton processing by a distant gin plant, while Yaakov was also ex-economic manager of his kibbutz. From another plant he brought Muli, an experienced technician with minimal technical education but an army captain in the reserves, as a hired TM.[12] Muli taught Yaakov and Aharon the basics of ginning; then experienced mechanics Levi joined and enhanced technical expertise, while in the fifth year Yaakov led the successful enlargement of the plant by adding of a new, higher-capacity second ginning unit.

Moav's considerable managerial experience could have been a referred expertise (Collins and Sanders 2007), helpful for learning the plant's problems, but he failed learning without shop floor involvement, which he avoided, and defended his authority by detached CCMI, according the Jewish saying, "a mute fool is reputed to be wise." Tens of interviewees described him as a conservative, stingy manager whose efforts at minimizing expenses irrationally barred many problems from being solved. Committed expert employees were minimally remunerated, only slightly more than lazy loafers retained because they made do with low salaries, while detached, ignorant Moav missed the difference (e.g., Collins and Weinel 2011). The formers suffered from Moav's retaining of loafers; they were pressed to work harder to overcome the idleness and mistakes of the latter. Moav used a loyalist loafer as a "two-way funnel" (Dalton 1959: 232): the latter supplied detached Moav with information about what was going on in the plant and gave him employees' views and information without requiring Moav's ignorance-exposing involvement while informing employees about his views; for these services the "funnel" was rewarded in various ways. Other immoral means were granting privileges and promotions based on personal loyalty rather than efficiency and effectiveness, of which he was ignorant. *Pe'ilim* who proved personal loyalty to Moav were appointed to the management committee, while critics were ousted and newcomers who did not actively prove their personal loyalty were not included. For instance, the new chief electrician *pa'il*, who did not bother to prove his personal loyalty to Moav as he was very busy with solving grave electrical problems left unattended by his predecessor, was not invited to the committee of which his inept but loyal predecessor was a member. Other examples: a new *pa'il* who did not seem sufficiently loyal did not get a company car and another one who became critical of Moav's dysfunction was left with an old, unreliable vehicle that encouraged his departure.

Moav managed the administration, *pe'ilim*'s manpower, finances and foreign relations, while Yaakov with Aharon, Muli, and Levi managed all operations. For them, Moav and the gin plant's Board were ignorant alien authorities to be manipulated in order to prevent damage to the plant's operations, which they achieved through trust and learning cycles of the ginning practitioners' community, similar to Orr's (1996) technicians versus Xerox executives. Moav was told only that needed to keep him satisfied and to receive his and the Board's approval for major decisions made by the four. Yaakov described the Board thus:

> "In the [gin plant] Board there were a variety of people who may have had skills in various domains but no professional know-how [of ginning]. Only two of us were capable of making professional decisions—myself and Aharon. When Aharon left, I felt I was only disruptive and could not change anything even though I had an understanding of almost everything and no one could sell me any old wives' tales . . . I knew every machine and all about the [cotton] business, but who else understood these? One can sell anyone any old wives' tale over there and the people are too embarrassed to ask questions so as not to reveal their ignorance. How come they're on the Board and don't understand a thing?"[13]

Management sessions were quite similar, according to the minutes: Moav rarely spoke, except when finances were discussed in an attempt to save on expenses. However, he was lavish with his own amenities: one of the first air-conditioned offices in the park, a nice small company car, and more.

Detached CEO Akerman Kept Dysfunctional Moav, Promoted Ignorant Yuval

When Moav finished a five-year formal term and a year after reaching retirement age (65), although everyone agreed that Yaakov as the plant's real leader should replace him, CEO Akerman, satisfied with Moav's staunch loyalty including as a member of Merkaz I-KRC Board of Directors,[14] rejected Yaakov and Aharon's demand for his succession. Versus Moav's unquestioned loyalty, Yaakov was empowered by the plant's successes (Klein 1998) that made him independent and promised less submissiveness on the I-KRC Board sessions if replacing Moav; hence Moav remained. His loyalty was ensured by total dependency on Akerman's will, as he could have been fired at any moment both on grounds of *rotatzia* norm and of retirement age.

Akerman's prolonging of Moav's tenure was a conspicuous Im-C move; the staff testified that Yaakov's highly trusted leadership ensured the plant's functioning despite dysfunctional Moav. The veteran store manager nostalgically remembered it: "Yaakov modeled committed leadership so convincingly that you could not but follow him." Only very few of the dozens of interviewees thought that Moav had been a good manager, these being only his loyalists whom he had promoted and rewarded. The best a ginning expert such as Levi could say of Moav was that his detachment spared degradation of professional decisions. The senior staff bitterly criticized his ignorant conservatism that let them suffer unsolved problems that they could have solved if freed of his conservative stinginess. Akerman himself admitted that "Yaakov was Moav's natural successor; he enjoyed the full trust of all those involved with the plant, which is of prime importance in this job." However, he declined to explain why the "natural successor" did not succeed. The only plausible explanation that Akerman refrained from doing so was own Im-C; retaining of staunch loyalist Moav kept I-KRC's Board docile, ignoring that the plant's functioning would deteriorate if the two frustrated deputies left, as indeed they did.

One year later Aharon left and Yaakov did so two years later, overburdened by taking on many of Aharon's tasks. The Im-C of both Moav and Akerman is further evident seeing how they let Yaakov exhaust himself when trying to prevent the plant's functioning from deteriorating without a proper successor to Aharon. Assumedly, Yaakov and Moav could not agree on any successor, as Moav sought a loyalist who would object to Yaakov's justified wish to replace him, while Yaakov sought an effective committed helper like Aharon.

When Yaakov left, Muli was empowered by expanding his jurisdiction to all of Yaakov and Aharon's tasks, while Moav's reaction to Yaakov's departure further proved his Im-C: in order to prolong his job, he "parachuted" young talented *pa'il* Yuval (aged 30) as deputy, ignorant of ginning and with minimal managerial experience, only two years as manager of a kibbutz cotton branch. Yuval could not be considered a proper successor without prolonged grooming; hence this served Moav's self-perpetuation aim rather than promoting a true leader (e.g., Haslam et al. 2011) capable of succeeding Yaakov, either an insider such as Levi or Amram, or importing a *pa'il* experienced in industrial management who after a shorter grooming period could have been a good successor. Experienced Muli was no match for Levi and Amram's expertise, lacking as he did a technical education while also busy settling the newly occupied territories, and he was not considered the heir apparent. Muli (aged 52) allowed young Yuval only minimal say in all practical domains. Yuval disliked this as his habitus from managing the kibbutz cotton branch was of involved autocratic control, as indicated by members of his kibbutz. As he opted for seductive-coercive autocracy that kept him ignorant of ginning, he frequently clashed with Muli's critique of mistakes exposed thanks to 17 years of ginning experience and his lengthy leadership as an army captain in the reserves.

Due to Yuval's ignorance and destructive conflicts with Muli (e.g., Deutsch 1969), the plant's functioning deteriorated so much that CEO Akerman replaced Moav with Yuval. Akerman presumably knew about Yuval's unsatisfactory record as Moav's deputy, but not about his CCMI; probing his suitability for PM required the CEO to consult plant expert staff and expose his ignorance of ginning problems, contrary to his habituated detached CCMI. He avoided this, though a few short interviews with the senior staff could have prevented the mistaken promotion. Senior technician Amram described Yuval's stupid autocracy thus:

> "Yuval entered the plant with too much brutal force; this was a major reason for my departure. He was the opposite of Yaakov; if some piston dysfunctioned—he went and tried to fix it with no consideration of experts; he never waited for them, never consulted them and after I left the staff rebelled against Yuval's excessive involvement in their work."

Regrettably, the CEO did not listen to plant staff when promoting Yuval, both due to detached CCMI and because Yuval's nomination promised to replace old Moav's staunch loyalty with a similar young loyalist on Merkaz's Board. Yuval's nomination promised this because:

1   Yuval's weakness as a young, inexperienced novice prevented much independence;
2   Yuval owed the CEO his loyalty due to his promotion despite problematic functioning;
3   Yuval as a member of Akerman's kibbutz had an interest in maintaining good relations with him.

These considerations, in addition to disregarding Yuval's failure as deputy and the previous avoidance of nominating Yaakov despite his suitability for the job, proves that self-serving Im-C dominated the CEO's decision-making.

Im-C of Second Gin PM Yuval and CEO Zelikovich

Yuval had some referred expertise as an ex-manager of a kibbutz cotton branch, which both Moav and Shavit lacked. But ignorant of ginning, with minimal managerial experience, and much younger than veteran local experts, he lacked the psychological safety (e.g., Nienaber et al. 2015) necessary to risk ignorance exposure by the vulnerable involvement required for a virtuous trust and learning cycle. He used CCMI by mostly distancing from employees; only occasionally did he interfere autocratically in deliberations, and he only minimally listened to experts as Amram depicted and others corroborated, leading to amateurish and foolish decisions that caused animosity, distrust, and secrecy (e.g., Costas and Grey 2014), such as the failed replacement of the electricity system. He roamed around seeking information like Gouldner's (1954) outsider, but as he was distrusted, employees never truly taught him. His ignorance was exposed, for instance, when he drove a forklift over a frail pit cup that had broken, and he and the machine fell into the pit.

Secrecy and ignorance similarly failed him in staff nominations. He sought empowerment and authority certainty by importing lieutenant *pe'ilim* like himself (Moore 1962: 109). At first he "parachuted" Karmi as deputy and as Muli's superior. Karmi was a little older than Yuval (34), and like him was an ex-manager of the kibbutz cotton branch, but he was less forceful, less self-assured, and seemingly less intelligent, choosing detached CCMI. His "parachuting" encouraged Muli's intention to leave, frustrating his expectation to become PM or at least deputy PM. Muli informed Yuval of his intentions and Yuval "parachuted" young *pa'il* Avi into a new job, deputy TM to groom him to replace Muli, keeping this intention secret to prevent resistance by expert staff who saw Amram as Muli's heir apparent.[15] Yuval said that he wanted a *pa'il* successor to care for kibbutzim's interests, but all informants denied this excuse, praised Amram's decisions and actions that were beneficial for kibbutzim cotton. The real reason was the threat of Amram's empowerment by promotion, particularly if Amram was aided by Levi: in addition to the professional advantages of the two and to Levi's role as shop steward, Levi was much older than his *pe'ilim* bosses, held a practical engineer certificate, was the best ginner, and a very experienced manager due to his 15 years as a pipe installation contractor. Yuval's "parachuting" of ignorant Avi and promise of promotion to TM was thus a clear Im-C move, aimed at his own empowerment rather than at promoting the best candidate to a managerial job.

Particularly fateful was Yuval's mistaken promotion of Avi to TM after a year and a half of supposed grooming for the job as Muli's deputy. Avi's miserable failure, which prompted the summoning of Thomas to the rescue, begs the question: how did such an intelligent involved boss make such a terrible mistake?

The answer is ignorance of one's own ignorance (Kruger and Dunning 1999) due to use of autocratic CCMI. Harvey and his colleagues (2001: 451) pointed out that ". . . specifying ignorance is possible only in those organizational contexts in which dialogue and inquiry into unknowns is an established cultural norm." Such dialogue and inquiry engender high-trust cultures, but Yuval's coerciveness caused distrust and ignorance cycles, denoted Im-C aimed at advance by self-serving means: concealing and/or camouflaging ignorance and abuse of intangible resources for coercing employees. In the absence of trust, suspicions inevitably emerge; there is no vacuum (Fox 1974). Yuval created a new managerial job specifically for Avi's "parachuting"; he did not define its jurisdiction and concealed his aim. Muli, Amram, and others soon suspected that Avi had been imported to replace Muli and to build Yuval's supporting clique (Dalton 1959: 58). Their secrecy due to distrusting Yuval deprived him of valid information, of "unshakeable facts" (Geneen 1984: 101) crucial for the decision concerning Avi's promotion. On his tours of the plant Yuval might have discerned Avi's detachment, but to know how ignorant he remained Yuval needed interactional expertise and knowledge of ginners' language, learned only by vulnerable involvement in the ginners' community deliberations.[16] But Yuval distrusted and detested the senior ginners and they closed ranks against him; he missed Avi's incompetence; when Muli left he promoted Avi to TM and he failed miserably.

Importing Thomas to the rescue, a successful mechanic and garage manager but with no ginning know-how and *phronesis*, rather than promoting knowledgeable insiders Amram or Levi, further proved Yuval's Im-C. Amram or Levi's empowerment by promotion would have dissolved Yuval's baseless assertions, wishful guesses, and amateurish suggestions. Such defeats might have ruined his authority versus Thomas, who would have to learn a lot before achieving the latter's expertise level, and until reaching this level he could not humiliate Yuval by exposing his ignorance and stupidity.

The next move, an even clearer mark of Im-C, was the sinecure that retained Avi's status parallel to Thomas's. Keeping Avi's status while Thomas was still in his initial trial period and his prospects of success were unknown seemed like a reasonable cautious move, not putting all his eggs in one basket. But Avi was a failed "egg" worth little; only the expertise of Amram, Levi, and others prevented complete failure until Thomas learned and became functional. One who cared about the plant's functioning should have acknowledged this and, for instance, promoted Amram to deputy TM. But Yuval cared about his own power; the fiction of "two technical managers" concealed Avi's incompetence for the TM job and spared Yuval his problematic firing,[17] while it enabled *divide-et-impera*: the dependency of Avi's sinecure on the boss's will ensured his support for Yuval's objections to Thomas's proposals.

Avi's automatic support invited mismanagement. Yuval barred access to the minutes of the management committee's sessions, but other sources told me of fiascos such as the failed electricity system whose ratification explained Yuval's automatic majority in the committee. Worse still, Avi's retention by a sinecure ruined employees' trust in the boss's benevolence and this in turn breached further communications with Avi, at an enormous cost, as in the S&GH debacle, or at a smaller cost, as in the automatic sampler case.

All the above do not mention the new CEO Zelikovich, who replaced Akerman a year after Yuval's promotion to PM. Zelikovich opted for detached CCMI. One reason was that despite dysfunctional Yuval, Muli and his aides kept the plant at a mediocre functioning level, sparing the CEO the urgent need to intervene. However, his detachment encouraged Yuval's self-serving actions: autocratic suppression of Muli and his aides, ignoring their critique of mistaken decisions, and Avi's promotion and retention beside Thomas. Yuval's immoral selfishness culminated in an irresponsible love affair in the midst of the high season when urgent major decisions must sometimes be reached in the 24/7 working plant. In the first high season of my observations, married Yuval and his young female unmarried secretary frequently disappeared for half a day to an unknown destination, with no way of contacting him. Everyone talked about this vicious romance, but the detached CEO whom I never saw visiting the plant ousted Yuval on the pretext of *rotatzia* only months after the season ended. CEO Zelikovich's detachment left Yuval with too much discretion for selfishness and seemingly also caused the CEO a very late reaction to it, which furthered employees' distrust in superiors.

Im-C of Third PM Shavit

The descriptions in Chapter 1 pointed out that plant manager Shavit also used detached CCMI like Moav as I witnessed: He rarely visited the shopfloor, and when visiting rarely spoke to knowledgeable staff and never discussed technical and operational problems with them. He asked only trivial questions, listened only to escorting TM *pa'il* Avi and ignorant loyalist Atad, ignoring comments of expert others and not trying to find out the truth when they contradicted Avi and Atad. His rare comments exposed that by his fourth year, he did not know certain ginning basics I had learned in my first week of work. Even more conclusive proof of his ignorance was his acceptance of Avi's false assertion that his mistaken design of the contour of the 30-inch pipe connecting the new S&GH to the previous machine only marginally impacted the recurring clogging of the S&GH, acceptance that delayed the repair of this major mistake for six weeks.

Shavit, after four years as plant manager, was unaware of the dangers of accepting Avi's assertion. Detachment kept him ignorant of ginning basics, know-how, and *phronesis*, which were inseparable parts of learning the gin operator job. If Shavit had experienced this job, he would have known how complex, intricate, and unforeseeable is the flow of cotton through the large serpentine pipes, such that even experts are often unsure how to solve a flow problem and require several trials until finding a solution. In the case of the S&GH problem, the solution was to add a tailored 10-meter serpentine pipe costing $US 1,000. Shavit as plant manager was expected to know these problems sufficiently to intelligently discuss them with ginners, to speak their language (Collins 2011), and have interactional expertise (Collins and Evans 2007) in order to receive their intelligent contributions to his decisions and actions. His authority could be legitimized by the ability to make the right decisions, which required his involvement in the ginning practitioner community deliberations. He does not need to know how to design gin piping, or all possible reasons for clogging, but he does need to be aware of the critical role of piping problems for gin plant functioning and he should have suspected and probed Avi's assertion that the mistaken pipe contour was marginal.

Shavit resembled the emperor in Andersen's legend, "The Emperor's New Clothes": just as the emperor did not dare check the swindlers' machines and fabrics himself, so Shavit did not dare expose his own ignorance by probing the pipe problem to check Avi's assertion. In fact, it was as simple as the emperor's checking that the swindlers' looms weaved nothing: if Shavit had climbed the S&GH and seen all the raw cotton concentrated on the left end and clogging it while the other 90% of its saws were empty of cotton, he would have suspected Avi, would have consulted inside and outside experts who would have unanimously supported the staff's rejection of Avi's claim as outside consultants did five weeks later, and would have left Avi no choice but to change the contour immediately.

But Shavit's detachment prevented this, while he also failed by consulting with his loyalist, ignorant informer/loafer Atad, the shop steward politician who was his "two-way funnel" (Dalton 1959: 232) and a conspicuous example of how lower participants' power (Mechanic 1962) was augmented by managerial ignorance. Atad's Im-C reflected Shavit's; though they clashed annually on demands for higher salaries when Atad became shop steward, after Atad achieved pay hikes for the staff by "Italian strikes" of ultra-slow work ahead of every ginning season, he served Shavit by keeping the industrial peace in return for nice salaries for himself and his dominant clique of foremen and technicians while neglecting the salaries of lesser employees. He used his job leeway as a repair technician to rally political support by walking around, talking, and pretending to work; an example of his irresponsible leadership was evident in the incident in which he led the morning shift that refused to help clean up the remnants of a 1 AM fire at 6 AM to enable resumption of processing (p. 60). The rise to power of such worthless incompetent "brambles" (thorn bushes) against which the Holy Bible warns us (Judges: Ch. 9, par. 8–16) reverberates in McGregor's (1960) warning of the rise of "worst trouble-makers." Levi depicted Atad thus:

> "Atad cursed me because when he was in my team he had to work. After every two weldings he'd run off to smoke a cigarette. He used to

do terrible things from the professional point of view. He went from one extreme to the other, plainly irresponsible. He walked around a lot, smelt here smelt there; he is a guy who knows how to get around [problematic] things. I would not rely on his welding if it had anything to do with carrying heavy weights. I would only gave him [welding] tin covers or [marginal] rods."[18]

The manager of a large store for technical supplies and an ex-foreman mentioned Atad as one of the gin plant's "people who really sabotage the work," and added:

"You say that Atad has become the head of the union committee? I can well imagine what the gin plant looks like now. I was one of the foremen who demanded to sack him. I refused to have him in my shift after all sorts of subterfuges against me."

The opinions of other employees were not more positive:

"Atad is one great chunk of subterfuges. He's the type who talks too much, kills time, talks much more than he does."
"Atad knows how to cook a stew, [he is] not the type on whose word you could count. Rabina was a member of the union committee when managers wanted to suck him. At first he fought for him but later he was sorry about it."
"Atad is a real louse. He's like a cow which gives milk and then kicks the bucket. He sometimes keeps a strict discipline but later he can agitate the workers [against management] for nothing at all . . . When Yaakov was here he acted as if he had a screw loose [in his brain]. Later he improved a bit."

Yaakov wanted to dismiss Atad; he knew about his subterfuges and abuses, but his hands were tied: Moav refused to terminate Atad and demanded that he be warned and given a second chance followed by a third, fourth, etc., since he made do with a relatively low salary as he came to Merkaz after he being fired from a number of previous jobs. Atad did not miss the chance, which Moav gave him; noticing the brain drain suffered by Merkaz due Israel's economic boom as against its modest salaries, he improved his behavior for a season and got greenhorn Yuval to grant him a permanent position. Then came Avi and "parachuted" his high-school friend Yiftach as foreman. Atad became a loyalist of the two and strengthened his position. Greenhorn Thomas was the next "jumper" whom Atad misled by his briefly improved behavior, receiving a promotion to foreman. After Levi left, veteran uneducated and weak foreman Rabina became shop steward; Atad agitated against the union committee, accused it of allowing Yuval to demote and cut the salary of an experienced operator who was injured in a work accident, and on a popular demand for work injury compensation insurance he rose to shop steward. In this capacity he met greenhorn Shavit, and pretending to be his loyalist, he became his "two-way funnel."

Atad enhanced the S&GH debacle by supporting Avi's assertion that the mistaken contour of the S&GH feeding pipe was marginal. As mentioned, detached Moav also used a "two-way funnel"; detached CCMI managers needed this tool to gain information by nurturing immoral, incompetent employees such as Atad. Atad supplied both real information and assumed information, telling Shavit what he wanted to hear in return for favors. Thus an executive's use of CCMI served not only her/his Im-C but also that of incompetent subordinates. Shavit rewarded Atad excessively, though he often shirked his tasks and duties, and Shavit knew that Atad's loyal image was largely fake, as both knowledgeable deputy PM Danton and seasonal Atad-organized "Italian strikes" reminded him. He knew that Atad's remuneration was unjustified and in effect deprived competent employees committed to their job, but he was dependent on Atad. Like Avi, he too was in a Kafkaesque situation, encircled by distrusting staff who he himself distrusted and kept uninformed; only a few supplied him with information. He was often paralyzed or mired in ineffective courses of action such as the "calming sessions," which appeared to calm him and Danton rather than Avi in the face of the S&GH debacle.

The choice of CCMI is integral to managers' Im-C, a disposition they often develop early due to career successes in authority jobs by use of immoral means. Shavit advanced career like Moav and dozens of other higher-ups in the kibbutz field: movement leaders, cabinet ministers, Knesset (parliament) members, CEOs of national and regional monopolies, and others.[19] Like many of these, both Moav and Shavit's managerial careers commenced early: Moav became the treasurer of a new kibbutz at age 22 and never returned to the ranks, while Shavit became an army platoon commander at the age of 19.5, a kibbutz branch manager at the age of 22, switched to managing the larger building branch at age 25, took a two-year condensed college managerial course at age 28, was promoted to kibbutz economic manager at age 30 and became plant manager at age 32. As with many other "meteoric" careers, both in the kibbutz field and in corporate world,[20] he advanced rapidly due to the patronage of Zelikovich, his kibbutz mate who was a veteran *pa'il* and executive of other I-KOs before Merkaz. Zelikovich nurtured him ever since his success as manager of the building branch; Shavit managed to achieve quicker and cheaper construction than his predecessors despite minimal building know-how, through rigorous control of costs and using outside building contractors who employed cheap Arabs after firing all the costly Jewish builders whom his predecessor had employed and managed. Then he repeated this control as kibbutz economic manager and achieved some successes, thus legitimizing his promotion to replace Yuval.

Intelligent, talented Shavit did not opt for detached CCMI because of his inability to acquire ginning know-how and *phronesis*, but rather in order to defend his authority while believing that he could succeed by repeating his rigorous control of costs and results. It was no coincidence that he chose to follow

Moav's detachment rather than Yuval's involved autocracy: Yuval repeated the autocracy used in the kibbutz cotton branch with moderate success, while Shavit tried repeating successful rigorous analysis of data reported by subordinate managers and contractors without involvement in their problem-solving. This personal strategy achieved moderate successes at the gin plant for certain periods: Moav for six years due to the high-moral leadership of vulnerably involved, talented, highly committed Aharon and Yaakov, cotton growing idealists interested in advancing this crop; and Shavit for two to three years with pragmatists Danton and Thomas, after each learned their job by vulnerable involvement—Danton among the drivers of tractors, forklifts, and lorries, and Thomas among ginners. But success in these two periods was moderate: while non-careerist lieutenants created virtuous trust and learning cycles, many of their efforts were tripped up by obstacles posed by conservative CCMI user bosses, quite similar to British industry bosses (Armstrong 1987). The two detached PMs ignored the mismanagement caused by their ignorance and low morality; both defended their own authority and jobs and also Shavit his career prospects. Every move that loosened or threatened to loosen their firm hold on the helm aroused defensive actions, for instance Shavit's prolonged delay of Thomas's innovative automatic feeder (below).

Senior employees were cognizant of Shavit's CCMI even before he failed, as described in Chapter 1, and Danton harshly criticized his ignorance. As he saw it,

"Shavit is a wizard of numbers who can prove everything using them but knows nothing about the things that create these numbers."

Nor did Danton appreciate Shavit's leadership skills; when he criticized the incessant turnover of *pe'ilim* to the detriment of hired employees, I asked if this rotation deprived them of a better, more trustworthy leadership, and he agreed and targeted Shavit, using his experience as an ex-platoon commander in the Parachuted Corps:

"Of course; what is needed is like a [good] commander who decides on the goal of the fighting, creates a team spirit, and then there are results, but for this good relations [between commander and soldiers] are required which Shavit never formed. I am considered the one [among *pe'ilim*] who has the best relationships with [hired] workers although I demand of them much more than others."

Implying Shavit's failed management, he later explained his point thus:

"The problem here is to devise a way for the workers to follow you, as a platoon commander [is followed] in battle."

Contrary to Yuval, who was quite asocial and disliked by both his kibbutz members and *pe'ilim*, just as he disliked and ignored them, as evident for instance from his wanton affair, Shavit was socially involved and liked by many of his kibbutz members and *pe'ilim*, but detached CCMI prevented open, trustful relationships at the plant like those created by Danton and Thomas with other *pe'ilim* and hired staff. Thomas, who unlike Danton was not an ex-army officer, criticized Shavit's mismanagement differently:

> "People here work hard, go out of their way to find and implement solutions to complicated problems, but all their efforts are worth nothing for Shavit who can trash their efforts with no hesitations."

Shavit "rode" on successes achieved by trusted servant transformational leader Thomas and trusted transactional leader Danton,[21] helped by two other involved *pe'ilim*, the chief electrician and the garage manager, along with some hired employees. As noted, Danton was Thomas's key supporter in the three-year conflict with Shavit over the automatic feeder (below), until last year when they clashed over the purchase of S&GH versus fiber cleaning machines. They related to Shavit much as Moav's two involved deputies related to their boss a decade earlier, as an ignorant alien authority to be manipulated to minimally hurt the plant's functioning. Thomas transformed the low-trust shop-floor culture that he found when coming to the failing plant into a local high-trust innovative culture by highly committed vulnerable involvement in problem-solving that engendered trust and learning cycles of local know-how and *phronesis* by reflection-in-action, solving problems in a community of practice with knowledgeable locals that created an "us" feeling.[22] This had happened both on the shop floor while coping with failed/clogged/broken machines and on the benches in the shade in front of the offices where mostly deputy PM Danton, who was in charge of yard operations, and less frequently Thomas, congregated with hired employees. Without prior knowledge, it was impossible to discern managers from foremen and workers—all wore dirty working clothes; only if one arrived towards the end of a discussion one could have seen that Danton or Thomas concluded what had to be done and all departed to do it. Most prior discourse was egalitarian and included an occasional dirty joke by a worker that sometimes pinned down a manager or foreman (Six and Sorge 2008). Less frequently, the other involved *pe'ilim*, the electrician and the garage manager dropped by, while neither Shavit nor Avi participated in these community of practitioners meetings. Previous research paid "limited attention to the conditions . . . that lead to supervisors offering high LMX to employees" (Wang and Clegg 2007: 151), while this case indicates that an egalitarian coffee drinking break with vulnerably involved managers creates such a condition.

Shavit's Im-C: Delaying Thomas's Major Innovation and Its Appropriation

Thomas gained power by succeeding through high-moral transformational leadership, which made him a well-known expert among Israel's cotton gin plants and then abroad, as efficiency and effectiveness soared. Shavit did not interfere, since the plant's functioning seemed to prove his capability, but it frightened him: successful Thomas gradually became dominant in managerial decisions at the expense of Shavit's power. When Thomas proposed developing and building an original automatic cotton-feeder at one-third to one-fourth of American firms' prices, $US 80,000 instead of $US 250,000–330,000, Shavit felt that this was too good to be true and used red tape with CEO Zelikovich's backing to tame Thomas and his supporter Danton. "Parachuted" Shavit had no prior industrial management experience, was unaware that practitioners had invented some 80% of industrial innovations (Bogers et al. 2010), and only knew that failure of the invention would damage his authority, prestige, and power, while a success would empower Thomas (Klein 1998). His postponing of Thomas's innovation for three years and his appropriation of the prestige generated by its success after the disenchanted inventor left is another example of his Im-C.

The three-year delay by Shavit was decisive: during these years most Israeli gin plants bought or ordered US-made Movers and automatic feeders. As explained, Israeli managers knew since 1971 that US gin plants used these innovations (pp. 11–12). Danton proposed buying a Mover soon after taking charge in 1976 but this also required an automatic feeder and a Yard Mover, which US manufacturers offered together at the above prices.[23] While it was unclear whether Israeli conditions would require modifications that would raise the price, another question was the possibility of modifying the existing transportation system and sparing most of the investment. Thomas and the cotton growers with which he consulted preferred this option and proposed building an original automatic feeder at a third of this price, one that would fit both current stretches and Movers. When Thomas proposed this solution to greenhorn Shavit, it seemed too good to be true. It was hard to believe that Thomas, who had only two years of experience at the plant and was not even an authorized engineer, could succeed with such a project. How could an ex-kibbutz garage manager who had repaired machines and who had never planned or constructed a machine himself construct a solution that would cost a third or quarter of the price of those offered by world-class manufacturers? Was it possible that Thomas would succeed so much better than numerous experienced engineers of large firms that had produced cotton equipment for decades?

Thomas was a professional, not a genius, who practiced the DUI (Doing, Using & Interacting) mode of innovation that relied on practitioners' experience-based learning of tacit know-how and *phronesis* (Jensen et al. 2007); my untested assessment is that Avi and Shavit were more intelligent than him, but he was a very experienced and expert mechanics manager who possessed the know-how and *phronesis* required to lead the creation of the original automatic feeder with a hydraulic pusher capable of pushing an eight-ton stack of raw cotton from a stretch. His solution combined some known elements used for years by the cotton industry with the original pusher that could be tried by an experiment costing some US$15,000.

The chief engineer of a known Israeli transportation equipment manufacturer offered to plan, build, and try the pusher, and then to plan, build, and install the feeder. He and Thomas assumed that all other plants would follow Merkaz and buy the machine, but Shavit's red tape frustrated them and cotton grower supporters. Shavit did everything he could to prevent approval of Thomas's proposal, to delay the needed experiment and construction and installation of the feeder. Discussions of the proposal on the plant's Board took a year until it was confirmed; the decision about the experiment dragged on for another year, and a third year was spent ordering the machine and planning it, while building, installing, and successful trial running took a few months and was completed ahead of season, days before my participant observation.

Thomas did not inaugurate the machine. He resigned after its successful tests, tired of the conflicts with Shavit. In the festive inauguration picture, careerist Shavit proudly stands at the control bench as if he had invented the original machine. The cover of the booklet published by the gin plant to sum up the season in which the machine was successfully operated and conveyed some 33,000 tons of raw cotton showed three pictures of the machine, one of them with Shavit while a picture of Thomas was absent; nor was his name mentioned inside. Only Shavit was mentioned, of course, with no mention of his three years of red tape. This was a clear immoral Machiavellian appropriation of Thomas's achievement, which reminds one of the Holy Bible's King Ahab, who killed Naboth the Jesreelite and appropriated his vineyard to be warned by the prophet: "Hast thou killed and also took possession? . . . In the place where dogs licked the blood of Naboth shall dogs lick thy blood, even thine" (Kings 1, Ch. 21, Par. 19). Comparing Shavit's deed to murder is justified when one realizes that he practically extinguished all prospects of other plants buying Thomas's innovation by delaying it for three years. Had it not been delayed for so long, Thomas's machine would have had a good chance of overcoming the costlier imported alternatives, as it enabled use of the old metal stretches beside Movers without the complications caused by imported feeders.

Shavit's low morality in this case was only slightly more extreme than his other immoral practices. He feared both the success and the failure of the innovation: its early success and adoption by all Israeli gin plants would have enhanced Thomas's power and possibly made him uncontrollable, promising Shavit more defeats as with the purchase of the S&GH rather than fiber cleaning machines, while its failure would have seriously damaged Shavit's prestige as a fantasist who tried to compete with world-class manufacturers. Distrusted, ignorant, and uninformed Shavit could neither estimate Thomas' chances of success nor would his career have benefitted much; hence he procrastinated. The annual booklet with Shavit's picture on the cover standing at the control bench of the automatic feeder with no mention of Thomas depicted a terrible season, with a negative record of 32% downtime, as a result of which an extra 3,000 tons of cotton were stored in the fields and growers lost considerable revenues due to the S&GH debacle. Shavit probably knew he was facing demotion; hence to improve his image ahead of seeking a new managerial job he appropriated Thomas's achievement and attributed it to himself.

Summary and the Concomitant Prevalence of Im-C and CCMI

The findings corroborate Chapter 1 and cited studies: local tacit know-how and *phronesis* essential for managerial competence were largely acquired by trust-creating vulnerable involvement in problem-solving efforts together with employees (e.g., Ingvaldsen et al. 2013). Without using the psychological dysfunction explanations of stupidity research, defense of authority, jobs, and careers by practicing CCMI and Im-C explained the plant's mismanagement and knowledge abuses, either by seductive-coercive autocracy as in the case of Yuval or by detachment as in the case of Moav, Karmi, Shavit, Avi, and others. The CCMI-Im-C complex retained incompetence and caused mistakes, wrongs, and failures, both directly and indirectly by negative managerial selection and promotion: rather than promoting competent knowledgeable insiders, weak incompetent CCMI-using executives concerned with empowered expert insiders imported outsiders of their own kind, *pe'ilim* according to loyalty or prospective loyalty, as in the "managerial homosexual reproduction" thesis (Kanter 1993[1977]: 49). Importees' loyalty enhanced superiors' power, but they mostly used CCMI, remained incompetent, and both they and their superiors practiced Im-C as they could not achieve performance, as in cited ethnographies that exposed organizations' dark side (p. 1).

In addition to the explanations presented in Chapter 1 for the choice of CCMI, there was also the temptation to use managerial power to conceal ignorance and incompetence as dark secrets and to survive in jobs by immoral means similar to fellow *pe'ilim*. An incoming *pa'il* often emulated others' CCMI unknowingly, as Avi initial chose to "wait and see" without knowing it would lead to CCMI, to the use of immoral means and to camouflaging/concealing them as dark secrets. Moreover, no managerial course had taught *pe'ilim* what others and I found, that managerial job competence requires sensitivity to the unique contours of circumstances that demand much local know-how and *phronesis* held exclusively by subordinates who would not share these with distrusted CCMI users. Often originating from kibbutzim with high-trust unit cultures that enhanced knowledge sharing (Shapira 2008: Chs. 15–17), *pe'ilim* were often not aware that using CCMI would discourage employees' trustful cooperation and sharing of knowledge. A "parachuted" *pa'il* often missed both his own ignorance and the avoiding of ignorance-exposing vulnerable involvement in practitioners' deliberations, preventing mutual trust with them and the achieving of job-competence by virtuous trust and learning cycles. The "jumper" knew that learning required asking questions, which exposed his ignorance and jeopardized his authority until proving effective, but easily missed fellow *pe'ilim*'s defensive use of CCMI, how it caused failures, and the successful learning by a few vulnerably involved *pe'ilim* (e.g., Thomas, Danton). One could be an ex-high-moral trustworthy manager of a kibbutz or a kibbutz branch but "parachuted" to an unknown I-KRC plant in which secrecy and mistrust prevailed and made learning ginning hazardous; in addition, the prospect of impending *rotatzia* within a few years encouraged opting for CCMI-Im-C.

Two factors, habituses and pertinent know-how and *phronesis*, including referred expertise, largely decided whether one opted to CCMI-Im-C or not. Many ex-kibbutz managers practiced Im-C, ingratiating/courting I-KO patrons, who then made them *pe'ilim*. The *pe'ilim* usually continued their Im-C in I-KO jobs, as patrons' auspices promised them career advancement without performance provided they were not grasped as complete failures. CCMI served this aim, while habitus often decided one's choice: previously detached kibbutz officers Avi and Shavit were detached in Merkaz as well; autocratically involved kibbutz branch manager Yuval behaved likewise in Merkaz, and previously vulnerably involved Yaakov, Aharon, Thomas, and Danton conducted themselves similarly as *pe'ilim*. One's know-how and *phronesis* affected the domain(s) in which he was vulnerably involved: Danton limited such involvement to his jurisdiction, for which he had pertinent knowledge, although as a management committee member he should have had interactional expertise in ginning. Lacking this, he mistakenly viewed Thomas's insisting on the S&GH rather than fiber cleaners as "a caprice" rather than as an intelligent choice based on complex considerations, and this conflict with the only true friend in Merkaz was the last straw that ousted Thomas.

Combining the two chapters' findings points to the prevalence of concomitant Im-C and CCMI among Merkaz executives. Their concomitance explains their etiological connection: the use of CCMI engenders vicious distrust and ignorance cycles that prevent career advancement by performance, hence leaving promotion-hungry *pe'ilim* only the Im-C alternative. The other direction is true as well: habituating Im-C encourages defending one's job, authority, and career prospects by using CCMI rather than taking the risk of ignorance exposure, resulting in a similar negative cycle that leaves Im-C as the sole option for advancing one's career. The prevalence of CCMI-Im-C at Merkaz reminds one of Wilson's (2011: 46) assertion that careerists "are so prevalent because bureaucracies are in effect designed by and for careerists," as well as Armstrong's (1987) assertion that British industry engineers suffered from divorce of executives from creative engineering labor of product and process improvement, much as Thomas suffered from Shavit's divorce from ginning labor. The finding that throughout the plant's 19 years CCMI-Im-C executives dominated, suggests that I-KRC bureaucracy was "designed by and for ['jumper'] careerists:" the auspices of two detached CEOs enabled one astute CCMI-user PM (Moav) to continue for 10 years by conservatism and "riding" on successes achieved by committed mid-levelers who overcame or circumvented his self-serving decisions; another PM (Yuval) continued for four years despite stupid autocracy failures due to a CEO detachment and some mid-levelers who overcame many of his stupid deeds until his excessive selfishness, hubris, and sex drive failed him; the third CCMI-Im-C PM Shavit survived for five years thanks to four years of effective mid-levelers, until the long-frustrated TM left and ignorant Shavit nominated ignorant successor Avi who caused a major failure and the succession of the two after a year's delay to save their nominator's image, enabling them further managerial careers elsewhere.

Although there is no research of I-KRCs' history, kibbutz research leaves little doubt that I-KRCs' founders in 1939–1940 were high-moral servant leaders and vulnerably involved pioneers who aimed for career advancement by performance rather than CCMI-Im-C. But as Chapter 6 will elucidate, with the enormous growth and success of the kibbutz field in the 1930s–1940s, its old guard prime leaders became immoral self-perpetuators who transformed it into one that was oligarchic, bureaucratic, and conservatively led.[24] Merkaz CEOs in the 1960s–1980s followed their lead and practiced Im-C, as did most other *pe'ilim*; only two deputy PMs and one TM were high-moral leaders, while one deputy PM (Danton) was an intermediate case who limited his trust-creating vulnerable involvement to his jurisdiction as did some other mid-level *pe'ilim*. The change to prevalent CCMI-Im-C with the growth and success of I-KOs facilitated the adoption of two norms, *rotatzia* and "parachuting." These two weakened mid-level *pe'ilim* as against CEOs who overruled *rotatzia* and stayed much longer, curbing mid-levelers' will to risk their authority by ignorance exposure in order to learn local knowledge that was bound to be unusable in their next jobs; their minimal learning and incompetence enhanced the dominance of self-perpetuating job-ignorant detached CEOs. The same negative impact of the two norms was found by the cited critical students of US armed forces (p. 48), leading to Wilson's (2011: 46) above cited assertion.

The next chapter will support this summary by using organizational literature to further clarify the concepts of trust, leadership, culture, and democratic management, the declared ideal of the kibbutzim contradicted by the reality of Merkaz, other I-KRCs, and other I-KOs.

Notes

1 Recent study: Aasland et al. (2010); corroborating others: Hollander (1998: 50); Thoroughgood et al. (2012).
2 Ailon (2015); Brown and Trevino (2006); Pullen and Rhodes (2015); Rhode (2006); Todnem and Burnes (2013).
3 Aryee and Chen (2004); Boddy et al. (2010); Starbuck (2007): 24; Weissberg (2002).
4 Ficarrotta (1988); Gabriel and Savage (1981); Henderson (1990); Mosier (1988); Segal (1981).

5 Dalton (1959); Hughes (1958); Jackall (1988); Maccoby (1976); Web and Cleary (1994). On such appropriation: Mehri (2005); Shapira (1987).
6 Helman (1987); Shapira (1995, 2001, 2005, 2008).
7 Also: Dalton (1959); Gouldner (1954); Whyte (1956).
8 I use the masculine form since all executives and managers were male.
9 In fact often it was not Thomas but a technician who drove it to a repair shop; Thomas mostly drove it to his home and back.
10 On this dependency see below; on the leader's impact on cooperative board members: Guerrero et al. (2014).
11 Beside the Merkaz general assembly there were assemblies for each plant, in which participation was permitted only for kibbutzim that used its services.
12 A captain in the reserves was normally on duty for 1.5 months every year in that era.
13 E.g., Parkinson (1957); Peter and Hull (1969).
14 All six plant managers were Merkaz Board members.
15 Levi was not considered heir apparent due to his crippled right hand, which made him workshop manager.
16 Respectively: Collins and Evans (2007); Collins (2011); Brown and Duguid (1991); Orr (1996).
17 Firing Avi after two years could not be presented as *rotatzia*, hence it accorded Levenson (1961: 374) and Martin and Strauss (1959: 96–97).
18 Atad is 'bramble' in Hebrew; using this nickname will be further justified by later testimonies.
19 Beilin (1984); Shapira (1990, 2001, 2005, 2008); Shure (2001); Tzimchi (1999).
20 Kibbutz: Shapira (2005, 2008). Corporate world: Dalton (1959); Johnson (2009); Kets De Vries (1993); Khurana (2002); Levenson (1961); Martin and Strauss (1959).
21 On such riding see: Armstrong (1987); on servant transformational vs. transactional leadership: pp. 79–83.
22 A firm's differing cultures: Orr (2006: 1807); Reflection-in-action: Schön (1983); Yanow and Tsoukas (2009); Community of practice: Orr (1996); Knowledgeable locals: Bennis (1989: 17); Us feeling: Haslam et al. (2011).
23 A Yard Mover moves stacks of raw cotton gathered in the yard to the automatic feeder.
24 See Chapter 6; for similar cases: Brumann (2000); Stryjan (1989). For the case of a radical innovative leader who financially rescued the kibbutz field and enabled resumed growth: Shapira (2011).

References

Aasland, Merethe S., A. Skogstad, et al. 2010. The prevalence of destructive leadership behaviour. *British Journal of Management* 21(4): 438–452.
Ailon, Galit. 2015. From superstars to devils: The ethical discourse on managerial figures involved in a corporate scandal. *Organization* 22(1): 78–99.
Alvesson, Mats, and Dan Kärreman. 2013. The closing of critique, pluralism, and reflexivity: A response to Hardy and Grant and some wider reflections. *Human Relations* 66(10): 1353–1371.
Armstrong, Peter. 1987. Engineers, management and trust. *Work, Employment and Society* 1(4): 421–440.
Arthurs, Jonathan D., and Lowell W. Busenitz. 2003. The boundaries and limitations of agency theory and stewardship theory in the venture capitalist/entrepreneur relationship. *Entrepreneurship Theory and Practice* 28(2): 145–162.

Aryee, Samuel, and Zhen X. Chen. 2004. Countering the trend towards careerist orientation in the age of downsizing: Test of social exchange model. *Journal of Business Research* 57(3): 321–328.

Beilin, Yosi. 1984. *Sons in the Shade of Fathers.* Tel Aviv: Revivim (Hebrew).

Bennis, Warren. 1989. *Why Leaders Can't Lead.* San Francisco: Jossey-Bass.

Boddy, Clive R. P., R. Ladyshewsky, and P. Galvin. 2010. Leaders without ethics in global business: Corporate psychopaths. *Journal of Public Affairs* 10(1): 121–138.

Bogers, Marcel, A. Afuah, and B. Bastian. 2010. Users as innovators: A review, critique, and future research directions. *Journal of Management* 36(4):857–875.

Bratton, Virginia K., and K. Michele Kacmar. 2004. Extreme careerism: The dark side of impression management. In: R. Griffin and A. O'Leary-Kelly (Eds.), *The Dark Side of Organizational Behaviour.* San Francisco: Jossey-Bass, 291–308.

Brown, John S., and Paul Duguid. 1991. Organizational learning and communities of practice. *Organization Science* 2(1): 40–57.

Brown, Michael E., and Linda K. Trevino. 2006. Ethical leadership: A review and future directions. *The Leadership Quarterly* 17(4): 595–616.

Brumann, Christoph. 2000. The dominance of one and its perils: Charismatic leadership and branch structures in utopian communes. *Journal of Anthropological Research* 56(4): 425–451.

Chiaburu, Daniel S., G. J. Munoz, and R. G. Gardner. 2013. How to spot a careerist early on: Psychopathy and exchange ideology as predictors of careerism. *Journal of Business Ethics* 118(3): 473–486.

Collins, Harry M. 2011. Language and practice. *Social Studies of Science* 41(3): 271–300.

Collins, Harry M., and Robert Evans. 2007. *Rethinking Expertise.* Chicago: University of Chicago Press.

Collins, Harry M., and Garry Sanders. 2007. They give you the keys and say 'drive it!'. Managers, referred expertise, and other expertises. *Studies in History and Philosophy of Science* 38(4): 621–641.

Collins, Harry M., and Martin Weinel. 2011. Transmuted expertise: How technical non-experts can assess experts and expertise. *Argumentation,* 25: 401–415.

Costas, Jana, and Christopher Grey. 2014. Bringing secrecy into the open: Towards a theorization of the social processes of organizational secrecy. *Organization Studies* 35(10): 1423–1447.

Curtis, Ron. 2009. Whewell's philosophy under dispute. *Philosophy of the Social Sciences* 39(3): 495–506.

Dalton, Melville. 1959. *Man Who Manage.* New York: Wiley.

Deutsch, Morton. 1969. Conflicts: Productive and destructive. *Journal of Social Issues* 25(1): 7–42.

Diefenbach, Thomas. 2013. Incompetent or immoral leadership? Why many managers and change leaders get it wrong. In: R. Todnem and B. Burnes (Eds.), *Organizational Change Leadership and Ethics.* New York: Routledge, 149–170.

Feldman, Daniel C., and Barton A. Weitz. 1991. From the invisible hand to the gladhand: Understanding the careerist orientation to work. *Human Resource Management* 30(2): 237–257.

Ficarrotta, Joseph C. 1988. Careerism: A moral analysis of its nature, types, and contributing causes in the military services. Retrieved 14.2.2013: www.isme. tamu.eduJSCOPE88Ficarrotta88

Flyvbjerg, Bent, N. Bruzelius and W. Rothengatter. 2003. *Megaprojects and Risk*. Cambridge: Cambridge University Press.

Fox, Alan. 1974. *Beyond Contract*. London: Faber.

Gabriel, Richard A., and Paul L. Savage. 1981. *Crisis in Command*. New Delhi: Himalayan.

Galbraith, John K. 1971. *The New Industrial State*. Boston: Houghton Mifflin.

Geneen, Herold. 1984. *Managing*. New York: Avon.

Goffman, Erving. 1959. *The Presentation of Self in Everyday Life*. Garden City (NY): Doubleday.

Gouldner, Alvin W. 1954. *Patterns of Industrial Bureaucracy*. New York: Free Press.

Guerrero, Sylvie, M. È. Lapalme and M. Séguin. 2014. Board chair authentic leadership and nonexecutives' motivation and commitment. *Journal of Leadership & Organization Studies* 22(1): 88–101.

Harvey, Michael G., M. M. Novicevic, et al. 2001. A historic perspective on organizational ignorance. *Journal of Managerial Psychology* 16(5/6): 449–468.

Haslam, S. Alexander, S. D. Reicher, and M. J. Platow. 2011. *The New Psychology of Leadership*. New York: Psychology Press.

Helman, Amir. 1987. The development of professional managers in the kibbutz. *Economic Quarterly* 33: 1031–1038 (Hebrew).

Henderson, Wiliam D. 1990. *The Hollow Army*. New York: Greenwood.

Hollander, Edwin P. 1998. Ethical challenges in leader-follower relationships. In: J. B. Ciulla (Ed.), *Ethics, the Heart of Leadership*. Westport (CN): Praeger, 49–62.

Hughes, Everett C. 1958. *Man and Their Work*. Glenco (IL): Free Press.

Ingvaldsen, Jonas A., Helvor Holtskog, and Geir Ringen. 2013. Unlocking work standards through systematic work observation: Implications for team supervision. *Team Performance Management* 19(5/6): 279–291.

Jackall, Robert. 1988. *Moral Mazes*. New York: Oxford.

Jensen, Morten B., B. Johnson, et al. 2007. Forms of knowledge and modes of innovation. *Research Policy* 36(5): 680–693.

Johnson, Craig E. 2008. The rise and fall of Carly Fiorina. *Journal of Leadership & Organizational Studies* 15(2): 188–196.

Johnson, Craig E. 2009. *Meeting the Ethical Challenges of Leadership*. Los Angeles: Sage.

Kanter, Rosabeth M. 1993[1977]. *Men and Women of the Corporation*. New York: Basic Books.

Kets De Vries, Manfred F. R. 1993. *Leaders, Fools, and Impostors*. San Francisco: Jossey-Bass.

Khurana, Rakesh. 2002. *Searching for a Corporate Savior*. Princeton (NJ): Princeton University Press.

Klein, Gary. 1998. *Sources of Power*. Cambridge (MA): MIT Press.

Kruger, Justin, and David Dunning. 1999. Unskilled and unaware of it: How difficulties in recognizing one's own incompetence lead to inflated self-assessments. *Journal of Personal and Social Psychology* 77(6): 1121–1134.

Levenson, Bernard. 1961. Bureaucratic succession. In: A. Etzioni (Ed.), *Complex Organizations*. New York: Holt, 362–375.

Luthans, Fred. 1988. Successful versus effective managers. *Academy of Management Executive* 2: 127–132.

Luttwak, E. 1984. *The Pentagon and the Art of War*. New York: Simon and Schuster.

Maccoby, Michael. 1976. *The Gamesman*. New York: Simon and Schuster.

Martin, Norman H., and Anselm L. Strauss. 1959. Patterns of mobility in industrial organizations. In: W. L. Warner and N. H. Martin (Eds.), *Industrial Man*. New York: Harper, 85–101.

McGregor, Douglas. 1960. *The Human Side of Enterprise*. New York: McGraw-Hill.

Mechanic, David. 1962. Sources of power of lower participants. *Administrative Science Quarterly* 7(3): 349–364.

Mehri, Darius. 2005. *Notes from Toyota-Land*. Ithaca (NY): ILR Press.

Moore, Wilbert E. 1962. *The Conduct of the Corporation*. New York: Random House.

Mosier, Michael L. 1988. Getting a grip on careerism. *Airpower Journal* 2(2): 52–60.

Nienaber, Ann-Marie, V. Holtorf, et al. 2015. A climate of psychological safety enhances the success of front end teams. *International Journal of Innovation Management* 19(2). DOI: 10.1142/S1363919615500279.

Orr, Julian. 1996. *Talking about Machines*. Ithaca (NY): Cornell University Press.

Orr, Julian. 2006. Ten years of talking about machines. *Organization Studies* 27(12): 1805–1820.

Parkinson, C. Nortcote. 1957. *Parkinson Law and Other Studies in Administration*. Boston: Hougton-Mifflin.

Peter, Lawrence J., and Richard Hull. 1969. *The Peter Principle*. London: Souvenier.

Pullen, Alison, and Carl Rhodes. 2015. Ethics, embodiment and organizations. *Organization* 22(2): 159–165.

Rhode, Deborah (Ed.). 2006. *Moral Leadership*. San Francisco: Jossey-Bass.

Robin, Corey. 2007. Dragon-slayers. *London Review of Books* 29(1): 18–20.

Schön, Donald A. 1983. *The Reflective Practitioner*. New York: Basic Books.

Segal, David R. 1981. Leadership and management: Organizations theory. In: J. H. Buck and L. J. Korb (Eds.), *Military Leadership*. Beverly Hills (CA): Sage, 41–69.

Shapira, Reuven. 1978/9. Autonomy of technostructure: An inter-kibbutz regional organization case study. *The Kibbutz* 6/7: 276–303 (Hebrew).

Shapira, Reuven. 1987. *Anatomy of Mismanagement*. Tel Aviv: Am Oved (Hebrew).

Shapira, Reuven. 1990. Leadership, rotation and the kibbutz crisis. *Journal of Rural Cooperation* 18(1): 55–66.

Shapira, Reuven. 1995. The voluntary resignation of outsider managers: Interkibbutz Rotation and Michels's 'Iron Law'. *Israel Social Science Research* 10(1): 59–84.

Shapira, Reuven. 2001. Communal decline: The vanishing of high-moral leaders and the decay of democratic, high-trust kibbutz cultures. *Sociological Inquiry* 71(1): 13–38.

Shapira, Reuven. 2005. Academic capital or scientific progress? A critique of the studies of kibbutz stratification. *Journal of Anthropological Research* 61(3): 357–380.

Shapira, Reuven. 2008. *Transforming Kibbutz Research*. Cleveland: New World Publishing.

Shapira, Reuven. 2011. Institutional combination for cooperative development: How trustful cultures and transformational mid-levelers overcame old guard conservatism. In: J. Blanc and D. Colongo (Eds.), *Co-Operatives Contributions to a Plural Economy*. Paris: L'Harmattan, 75–90.

Shure, Khaim. 2001. *I Bring Him Down From Heaven*. Tel Aviv: Ministry of Defense (Hebrew).

Six, Frederique, and Arndt Sorge. 2008. Creating a high-trust organization: An exploration into organizational policies that stimulate interpersonal trust building. *Journal of Management Studies* 45(5): 857–884.

Starbuck, William A. 2007. Living in mythical spaces. *Organization Studies* 28(1): 21–25.

Stryjan, Yohanan. 1989. *Impossible Organizations*. New York: Greenwood.

Thoroughgood, Christian N., W. T. Brian, et al. 2012. Bad to the bone: Empirically defining and measuring destructive leader behaviour. *Journal of Management and Organizational Studies* 19(2): 230–255.

Todnem, Rune, and Bernard Burnes (Eds.). 2013. *Organizational Change, Leadership and Ethics*. New York: Routledge.

Tzimchi, No'a (Ed.). 1999. *Dan Tzimchi*. Kibbutz Dalia: Maarechet (Hebrew.).

Wang, Karen Y., and Stewart Clegg. 2007. Managing to lead in private enterprise in China: Work values, demography and the development of trust. *Leadership* 3(2): 149–172.

Webb, Janette, and David Cleary. 1994. *Organizational Change and the Management of Expertise*. London: Routledge.

Weissberg, Robert. 2002. Administrative careerism and PC. *Academic Questions* 15(2): 58–68.

Whyte, William H. 1956. *The Organization Man*. New York: Simon and Schuster.

Wilson, George C. 2011. Careerism. In: W. T. Wheeler (Ed.), *The Pentagon Labyrinth*. Washington (DC): Center for Defense Information, 43–59.

Yanow, Dvora, and Haridimous Tsoukas. 2009. What is reflection-in-action? A phenomenological account. *Journal of Management Studies* 46(8): 1339–1364.

3 The Concepts of Trust, Leadership, Culture, and Democratic Management

According to renowned economist J. K. Galbraith (1971: 69–70), in today's large firm

"... a large number of decisions, and *all* the important decisions (original emphasis), draw on information possessed by more than one man. Typically they draw on the specialized scientific and technical knowledge, the accumulated information or experience and the artistic or intuitive sense of many persons. And this is guided by further information, which is assembled, analyzed and interpreted by professionals using highly technical equipment. The final decision will be informed only as it draws systematically on all those whose information is relevant. Nor, human beings what they are, can it take all of the information that is offered at face value. There must, additionally, be a mechanism for testing each person's contribution for its relevance and reliability as it is brought to bear on the decision."

Neither Galbraith nor the voluminous literature on organizational learning, knowledge management, and intellectual capital specify such a mechanism. Hence, higher-ups consider the relevance and reliability of the information and knowledge of each contributor, and decide who is knowledgeable, whose analysis and assembly of information is valid, and which of expert opinions better integrates the variety of contributions. Nobel laureate Simon presented a case of an ideal managerial decision-making process:

"... the [battleship] planning procedure permits expertise of every kind to be drawn into the decision without any difficulties being imposed by the lines of authority in the organization. The final design undoubtedly received authoritative approval; but, during the process of formulation suggestions and recommendations flowed freely from all parts of the organization ... So long as the appropriate experts are consulted, their exact location in the hierarchy of authority need not much affect the decision"

(Simon 1957: 230).

Unfortunately Simon's ideal is never realized; at the end of the day, the status, authority, prestige, and power of participants, as well as other political, social, psychological, and cultural factors, determine if and to what extent each view is considered. Worse still, according to Heifetz (1995) leaders determine decisions by holding the environment of deliberations, by directing attention, by controlling access to information and its flow, by framing issues, orchestrating conflicts, and shaping decision processing.[1] They decide who is knowledgeable, usually excluding operators, although in the above battleship case it is the operators who have the relevant experience to know best, for instance, the problems of current fighting positions that a new design may solve. Unfortunately, even if the latter are heard, their influence tends to be minimal versus that of managers and those considered experts who dominate deliberations and decide whether to use participants' contributions.[2] An executive who seriously tries to consider lower participant contributions must be locally knowledgeable (pp. 2–3), needs interactional expertise that enables fruitful communication with experts in the language of their practice as well as having referred expertise.[3] In order to acquire these expertises one has to be cognizant of own's ignorance, a fairly rare state (Kruger and Dunning 1999). Whether one is cognizant or not, only if s/he practices vulnerable involvement in subordinate deliberations, exposes his/her own ignorance, and gains subordinates' trust, may they teach her/him. Then s/he may be able to appreciate operators' contributions due to their exclusive know-how and *phronesis*, acquired by coping with tasks in ways s/he never experienced. But in order to initiate a virtuous trust and learning cycle, a manager's involvement must prove intention to learn and justly and fairly consider employees' analyses, views, and suggestions, rather than only to control them as Merkaz PMs did. A superior can gain subordinates' trust only if s/he proves high-morality, assuring them that her/his learning will serve the common good, and not just her/his own interests (Hosmer 1995).

Trust is thus the decisive factor, as in the model presented in Chapter 1. A high level of mutual trust between hierarchic ranks enables the executive to practice Galbraith's (1971) and Simon's (1957) ideal decision-making. For example, the need to gain know-how and *phronesis* for his task only partially explained CEO Grove's (1996: 144) choice to risk his authority by exposing his ignorance to Intel programmers; a major encouraging factor was mutual trust engendered by his previous successful leadership of Intel, which ensured that they would not use his mistakes during learning against him. Unlike trusted insider Grove, outsider HP CEO Carly Fiorina had to gain the trust of hitherto unknown employees; hence such ignorance exposure was more risky for her authority and she seemed to avoid it while hastening to introduce major changes that contradicted entrenched HP culture, causing much resistance and distrust, and contributing meaningfully to her failure (Johnson 2008). But trust is a problematic concept; its uses and meanings differ much within and between disciplines.

Trust

Since 1958 a few scholars have alluded to the decisiveness of trust for managerial functioning, then autobiographies by successful business leaders supported this, and since the 1990s trust research has surged.[4] However, due to 40 years of separation between organizational ethnographers and organizational behaviorists and sociologists, the theories and methods of the latter have remained inappropriate for the study of organizational cultural dynamics and trust impact on these dynamics.[5] This led to the bypassing of ethnographies and leader autobiographies pointing to trust between echelons, as requiring a high-trust culture which differs structurally from a low-trust one as in the Chapter 1 model,[6] much as Korczynski (2000: 16) differentiates between high- and low-trust economies (a partial table):

Table 3.1 Low-Trust Versus High-Trust Economies

Dimension	Low-trust economy	High-trust economy
Agents' motivation	Economic, opportunistic	Economic, social and ethical
Agents' time horizon	Short	Long
Agents' level of rationality	Narrowly rational calculativeness	Trust even [without] . . . basis for expectation
Key property of the market	Creates power imbalance; threatens agents' economic existence	Provides information to allow knowledge of trusting behavior

A contrasting paradigm is employed by Bradach and Eccles (1989): trust, market, and hierarchy are three equal alternatives used in various combinations. However, this paradigm misses the tendency of both markets and hierarchies to cause mistrust contrary to organizing by trust and consent.[7] Market competition creates power differentials by which some seduce-coerce others to do their will by means of hierarchies while trust is minimal, as those seduced-coerced perform narrowly defined contractual obligations with minimal discretion (Fox 1974). A plurality image creates a large proportion of specializing employees on whose intangible resources today's knowledge-rich organization depends; hence, they are empowered, and seducing-coercing them is ineffective. Psychologist Kipnis (1976) found that "jumper" managers often distrust subordinates' obedience, hence they use seduction-coercion. But this strategy may fail even in a not-so-sophisticated firm; hence failure may encourage the "jumper" to turn to trustful practices. For instance, the known leadership scholar Warren Bennis, after some initial failed change efforts as a "jumper" university president, changed his strategy, established a "constellation" of influential knowledgeable insiders with which he shaped all major decisions and led their implementation, and only then did he achieve major changes (Bennis 1989: 17).

Bradach and Eccles's (1989) mix of trust, market, and hierarchy is elusive also because while high- and low-trust organizational cultures tend towards parallel economies, economies encompass many incoherences due to practical requirements, such that high-trust firms are found in low-trust economies and vice versa.[8] Similarly, high-trust units are found within low-trust firms, as for instance when Guest's (1962) new manager created a high-trust plant culture contrary to corporate conventions. Chapters 1 and 2 explained managers' choices by three factors: habituses, amount of pertinent know-how and *phronesis*, and emulation of other *pe'ilim*, while a fourth major factor is a grasp of employees' situation. If their tasks are grasped as simple and routine, requiring minimal trust since outcomes are measureable and easy-to-control while labor markets offer many substitutes, a manager tends to coerce employees as replacing them seems easy. This may have been a critical mistake, as that of Gouldner's (1955) outsider who grasped miners as a replaceable commodity but found no substitutes for striking miners. Had he gained miners' trust by vulnerable involvement, he might have learned this *phronesis* and chosen to use his predecessor's trustful management.

Gouldner's outsider situation was not that exceptional (e.g., Nichols et al. 2009: 261). A similar case is that of managers of firms or units that use sophisticated equipment for mature technologies that require a lot of operator specialization through expertises acquired on the job, as was the case in cotton gin plants. Often no market offers true substitutes for employees with precious firm-specific expertises, for which nurturing genuine replacements is a long and costly process. Even more costly can be disgruntled experts who exit with precious know-how and create competing firms.[9] Their control by hierarchy- and market-based seduction-coercion is ineffective, unlike control of low, unskilled echelons such as packers, porters, and janitors. It is also ineffective control of expert operators of sophisticated automatic processes who can defeat it by using their expertise to the firm's detriment: my registrar colleagues caused the automatic sampler to clog without being noticed when they concluded that no one was truly trying to solve the machine's problems that caused them much suffering; their actions helped the abandoning of this machine. Thus, use of CCMI can be fateful, as it enhances the Kruger-Dunning (1999) effect: in addition to the manager's failure to notice that his/her own ignorance negatively impacts job functioning and engenders distrust, employees of such a manager tend to use their knowledge advantage for their own benefit, as untangled by Roy (1952, 1955) and subsequent ethnographers. A manager may realize this only in a crisis situation or in other bad circumstances when s/he faces only bad action options.

However, while seduction and coercion are unilateral managerial choices, as explained in Chapter 1, high-trust cultures result from the mutual process of a virtuous ascending trust spiral (Fox 1974), in which a manager's trusting practice of vulnerable involvement is a cue that encourages employees to reciprocate by the trusting practice of knowledge sharing that enables her/his learning and engenders a trust and learning cycle (Six and Sorge 2008). Such a cycle also requires that a manager indicate his/her trust by granting discretion to employees (Siebert et al. 2015). For instance, in the automatic sampler case, Avi's decision to bar technicians from visiting another plant to learn solutions to the sampler's problems denied them their rightful discretion and exhibited distrust that led to desertion of the machine.

Yuval's case points to another reason that outsider executives opt for autocratic seduction-coercion: they tend to assume that in a mature technology (e.g., ginning), markets can offer substitutes for recalcitrant operators. This assumption may prove wrong not only concerning automatic plant operators such as ginners, but even for a simpler technology such as mining because of mine work hazards that Gouldner's (1955) outsider missed for lack of experiencing it. Likewise, high-tech firms often had low-status employees known as Rudies who knew which knowledge was held by whom due to their roles and long experience, rather than title or credentials; hence they were an essential, hard-to-replace asset for firms' internal knowledge-seekers. Unfortunately, they were often fired during downsizing by executives ignorant of their importance (Stewart 1997: 99), seemingly due to executives' ignorance of their own ignorance, as they practiced CCMI and no employee told them this fact (e.g., Milliken et al. 2003).

The opposite is a vulnerably involved servant transformational leader who engenders a virtuous trust and learning cycle. In the literature, servant and transformational leaderships are often differentiated: servant leaders work primarily by satisfying followers' needs for autonomy, competence, and relatedness (Chiniara and Bentein 2016), versus transformational leaders' emphasis on rousing vision, innovativeness, commitment to tasks, and modeling their own skilled performance (Van Dierendonck et al. 2014). However, in both types a leader creates mutual trust by modeling high-moral commitment for the common good, hence s/he is vulnerably involved, discerning true experts from others and becoming cognizant of their precious tacit knowledge (Collins 2007); s/he encourages contributions to problem-solving and decision-making by openness to their critique, suggestions, and innovations. S/he shares knowledge and information with them so that their trust is rational, based on proved trustworthiness. High-trust culture endures if high-moral leaders aim for the common good, enhance employees' contributions to decision-making and innovation, care for employees' interests according to ethical considerations, while the time horizon of employment relations is long, offering secure employment and prospects of career advancement.[10]

High-trust cultures are common in egalitarian communal/small cooperative settings, with minimal hierarchy, democratic management, and irrelevant labor markets as members do all work. Though seductive-coercive control is illegitimate in such cases, with growth and success hired labor is often introduced; then democracy and egalitarianism dwindle and high-trust cultures tend to disappear, while members often do not notice this fundamental change, which is gradual and undeclared.[11] High-trust cultures may persist if decentralization takes place and unit managers are allowed much discretion, while their high-morality is promoted by a servant transformational leader's practices which a proper constitution encourages, empowering members to replace her/him when he/she enters the dysfunction phase and becomes an immoral oligarch.[12] The scarcity of such leaders in Merkaz and in other I-KRCs studied (next chapter) largely explains gin plants' distrustful mismanagement, missed by Niv and Bar-On (1992) as well as other kibbutz students.

Leading trustfully is more complex than low-trust seductive-coercive autocracy based on market forces and hierarchy, another reason for outsiders to avoid it. The creation of trust between hierarchical ranks is often slow and hazardous, requires building a consensus concerning ends, means, task allocation, duties, rewards, and career prospects. Managers must prove integrity, competence, predictability, and benevolence towards employees' interests, needs, and wants, while allowing them the discretion to succeed in complex tasks, coordinating their participation in problem-solving and suppressing fools, impostors, and bootlickers.[13] This does not contradict Covey's (2006) bestseller, *The Speed of Trust*: minimally dealing with the relatively slow building of mutual trust by an ascending trust spiral (Fox 1974), he describes how full trust speeds up actions and transactions by minimizing negotiations, delays, tricks, and disobedience. The decision-making at trust-aimed Japanese firms was found slow due to consensus-seeking efforts, but decision implementation was rapid, versus non-Japanese firms' fast decision-making but slow implementation, if at all, due to obstacles and objections by parties whose interests were ignored or even not considered by executives (Dore 1973; Vogel 1975).

Trust requires qualities that are rare among US corporate managers, the largest group of management research subjects: honesty, integrity, sincerity, friendliness, and openness of information, such as admitting their own mistakes and failures.[14] This scarcity helps explain the recent US business scandals, but more importantly it helps explain the dominance of seductive-coercive low-trust cultures in which knowledge is a control tool used by superiors to defend and advance their own interests rather than organizational ones. According to Diefenbach (2013: 150) empirical evidence suggests that managerial abuse of power and of employees, petty tyranny, and downward workplace mobbing are much more widespread than usually recognized or acknowledged. Workers use exclusive know-how for "making out" a counter-system by which they defend their interests against managers' unilateral action (Roy 1952). Suspicious of employees' "making out," managers tend to further restrict information, but then employees do likewise, resulting in secrecy from which everyone suffers, as well as a descending trust spiral: each side defends interests grasped as threatened by the other, conceals information, and tries to curtail the other's discretion; these signal distrust, the other retaliates, *ad infinitum*.[15] Thus, in accord with Whitener and colleagues (1998), Zolin and colleagues (2004), and Six and Sorge (2008), and as exemplified by Guest's (1962: Ch. 4) incoming leader, the initial act of trusting subordinates is decisive for initiating an ascending trust spiral. Unfortunately, deficient ethnographic study of executives, their glorification, and an unclear concept of leadership often lead to omission of this decisiveness.[16]

Leadership

For Grint (2000) leadership is a collection of arts barely accessible to scientific approaches, while Sergiovanni (1992: 2) asserted that "the topic of leadership represents one of social science's greatest disappointments." Barker (1997) asks, "How can we train leaders if we do not know what leadership is?" According to McGill and Slocum (1998), all those who add answers to today's "leadership crisis" help little in resolving it, as they are not asking the right questions. Gini (1997) found that most leadership studies lack clarity and consensus regarding the very meaning of the term, since "Any attempt to describe a social process as complex as leadership inevitably makes it seen more orderly than it is" (p. 323); ". . . leadership is a delicate combination of the *process*, the *techniques* of leadership, the *person*, the specific *talents and traits* of a/the leader, and the general requirement of the *job* itself" (italics original; p. 329).[17]

However, Gini's list misses other pertinent factors, such as know-how and *phronesis*, habituses (Bourdieu 1977), and trust, emphasized by Chapters 1 and 2, as well as the followers and environmental factors.[18] Destructive leadership, for instance, is explained by the toxic triangle of destructive leaders, susceptible followers, and conducive environments.[19] A major factor missed by most leadership authors is the manager's trust in subordinates, which has a unique positive effect beyond the effect of trust in the manager (Brower et al. 2009). According to Bass (1998: 173) "trust is the single most important variable moderating the effects of transformational leadership," but he ignores the decisivenes of leaders' trust in employees: only a manager who trusts employees may opt for vulnerable involvement that exposes her/his inevitable ignorance of at least part of their know-how and *phronesis*, allows them much discretion, and engenders an ascending trust spiral (Fox 1974) in virtuous trust and learning cycles; a distrusting leader tends to cause distrust and ignorance cycles that often cannot be subsequently changed (Whitener et al. 1998). Many users of the transformational leadership concept ignored Burns's (1978) emphasis on a leader's high-moral attributes that indicate her/his trust in followers, such as admitting mistakes, open information, and readiness to perform even humble tasks if required.[20] Similarly, others defined a true leader as one who gains followers' trust and will to follow group/firm aims by policies and practices proving that s/he is part of the group/firm, trusts its members, and serves its aims, unlike the false leader whose concealed selfish deeds contradict talk of advancing common aims.[21] Poulin and his colleagues (2007) called the former "socialized leader," as against the latter type, a "personalized leader." Others also used this differentiation but missed the common distrust of followers by many personalized leaders who use CCMI and practice Im-C.

However, it is hard to discern in real time which type a leader is and whether s/he advances the group aims or camouflages it to advance his or her own interests. One reason for this difficulty is leaders' practice of changing their personal strategies: with success and tenure leaders become immoral, oligarchic, and use followers' trust created in their effectiveness phase for self-perpetuation (Michels 1959[1915]); they reach the dysfunction phase in accord with Leadership Life Cycle Theory (hereafter: LLCT; Hambrick 2007) and abuse followers' trust for power perpetuation, while students may mistake this for charisma (Shapira 2008: 90), as they mostly confuse transformational and charismatic leadership or use the problematic concept of charismatic-transformational leadership.[22] Many true socialized leaders generated transformation without charisma and were trusted due to their successes achieved because they trusted followers despite the latter's initial reservations by proving talent, knowledge, and competent learning, asserting a high-moral vision of lofty goals, inspiring followers to make extra efforts to attain them, modeling high-moral commitment to tasks, and encouraging use of followers' faculties for innovative problem-solving, which they took care to implement.[23] Collins and Porras (1995: 88) concluded that a high-profile, charismatic style is absolutely not required to successfully shape an innovative visionary company and O'Toole (1999: 129) emphasized that transformational leaders succeed by trusting everyone down the line with a "map," the vision of where the firm is headed, and what behaviors are needed to get there.

Leading by one's charisma tends to be personalized, and one seeks unilateral trust, having little trust in followers who fail to solve their problems; s/he offers a radical solution and creates trust in it by the appeal of her/his own exceptional qualities.[24] The transformational leader's trust is mutual: s/he trusts followers to use their faculties and ingenuity for innovative problem-solving. Charismatic leader distrust of employees contradicts the mutual trust that engenders virtuous learning cycles and innovation-prone high-trust cultures especially in knowledge-rich firms. Such a firm in case of a crisis may need an unconventionally thinking leader in a crisis and having charisma helps such one convincing followers of her/his radical solution, but similar to Guest (1962), Bennis (1989), and Washburn's (2011) cases, in all organizational ethnographies known to me rescuers were high-moral transformational leaders, with more or less charisma but an irrational following due to a belief in their "magical gift" was negligible. They all achieved turnarounds by a "change [that] only really comes about when those involved actively engage in the work of change, and are part of the cognitive shift often necessary to start turning the organization around" (Grint and Holt 2011: 92). They were followed because of a rational belief in their high-moral true leadership,[25] as they created "a complex moral relationship between people, based on trust, obligation, commitment, emotion, and a shared vision of the good" (Ciulla 2004: xv), through convincing visions and their ability to advance these.[26] Thus, only by reviewing the practices of a leader and followers, as well as their contexts and processes, may one distinguish for certain between a socialized, true high-moral transformational leader and a personalized and/or charismatic one who conceals her/his ignorance and Im-C.

Unfortunately, the trust and leadership literature tends to disregard the long-range perspective: the initial mutual trust of a high-moral effective leader by followers engenders successes; then s/he reaches a dysfunction phase, covertly diverts real organizational aims to those serving her/his perpetuation, and nurtures unilateral trust in her/his leadership until reaching a charismatic image, as did prime kibbutz leaders Tabenkin and Yaari.[27] LLCT studies found that the dysfunction phase of CEOs commenced after 3–12 years on the job, while the dysfunction of prime kibbutz leaders commenced after 12–15 years.[28] Despite these studies, as well as Lord Acton's dictum that "power corrupts and total power corrupts totally," leadership studies mostly missed how some leaders remained for prolonged periods as their firms thrived due to unique circumstances and/or because of mid-levelers' successes due to entering the leadership vacuum created by old-guard dysfunction and solving some major problems. As Chapter 6 explains, after 12–15 years of effective leadership prime kibbutz leaders became oligarchic conservatives but retained their power and prestige by immoral means for another three decades, as mid-level I-KO *pe'ilim* achieved successes that camouflaged their dysfunction.[29]

Due to their relatively short length of observation and social distance from executives, anthropologists tend to miss such changes by veteran leaders. For example, from 1957 DEC (Digital Equipment Corporation) CEO Olsen led a high-trust, innovative-prone culture to impressive success and growth by high-moral transformational leadership. However, after a decade he commenced dysfunctioning, never decided major issues and ignored pressing problems, often left executives in shambles, causing much distrust, destructive conflicts, and brain drain (Rifkin and Harrar 1988: Chs. 9–12). DEC was later revived by mid-levelers who entered the leadership vacuum and solved some major problems, though not others due to Olsen's conservatism. However, trust in Olsen's high-moral leadership was retained among the lower ranks as he allowed mid-levelers to exercise their discretion and never used fiats, while rewarding fairness and integrity.[30] Unfortunately, Kunda (1992) missed Olsen's dysfunction, which largely explained DEC's negative late culture. Like the above kibbutz case, the long era of DEC thriving while Olsen dysfunctioned was explicable by combining a historical and ethnographic view. Thus, untangling leadership complexities requires ethnographying of a much lengthier period than the usual industrial ethnography as was done here.

"Parachuted" Outsiders, Distrust, CCMI, and Im-C through "Jumping"

DEC's case also demonstrates a prime problem of leading knowledge-based firms, including automatic processing plants: dependency of superiors' decisions and actions on the exclusive knowledge and expertises of inferiors, which give the latter extra power. Then coercion becomes ineffective and encourages opting for trust, but a superior may choose to suppress opposing experts by importing loyalists or prospective loyalists, in Israel called "parachuting." In 1968 DEC's Olsen did so to engineer De Castro, the heir apparent of the R&D department, who had led the development of major DEC computers. De Castro insisted on a major technological reshuffle, which Olsen grasped as too hazardous. He "parachuted" an outsider as De Castro's boss, De Castro left with his team to establish a successful competitor, while Olsen's use of coercive power curbed the trust with other seniors who became docile and conservative, menaced by a possible similar suppression (Rifkin and Harrar 1988: Chs. 9–11). By "parachuting," Olsen consolidated his power but diminished trust and changed DEC's culture for the worst in innovativeness terms, much as most of the Merkaz "parachutings" aside from that of Thomas. The longitudinal ethnography exposes leaders' destructive use of "parachutings" to coerce employees to their will, untangling the falseness of its excuses often discerned by employees, resulting in enhanced distrust of superiors.

"Jumpers" suffer larger knowledge gaps than insiders and especially a lack of essential local knowledge, which discourages ignorance exposure, which engenders a negative low-trust cycle. They may have other knowledge advantages, but half a century of research failed to conclude whether they are preferable over insiders, as this research is mostly ignored by oligarchy theory, LLCT, and succession norms such as *rotatzia* + "parachuting."[31] For instance, in the US outsider CEOs introduced more successful innovations and strategic changes in succession-stable corporations with long-tenured successful predecessors than in less stable ones (Karaevli and Zajac 2013). Long-tenured in the US means more than 9–10 years (Brouwer 2008: 129), double than *rotatzia*'s formal terms. Thus, by causing instability and more non-ordinary successions due to failures, *rotatzia* and "parachutings" helped explain Merkaz's mismanagement.

"Parachuting" is also problematic since "jumpers" must choose their personal strategy upon taking charge, leading to either a virtuous or a vicious cycle; if a "jumper" does not opt for trust-creating vulnerable involvement from the beginning, and rather only attempts it later on, he or she may not succeed (Whitener et al. 1998), as initial choice leads to sticky and vicious distrust and ignorance cycles; only one case of a "jumper's" change from detachment to vulnerable involvement was found in the literature (Holtskog 2014: 161–162). Besides, an outsider who is at first detached and/or seductive-coercive and begins to trust employees only later on may also be suspected of seeking power gains, grasped as insincere and opportunistic rather than a trustworthy, authentic leader.

Newcomers who take charge of unacquainted employees tend to use seduction-coercion (Kipnis 1976), a strategy that fits their interests: it is simpler than trust-building, requires neither ignorance exposure, nor long-term commitment, nor employees' consent, nor care for their interests beyond a working place and market-level wages. Unfortunately, these are often insufficient to generate essential employees' contributions. According to Dalton (1959: 213), "The diversity and range of contributions required of an administrative or functional group cannot be exactly reflected in the official system of rewards. This is inherent, not a diabolical shortcoming"; hence, Dalton's managers often elicited employees' essential contributions by using unofficial rewards that often seemed illegitimate or even immoral.[32] But how can an outsider who uses CCMI ascertain whose contribution is essential and which unofficial reward adequate? Often even insiders are not sure how to weigh a contribution's value and reward it proportionally (Dalton 1959: Ch. 7) because intangible rewards defy quantification and each actor evaluates rewards subjectively; hence their value for her/him is hard to asses. Worse still, rewards tend to go more to those who already have some rather than to those who deserve them (Goode 1978); hence to achieve trust-creating fair and just rewarding (Hosmer 1995) an executive must be able to assess subordinates' contributions. The use of CCMI by Merkaz managers prevented such assessment, and led to the loss of both trust and the potential contributions of major experts such as Levi and Amram.

Ethnography may untangle and explain rewarding. Lazega (2001), for instance, found that major rewards at a collegial US law firm were fame and prestige while tangible remuneration was accorded by seniority. Some leaders received less remuneration than more veteran lawyers, but were rewarded much more intangibly by winning prestigious legal battles that brought in most of the revenues and enhanced their power and authority; firm management was rotated among seniors, endowing little prestige and power.

Merkaz was different, as were other industries; executives were both best remunerated and received most of the prestige and fame, often usurping experts' successes and using them to leverage a "jump" and "parachute" into higher-level jobs elsewhere, as Shavit, for instance, usurped Thomas's success with the automatic feeder and "jumped" to manage another, larger plant with Zelikovich's help.[33] Even the modest success of a manager's unit may enable a successful "jump" with an enhanced image, using authority and power to camouflage and conceal both one's failures and others' contributions to successes.[34] Ample "jumpings" (e.g. Geneen 1984) help explain why in the US ineffective managers tend to have more successful careers than effective ones (Luthans 1988): outsider CEOs and executives who choose CCMI are susceptible to ineffective subordinate managers' ingratiation, subterfuges, and faked loyalty, using executives' failing to discern them from effective ones who invest efforts in performing. Moreover, the latter, empowered by successes, tend to criticize superiors' mistakes, while CCMI-Im-C loyalists abide by the mistaken decisions of ignorant bosses. This obedience pays back nicely since an ignorant outsider boss needs insiders to learn the ropes, which such loyalists know best by investing energies in politics rather than performance, becoming politics experts (Buchanan and Badham 2008: 304) as was Atad. The outsider who rewards them by promotion often faces shrewdness: after promotion they "jump" elsewhere, a strategy that often succeeds since the target firm's CEO knows little about "jumpers" functioning in previous firms aside from their positions, and often s/he cannot skillfully assess this also due to ignorance of their own ignorance.[35] A CCMI-user outsider often gains power by replacing deputies with ignorant loyalists, imported ones or insiders who suppress and oust effective insiders as did Merkaz PMs, while various circumstances may let such an ignorant ruling clique continue for long periods despite major failures.[36]

Discerning Leaders' Immoral Change and Exposing Im-C and CCMI

According to oligarchy theory, a leader becomes a self-serving dysfunctional oligarch with tenure and the firm's success and growth. As mentioned, both the trust and leadership literatures mostly ignored this negative change although growth makes pertinent Scharfstein's (1995) conclusion that amorality is integral to the wielding of authority in large entities. Even ethnographers who alluded to the dysfunction of old guard leaders mostly missed its self-serving nature and the vicious distrust and ignorance cycles enhanced by the promotion of ingratiating, ignorant imposter incompetents rather than talented critical thinkers and innovators. One explanation of such an omission by Kunda (1992) is the creativity of human action (Joas 1996): DEC's Olsen was an unconventional autocrat who dominated by subtle means with no dismissals, a few "parachutings," and minimal privileges to himself and senior staff; he retained a humble personal lifestyle, unknown among such CEOs, which preserved the trust-enhancing "we" feeling (Haslam et al. 2011) of most DEC employees. But trust-enhancing practices did not prevent his decision-making dysfunction, which failed innovation in an innovation-prone industry and caused brain drain and failures until DEC collapsed.

A longitudinal ethnography of DEC's top echelons and use of oligarchy theory and LLCT was required to discern and explain this leadership decline. A longitudinal perspective is essential because the successors of veteran dysfunctioning leaders tend to be their conformist loyalists who lack critical thinking (Hirschman 1970) and use CCMI-Im-C all the way to the top. Thus, its exposure is difficult as is the exposure of the Im-C of a "parachutist." Successful Merkaz non-careerist effective mid-levelers such as Thomas, Levi, and Amram spoke eagerly of their own functioning and admitted mistakes and failures, while exposing the dark secrets of CCMI and Im-C of detached/seductive-coercive "jumpers" required a prolonged effort as they were secretive and offered fake excuses for failures if they agreed to discuss them at all. But observations of mistakes and failures, plus ample interviews and reading of management minutes and other archival materials, proved CCMI and Im-C, which resembled many of the findings of destructive leadership studies.[37]

Users of seduction-coercion may not try to conceal the observable, seeking culprits rather than trying to learn from failures (Gittell 2000), unlike users of detached CCMI. But some of the latter practices that suggested CCMI-Im-C were observable: secrecy, distancing oneself from practitioners' deliberations, avoidance of employees who sought a manager's help with problem-solving, minimizing dependency on employees' expertise by conservatism, and using outside consultants rather than expert insiders, as well as various subterfuges, such as bluffing, scapegoating, and the like (e.g., Dalton 1959). Immorality was also discernible as it spread from leaders to followers, as in the saying "the fish stinks from the head,"[38] and was inferred from superiors' discouraging of high-moral behaviors such as honesty and sincerity by modeling their opposites (Maccoby 1976: 190). Many interviews of past *pe'ilim* and hired staffs free to criticize higher-ups also untangled this.

Cultures and Sub-Cultures

Chapters 1 and 2 pointed to contrasting managerial choices, which engender either high- or low-trust cultures. While the study of cultures has become of central interest for many disciplines, the definition of culture remains varied. For Geertz (1973), cultures are meaning structures that control human behavior, while for Harris (1990), Vaughan (1996), and Swidler (2001), they are collections of behavioral tools and practical solutions for existential problems. Bourdieu's (1990: 86) view connects these views by defining cultures as "symbolic systems" that are products of practices that implement principles that are "coherent and compatible with the objective conditions— but also practical, . . . easy to master and use, because they obey a 'pure' economic logic."

However, what is practical and logical for one firm may be impractical and illogical for another with the same formal aims and objective conditions but with a different market niche, strategy, technology, employees' tenure, and their knowledge and skills.[39] In the same vein, Hawthorn (1991) has pointed out that there are often some plausible practical alternative solutions for a problem, which are forgotten once the incumbent has been chosen and succeeded or seemed to. These alternatives might have succeeded as well, or may after a while with new know-how and technologies, which human creativity develops (Joas 1996). Human creativity changes both the practicality of solutions and the viability of cultures as solution collections, while the adoption of new practices is affected by the cultural context. For instance, the "Iron Cage" hypothesis of the new institutional approach asserts that an organization succeeds only if it conforms to societal norms.[40] However, the many high-trust organizations that thrive in low-trust societal cultures and economies, as well as many low-trust firms that succeed in high-trust economies,[41] limit the applicability of this hypothesis, as do findings of quite different cultures in firms' various units (Parker 2000). The finding of contrary cultures of successful British rayon firms versus successful electronic firms likewise limit its applicability: the latter's "organic," innovative cultures were clearly high-trust contrary to the low-trust "mechanical," conservative rayon firm cultures (Burns and Stalker 1961). One may point to some common British cultural attributes and call both above cultures "subcultures," but as both the discussion and Merkaz findings show contrary organizational functioning of high- versus low-trust cultures, it makes little sense to designate them as sub-cultures.

High-trust culture can thrive if managers are grasped as high-moral leaders who prefer the common good over their own and allocate rights, duties, and rewards, in right, just, and fair manner in accord with societal mores and norms (Hosmer 1995). Hosmer only questions whether "there is a connection—through trust—between the moral duty of officers and the output performance of organizations" (p. 400). My findings on the success of high-moral Moav's deputies and of Thomas and his colleagues, as well as further evidence in next chapters plus cited literature, answer this query in the affirmative. High-moral managers mostly enhance performance by trustful practices: performance is enhanced by trust-creating ignorance-exposing vulnerable involvement, openness, honesty, and sincerity, which engender learning cycles, managerial effectiveness, and positive communication with employees who are granted discretion for innovative problem-solving that encourages their involvement, cooperation, and commitment.[42] Many leadership studies missed the decisive role of morality by ignoring ethnographies or because ethnographers did not penetrate executives' dark secrets and missed Im-C practices.[43] Lacking ethnographies of executives, their morality is often not grasped as a personal strategic choice (Mintzberg 1987) and was not associated with vulnerably involved effective management, which researchers mostly missed as those who practiced it (Kanter 1993[1977]: 33) lost promotion competitions to rivals who became immoral CEOs and like Shavit and Mehri's (2005) manager appropriated the prestige of the formers' achievements, barring students knowing the true achievers.

Outsiders' knowledge gaps encouraged CCMI, but even an insider who experienced some of her/his subordinates' jobs years ago tends to be ignorant of them now as employees use new technologies, tools, and machines, and s/he faces the ignorance exposure dilemma. This dilemma is aggravated by the care for employee needs and interests required to create trust; these are hard to know since if they are asked about these "they almost always reply with what they want" (O'Toole 1999: 192). An executive must actively seek employee needs and interests in order to care for them and gain their trust, but this puts her/him in an uneasy position of dependence. Worse still, s/he must be grasped as high-moral in whose "decisions and actions . . . interests of society take the degree of precedence that is right, just and fair" over his own interests (Hosmer 1995: 339). Unfortunately, this degree is hard to judge as it depends on the specific situation and its contexts, organizational values and norms, the field's gravity, and societal gravity (Bourdieu and Wacquant 1992). All these unknowns require of a newcomer considerable effort, while a major motivation for this can be the belief in employees' potential contributions to one's job functioning. However, such a belief creates awareness of their intangible resources, which requires vulnerable indwelling and assimilating in their deliberations; thus, managers' personal strategy choices are decisive in the shaping of local cultures.[44]

However, there is another major obstacle to creating high-trust cultures: full trust means that each participant is allowed much discretion to contribute for common aims (Fox 1974). Allowing much discretion may cause serious coordination problems; it requires considerable consensus concerning aims, means, and allocation of duties and rewards, and this becomes harder the more knowledge-rich the organization, with its variety of jobs, specializations, and expertise levels. Neither communities of practice literature nor research of high-performance work systems that vindicates discretion alluded to this problem.[45] Merkaz findings point to a huge difference in the expertise level of detached/seductive-coercively involved *pe'ilim* as against that of vulnerably involved ones. These differences prevented consensus concerning major problems required for trust relations. A major source of differences is importing outsiders with a variety of cultural habits, as exemplified by the difference between Avi and Thomas's habituses due to their contrasting types of careers: Avi advanced by replacing action domains, while Thomas advanced within a single domain. Further incoherence generates outsiders who opt for CCMI-Im-C, which enhances distrust and secrecy that helps advance the career of "brambles" who use political acumen to unduly reap rewards at the expense of effective mid-levelers, busy with achieving performance (see pp. 152–155). In theory, promoters of "brambles" are punished by both brain drain and failures, but many obstacles stop disappointed effective mid-levelers from leaving; similar to Thomas who waited three years to build an innovative automatic feeder under despised Shavit, many reasons lead to the retention of mid-levelers who contribute to the firm's functioning despite despised leaders who promote "brambles." Such mid-levelers retain local high trust within their jurisdiction, as did Thomas and Danton, while in the rest of the firm/ plant a low-trust secrecy culture prevails. In this culture both leaders and researchers missed who of the mid-levelers led to successes and who tried to block them, caused failures, wasted resources, and camouflaged all of the above.

Organizational Commitment, Autocracy, and Oligarchy vs. Democracy

Seeking loyalists to enhance a superior's power encourages the "parachuting" of outsiders. This encourages the attrition of frustrated insiders and their loyalists, like DEC's De Castro and his team, but other employees also "jump" out if they find good opportunities and detest the current job. Watson (2004) discerns between high- and low-commitment cultures and points to the brain drain that the latter tend to suffer. High-commitment cultures are usually led by highly trusted knowledgeable insider executives who succeed without using the "parachuting" of mid-levelers, creating high-trust cultures, as Dore (1973) and Ouchi (1981) explained the success of many Japanese firms.[46] However, some insider CEOs succeeded in the US as well: Jim Collins (2001) compared 20 years of performance of the best 11 firms, each in its respective industry, to the second best. Some 95.2% of best firms CEOs were insiders versus only 69% of the second-best firms. The depictions of best firm CEOs untangle servant, highly committed, and high-moral leaders who created high-trust cultures, but Collins avoided these concepts. His insider CEOs catalyzed commitment to and vigorous pursuit of their vision by employees (Collins, J. 2001: 20), created mutual trust with them by modeling high-moral commitment to tasks (Collins, J. 2001: 21), by personal modesty (Collins, J. 2001: 27), and by being "contributing team members" together with deputies (Collins, J. 2001: 20), all features of servant transformational leaders who engender high-trust cultures.[47] For Collins the "culture of discipline" explained successes, but discipline achieved by seductive-coercive autocracy such as Yuval's could not engender the high commitment required for the "vigorous pursuit" of a leader's vision by employees; it could only be achieved by the trust and consent of a servant transformational leader, as were Collins's successful CEOs, according to his depictions though not his analysis.

More insider than outsider CEOs enhance organizational commitment, as their careers are often models of such commitment, while outsiders' careers, consisting of frequent "jumpings" to new firms, model a lack of such commitment, rather a commitment to their own career advancement. Many authors grasp transformational leadership as simpler than it is in fact, as firm's high-moral commitment factor is often neglected. On the battlefield, highly committed servant leadership is evident when an officer leads soldiers to storm enemy positions by running ahead and risking his life against enemy fire. In business it is harder to assess what personal risks a leader takes when pursuing innovation; for example, ITT CEO Geneen (1984: 124–127) kept his job despite two failed initiatives costing $US 1 billion.

At the apex of the business world even demotion is not much of a risk, as one receives a huge "golden parachute" and can remain in the business elite; Carly Fiorina was remunerated for her six failing years as HP CEO by more than $US 110 million (Johnson 2008: 191). Such a huge remuneration for failed leadership, which took her successor years to correct (Johnson 2008), deters true leadership with which employees could identify (Haslam et al. 2011). Such reward for failure encourages immoral, oligarchic autocracy; hubris; and other types of corrupt and destructive leadership. This begs the question: how can we explain the dominance of such oligarchic and autocratic corporate practices in democracies?

Michels's (1959[1915]) classic answer, given above in both kibbutz and DEC cases, was that the extra-long tenure of successful leaders caused oligarchization and autocracy, but in corporate US such tenure was rare; 87% of CEOs retired within 12 years (Vancil 1987: 79). However, while some CEOs retired early due to failures and to other incapacitating reasons, many others retired due to the oligarchic measure of "golden parachutes" allotted by the directorate without any say for non-director executives and managers who knew best who deserved generosity and who did not. Thus, powerful business elites appropriated huge sums of money even if failed in jobs by an oligarchic practice that replaced another, i.e., indefinite tenure, while reiterating the primacy of the elite's autocratic power.

Feenberg (1995) explains this power thus: "modern technology lends itself to authoritarian administration, but in different social context it could just as well be operated democratically" (Feenberg 1995: 4). This does not happen because "[T]echnologies are selected by these interests [of social agencies and powers] from among many possible configurations"; "once introduced, technology offers a material validation of the cultural horizon to which it has been performed" (Feenberg 1995: 12). This horizon was shaped by two widely held false beliefs, "that technical necessity dictates the path of development, and that the pursuit of efficiency provides the basis for identifying that path." These beliefs are "employed to justify restrictions on opportunities [of employees] to participate in the institutions of industrial society . . . we can achieve a new type of technological society which can support . . . [D]emocracy" (Feenberg 1995: 18).[48]

Altman (2002) explains autocracy by the economic advantages of low-trust, autocratic firms. Firms with superior, more cooperative work cultures (i.e., high-trust, democratic, participative) are more efficient, but their labor costs are higher as an empowered work force is paid higher wages than powerless workers of inferior, less cooperative work cultures (i.e. low-trust, autocratic, oligarchic). Globalization enhances the economic advantages of the autocratic firms: they close factories and fire costly employees in home country to move less specialized work to third world countries with minimal wages where local contractors and collaborating governments repress workers' efforts to unionize and receive decent wages. Worse still, if such repression fails, work is moved to another, even lower-wage country, while the extra profits gained are used to finance ultra-costly advertising campaigns (Klein 2000). Instead of risking innovation, these firms use innovations created by firms of the former type, while they dominate markets due to the above advantages, and their dominance interferes with the creation of more cooperative work cultures.

A fourth explanation is the oligarchization and bureaucratization of the organization's field with growth and success, which leaders use for entrenchment if no democratic constitution ensures their timely succession before it becomes impossible. As cited, kibbutz cultures were initially democratic and egalitarian, but success-empowered prime leaders violated these principles and stayed for good, helped by senior *pe'ilim* loyalists who as privileged I-KO officials accumulated power, prestige, and intangible capitals and prevented their own *rotatzia*, "riding" on the successes of *rotational* mid-levelers, as Moav "rode" on Yaakov's and Aharon's successes. *Rotatzia* was officially aimed at preventing oligarchization, but in reality it did the opposite and the kibbutzim declined due to life-long dysfunctioning oligarchic leaders, quite similar to other successful communes and cooperatives.[49] Use of modern technologies by kibbutzim also negatively affected democracy (e.g., Feenberg 1995) and likewise affected the use of cheap hired labor by many kibbutzim and I-KRCs (e.g., Altman 2002). Worse still, *pe'ilim* as outsider "parachuted" I-KRC managers tended to use CCMI and to pursue Im-C, which enhanced non-democratic cultures (Shapira 1987, 2013).

A fifth explanation is offered by Darr and Stern (2002), who ask why the democratic election of leaders, which is such a fundamental institution in the political domain of Western society, is rejected in the economic domain. They found that democracy stops at the factory gates partly because of the practices and ideologies of the professionals who construct and maintain the boundaries between the workplace and the larger political sphere; lawyers, accountants, and academics act as structural constraints on workers' democratizing attempts.

Thus, all these beg the question of whether the ethnographic study of I-KRCs and their plants can help develop a theory of management and leadership that can create and maintain for long trustful, effective democratic corporate cultures.

Can Multi-Ethnography Offer a Theory of Managerial Trust as an Alternative to Detachment/Seduction-Coercion?

Ethnography is a problematic method for building a new theory; it tends to be limited by the perspective chosen and by the specifics of a studied culture.[50] Anthropologists also tend to miss the effects of contexts on their field of study (Marx 1985: 145). However, the above discussions pointed to the potential of combining multiple ethnographies and a prolonged one with a historical gaze to create a new theory. Supporting it are Burns and Stalker's (1961) multiple ethnographies that led to an innovation theory, Dore's (1973) ethnographies which delineated the contours of a theory of high- and low-trust organizational cultures, and Fox's (1974) theory of low- and high-trust industrial relations stemming from the comparison between historical cases and Hoon's (2014) meta-synthesis of case studies. Then many authors furthered the trust theory, as cited. In this literature, leaders shaped local cultures by their choices of practices; thus, ethnographies aimed at explaining this shaping must compare between opposing managerial practices:

A High-moral vulnerably involved managers committed to plants' and employees' interests, seeking trust and consent by openness and knowledge sharing, learning and innovation as the highway to performance and internal career advancement.

B Managers who seek a faked image of success wherever a real one requires risk-taking and hardships, preferring personal interests over common ones, advancing careers by immoral and even Machiavellian means, using detachment and/or seduction-coercion to defend authority and gain advantages and for "jumping" when finding opportunity.

For a good theory, such ethnography must untangle the etiology of the contrasting personal strategies. Four explanations of managers' choices were suggested above:

1 How much pertinent knowledge and competencies they have;
2 Their habituses;
3 Their grasping employees as either replaceable by market substitutes or irreplaceable due to internally acquired skills;
4 Their tendency to emulate practices used by other successful *pe'ilim* and the kibbutz field's higher-ups.

However, the above discussions pointed also to:

5 Their mutual trust with employees based on past relationships or their lack thereof.

Outsiders may not have such pasts and trust, but Saxenian (1994: Ch. 2), for instance, found that Silicon Valley's innovativeness explained trustful relationships and camaraderie among entrepreneurs and managers in close-knit small-town networks that enhanced frequent positive "jumpings." Likewise helpful are former acquaintances, which explain the opposite results of seemingly similar "parachutings": Gerstner and Fiorina were "parachuted" to head IBM and HP, respectively, after successfully leading corporations in quite different industries, while only Gerstner succeeded. The literature's critique of the assumption of managerial skills' portability is not enough to explain the difference,[51] while my analysis explains it: Gerstner did not use CCMI as he had been familiar with IBM executives for many years. Trusting them when taking charge, he brought no loyalists with him, whom locals tend to distrust (Gouldner 1954), coped with problems together with them like Guest's (1962) outsider, and made massive changes only after two years on the job, the same period it took for Guest's (1962) outsider and Elena Kagan at the Harvard Law School (Washburn 2011) to make a turnaround:

"Gerstner critically evaluated the existing policies and strategies before making any attempt to change them. This approach not only gave him the necessary time to gain expertise about several aspects of the firm and its business, but also helped him gain the necessary power base, and social and political capital . . ."

(Karaevli 2007: 691).

"Gain expertise" meant that for two years he learned by ignorance exposure, furthered the trust he commenced with, reviewed problems, and chose successful solutions that gained him power, and only then made major changes. Fiorina was the opposite, with little learning and suspected by HP executives, she did not built trust in her leadership, learned little before introducing sweeping changes aimed at proving herself (e.g., Watkins 2003), which instead caused vicious distrust and ignorance cycles, mistakes, and failures (Johnson 2008), much like Merkaz's Yuval and Gouldner's (1954, 1955) "parachutist."

However, as mentioned, recent organization studies rediscovered the concept of practice and the major advantage of the "practice lens" is its critical power. Through this lens the practice of importing outsider executives requires explanation as a relatively new practice; it was rare in Dalton's (1959) and Levenson's (1961) days and "jumping" was first described by Downs (1966). It only became an institutionalized practice with its specialized institutions such as headhunting firms in recent decades (Khurana 2002). Institutionalization of a new practice is not necessarily due to its superiority over an old one, only enough that contextual pressures join internal circuits to cause it (Gherardi and Perrotta 2013). The prime context of the I-KRCs studied is the kibbutz field, which despite mistaken canonical research is now being explained through others' and my own ethnographies and critical studies. Further explanation of gin plants and I-KRCs' mismanagement requires explanation of the institutionalization of *rotatzia* and "parachutings" in the kibbutz field despite their negative, effects necessitating a Strathernian contextualization that discerns impacting contexts and their interrelations helped by historical analysis.[52] This will be done by Chapter 6. Chapter 5 will analyze other negative processes of plants' low-trust cultures that deepened immoral mismanagement, and Chapter 4 analyzes the four other plants that corroborate Merkaz's findings. The use of genealogical Boasian ethnographying (Bunzl 2004) of the five cases will expose more of I-KRCs' dark sides, further explaining executives' control and how some mid-levelers overcame the negative effects of PMs' CCMI-Im-C.

Notes

1 See also Grint (2005) on leaders' ability to construct/shape contexts that would legitimize chosen actions.
2 Heifetz (1995); Swidler and Arditi (1994).
3 See respectively: Collins and Evans (2007); Collins (2011); Collins and Sanders (2007).

4 Trust pioneers: Argyris (1962); Banfield (1958); Deutsch (1958, 1962); Fox (1974); Hollander (1978); Jay (1972); Likert (1967); McGregor (1960); Riker (1974); Shapira (1982); Zand (1972). CEO Autobiographies: Geneen (1984); Harvey-Jones (1988); Sieff (1986). Research surging: Dodgson (1993); Fairholm (1994); Fukuyama (1995); Wagner (1995); Hosmer (1995); Kramer and Tyler (1996); Ring and Van de Ven (1992); Sako (1992).

5 Bypassing ethnographies: Bate (1997). Inappropriate methods: Barley and Tolbert (1997).

6 E.g., Dore (1973); Fox (1974); Guest (1962); Ouchi (1981); Powell (1990); Rohlen (1974); Shapira (1995b).

7 Courpasson and Clegg (2006); Gouldner (1955); Rosner (1993).

8 For instance, high-trust communes and cooperatives in low-trust economies: Rosner (1993); Russel (1995); Semler (1993); Shapira (2008); Whyte and Whyte (1988). For a contrasting case see below.

9 Mehri (2005); Pettigrew (1973); Webb and Cleary (1994). Creating competition: Rifkin and Harrar (1988: Ch. 10).

10 Bourhis et al. (2005); Ciulla (1998a); Dore (1973); Fairholm (2004); Fox (1974); Geneen (1984: Ch. 4); Hosmer (1995); Ouchi (1981); Raelin (2011); Rohlen (1974); Schröder (2013: 558–559); Shapira (1987, 2012a); long time horizon and creativity: Jaques (1990).

11 Brumann (2000); Rosner (1993); Russell (1995). On this change: Errasti (2014); Shapira (2008); Stryjan (1989).

12 High morality: Hosmer (1995); Dysfunction phase: Hambrick (2007); Michels (1959[1915]). Decentralized organization: Brumann (2000); Erdal (2011); Semler (1993); Shapira (2001, 2008, 2013).

13 On trust see: Ardichvili (2008); Colquitt et al. (2007); Covey (2006); Dietz and Den Hartog (2006); Eggs (2012); Fairholm (2004); Fox (1974); Mayer et al. (1995); Preece (2004); Raelin (2013); Simons (2002); Six and Sorge (2008); on participation see: Brøgger (2010); Cloke and Goldsmith (2002); Emery (1995); Gollan and Xu (2015); Heller et al. (1998); McLagan and Nel (1997); Perkins and Poole (1996); Semler (1993); Sen (2003); on satisfying employees' needs see; O'Toole (1999: 192).

14 Ciulla (1998b); Dalton (1959); Hill (2006); Jackall (1988); Keltner et al. (2006); Maccoby (1976); Stein (2001).

15 Burawoy (1979); Crozier (1964); Dalton (1959); Fox (1974); O'Mahoney (2005); Roy (1952, 1955).

16 Ailon (2015); Villette and Vuillermot (2009); Welker et al. (2011).

17 See support by other critics: Alvesson and Spicer (2012); Banks (2008); Buckingham and Coffman (1999: 63); Van Knippenberg and Sitkin (2013); Watson (2013).

18 Fraher (2016); Gardner (1990): 23; Hollander (2009); Howell and Shamir (2005); Maccoby (2015: 38).

19 Aasland et al. (2010); Fraher (2016); Lipman-Blumen (2005); Padilla et al. (2007); Thoroughgood et al. (2012).

20 Badaracco and Ellsworth (1989); Barbuto (1997); Bass (1985); Beyer (1999); Colquitt et al. (2007); Eseryel and Eseryel (2013); Kanter (1993[1977]: 33); Mishra and Mishra (2015); Norman et al. (2010); Wren (1998); Yukl (1999).

21 True vs. false leaders: Bass and Steidlmeier (1999); Bennis (1989); Haslam et al. (2011); above cited works on destructive leaders. Talks negate deeds: Robison (2010); Simons (2002).

22 Barbuto (1997); Beyer (1999); Shapira (2008); Van Knippenberg and Sitkin (2013); Yukl (1999).

23 On decisiveness of modeling See: Gamson (1991); on such leaders see footnotes 25–26.

24 Adair-Toteff (2005); Barbuto (1997); Tucker (1970).

25 Avolio and Gardner (2005); Bass and Steidlmeier (1999); Haslam et al. (2011); Hmieleski et al. (2011); Sosik et al. (2009); Terry (1993).

26 Downton (1973); Giuliani (2002); Goleman et al. (2002); Graham (1991); Harvey-Jones (1988); Heskett (2011); Kotter and Heskett (1992); O'Toole (1999); Poulin and Siegel (2005); Sankar (2003); Sergiovanni (1992); Shapira (2001, 2008); Sieff (1986); Useem et al. (2011).

27 Hirschman (1982); Jay (1969); Kets De Vries (1993); Lenski (1966); Michels (1959[1915]); on kibbutz leaders see Shapira (2008) and Ch. 6.

28 Hambrick (2007); Hou et al. (2014); Miller and Shamsie (2001); Ocasio (1994); Wulf et al. (2011).

29 Shapira (2008, 2011). See Graham (1991) and Grint (2014) for cases of mid-level innovative rescuers.

30 Badaracco and Ellsworth (1989); Dineen et al. (2006); Kunda (1992: 174); Simons (2002); Smollan and Parry (2011).

31 Cannella and Rowe (1995); Jung (2014); Karaevli (2007); Miller (1993); Poulin et al. (2007); Shen and Cannella (2002); White et al. (1997); insiders were better: Bower (2007); Collins, J. (2001); Groysberg et al. (2006); Khurana (2002); Kotter (1982); Shapira (1987, 2013); Townley (2002).

32 Dalton (1959: 213); Kunda (1992: 40–44).

33 "Jump" see: Downs (1966). Advance by "jumps": Geneen (1984: Ch. 3); Murrell et al. (1996); Rifkin and Harrar (1988: Ch. 20); Shapira (2013). Usurpation: Mehri (2005).

34 Dalton (1959); Hughes (1958); Levenson (1961); Lynn and Jay (1986); Martin and Strauss (1959).

35 Dore (1973: Ch. 9); Graham (1991: 114–115).

36 Dalton (1959); Gouldner (1954); Kanter (1993[1977]); Mehri (2005).

37 Aasland et al. (2010); Fotaki and Hyde (2015); Fraher (2016); Lipman-Blumen (2005); Thoroughgood et al. (2012).

38 For Gini (2004: 9) the Russian proverb is "A fish rots from the head." See also: Liu et al. (2012).

39 See: Perrow (1970); also Cappelli and Crocker-Hefter (1996).

40 DiMaggio and Powell (1983); Powell and DiMaggio (1991).

41 Barkai (1977); Clark (1979); Erdal (2011); Saxenian (1994); Semler (1993); Spiro (1983); Whyte and Whyte (1988).

42 Previous footnote and Golemen et al. (2002), Grint (2000), Norman et al. (2010) and Thomas et al. (2009).

43 Low-moral leaders: Banfield (1958); Brockner et al. (1997); Jackall (1988); recent business scandal studies; on destructive leadership see footnote 37.

44 Gouldner (1954); Guest (1962); Mehri (2005); O'Mahoney (2005); Shapira (1995b, 2013, 2015).

45 Communities of practice: Lave and Wenger (1991); Orr (1996); Wenger (1998); high-performance work systems: Jensen et al. (2007).

46 Versus these see low-trust Japanese firms' ethnographies: Clark (1979); Mehri (2005).

47 Barbuto (1997); Burns (1978); DePree (1990); Graham (1991); Greenleaf (1977); Sendjaya (2005).

48 See support by: Clarke and Butcher (2006); Cloke and Goldsmith (2002); Darr and Lewin (2001); Erdal (2011); Estrin and Jones (1992); Heller et al. (1998); Hirschman (1984); McLagan and Nel (1997); Semler (1993); Sen (2003); Shapira (1987, 2008); Whyte and Whyte (1988).

49 Shapira (1978/9, 1980, 1995a, 2001, 2005, 2008, 2013); e.g. Brumann (2000); Russell (1995); Stryjan (1989).

50 Hammersley (1992); Martin (1992); Van Maanen (1995).

51 Bower (2007); Gabarro (1987); Groysberg et al. (2006); Khurana (2002); Watkins (2003).
52 Strathernian contextualization: Huen (2009); Morita (2014); Shapira (2015); Strathern (2004); historical analysis: Wallerstein (2004).

References

Aasland, Merethe S., A. Skogstad, et al. 2010. The prevalence of destructive leadership behaviour. *British Journal of Management* 21(4): 438–452.

Adair-Toteff, Christopher. 2005. Max Weber's charisma. *Journal of Classical Sociology* 5(2): 189–204.

Ailon, Galit. 2015. From superstars to devils: The ethical discourse on managerial figures involved in a corporate scandal. *Organization* 22(1): 78–99.

Altman, Morris. 2002. Economic theory and the challenge of innovative work practices. *Economic and Industrial Democracy* 23(1): 271–290.

Alvesson, Mats, and Andre Spicer. 2012. A stupidity-based theory of organizations. *Journal of Management Studies* 49(7): 1194–1220.

Ardichvili, Alexander. 2008. Motivators, barriers, and enablers. *Advances in Developing Human Resources.* 10(4): 541–554.

Argyris, Chris. 1962. *Interpersonal Competence And Organizational Effectiveness.* Homewood: Dorsey.

Avolio, Bruce J., and William L. Gardner. 2005. Authentic leadership development: Getting to the root of positive leadership development. *The Leadership Quarterly* 15(3): 315–338.

Badaracco Joseph L.,Jr., and Richard R. Ellsworth. 1989. *Leadership and the Quest for Integrity.* Boston: Harvard Business School Press.

Banfield, Edward D. 1958. *The Moral Basis of a Backward Society.* New York: Free Press.

Banks, Stephan P. 2008. *The Troubles with Leadership.* Cheltenham (UK): Edward Elgar.

Barbuto, John E., Jr. 1997. Taking the charisma out of transformational leadership. *Journal of Social Behaviour and Personality* 12(3): 689–697.

Barkai, Haim. 1977. *Growth Patterns of the Kibbutz Economy.* Amsterdam: North-Holland.

Barker, Richard L. 1997. How can we train leaders if we do not know what leadership is? *Human Relations* 50(4): 343–362.

Barley, Stephen R., and Pamela S. Tolbert. 1997. Institutionalization and structuration: Studying the links between action and institution. *Organization Studies* 18(1): 93–117.

Bass, Bernard M. 1985. *Leadership and Performance beyond Expectations.* New York: Free Press.

Bass, Bernard M. 1998. The ethics of transformational leadership. In: J. B. Ciulla (Ed.), *Ethics, the Heart of Leadership.* Westport (CN): Praeger, 169–192.

Bass, Bernard M., and Paul Steidlmeier. 1999. Ethics, character, and authentic transformational leadership behaviour. *Leadership Quarterly* 10(2): 181–217.

Bate, Paul S. 1997. Whatever happened to organizational anthropology? A review of the field of organizational ethnography and anthropological studies. *Human Relations* 50(9): 1147–1175.

Bennis, Warren. 1989. *Why Leaders Can't Lead.* San Francisco: Jossey-Bass.

Beyer, Janice M. 1999. Taming and promoting charisma to change organizations. *Leadership Quarterly* 10(2): 307–330.

Bourdieu, Pierre. 1977. *Outline of a Theory of Practice.* Cambridge: Cambridge University Press.

Bourdieu, Pierre. 1990. *The Logic of Practice.* Cambridge: Polity.

Bourdieu, Pierre, and Loic J. D. Wacquant. 1992. *An Invitation to Reflexive Sociology.* Cambridge: Polity.

Bourhis Anne, L. Dubé, and R. Jacob. 2005. The success of virtual communities of practice: The leadership factor. *The Electronic Journal of Knowledge Management* 3(1): 23–34. Online: www.ejkm.com

Bower, Joseph L. 2007. *The CEO Within.* Boston: Harvard Business School Press.

Bradach, Jeffery L., and Robert G. Eccles. 1989. Price, authority, and trust: From ideal types to plural forms. *Annual Sociological Review* 15: 97–118.

Brockner, Joel, P. A. Siegel, et al. 1997. When trust matters: The moderating effect of outcome favorability. *Administrative Science Quarterly* 42(3): 558–583.

Brøgger, Benedicte. 2010. An innovative approach to employee participation in a Norwegian retail chain. *Economic and Industrial Democracy* 31(4): 477–495.

Brouwer, Maria. 2008. *Governance and Innovation.* London: Routledge.

Brower, Holy H., S. W. Lester, et al. 2009. A closer look at trust between managers and subordinates: Understanding the effects of both trusting and being trusted on subordinate outcomes. *Journal of Management* 35(2): 327–347.

Brumann, Christoph. 2000. The dominance of one and its perils: Charismatic leadership and branch structures in utopian communes. *Journal of Anthropological Research* 56(4): 425–451.

Buchanan, David A. and Richard A. Badham. 2008. *Power, Politics, and Organizational Change.* Los Angeles: Sage.

Buckingham, Marcus, and Curt Coffman. 1999. *First Break All the Rules.* New York: Simon and Schuster.

Bunzl, Matti. 2004. Boas, Foucault, and the "Native Anthropologist": Notes toward a Neo-Boasian Anthropology. *American Anthropologist* 106(3): 435–442.

Burawoy, Michael. 1979. *Manufacturing Consent.* Chicago: University of Chicago Press.

Burns, James M. 1978. *Leadership.* New York: Harper.

Burns, Tom, and Gerald M. Stalker. 1961. *The Management of Innovation.* London: Tavistock.

Cannella, Albert A., and W. Glen Rowe. 1995. Leader capabilities, succession, and competitive context: A study of professional baseball teams. *Leadership Quarterly* 6(1): 69–88.

Cappelli, Peter, and Ann Crocker-Hefter. 1996. Distinctive human resources are firms' core competencies. *Organizational Dynamics* 24(3): 7–22.

Chiniara, Myriam, and Kathleen Bentein. 2016. Linking servant leadership to individual performance: Differentiating the mediating role of autonomy, competence, and relatedness need satisfaction. *Leadership Quarterly* 27(1): 124–141.

Ciulla, Joanne B. (Ed.). 1998a. Leadership ethics: Mapping the territory. In: J. B. Ciulla (Ed.), *Ethics, the Heart of Leadership.* Westport (CN): Praeger, 3–26.

Ciulla, Joanne B. 1998b. Leadership and the problem of bogus empowerment. In: J. B. Ciulla (Ed.), *Ethics, the Heart of Leadership.* Westport (CN): Praeger, 63–86.

Ciulla, Joanne B. (Ed.). 2004. *Ethics, the Heart of Leadership,* 2nd edition. Westport (CT): Praeger.

Clark, Rodney. 1979. *The Japanese Company.* New Haven: Yale University Press.

Clarke, Martin, and David Butcher. 2006. Reconciling hierarchy and democracy. *Management Learning* 37(3): 313–333.

Cloke, Kenneth, and Joan Goldsmith. 2002. *The End of Management and the Rise of Democracy.* San Francisco: Jossey-Bass.

Collins, Harry M. 2001. Tacit knowledge, trust and the Q of sapphire. *Social Studies of Science* 31(1): 71–85.

Collins, Harry M. 2007. Bicycling on the moon: Collective tacit knowledge and somatic-limit tacit knowledge. *Organization Studies* 28(2): 257–262.

Collins, Harry M. 2011. Language and practice. *Social Studies of Science* 41(3): 271–300.

Collins, Harry M., and Robert Evans. 2007. *Rethinking Expertise.* Chicago: University of Chicago Press.

Collins, Harry M., and Garry Sanders. 2007. They give you the keys and say 'drive it!'. Managers, referred expertise, and other expertises. *Studies in History and Philosophy of Science* 38(4): 621–641.

Collins, James, and Jerry J. Porras. 1995. Building a visionary company. *California Management Review* 37(1): 80–100.

Collins, Jim. 2001. *Good to Great.* New York: HarperCollins.

Colquitt, Jason A., B. A. Scott, and J. A. LePine. 2007. Trust, trustworthiness, and trust propensity: A meta-analytic test of their unique relationships with risk taking and job performance. *Journal of Applied Psychology* 92(4): 909–927.

Courpasson, David, and Stewart Clegg. 2006. Dissolving the Iron Cages? Tocqueville, Michels, bureaucracy and the perpetuation of elite power. *Organization* 13(3): 319–343.

Covey, Stephen M. R. 2006. *The Speed of Trust.* New York: Simon and Schuster.

Crozier, Michel. 1964. *The Bureaucratic Phenomenon.* Chicago: University of Chicago Press.

Dalton, Melville. 1959. *Man Who Manage.* New York: Wiley.

Darr, Asaf, and Alisa Lewin. 2001. Democratic justice regimes in work organizations: The case of Israeli taxi cooperatives. *Economic and Industrial Democracy* 22(3): 383–405.

Darr, Asaf, and Robert N. Stern. 2002. Coopting change toward industrial democracy: Professionals as agents of structural constraint. *Sociological Inquiry* 72(2): 171–194.

DePree, Max. 1990. *Leadership is an Art.* New York: Dell.

Deutsch, Morton. 1958. Trust and suspicion. *Journal of Conflict Resolution* 2(2): 265–279.

Deutsch, Morton. 1962. Cooperation and trust: Some theoretical notes. In: M. R. Jones (Ed.), *Nebraska Symposium on Motivation.* Lincoln: University of Nebraska Press, 275–319.

Diefenbach, Thomas. 2013. Incompetent or immoral leadership? Why many managers and change leaders get it wrong. In: R. Todnem and B. Burnes (Eds.), *Organizational Change Leadership and Ethics.* New York: Routledge, 149–170.

Dietz, Graham, and Deanne N. Den Hartog. 2006. Measuring trust inside Organizations. *Personnel Review* 35(5): 557–588.

DiMaggio, Paul J., and Walter W. Powell. 1983. The Iron Cage revisited: Institutional isomorphism and collective rationality in organizational fields. *American Sociological Review* 48(2): 147–160.

Dineen, Brian R., R. J. Lewicki, and E. C. Tomlinson. 2006. Supervisory guidance and behavioural integrity: Relationships with employee citizenship and deviant behaviour. *Journal of Applied Psychology* 91(3): 622–633.

Dodgson, Mark. 1993. Learning, trust, and technological collaboration. *Human Relations* 46(1): 77–95.

Dore, Ronald. 1973. *British Factory—Japanese Factory.* Berkeley (CA): University of California Press.

Downs, Anthony. 1966. *Inside Bureaucracy.* Boston: Little, Brown.

Downton, James V. Jr. 1973. *Rebel Leadership.* New York: Free Press.

Eggs, Cindy. 2012. Trust building in a virtual context: Case study of a community of practice. *The Electronic Journal of Knowledge Management* 10: 212–222. Online at: www.ejkm.com

Emery, Fred E. 1995. Participative design: Effective, flexible and successful, now! *Journal for Quality and Participation* 18(1): 6–9.

Erdal, David. 2011. *Beyond the Corporation.* London: Bodley Head.

Errasti, Aniel. 2014. Mondragon's Chinese subsidiaries: Capitalist multinationals in practice. *Economic and Industrial Democracy* 36(3): 479–499.

Eseryel, U. Yeliz, and Deniz Eseryel. 2013. Action-embedded transformational leadership in self-managing global information systems development teams. *Journal of Strategic Information Systems* 22(2): 103–120.

Estrin, Saul, and Derek C. Jones. 1992. The viability of employee-owned firms: Evidence from France. *Industrial and Labor Relations Review* 45(2): 323–338.

Fairholm, Gilbert W. 1994. *Leadership and the Culture of Trust.* Westport (CN): Praeger.

Fairholm, Matthew R. 2004. A new sciences outline for leadership development. *The Leadership and Organization Development Journal* 25(4): 369–383.

Feenberg, Andrew. 1995. Subversive rationality: Technology, power, and democracy. In: A. Feenberg and A. Hannay (Eds.), *Technology and the Politics of Knowledge.* Bloomington: Indiana University Press, 3–22.

Fotaki, Marianna, and Paula Hyde. 2015. Organizational blind spots: Splitting, blame and idealization in the National Health Service. *Human Relations* 68(3): 441–462.

Fox, Alan. 1974. *Beyond Contract.* London: Faber.

Fraher, Amy L. 2016. A toxic triangle of destructive leadership at Bristol Royal Infirmary: A study of organizational Munchausen syndrome by proxy. *Leadership* 12(1): 34–52.

Fukuyama, Francis. 1995. *Trust.* New York: Free Press.

Gabarro, John J. 1987. *The Dynamics of Taking Charge.* Boston: Harvard Business School Press.

Galbraith, John K. 1971. *The New Industrial State.* Boston: Houghton Mifflin.

Gamson, William A. 1991. Commitment and agency in social movements. *Sociological Forum* 6(1): 27–50.

Gardner, John W. 1990. *On Leadership.* New York: Free Press.

Geertz, Clifford. 1973. *The Interpretation of Cultures.* New York: Basic Books.

Geneen, Herold. 1984. *Managing.* New York: Avon.

Gherardi, Silvia, and Manuela Perrotta. 2013. Egg dates sperm: A tale of a practice change and its institutionalization. *Organization* 18(5): 595–614.

Gini, Al. 1997. Moral leadership: An overview. *Journal of Business Ethics* 16(3): 323–330.

Gini, Al. 2004. Business ethics and leadership in a post Enron Era. *Journal of Leadership & Organization Studies* 11(1): 9–15.

Gittell, Judy H. 2000. Paradox of coordination and control. *California Management Review* 42(3): 101–117.

Giuliani, Rudolf W. (with Ken Kurson). 2002. *Leadership*. New York: Talk Miramax.

Goleman, Daniel, R. Boyatzis, and A. McKee. 2002. *Primal Leadership*. Boston: Harvard Business School Press.

Gollan, Paul J., and Ying Xu. 2015. Re-engagement with the employee participation debate: Beyond the case of contested and captured terrain. *Work, Employment and Society* 29(2): NP1–NP13.

Goode, William J. 1978. *The Celebration of Heroes*. Berkeley (CA): University of California Press.

Gouldner, Alvin W. 1954. *Patterns of Industrial Bureaucracy*. New York: Free Press.

Gouldner, Alvin W. 1955. *Wildcat Strike*. New York: Harper & Row.

Graham, Jill W. 1991. Servant-leadership in organizations: Inspirational and moral. *Leadership Quarterly* 2(2): 105–119.

Greenleaf, Robert K. 1977. *Servant Leadership*. New York: Paulist Press.

Grint, Keith. 2000. *The Arts of Leadership*. New York: Oxford University Press.

Grint, Keith. 2005. Problems, problems, problems: The social construction of 'leadership'. *Human Relations* 58(11): 1467–1494.

Grint, Keith. 2014. The hedgehog and the fox: Leadership lessons from D-Day. *Leadership* 10(2): 240–260.

Grint, Keith, and Clare Holt. 2011. Leading questions: If 'Total Place', 'Big Society' and local leadership are then answers: What's the question? *Leadership* 7(1): 85–98.

Grove, Andrew S. 1996. *Only the Paranoid Survive*. New York: Doubleday.

Groysberg, Boris, A. N. McLean, and N. Nohria. 2006. Are leaders portable? *Harvard Business Review*, May, reprint R0605E, Retrieved 11.1.2013: www.hbr.org

Guest, Robert H. 1962. *Organizational Change*. London: Tavistock.

Hambrick, Donald C. 2007. Upper echelons theory: An update. *Academy of Management Review* 32(2): 334–343.

Hammersley, Martyn. 1992. *What's Wrong with Ethnography*. London: Routledge.

Harris, Marvin. 1990. *Our Kind*. New York: Harper.

Harvey-Jones, John. 1988. *Making It Happen*. London: Fontana.

Haslam, S. Alexander, S. D. Reicher and M. J. Platow. 2011. *The New Psychology of Leadership*. New York: Psychology Press.

Hawthorn, Geoffrey. 1991. *Plausible Worlds*. Cambridge: Cambridge University Press.

Heifetz, Ronald A. 1995. *Leadership without Easy Answers*. Cambridge (MA): Belknap.

Heller, Frank, E. Pusic, et al. 1998. *Organizational Participation*. Oxford: Oxford University Press.

Heskett, John. 2011. *The Culture Cycle*. Upper Saddle River (NJ): FT Press.

Hill, Linda A. 2006. Exercising moral courage: A developmental agenda. In: D. L. Rhode (Ed.), *Moral Leadership*. San Francisco: Jossey-Bass, 267–300.

Hirschman, Albert O. 1970. *Exit, Voice and Loyalty*. Cambridge (MA): Harvard University Press.

Hirschman, Albert O. 1982. *Shifting Involvement*. Oxford: Martin Robertson.

Hirschman, Albert O. 1984. *Going Ahead Collectively*. New York: Pergamon.

Hmieleski, Keith M., M. S. Cole, and R. A. Baron. 2012. Shared authentic leadership and new venture performance. *Journal of Management* 38(5): 1476–1499.

Hollander, Edwin P. 1978. *Leadership Dynamics*. New York: Free Press.

Hollander, Edwin P. 2009. *Inclusive Leadership: The Essential Leader-Follower Relationship*. New York: Routledge.

Holtskog, Halvor. 2014. *How Industry Makes Knowledge*. PhD Thesis, Norwegian University of Science and Technology, Trondheim.

Hoon, Christina. 2014. Meta-synthesis of qualitative case studies: An approach to theory building. *Organizational Research Methods* 16(4): 522–556.

Hosmer, Larue T. 1995. Trust: The connecting link between organizational theory and philosophical ethics. *Academy of Management Review* 20(3): 379–403.

Hou, Wanrong, R. L. Priem, and M. Goranova. 2014. Does one size fit all? Investigating pay—future performance relationships over the seasons of CEO tenure. *Journal of Management*. DOI 10.1177/0149206314544744

Howell, Jane M., and Boas Shamir. 2005. The role of followers in the charismatic leadership process: Relationships and their consequences. *Academy of Management Review* 30(1): 96–112.

Huen, Chi W. 2009. What is context? An ethnophilosophical account. *Anthropological Theory* 9(2): 149–169.

Hughes, Everett C. 1958. *Man and Their Work*. Glenco (IL): Free Press.

Jackall, Robert. 1988. *Moral Mazes*. New York: Oxford University Press.

Jaques, Elliot. 1990. *Creativity and Work*. Madison (CN): International Universities.

Jay, Anthony. 1969. *Management and Machiavelli*. New York: Bantam.

Jay, Anthony. 1972. *Corporation Man*. London: Jonathan Cape.

Jensen, Morten B., B. Johnson, et al. 2007. Forms of knowledge and modes of innovation. *Research Policy* 36(5): 680–693.

Joas, Hans. 1996. *The Creativity of Action*. Cambridge: Polity.

Johnson, Craig E. 2008. The rise and fall of Carly Fiorina. *Journal of Leadership & Organizational Studies* 15(2): 188–196.

Jung, Jiwook. 2014. Political contestation at the top: Politics of outsider succession at U.S. corporations. *Organization Studies* 35(5): 727–764.

Kanter, Rosabeth M. 1993[1977]. *Men and Women of the Corporation*. New York: Basic Books.

Karaevli, Ayse. 2007. Performance consequences of new CEO 'outsiderness': Moderating effects of pre-and post-succession contexts. *Strategic Management Journal* 28(4): 681–706.

Karaevli, Ayse, and Edward J. Zajac. 2013. When do outsider CEOs generate strategic change? The enabling role of corporate stability. *Journal of Management Studies* 50(7): 1267–1294.

Keltner, Dacher, C. A. Langer, and M. L. Allison. 2006. Power and moral leadership. In: D. L. Rhode (Ed.), *Moral Leadership*. San Francisco: Jossey-Bass, 177–194.

Kets De Vries, Manfred F. R. 1993. *Leaders, Fools, and Impostors*. San Francisco: Jossey-Bass.

Khurana, Rakesh. 2002. *Searching for a Corporate Savior*. Princeton (NJ): Princeton University Press.

Kipnis, David. 1976. *The Powerholders*. Chicago: University of Chicago Press.

Klein, Naomi. 2000. *No Logo*. New York: Picador.

Korczynski, Marek. 2000. The political economy of trust. *Journal of Management Studies* 37(1): 1–21.

Kotter, John P. 1982. *The General Managers*. New York: Free Press.

Kotter, John P., and James L. Heskett. 1992. *Corporate Culture and Performance.* New York: Free Press.

Kramer, Roderick M., and Tom R. Tyler (Eds.). 1996. *Trust in Organizations.* Thousand Oaks (CA): Sage.

Kruger, Justin, and David Dunning. 1999. Unskilled and unaware of it: How difficulties in recognizing one's own incompetence lead to inflated self-assessments. *Journal of Personal and Social Psychology* 77(6): 1121–1134.

Kunda, Gideon. 1992. *Engineering Culture.* Philadelphia: Temple University Press.

Lave, Jean, and Etienne Wenger. 1991. *Situated Learning.* Cambridge: Cambridge University Press.

Lazega, Emmanuel. 2001. *The Collegial Phenomenon.* Oxford: Oxford University Press.

Lenski, Gerhard. 1966. *Power and Privilege.* Glenco (IL): Free Press.

Levenson, Bernard. 1961. Bureaucratic succession. In: A. Etzioni (Ed.), *Complex Organizations.* New York: Holt, 362–375.

Likert, Rensis. 1967. *The Human Organization.* New York: McGraw-Hill.

Lipman-Blumen, Jean. 2005. *The Allure of Toxic Leaders.* New York: Oxford University Press.

Liu, Dong, H. Liao, and R. Loi. 2012. The dark side of leadership: A three-level investigation of the cascading effect of abusive supervision on employee creativity. *Academy of Management Journal* 55(5): 1187–1212.

Luthans, Fred. 1988. Successful versus effective managers. *Academy of Management Executive* 2: 127–132.

Lynn, Jonathan, and Anthony Jay. 1986. *Yes, Prime Minister.* London: BBC Publications.

Maccoby, Michael. 1976. *The Gamesman.* New York: Simon & Schuster.

Maccoby, Michael. 2015. *Strategic Intelligence.* Oxford: Oxford University Press.

Martin, Joanne. 1992. *Cultures in Organizations.* New York: Oxford.

Martin, Norman H., and Anselm L. Strauss. 1959. Patterns of mobility in industrial organizations. In: W. L. Warner and N. H. Martin (Eds.), *Industrial Man.* New York: Harper, 85–101.

Marx, Emanuel. 1985. Social-anthropological research and knowing Arab society. In: Aluf Har'even (Ed.), *To Know Neighboring People.* Jerusalem: Van Lear, 137–152 (Hebrew).

Mayer, R. C., J. H. Davis, and F. D. Schoorman. 1995. An integrative view of organizational trust. *Academy of Management Review* 20(4): 709–734.

McGill, Michael E., and John W. Slocum, Jr. 1998. A little leadership, please? *Organizational Dynamics* 26(3): 39–49.

McGregor, Douglas. 1960. *The Human Side of Enterprise.* New York: McGraw-Hill.

McLagan, Patricia, and Christo Nel. 1997. *The Age of Participation.* San Francisco: Berret-Koehler.

Mehri, Darius. 2005. *Notes from Toyota-Land.* Ithaca (NY): ILR Press.

Michels, Robert. 1959[1915]. *Political Parties.* New York: Dover.

Miller, Danny. 1993. Some organizational consequences of CEO succession. *Academy of Management Journal* 36(3): 644–659.

Miller, Danny, and J. Shamsie. 2001. Learning across the life cycle: Experimentation and performance among the Hollywood studio heads. *Strategic Management Journal* 22(8): 725–745.

Milliken, Frances J., Elizabeth W. Morrison, and Patricia F. Hewlin. 2003. An exploratory study of employee silence: Issues that employees don't communicate upward and why. *Journal of Management Studies* 40(6): 1453–1476.

Mintzberg, Henry. 1987. The strategy concept 1: 5 Ps for strategy. *California Management Review* 30(1): 11–21.

Mishra, Anil K., and Karen E. Mishra. 2015. Leaders—born or made? In: Ronald E. Riggio (Ed.), *Becoming a Better Leader*, 31–43. International Leadership Association and Routledge's E-Book.

Morita, Atsuro. 2014. The ethnographic machine: Experimenting with context and comparison in Strathernian Ethnography. *Science, Technology & Human Values* 39(2): 214–235.

Murrell, Audrey J., I. H. Frieze, and J. E. Olson. 1996. Mobility strategies and career outcomes: A longitudinal study of MBAs. *Journal of Vocational Behaviour* 49(3): 324–335.

Nichols, Theo, A. Danford, and A. C. Tasiran. 2009. Trust, employer exposure and the employment relation. *Economic and Industrial Democracy* 30(2): 241–265.

Niv, Amitai, and Dan Bar-On. 1992. *The Dilemma of Size from a System Learning Perspective: The Case of the Kibbutz.* Greenwich (CN): JAI.

Norman, Steven M., Bruce J. Avolio, and Fred Luthans. 2010. The impact of positivity and transparency on trust in leaders and their perceived effectiveness. *The Leadership Quarterly* 21(3): 350–364.

Ocasio, William. 1994. Political dynamics and the circulation of power: CEO succession in U.S. industrial corporations 1960–1990. *Administrative Science Quarterly* 39(2): 285–312.

O'Mahoney, Joseph K. 2005. Trust, distrust and anxiety: The new manufacturing philosophy at Gearco. Retrieved 17.8.2008: http://joeomahoney.googlepages.com/JOM_FinalPaper.doc

Orr, Julian. 1996. *Talking about Machines.* Ithaca (NY): Cornell University Press.

O'Toole, James. 1999. *Leadership from A to Z.* San Francisco: Jossey-Bass.

Ouchi, William G. 1981. *Theory Z.* Reading (MA): Addison-Wesley.

Padilla, Art, R. Hogan, and R. B. Kaiser. 2007. The toxic triangle: Destructive leaders, susceptible followers, and conducive environments. *Leadership Quarterly* 18(2): 176–194.

Parker, Martin. 2000. *Organizational Culture and Identity.* London: Sage.

Perkins, Kennth B., and Darryl G. Poole. 1996. Oligarchy and adaptation to mass society in an all-volunteer organization: Implications for understanding leadership, participation, and change. *Nonprofit and Voluntary Sector Quarterly* 25(1): 73–88.

Perrow, Charles. 1970. *Organizational Analysis.* London: Tavistock.

Pettigrew, Andrew M. 1973. *Organizational Decision-Making.* London: Tavistock.

Poulin, Bryan J., M. Z. Hackman, and C. Barbarasa-Mihai. 2007. Leadership and succession: The challenge to succeed and the vortex of failure. *Leadership* 3(3): 301–325.

Poulin, Bryan J., and Sam Siegel. 2005. Nucor Corporation 1965–1995: After 30 years of success, what next? Unpublished case study, Faculty of Business Administration, Lakehead University, Canada.

Powell, Walter W. 1990. Neither markets nor hierarchy: Network forms of organization. *Research in Organizational Behaviour* 12: 295–336.

Powell, Walter W., and P. J. DiMaggio (Eds.). 1991. *The New Institutionalism in Organizational Analysis.* Chicago: University of Chicago Press.

Preece, Jennifer. 2004. Etiquette, empathy and trust in communities of practice: Stepping-stones to social capital. Retrieved 15.7.2005: www.ifsm.umbc.edu/~preece/papers

Raelin, Joseph. 2011. From leadership-as-practice to leaderful practice. *Leadership* 7(2): 195–211.

Raelin, Joseph. 2013. The manager as facilitator of dialogue. *Organization* 20(6): 818–839.

Rifkin, Glenn, and George Harrar. 1988. *The Ultimate Entrepreneur.* Chicago: Contemporary Books.

Riker, William H. 1974. The nature of trust. In: J. T. Tedeschi (Ed.), *Perspectives on Social Power.* Chicago: Aldine, 63–81.

Ring, Peter S., and Andrew Van de Ven. 1992. Structuring cooperative relationships between organizations. *Strategic Management Journal* 13(4): 483–498.

Robison, Jennifer. 2010. Leading engagement from the top. *Gallup Management Journal Online.* Retrieved: 27.7.2011: http://findarticles.com/p/articles/mi_6770

Rohlen, Thomas P. 1974. *For Harmony and Strength.* Berkeley (CA): University of California Press.

Rosner, Menachem. 1993. Organizations between community and market: The case of the kibbutz. *Economic and Industrial Democracy* 14(4): 369–397.

Roy, Donald F. 1952. Quota restriction and goldbricking in a machine shop. *American Journal of Sociology* 57(4): 427–442.

Roy, Donald F. 1955. Efficiency and the fix: Informal intergroup relations in a piecework shop. *American Journal of Sociology* 60(3): 255–266.

Russell, Raymond. 1995. *Utopia in Zion.* Albany (NY): SUNY Press.

Sako, Mary. 1992. *Price, Quality and Trust.* Cambridge: Cambridge University Press.

Sankar, Y. 2003. Character not charisma is the critical measure of leadership excellence. *Journal of Leadership & Organizational Studies* 9(4): 45–55.

Saxenian, Anna Lee. 1994. *Regional Advantage.* Cambridge (MA): Harvard University Press.

Scharfstein, Ben-Ami. 1995. *Amoral Politics.* Albany (NY): SUNY Press.

Schröder, Martin. 2013. How moral arguments influence economic decisions and organizational legitimacy—the case of offshoring production. *Organization* 20(4): 551–576.

Semler, Ricardo. 1993. *Maverick.* New York: Warner.

Sen, Asim. 2003. *Democratic Management.* Lanham (MD): University Press of America.

Sendjaya, Sen. 2005. Morality and leadership: Examining the ethics of transformational leadership. *Journal of Academic Ethics* 3(1): 75–86.

Sergiovanni, Thomas J. 1992. *Moral Leadership.* San Francisco: Jossey-Bass.

Shapira, Reuven. 1978/9. Autonomy of technostructure: An inter-kibbutz regional organization case study. *The Kibbutz* 6/7: 276–303 (Hebrew).

Shapira, Reuven. 1980. *The Absorption of Academicians in Kibbutz Industry.* Tel Aviv: KIA.

Shapira, Reuven. 1982. Workers, Managers and Expertise: Trust and Market Relations in an Automatic Processing Plant. PhD. Thesis, Tel Aviv University.

Shapira, Reuven. 1987. *Anatomy of Mismanagement.* Tel Aviv: Am Oved (Hebrew).

Shapira, Reuven. 1995a. The voluntary resignation of outsider managers: Interkibbutz rotation and Michels's 'Iron Law'. *Israel Social Science Research* 10(1): 59–84.

Shapira, Reuven. 1995b. 'Fresh blood' innovation and the dilemma of personal involvement. *Creativity and Innovation Management* 4(2): 86–99.

Shapira, Reuven. 2001. Communal decline: The vanishing of high-moral leaders and the decay of democratic, high-trust kibbutz cultures. *Sociological Inquiry* 71(1): 13–38.

Shapira, Reuven. 2005. Academic capital or scientific progress? A critique of the studies of kibbutz stratification. *Journal of Anthropological Research* 61(3): 357–380.

Shapira, Reuven. 2008. *Transforming Kibbutz Research.* Cleveland: New World Publishing.

Shapira, Reuven. 2011. Institutional combination for cooperative development: How trustful cultures and transformational mid-levelers overcame old guard conservatism. In: J. Blanc and D. Colongo (Eds.), *Co-operatives Contributions to a Plural Economy.* Paris: L'Harmattan, 75–90.

Shapira, Reuven. 2012. High-trust culture, the decisive but elusive context of shared co-operative leaderships. In: J. Heiskanen et al. (Eds.), *New Opportunities for Co-Operatives: New Opportunities for People.* Mikkeli, Finland: University of Helsinki Press, 154–167.

Shapira, Reuven. 2013. Leaders' vulnerable involvement: Essential for trust, learning, effectiveness and innovation in inter-co-operatives. *Journal of Co-operative Organization and Management* 1(1): 15–26. http://dx.doi.org/10.1016/j.jcom.2013.06.003

Shapira, Reuven. 2015. Prevalent concealed ignorance of low-moral careerist managers: Contextualization by a semi-native multi-site Strathernian ethnography. *Management Decision* 53(7): 1504–1526. http://dx.doi.org/10.1108/md-10-2014-0620

Shen, Wei, and Albert A. Cannella. 2002. Revisiting the performance consequences of CEO succession: The impacts of successor type, post succession senior executive turnover, and departing CEO tenure. *Academy of Management Journal* 45(4): 717–733.

Siebert, Sabina, G. Martin, et al. 2015. Looking 'Beyond the Factory Gates': Towards more pluralist and radical approaches to intraorganizational trust research. *Organization Studies* 36(8): 1033–1062.

Sieff, Marcus. 1986. *Don't Ask the Price.* London: Weidenfeld and Nicolson.

Simon, Herbert. 1957. *Administrative Behaviour.* New York: Free Press.

Simons, Tony. 2002. Behavioural integrity: The perceived alignment between managers' words and deeds as a research focus. *Organization Science* 13(1): 18–35.

Six, Frederique, and Arndt Sorge. 2008. Creating a high-trust organization: An exploration into organizational policies that stimulate interpersonal trust building. *Journal of Management Studies* 45(5): 857–884.

Smollan, Roy, and Ken Parry. 2011. Follower perceptions of the emotional intelligence of change leaders: A qualitative study. *Leadership* 7(4): 435–462.

Sosik, John J., D. Jung, and S. L. Dinger. 2009. Values in authentic action: Examining the roots and rewards of altruistic leadership. *Group & Organization Management* 34(4): 395–431.

Spiro, Melford E. 1983. Introduction: Thirty years of kibbutz research. In: E. Krausz (Ed.), *The Sociology of Kibbutz.* New Brunswick (NJ): Transaction, 1–6.

Stein, Howard F. 2001. *Nothing Personal, Just Business.* Westport (CN): Quorum.

Stewart, Thomas A. 1997. *Intellectual Capital.* New York: Doubleday.

Strathern, Marilyn. 2004. *Partial Connections*. Savage (MD): Rowman & Littlefield.

Stryjan, Yohanan. 1989. *Impossible Organizations*. New York: Greenwood.

Swidler, Ann. 2001. *Talk of Love*. Chicago: University of Chicago Press.

Swidler, Ann, and Jorge Arditi. 1994. The new sociology of knowledge. *Annual Review of Sociology* 20: 305–329.

Terry, Robert W. 1993. *Authentic Leadership*. San Francisco: Jossey-Bass.

Thomas, Gail F., R. Zolin and J. L. Hartmen. 2009. The central role of communication in developing trust and its effect on employee involvement. *Journal of Business Communications* 46(3): 287–310.

Thoroughgood, Christian N., W. T. Brian, et al. 2012. Bad to the bone: Empirically defining and measuring destructive leader behaviour. *Journal of Management and Organizational Studies* 19(2): 230–255.

Townley, Barbara. 2002. Managing with modernity. *Organization* 9(4): 549–573.

Tucker, Richard H. 1970. The theory of charismatic leadership. *Daedalus* 97(3): 731–756.

Useem, Michael, R. Jordan, and M. Koljatic. 2011. How to lead during a crisis: Lessons from the rescue of the Chilean miners. *Sloan Management Review* 53(1): 48–55.

Van Dierendonck, Dirk, D. Stam, et al. 2014. Same difference? Exploring the differential mechanisms linking servant and transformational leadership to follower outcomes. *Leadership Quarterly* 25(3): 544–562.

Van Knippenberg, Daan, and Sim B. Sitkin. 2013. A critical assessment of charismatic-transformational leadership research: Back to the drawing board? *The Academy of Management Annals* 7(1): 1–60.

Van Maanen, John (Ed.). 1995. *Representation in Ethnography*. Thousand Oaks (CA): Sage.

Vancil, Richard F. 1987. *Passing the Baton*. Boston: Harvard Business School Press.

Vaughan, Diane. 1996. *The Challenger Launch Decision*. Chicago: University of Chicago Press.

Villette, Michel, and Catherine Vuillermot. 2009. *From Predators to Icons*. Ithaca: ILR Press.

Vogel, Ezra. 1975. *Modern Japanese Organization and Decision-Making*. Berkeley (CA): University of California Press.

Wagner, Cynthia. 1995. Would you want Machiavelli as your CEO? Implications of autocratic versus empowering leadership styles to innovation. *Creativity and Innovation Management* 4(2): 120–127.

Wallerstein, Immanuel. 2004. *The Uncertainties of Knowledge*. Philadelphia: Temple University.

Washburn, Kevin K. 2011. Elena Kagan and the miracle at Harvard. *Journal of Legal Education* 61(1): 67–75.

Watkins, Michael. 2003. *The First Ninety Days*. Boston: Harvard Business School.

Watson, Kate. 2013. The ironies of leadership: Insights from a narrative analysis of the TV Western drama series, Rowhide. *Organization* 20(6): 924–935.

Watson, Tony J. 2004. HRM and critical social science analysis. *Journal of Management Studies* 41(3): 447–467.

Webb, Janette, and David Cleary. 1994. *Organizational Change and the Management of Expertise*. London: Routledge.

Welker, Marina, D. J. Partridge, and R. Hardin. 2011. Corporate lives: New perspectives on the social life of the corporate form. *Current Anthropology* 52(S3): S3–15.

Wenger, Etienne. 1998. *Communities of Practice*. Cambridge: Cambridge University Press.

White, Michael C., M. Smith, and T. Barnett. 1997. CEO succession: Overcoming forces of inertia. *Human Relations* 50(7): 805–828.

Whitener, Ellen M., S. E. Brodt, et al. 1998. Managers as initiators of trust: Exchange relationships framework for understanding managerial trustworthy behaviour. *Academy of Management Review* 23(3): 513–530.

Whyte, William F., and Kathleen K. Whyte. 1988. *Making Mondragon*. Ithaca (NY): ILR Press.

Wren, J. Thomas. 1998. James Madison and the ethics of transformational leadership. In: J. B. Ciulla (Ed.), *Ethics, the Heart of Leadership*. Westport (CN): Praeger, 145–168.

Wulf, Torsten, S. Stubner, et al. 2011. Performance over the CEO lifecycle—a differentiated analysis of short and long tenured CEOs. *Problems and Perspectives in Management* 4: 98–108.

Yukl, Gary. 1999. An evaluation of conceptual weaknesses in transformational and charismatic leadership theories. *The Leadership Quarterly* 10(2): 285–305.

Zand, Dale E. 1972. Trust and managerial problem solving. *Administrative Science Quarterly* 17(2): 229–239.

Zolin, Roxanne, P. J. Hinds, et al. 2004. Interpersonal trust in cross-functional, geographically distributed work: A longitudinal study. *Information and Organization* 14(1): 1–26.

4 Effective, Innovative Northern Gin Versus Four Mostly Mismanaged Plants

As stated, ethnography is a problematic method for building a new theory. It is often overly influenced by the specifics of a studied culture. But the present study is longitudinal and multi-site, and it analyzes a variety of ginning industry cultures (e.g., Parker 2000):

1 The cultures of an internal sectorial plant: the high-trust Thomas- and Danton-led shop-floor culture versus the low-trust one of Shavit and most other *pe'ilim*;
2 The different cultures of the focal plant throughout its history: the high-trust ones of Yaakov-Aharon's era and of Thomas-Danton's era versus the low-trust eras;
3 Similarly, high- versus low-trust cultures in four other gin plants.

The latter cultures were not studied as intensively and thoroughly as Merkaz's, but they were all I-KRC cultures, hence their contexts, practices, problems, and solutions mostly resembled Merkaz's and their interpretation was greatly facilitated by Merkaz's findings. Thus, by conducting visits to plants, 63 interviews of present and past executives, managers, and foremen, and reading plant annuals and Cotton Marketing Council publications,[1] I was able to identify cultural types in different eras and sectors and link the changes to executives' and managers' practices and habituses, as well as their know-how and *phronesis*, which in the study of Merkaz were found to be prime factors. The review of the four other plants studied will show that Merkaz's findings were quite representative of the immoral mismanagement at three of them, and even at the fourth, Northern Gin, in which PM 1 and 2 created a high-trust, innovative-prone, effectively managed plant culture for 12 years, three other PMs mismanaged by using CCMI-Im-C, similar to Merkaz's PMs. The information in the 331-folio-page journal is detailed enough to support the hypothesis that the three other gin plants were mostly characterized by immoral mismanagement. However, much like Thomas, TMs in these plants mostly opted for vulnerable involvement, contrary to their bosses: all CEOs were detached and ignorant of gin plant problems, which helped explain PMs' CCMI-Im-C choices, while "parachutings" and *rotatzia* further explained the prevalence of these choices.

Three of the four plants resembled Merkaz, each with two high-capacity processing units that processed 500–700 tons daily, while the smallest Northern Gin had one unit that processed 250–300 tons daily. However, Northern was for many years, up to the mid-1970s, among the best gin plants with both high cotton fiber quality and minimal downtime, only 3–5% versus 10–12% at most other plants and Merkaz's 32% in my season as registrar. Northern's PM-2 Gabi was the prime leader of this achievement due to 7.5 years of vulnerably involved management, while predecessor PM-1 also practiced involvement and nurtured employees' professionalism and organizational commitment by using a high-trust culture, backed by somewhat involved CEO 1 and then by fully involved CEO 2 Dan.

The Socialized Leadership of Gabi and Two Other PMs at Northern Gin Plant

Of the 22 plant managers studied, only Northern's certified practical engineer Gabi learned ginning thoroughly by vulnerable involvement that created virtuous trust and learning cycles, and was able to operate the ginning process and overcome its problems. I did not witness these, coming to Northern years after his succession and leaving his kibbutz, frustrated by the region kibbutzim's choice of a new CEO who replaced committed, effective PMs with his ignorant detached Im-C loyalists. However, I interviewed Northern I-KRC's two CEOs, Gabi's predecessor, and three successors, plus 13 Northern gin staff, as well as Gabi twice at length at his home since he knew a lot about his successors and about PMs of other gin plants. He eagerly reviewed my data on Merkaz and other plants and elucidated technical questions left unanswered. Gabi's practical engineering education plus vulnerable involvement helped him achieve ginning contributory expertise (Collins and Evans 2007) that was unique among all the 22 PMs, while only deputies Yaakov, Aharon, and Danton, as well as a few TMs, likewise replicated his participative democratic management, mostly learned in their kibbutz managerial jobs (Shapira 2008). Gabi's last kibbutz job was deputy to an older member charged with establishing a new plant; he soon realized that the plant's concept and proposed process and equipment offered by outsider consultants were fraudulent and bound to fail. He tried to convince his boss and kibbutz managers of this and proposed alternative experts but to no avail. They grasped him as a troublemaker and urged him to leave for a job in Northern I-KRC. The first I-KRC CEO was high-moral non-careerist as signaled by his humble car; he was involved enough to discern that, despite his best intentions, PM-1 achieved mediocre results, and by citing *rotatzia* Gabi replaced him after 4.5 years on the job. Northern Gin excelled during Gabi's 7.5 years until his succession on all efficiency and effectiveness measures, primarily high fiber quality and length, which was cotton growers' prime concern as it decided fiber prices, in addition to minimal downtime, which meant enabling timely harvesting before autumn rains could cause damages.[2] The other nine Israeli gin plant managers acknowledged Gabi's excellence and chose him as their association head and representative vis-a-vis the authorities. All the dozens of interviewees who knew Gabi, both Northern employees and those of other gin plants, praised his excellent functioning as PM.

Gabi's high-moral innovative leadership resembled Guest's (1962) successful outsider, although he did not achieve a similar turnaround since his predecessor had already commenced high-trust culture. However, his technical expertise and thorough learning of ginning while nurturing professional TMs and staff led to excellent functioning; his competent socialized leadership achieved effectiveness (Poulin et al. 2007) versus personalized gin PMs' immoral mismanagement, defending their jobs by either detachment or by seduction-coercion. Gabi followed in the footsteps of founding high-moral I-KRC CEO, who was replaced by the even more vulnerably involved CEO Dan, a highly trusted executive, unlike the other I-KRC CEOs on whom I have information (below). I was not able to interview Dan, but many testified to his involvement and knowledge of the plant, which was essential because Gabi used high-moral unconventional practices: he consecutively promoted two highly competent hired technicians as TMs, of which one was the above-cited certified practical engineer Arbiv (p. 9), not concerned about their empowerment by successes. His technical and managerial competencies due to education, experience, and vulnerable involvement in TMs' deliberations created virtuous trust and learning cycles and a high-trust culture, ensuring that conflicts with them would be productive (Deutsch 1969). His sincerity, open knowledge, and information prevailed and enhanced cooperation, learning, and creative problem-solving due to the long time horizon (Jaques 1990) that CEO Dan promised Gabi, contrary to *rotatzia* (see pp. 13–14). Gabi replaced the mediocre TM-1 with brilliant TM-2 Arbiv, whose successes eventually led him to leave for the US to be R&D engineer at WLGEP, while his experienced deputy became TM-3. The superb expertise of the latter two untangled lengthy repeated interviews that taught me much ginning know-how and *phronesis*, while TM-3 also described the radical negative shift to a low-trust culture after Gabi and Dan's succession by three politics-prone CCMI users, PMs 3, 5, and 6, who practiced Im-C similar to Merkaz CEOs and PMs.

Gabi's immediate successor, PM-3, whom I call Mikha, failed in his job and was replaced within two years by PM-4 Emanuel who was Gabi's friend and followed his socialized leader practices for four years. Thus, for 15 of Northern's 21 years studied it had three socialized high-moral PMs who opted for virtuous trust and learning cycles and the high-trust culture that Emanuel only partially restored after it was ruined by Mikha. Both vulnerable involvement in work problems and caring for employees' needs created trust. These practices were described by Northern PM-1:

"For me it was clear that as a small plant I could not pay high salaries, hence I found them [the employees] jobs [to earn more] between seasons in nearby I-KRC factories as [seasonal] tractor drivers, mechanics, etc. I commenced [nurturing staff] with an experienced ginner that I recruited from the Valley Gin [as TM-1] and with youngsters who had technical leaning but little or no experience, and from them I built a team that worked like a family. There was comradeship among them and they were highly committed, always took risks to extinguish fires and to make dangerous repairs, giving to the plant as much as they could without thinking twice [before taking risks]. They were proud of their teamwork, which became a model for other [I-KRC] plants. We cared for their professional advancement, sent them to short courses, and organized evening classes and paid for [expensive] driving courses and licenses, while also helping them find apartments [in a nearby town], especially when they married and had children. As my family was not much older than theirs, friendship relationships were created with some of the families, they often visited us [at my kibbutz a distance of 2 km.] and we them.

Due to trust relationships with them I could ensure other [I-KRC] plant managers of their trustworthiness and committed work when asking to employ them between seasons, while after Arbiv graduated practical engineering and became our TM [-2] he was trusted by neighboring plants to plan automated production systems which my employees built. I also used my ties with other gin PMs to visit their plants in order to further the ginning knowledge of my employees. This enhanced their morale when they realized their professional superiority over many of their hosts, but it also sometimes had a negative effect when they equated their humble salaries to the better ones of their hosts. But I did not stop the visits [although unable to raise salaries] since it afforded them possibilities for learning and advancing their professionalism which I could not achieve any other way."

His testimony was supported by other interviewees. For instance, a young promising technician who later became deputy TM, and when Arbiv left became TM-3, decided to marry his fiancé but they could not find an apartment in the nearby town; when interviewed 20 years later he remembered how PM-1 used his ties in the dominant Mapay party and personally begged its officials until finding an apartment. Both Gabi and Emanuel continued this caring for employees' needs. Gabi also helped arrange the weddings of young employees:

"Once one employee, S. B.-Z., had a small Gogomobil car which stood by the pesticide store; I caught him flirting there with a 17-year-old girl. I took him to the office and asked him if it is a serious affair, whether he aimed to marry her. He said that although he would be happy to do so he can't as he can't afford a wedding. I organized an appeal among all employees and the couple soon married, and now have three children; I was the godfather of their first son."

As against this lovely tale, Gabi also made sure to get rid of immoral employees even if this meant, for instance, losing a best ginner and required spying in the plant out of season on Friday night, which is a part of the Jewish Sabbath holiday:

"S. S. was a proficient ginner who knew all the jobs perfectly and even replaced shift foremen for meals. He was an attractive guy with a pretty wife, but he was also immoral and selfish, detested by both colleagues and bosses, hence I could not promote him to foreman. Workers called him 'pimp', hinting that this was how he earned extra money at night without his wife's knowledge. One Saturday, at 2 am, a foreman phoned and directed me to the furnaces room, where I found S. S. having sex with a young, maybe 13-year-old teenager, a known way to introduce girls to prostitution. I had no legal basis for firing him as she confirmed that it had been her initiative, thus I informed a relative, the family interfered, stopped his pimping by close surveillance, and it was not long before he left the country."

In accord with Leader-Member Exchange theory (LMX), Gabi was fully informed of every meaningful event due to positive relationships with employees: he helped them function effectively and they supplied him with information that helped his leadership; its success enhanced their trust and help, and so on (Norman et al. 2010). Avoidance of feedback by incompetent employees (Moss et al. 2009) succeeded, since well-informed Gabi discerned incompetents and immoral self-servers and got rid of them (Collins and Weinel 2011).

Gabi's successor Mikha failed as he resembled Yuval, trying autocratically to coerce employees without minimal knowledge of the industry. He was distrusted by all and fired by the CEO after the plant's fiber quality plummeted to the worst level of all Israeli plants. Then PM-4 Emanuel, as Gabi's close friend, worked hard to restore the high-trust culture by caring for employees' needs, for instance initiating the building of a new dining hall for the I-KRC's hired employees, since his open door policy bred many complaints about the old shabby dining hall. However, this policy required strict adherence to retain trust:

"Every employee could enter my office whenever they wanted unless I was busy. In such a case I would promise to call them as soon as I finish my current chore, but such promises must always be kept, otherwise no employee would ever turn to you again."

Keeping one's word proves integrity, an essential ingredient of trustworthiness (Simons 2002), but while Chapters 1 and 2 emphasized trust and learning cycles created by vulnerable involvement or their opposites that impacted managers' know-how and *phronesis*, the above examples indicate that such involvement also enhanced inter-rank trust and work commitment as managers learned and solved employees' social problems. Unlike Taiwan (Chan 2014), such paternalism was rare among Israeli executives; it enabled managers to penetrate the plant's dark social secrets helpful for recognizing and weeding out bums, fools, impostors, and troublemakers (McGregor 1960), contrary to the successful career of "bramble" Atad at ignorantly managed, low-trust Merkaz.

Gabi's high-moral leadership succeeded also due to his backing by involved knowledgeable CEO Dan; such backing is essential, for instance when contextual pressures interfere with the selection of personnel, as was often the case in I-KRCs concerning *pe'ilim*: Managers of kibbutzim often tried to send to I-KRCs members who lacked a permanent kibbutz job as they were bums, fools, impostors or incompetent (Shepher 1983). By being involved and an expert in ginning, Gabi, with Dan's help, barred introducing or soon weeded out such *pe'ilim*. While the rejection of a *pa'il* who was clearly unsuited for the job was no problem, it was quite hard to get rid of a *pa'il* who was formally qualified for the job and functioned reasonably at first but later became lazy or a drifter; this required the backing of an involved and knowledgeable CEO such as Dan, further explaining Gabi's success. Gabi described the contrary practice of Dan's successor:

> "In our day [mine and Dan's] we never accepted kibbutz members sent by the kibbutzim only because they were superfluous, as they [kibbutzim] do now. Later CEOs did not recruit good staff, hence they manned plants with lesser *pe'ilim* for whom kibbutzim could not find what to do."

This was one reason that Gabi left, shortly after CEO Dan's succession by a detached Im-C *pa'il* who "parachuted" his own loyal *pe'ilim* to key I-KRC positions. Previously, Gabi's expertise and employees' knowledge had enabled manning jobs with qualified people, either *pe'ilim* or hired employees. He was not concerned about employees' empowerment by successes (Klein 1998), nor did he need to "parachute" loyalist *pe'ilim* to defend his authority; his nurturing of trustworthy TM Arbiv and his deputy, and later promoting his deputy as TM-3, enhanced the high-trust culture in which opinion differences were considered bona fide and solved pragmatically (Fox 1974: Ch. 2). As a certified practical engineer and ex-garage manager like Thomas, Gabi involved himself in the ginners' shop floor problem-solving much more than Northern's PMs 1 and 4, and he gained more ginning expertise than all other 21 PMs. In Collins and Evans's (2007) terms, he achieved both interactional and contributory expertises by involvement in shop-floor problem-solving versus Northern PMs 1 and 4 who, like Yaakov and Aharon, were less proficient ginners due to less participation in shop floor problem-solving, lacking a technical education and mechanics' experience. In Flyvbjerg's (2001: 13–17) terms, Gabi achieved the highest, fifth grade of "expertise" similar to Thomas, versus the four who only achieved third or fourth grades of ginning expertise.

Further Explanations of Gabi and Northern Gin's Success

Following the discussion of transformational leadership in Chapter 3, one can ask of Gabi's achievements (also below): Was he such a leader? On one hand, he did not make a turnaround like Guest's (1962: Ch. 4) car plant manager or like Kagan at Harvard Law School (Washburn 2011) as already PM-1 shaped a high-trust culture, but on the other hand his leadership radically changed the plant's functioning like theirs, and exceeded Thomas's, which was constricted by Shavit and the surrounding low-trust culture. His leadership enhanced shop-floor collaborative learning, problem-solving, and innovating efforts, which he led while others contributed significantly (Bennis 1989: 17). His leadership also enhanced the plant's functioning, because Emanuel followed him. Which elements of transformational leadership did Gabi use that resulted in Northern's exceptional success?

Gabi resembled Thomas, who was neither a genius nor a charismatic leader, less handsome and less sociable than Shavit. He was talented, educated, held pertinent experience, acquired ginning know-how and *phronesis* through vulnerable involvement, and was a critical thinker whose critique of his assumed fraudulent kibbutz boss pushed him out to the I-KRC. Critical thinking encouraged vulnerable involvement aimed at learning, also encouraged by a habitus of participative democratic management in the kibbutz field crops branch, in the agricultural machinery garage, and other kibbutz managerial jobs. His expertise as a practical engineer and mechanic of cotton machinery gave him the psychological safety that enabled thorough learning of ginning and nurturing highly professional TMs and staff, not only Arbiv and his deputy and later successor TM-3, but also others such as the Deputy TM with whom I toured the plant. TM-3 served as Arbiv's deputy for 12 years; he lacked a practical engineering certificate but learned the profession both in technical high school and in evening courses, and with prolonged experience of Northern's high-trust culture of knowledge sharing and learning he became a major ginning expert, as Thomas and other experts testified and as I witnessed. His deputy showed me many small but significant technical improvements of the plant's machinery which prevented blockings, like those from which we suffered so often at Merkaz, initiated by TM-3, by technicians, and by operators who suffered the predicament of coping with blockings. Due to vast know-how and *phronesis*, Gabi enhanced successes by allowing discretion and by brokering and buffering (Soekijad et al. 2011). This grassroots innovation is reminiscent of 18th-century anthropologist Johann Herder, who pointed out the prevalence of creativity beyond the confines of what he called "the reading room," i.e., deliberations of the educated elites and academia:

"Every man of noble and vivacious sentiments is a genius in his work, to his destiny, and truly the best geniuses are to be found outside the reading room. Whatever human nature has brought forth in genius manner, be it science or art, an institution or action, is the work of the *genius*, and *any* ability to awaken human gifts and encourage them to fulfil their purpose is precisely *genius*"

(Italics original; cited by Joas 1996: 81, 84).

Gabi targeted employees' creativity by a clear "map" (O'Toole 1999: 129): best fiber quality achieved through competent ginning by committed teams, which minimized downtime and maximized productivity in the best interests of cotton growers by competent operating, agile repair of machines, and immediate fire extinguishing. Gabi trusted that employees' ingenuity would serve these aims; he granted them discretion to effect improvements, unconcerned that hired employees empowered by successes would diminish his authority, testifying to the high-trust local culture. He modeled "continual efforts to teach others to seek the highest ideals of public service and thereby to leave to citizens [employees] a legacy of trust, integrity, and responsibility, as well as high-quality service delivery and accountability" (Fairholm 2004: 587). Creativity was also encouraged by the lengthy time horizon (Jaques 1990), due to both Gabi and CEO Dan's overruling of *rotatzia* for several years. Gabi's trust in subordinates exceeded that of other PMs: in his early days his car was the only plant car and permanent employees could use it during the day, for instance for a visit to the doctor or to give one's wife a lift, providing it stood idle and received the approval of Gabi's secretary, who kept his schedule. Since a car can be used for vicious ends as well, this practice proved Gabi's full trust of employees as a transformational leader, rather than a unilaterally trusted charismatic one (Chapter 3). Similarly, Gabi trusted employees to care for Northern's cotton fiber quality, which was almost always the best in Israel, as interviewees proudly emphasized. Arbiv, for instance, said:

"The first PM infused this [fiber quality importance] into our blood and Gabi continued. My successor [TM] may now cause riots about salaries, but when it comes to discussing the plant what's best for the cotton will always receive the highest priority."

However, the Cotton Production and Marketing Council annuals only partially support this assertion concerning the post-Gabi era. Their numbers indicate that the worst era was that of PM-3 Mikha, when fiber quality plummeted to the worst of all 12 ginning units. Mikha was autocratic like Yuval, but unlike Yuval, who was an ex-cotton grower, he came from a kibbutz vegetable branch, knew little about cotton, nothing of mechanics, and caused bitter conflicts with TM-3 and the staff. He stopped Gabi's practice of taking TMs and Deputy TMs to ginners' professional meetings in Israel and barred their tours abroad. His successor Emanuel partially regained employees' trust and commitment by renewing participation of the TM and his deputy in these meetings, as he trusted them, due to his acquaintance with them from the many years of managing his kibbutz cotton branch. Emanuel elevated fiber quality to midway on the gin plants' fiber quality list, but then came detached "jumper" PM-5 and due to his mismanagement it plummeted again, lagging behind Merkaz during Thomas's late era, when he was a trusted expert who competently led the high-trust shop-floor culture.

One clear explanation of plummeting fiber quality are repeated conflicts between hired employees and PMs, which often culminated in strikes or "Italian strikes" that delayed completion of plant overhaul ahead of a harvesting season. During Gabi's years there were no strikes; the first strikes appeared during Emanuel's late era, despite his caring for employees' well-being. He failed due to absenteeism, when he also took charge of another I-KRC's plant with an April–September high season and imported a ginning-ignorant *pa'il* as Deputy PM to manage Northern's overhauling during this period while he managed the other plant. This *pa'il* opted for detached CCMI and his substitution of Emanuel was a failure, added hierarchy, and caused mistrust of both Emanuel and the deputy. Bitter conflicts erupted, culminating in "Italian strikes" ahead of ginning seasons, similar to those led by Atad in Merkaz.

Emanuel's trust-diminishing absence emphasized the decisiveness of Gabi's vulnerable involvement for a high-trust culture like Guest's (1962: Ch. 4) new leader: such a leader deals personally with any problem not solved by subordinates, learns it together with them, and solves it by using acquired knowledge, power advantage, and overall authority. For instance, Gabi successfully solved the problem of raw cotton variable humidity by involving cotton growers in the solution: gin plants' prime goal was best fiber quality to maximize growers' revenues; a major factor that impacted quality was drying treatment, which had to accord varied humidity of each eight-ton stack, and to accord varied air humidity and heat. For example, during my participant observation on some hot November days with dry eastern winds of only 10–15% humidity and a temperature of 35° Celsius, Merkaz operators did not light furnaces to dry the raw cotton; the airflow of powerful fans was sufficient. Differential treatment required measuring the humidity of each stack, a time-consuming task which I never saw anyone doing at Merkaz; drying treatment was decided intuitively during processing when processing a stack took 20 minutes, meaning that a large part of the stack was processed before the operator could discern whether there was need to change the drying treatment, and hence often half a stack was not dried properly. Gabi concluded that since fiber quality was in the interest of cotton growers they would do it; he bought and gave each grower a hygrometer and each stack was brought to the plant yard with a known humidity, helping operators greatly. Moreover, Gabi's innovation demonstrated in practice his words concerning the plant's prime goal, excellent fiber quality, proving his integrity. Only the PM's authority could introduce such a change, further explaining the failure generated by Emanuel's absence and that of Lowland's half-detached PM David (below, p. 131).

Gabi's initiative accorded Chapter 3's emphasis on transformational leaders' high-moral trust of practitioners signaled by immersion, learning, and innovative problem-solving. Similarly, high-moral were PMs 1 and 4, who were also socialized leaders (Poulin et al. 2007), but unlike Gabi they avoided some of employees' deliberations as lacking Gabi's technical knowledge they could not help solve some mechanical problems. Thus, while PMs 1 and 4 were trusted, unlike distrusted PMs 3, 5, and 6, this was all the more true of Gabi, as his full immersion made it even clearer that in his actions and decisions "the interests of society t[ook] the degree of precedence that [wa]s right, just, and fair over the interests of the individual" (Hosmer 1995: 399); his practices enhanced problem-solving, decision-making, and making changes, which were always aimed at serving the plant's overall goal (Goldratt 1992).

Gabi's high morality was backed by vulnerably involved, highly trusted CEO Dan, contrary to eight other detached or minimally involved CEOs on whom I have verified information. I did not interview Dan, but Gabi and others testified to his considerable involvement and lack of any attempt to distance himself from lower echelons (Collinson 2005a); his involved backing was essential because innovative Gabi used unconventional practices. For instance, almost all gin plants imported *pe'ilim* for the job of TM, such as Avi, Yehu, and Gornitzki, while Gabi retained hired TM Arbiv, nominated by his predecessor, and later promoted to TM his hired deputy. Inside promotion of an experienced deputy enhanced the high-trust culture in which "what's best for the cotton will always receive the highest priority" (Arbiv) and no one's job success could make him forget this dictum to which three PMs and two consecutive TMs adhered. Other plants mostly did not adhere to such a dictum, rather to power politics in which one's power serves one's own interests, defending authority and advancing careers, and as in Merkaz this was camouflaged as serving the plant's interest, which was suspected but concealed by secrecy. Gabi avoided such low morality by trustful practices; his words were followed by deeds, proving his integrity. Most clear was the rewarding of commitment to the fiber quality goal by proper promotion and remuneration. Many authors reiterated that leaders' actions talk louder than their words; ITT's CEO Geneen asserted that

> ". . . the best way to inspire people to superior performance is to convince them by everything you do and by your everyday attitude that you are wholeheartedly supporting them. You have got to mean it and demonstrate it"

(Geneen 1984: 149).

By practicing vulnerable involvement, CEO Dan and PM Gabi proved their wholehearted support of employees' coping with the complex ginning system; Gabi and employees "constituted and reconstituted" ginning know-how and *phronesis* by "engaging the world of practice" (Orlikowski 2002: 249), while Gabi successfully honed knowledge assets into sharper resources aimed at the plant's prime goal (e.g., Wagner 2002). The superb ginning expertise untangled lengthy repeated interviews with Gabi, Arbiv, and TM-3.[3] Gabi's trust in the two was evident when he took them to professional meetings of gin PMs and TMs in which they were the only non-*pe'ilim* present; this deed echoed the cited critique of the ex-head of the national cotton fiber-grading laboratory (p. 9) that "to learn the subject [of ginning one] . . . needs at least 5–6 years. The professionals who carried out the ginning, its changes and innovations were hired mechanics . . . who knew nothing about cotton . . ."; in contrast, Northern Gin professionals were PM Gabi, who learned ginning for 7.5 years; hired Arbiv, who did it for a decade before leaving for WLGEP's R&D; and hired TM-3, who did it for two decades. They knew a lot about cotton and ginning, as proved by the outcomes of their management.

Both interviews with *pe'ilim* and with hired employees corroborate the analysis of this ex-head concerning PMs 3, 5, and 6. These PMs concealed their ignorance by not taking hired TMs and Deputy TMs to professional meetings of the Gin Plant Association, including those that hosted American experts. Much as Avi prevented hired technicians from traveling to another plant to see a sampler that worked smoothly in order to conceal his own ignorance, these PMs prevented TMs from witnessing their own ignorance at such meetings. Both Gabi and Emanuel testified that other plant managers were astonished to see their hired TM and his deputy accompanying them to such meetings as well as on business trips abroad. Thus, an additional clue to Northern Gin's success in Gabi's era was his TM and his deputy's active participation in and learning of the expertise of automatic cotton processing, plants' process planning, equipment choice, purchase, installation, and problem-solving deliberations. In other plants, hired TMs, deputies, foremen, and technicians, "[t]he [presumed] professionals who did the ginning, its changes and innovations" mostly "did not have enough know-how to overcome the complex problems" (cotton grading expert, p. 9) of ginning, since their superiors defended their own authority by concealing their ignorance through barring their participation in the learning from experts.

This conclusion is supported by one exceptional category of hired TMs who were given more discretion and more opportunities to learn ginning than other hired TMs; these were the first TMs of new plants, such as Muli. In all five plants the founding PM was an experienced but ginning-ignorant manager who recruited a technician of a current plant elsewhere and appointed him as TM. The promoted technician was empowered by exclusive knowledge lacked by *pe'ilim* managers; he was granted much discretion, including travels abroad to choose and purchase equipment. Subsequently, however, discretion was mostly curtailed, as either involved *pe'ilim* such as Yaakov and Aharon became knowledgeable, or a "parachuted" *pa'il* succeeded the hired TM (Thomas, Avi, cases below). Only Northern Gin PMs promoted insider hired TMs as they were vulnerably involved, trusted the expertise and high morality of TMs, and were not concerned about their empowerment by successes. In other plants, successor PM *pe'ilim* mostly replaced hired TMs by *pe'ilim* or limited their discretion and barred their participation in outside meetings and abroad as this could have exposed their CCMI.

Northern's success was compromised by PMs 3, 5, and 6, who practiced CCMI-Im-C. PM 3 Mikha's autocracy failed, PM 4 Emanuel only very partially managed to resume the high-trust culture, and detached CCMI-user PM-5 distrusted veteran staff who confronted him concerning many ignorant and amateurish decisions. Top expert TM-3 demonstrated:

> "Northern's 5th PM does not allow me any discretion of the kind I have with Emanuel; the truth is that I am always worried about him, I don't really know what his intentions are, what he will dream up at night and then try to implement in the morning. His decisions are strange; for instance one kibbutznik was abroad and saw yellow covers for cotton stacks that are presumably better [than the current red covers] but would double the cost. With no trial or consultation the manager ordered hundreds of such covers, which proved bad for the cotton and had to be replaced."

A bitter conflict erupted just ahead of my visit concerning staff downsizing due to the reduction of cotton growing because of low cotton prices. TM-3 and his union committee offered some solutions, but would not fire veterans aged over 50 as their prospects of finding new jobs at their advanced age were almost nonexistent. PM-5 opened the interview by stating: "We are a small gin plant but a good one," but then adding a contrasting statement: "We have a permanent staff of 17 people, which is too large, and I want to reduce it and to introduce new people." But why should new people be added if one seeks to reduce the staff? Not answering my question, his assertions untangled the intention to replace costly powerful professional veterans with cheaper youngsters whose minimal salaries would give the CEO and the Board an image of a PM who promoted "efficiency." He clearly disregarded the fact that the professionalism of the formers made the plant "a good one," but admitted that only ignorant lesser youngsters with Atad-like capabilities could be found with the mini-salaries he would offer. TM-3 was the prime obstacle to his plan, hence he tried to get rid of him but failed as the entire staff was united behind him, as were politicians from the nearby town.

Summary of the Northern Gin Case

As mentioned, studies of destructive leadership explain it by the toxic tri-angle of destructive leaders, susceptible followers, and conducive environ-ments (p. 81). In the same vein, the constructive triangle of Northern Gin's successful leadership consisted of:

1 Leaders' high-moral ignorance-exposing vulnerable indwelling in staff's deliberations enhanced learning and innovating by trustful cooperating with practitioners' problem-solving and expertise nurturing;
2 High-moral trusting and talented TMs and expert staff, including vet-eran operators, were committed to the plant's mission clearly explicated by leaders' words and deeds;
3 The supporting context that included the backing of a trusting knowl-edgeable and involved CEO.

Dan and Gabi generated a positive "change [that] only really comes about when those involved actively engage in the work of change, and are part of the cognitive shift often necessary to start turning the organization around" (Fairholm 2004: 92). Northern's high-trust culture resembled Cunha's (2002) "Best Place to Be": it had "good leaders who were able to stimulate participation and who communicated intensely with their subordinates"; they led by "esprit de corps, performance orientation, diversity, orientation toward the future, innovation, efficiency, personal development, and com-petence . . . trust and entrepreneurship . . . points out the need to give people enough space and freedom to allow them to pursue their own ideas. . . . a climate of informality and diversity in order to preserve trust and teamwork while emphasizing goal orientation and performance (2002: 487–488; also: Ingvaldsen et al. 2013).

However, Northern's findings corroborate those of Merkaz by untangling the emergence of similar immoral mismanagement when detached CCMI-Im-C practitioner CEOs succeeded Dan and "parachuted" their ginning-ignorant loyalists or prospective loyalists as PMs who cancelled all these, engendered vicious distrust and ignorance cycles, and turned Northern almost into a twin of Merkaz. The difference that helped prevent a com-pletely negative turnaround was the entrenched veteran ginning profes-sional staff headed by expert TM-3 and his expert deputy, whom PMs 5 and 6 failed in firing. Northern's case points to additional positive effects of executives' vulnerable involvement and virtuous trust and learning cycles:

1 High-moral trusting executives granted expert employees discretion, non-materially incentivized their functioning on the job and nurtured their expertise, which enhanced the plant's effectiveness through their ingenuity in problem-solving and innovating, as asserted by anthropol-ogist Herder two centuries ago (p. 116).

2   Due to virtuous trust and learning cycles, knowledgeable executives and managers successfully socialized employees to consistently pursue the plant's prime goals of minimal downtime, highest product quality, and minimal quantity loss.

3   Vulnerably involved executives successfully discerned and promoted knowledgeable deserving insiders to management ranks, preventing mistakes and failures by CCMI-Im-C practicing "parachuted" managers that troubled Merkaz and other plants (below).

4   PMs did not need loyal Atad-like "bramble" informers, because vulnerable involvement plus employees' openness due to the high-trust culture well informed them of what was going on at the plant.

5   Knowledgeable executives defended the high-trust culture by recognizing, suppressing, and ousting bums, fools, ingratiating impostors, criminals, and Im-C troublemakers.

6   Trustful, open communication enhanced executives' learning and caring for employees' social and other non-work problems, which enhanced employees' trust, committed work, and OCB (organizational citizenship behavior; e.g., Dineen et al. 2006).

7   Care of employees' personal and social problems by trusted involved executives curbed turnover, brain drain, and use of industrial action; conflicts were solved constructively, preventing conflict-driven failures and losses.

However, Northern's case also shows that even the industry's best plant suffered in its late years mismanagement by "parachuted" *rotational* CEOs and PMs who used CCMI, one PM by coerciveness and two by detachment, while both practices served *pe'ilim*'s Im-C, caused distrust and negativism among hired employees, and incited destructive conflicts. Executives who practiced CCMI and were ignorant of their own ignorance (Kruger and Dunning 1999) explain the destructiveness of conflicts; PMs 3, 5, and 6 missed decisive information: they did not notice that the "good plant" achieved their predecessors by nurturing the staff's expertise, high morality, and work commitment. This omission increased their wish to get rid of these staff members and their leader, TM-3, and to suppress him and his deputy by barring participation in professional meetings that further heated conflicts, inflamed by efforts to fire staff. PMs emphasized their own superior status by exclusive participation in these meetings, prevented ignorance exposure vis-á-vis their subordinates, but ruined the trust required to end conflicts by consent (Deutsch 1969). They enhanced suspicions of their incompetence, exposed by stupid amateurish decisions, inflamed conflicts, and shattered information-sharing required to break vicious circles of conflict.

"Parachuted" Executives' Im-C and Use of CCMI in Three Other Plants

Analyses of mismanagement in three more gin plants will corroborate the above findings and the negative impact of management systems predicated on *rotatzia* + "parachuting" of executives and managers from owner kibbutzim to I-KRCs and gin plants. Similar to the former plants, all were established in late 1950s–early 1960s, studied in the 1980s, and owned by I-KRCs; only Lowland Gin was at first a cooperative of kibbutzim, moshavim,[4] and private farmers. For ginning expertise, two plants encouraged technicians to "jump" from older plants to become TMs, while American engineers supervised plant erection and trial running, while in a third plant such engineer elevated to TM and coached a technician from among the plant-building crew. During the late 1960s–early 1970s all three plants were enlarged by adding a second processing unit to each one, as done in Merkaz in 1966. The growth of the cotton industry ceased in the early 1980s and it gradually dwindled; most plants were closed and currently only two remain.

Lowland Gin Plant

The plant's initiator was Avraham, head of the Lowland Regional Council;[5] he contacted two other heads of adjacent regional councils and a group of private farmers, and together they established the gin plant with a hired PM. He failed and was fired after the first season and Avraham took the helm as an absentee manager, since he remained full-time head of the Regional Council; he authorized the hired TM (called L-TM-1) to manage the plant de facto. L-TM-1 had seven years of experience in ginning: he "jumped" from the same job at another plant, to which he "jumped" from a technician's job at a third plant. L-TM-1 only involved Avraham in major decisions such as equipment purchasing, promotions, salaries and plant development. In this latter function Avraham was active, initiated adding a fruit dehydrating facility and a facility for removing down from cotton seeds, which supplied the gin staff with work between seasons and added income through better compensated evening and night shifts in the downing department.

At first, the knowledgeable L-TM-1 served as a highly committed substitute PM, who remained even until midnight if needed to solve a major technical problem, managing work reasonably. But after two successful "jumpings" he tended to Im-C; he for instance usurped others' proposed innovations by first rejecting them and after a while proposing them as his own, similar to Mehri's (2005: 142) manager. Backed by Avraham, he centralized control, became autocratic, causing distrust and a turnover of talented mechanics and foremen who were never taken to learn from other plants. Their limited know-how enhanced his power but required of him extra efforts to overcome operational problems. Employees also suffered from the inability to communicate with the PM to solve personal and social problems, which L-TM-1 failed to solve or worse, did not try to solve. For instance, L-TM-1 told an employee who complained about unfair deductions from his salary that he was not authorized to deal with the issue, without suggesting how to deal with it, while the PM rarely appeared at the plant to solve such problems because L-TM-1 drew a rosy picture: "no problems." The PM's absence caused employee dissatisfaction, turnover, and brain drain. To replace the departing Jews, L-TM-1 recruited less educated Arabs who were satisfied with lower salaries and were more committed to work than Jews, enabling good ginning results, another reason for Avraham's absenteeism.

After six years Avraham left his kibbutz and a *pa'il* replaced him as the council head and kept Avraham as Lowland's hired PM. However, he remained detached and ignorant of ginning, while L-TM-1's functioning deteriorated both because of his extra efforts to run the plant with mostly ignorant uneducated staff and because of empowerment that encouraged oligarchic dysfunctional self-perpetuating conservatism (Michels 1959[1915]), in accord with LLCT (Hambrick 2007). Avraham's presence in the plant's office slightly improved treatment of employee problems, but L-TM-1 used his presence for purposes of absenteeism, traveling frequently abroad: "I traveled abroad dozens of times for teaching and guiding." However, in the absence of any expert deputy and with a detached and ignorant PM, work suffered during these travels, as an ad-hoc chosen foreman or technician substituted for L-TM-1. L-TM-1 also usurped the authority of the detached, inept old PM concerning salaries, then the buying of new machines, and more. A forklift driver remembered that when he joined the plant in its eighth year L-TM-1 was

> ". . . omnipotent in the plant, he could come to work at 3 PM with no excuse. Yatzek [Avraham's successor] demanded that he come at 6:30 AM but he refused; [his successor] L-TM-2, for instance, always comes at 6:00. And even when coming at 3 PM L-TM-1 could disappear with no one knowing where he had gone."

Plant functioning deteriorated with such low morality of its powerful, untrustworthy leader. If Avraham did anything to stop this negative behavior, this was not felt by any of the interviewees; L-TM-1 continued for another five years until fired by a Yuval-like, coercively involved *pa'il* PM, Yatzek. At first Yatzek was a director on the plant's Board, as the economic manager of his kibbutz, and then he became a Deputy PM as a *pa'il*, when in its 11th year plant ownership was shifted from the three Regional Councils and private farmers to the region's I-KRC. A year and a half later Yatzek replaced Avraham. As deputy, he was L-TM-1's friend and together they bought and established a second ginning unit, but as he took charge he subdued his ex-friend autocratically; similar to Yuval he sauntered around, yelled at employees publicly even for minor mistakes or seemingly mistakes, and ignorantly interfered in technical decisions, stupidly overruling L-TM-1's decisions with amateurish ones and then firing him. Interviewed after eight years on the job, he proved ignorant of ginning complexity, and said of L-TM-1's replacement by the "parachuted" *pa'il* L-TM-2, an ex-kibbutz cotton branch manager ignorant of ginning:

> "I took a lad from the [cotton] field, made him TM, and did not allow any overlapping between the two [him and L-TM-1]. Board members

told me that I was playing [taking a risk] with their precious cotton—this was really a bold move hitherto unknown in Israel. They thought a TM in a gin plant is God himself, did not understand that it was only some bolts, metal sheets, and bearings, and since I knew what a bearing is, I was born on a tractor and my harvester combine never stopped working because I could always found a bolt or an iron wire to repair it, hence I was not concerned of any technical problems [due to this step]."

Yatzek bluffed about the succession process (see below), but even worse was his ignorance: no knowledgeable ginner would accept that a gin plant is "only some bolts, metal sheets, and bearings," and that experience with driving a tractor and a harvester combine teaches one how to fix plant's problems by "a bolt or an iron wire." This claim contradicts my findings that show gin plant complexity and accords the critique by Arbiv and the ex-head of the national cotton fiber grading laboratory of PMs' ginning ignorance (p. 9). Valley Gin TM, with 27 years of experience (below), cited the American engineer who in 1956 supervised his first gin plant erection and before leaving for home heard the staff complaining that he had not taught them enough ginning:

"You'll work and learn the hard way; I have been in the trade for 25 years and I am still learning ginning."

But learning is minimal in a culture of secrecy, bluffs, subterfuges, and other abuses, due to seductive-coercive autocracy as practiced by L-TM-1 most of his years and in all Yatzek years, i.e., some 80% of Lowland's studied years. Its veteran garage manager, who learned mechanics from his teens at his father's garage in Poland, explained Yatzek's ignorance of ginning complexity by his rewarding and promoting yes-men ingratiatory bums rather than knowledgeable, competent, truth-telling, hard-working employees:

"The problem here is that good work is not paid for, only talking and image building are paid, ingratiating the boss instead of doing good work. Many incompetents came here and remained who only knew how to drill a hole but pretended to be professional [mechanics]. Yatzek sought and rewarded spies who told him what was going on the shop floor. I refused [to do this] as I did [previously] when I managed a large Siberian work camp, and I was punished [for my integrity] by Yatzek. Earlier, L-TM-1 used bluffs and I said this bluntly in his face. Bosses unfairly punished me and I complained to the union committee but they merely mocked me, said 'we will redress your grievance' and did nothing. I have no contact with all these incompetents who only know how to ingratiate bosses."

L-TM-2 supported this description by asserting that "I did not learn anything from them [hired staff]," but veterans contradicted his assertion, telling they had taught him ginning, although only after gaining their trust through vulnerable involvement. His contrary assertion seemed to represent his traumatic entry period, when he faced distrust and a culture of secrecy unknown in previous kibbutz managerial jobs, while lacking any defined status, until replacing L-TM-1 caused his isolation by suspicious staff, similar to Avi's entrance to Merkaz:

> "In the first year I came more for observation rather than actual entrance until he [L-TM-1] left and then it was a real 'parachuting' into the job with no mentoring and no contact [with L-TM-1] for conveying working knowledge. . . . It was a hard time (Why?), not because others tried to trip me up but since none wanted to help me"
>
> (e.g., Milliken et al. 2003).

L-TM-2 arrived at the age of 35 with previous successful experience in managing the cotton branches of two kibbutzim, hence he enjoyed psychological safety that encouraged vulnerable involvement. This happened only after a year with L-TM-1, contrary to Yatzek's bluff that there was no overlapping, but like Avi's overlapping Muli he learned little, and L-TM-1 suspected him of being a prospective successor and did not teach him ginning, while in the low-trust secrecy culture his undefined status prevented employees' trust and teaching him. Only after taking charge did his vulnerable involvement gradually gain employees' trust and knowledge sharing, but he did not achieve Thomas's level of expertise due to his failure to create a high-trust shop floor culture as a result of Yatzek's ignorant prevailing by seductive-coercive autocracy. L-TM-1 described the situation:

> "Yatzek tried to control every move [of people]; he became hysterical if any guy was seen wandering around for a minute without doing anything; he yelled at people, put them down in front of everyone."

Yatzek's autocracy retained a low-trust culture of secrecy, knowledge abuses, bluffs, and other subterfuges, which his loyalist *pe'ilim* supported contrary to L-TM-2's critique of their using power to suppress hired employees:

> "They [*pe'ilim*] kept [hired] employees low, gave them the feeling that their job depended on them. They knew very well to spread this insecurity, but this caused fears [also] among foremen, hence they told stories, non-based things, only to prove that what they did was right and arranged the numbers [to prove this] as they wished. I thought it was a mistake [to suppress them] but now I see that Yatzek was right [with suppression]."

L-TM-2 changed his mind during his nine years on the job: due to Yatzek's autocracy he lacked the discretion to try to innovate and learn, while unlike

Thomas he lacked involved *pe'ilim* partners, like Danton, with which to nurture a high-trust shop floor culture, while Yatzek and his loyalist *pe'ilim* antagonized the hired staff and maintained defensive secrecy. Yatzek fought employees' counter-secrecy by punishing anyone caught concealing information, but this just encouraged it. L-TM-2's disappointment with this debilitating secrecy led him to praise his boss's policy of distrust only two sentences after criticizing *pe'ilim*'s support of this boss. Another reason for the praise was Yatzek's successful career: two years before the interviews he advanced to manage a much larger plant, owned by two I-KRCs, with hundreds of employees; in his last year in Lowland when he was busy lobbying for this "jump" he granted L-TM-2 more discretion, but after over 16 years of brain drain and selective retention of docile, lesser employees who settled for lower salaries (below) L-TM-2 could barely use this leeway productively, since he lacked experts with whom to change and innovate, nor could he trust the information received from bums, fools, and impostors used to managers uninterested in their inputs (Fast et al. 2014). He frequently consulted highly expert ginner, veteran Southern Gin's TM-2 Yunus (below) by phone, and sometimes visited his plant. He gradually achieved improved functioning: in his third year fiber quality improved from seventh to fourth place among the 10 plants, a little better than the national average. But Yunus's advice was a meager substitute for an open, sincere, and trustful cooperative relationship with a knowledgeable staff. Concerning his staff he felt that he had failed to

". . . make them think. It might have been my naivety, but I never felt that they tried to fail me, to intentionally subvert my efforts. But they knew nothing; there were three [bad] foremen whom we tried to get rid of, while we painfully suffered the departures of some good ginners who could have replaced them but found better salaries elsewhere."

Employee interviews supported this bleak picture that Yatzek's autocracy left to his successor PM-4 and L-TM-2. Brain drain also explained PM-4's finding that Lowland's salaries were lower than at most other gin plants. Worse still, PM-4's downsizing led to the firing of 12 veteran Arab workers, although "they were excellent workers; they did all types of work, were hardworking, although they could not do every job our [Jewish] lads do." However, PM-4, as a detached and ignorant "parachutist," did not ask why these excellent workers could not do Jewish lads' work; all signs showed that dominant veteran incompetent Jews, including the above three foremen, blocked Arabs' promotion, which legitimized the all-Arab firing list prepared by the all-Jewish union committee. Under Yatzek, autocratic coercive-seductive ignorant management and suppression of hired employees by *pe'ilim*, L-TM-2's involvement failed to nurture talented Arabs to replace mediocre Jews; in fact he did not even mention the firing of excellent Arab workers. As will be learned from the case of Merkaz's Nekhas (pp. 169–170), this was probably a loss of considerable talent potential.

All the above raises the question: What did the I-KRC CEO do about this bleak picture? Was he aware of it? He was interviewed before I knew about this negative situation, hence I did not ask him nor did he mention it, but reading the 24 Lowland interviews provided an answer: he was so detached that no interviewee mentioned him aside from Yatzek, who only said that good ties with the CEO helped his recent promotion. The CEO's headquarters were 30 kilometers away in a large city; in the six-page-long interview only two sentences mentioned Lowland, and only its finances, nothing about its mismanagement, versus extensive discussion of the managerial problems of other I-KRC plants. Clearly unaware of its mismanagement, it is no wonder that the CEO promoted loyalist Yatzek as PM of the larger plant with hundreds of workers.

Discussion and Summary of the Lowland Gin Case

Lowland Gin's 22 years were dominated by one TM (L-TM-1) and one PM (Yatzek). PM Avraham used detached CCMI and practiced Im-C, as indicated by his detachment that also let him hold the job of head of a Regional Council. This was very unusual; I know of no one else who held these two full-time executive jobs at once. This was rare for good reasons, as evident from the negative impact of his absence, which empowered L-TM-1, and within a few years turned him into an immoral, autocratic oligarch. At first, L-TM-1's careerism led to genuine efforts to cope with problems that motivated staff, but with entrenchment he reached a dysfunction phase and often came to work very late, with no intervention by PM Avraham. The result of the two's combined detached mismanagement was turnover and brain drain, minimal staff expertise, inefficiency, and ineffectiveness. Even when Avraham abandoned his double jobs it changed little, just his detached mismanagement became clearer, backing L-TM-1's oligarchic dysfunctional rule over mediocre staff with no expert deputy to replace him on his frequent absences abroad. Much like Merkaz's Moav, Avraham retained his job for 12 years by distrustful detached immoral CCMI, which did not change after he became a full PM, since the distrust relations formed over six years of absentee rule from which employees suffered could not be changed without great efforts, which old Avraham never tried, letting L-TM-1's negative autocracy reign until Yatzek fired him.

Ignorant autocratic "parachuted" *pa'il* PM Yatzek changed little by replacing L-TM-1 with a *pa'il* L-TM-2 with minimal technical qualifications as if he was trying to overcome L-TM-1's mismanagement, although in reality he primarily sought to empower his autocracy. He was not completely ignorant as was Yuval due to four years as a director on the Board and 1.5 years as Deputy PM working with L-TM-1 on establishing a new ginning unit. Hence, he replaced L-TM-1 with an experienced manager while not concerned about his ginning ignorance, restricting his discretion, unlike Thomas who enjoyed Shavit's detachment, had ample mechanical know-how, and enjoyed the collaboration of three other involved *pe'ilim* with whom he created a trustful shop-floor culture—all advantages that L-TM-2 lacked. Without mechanical education and little experience, L-TM-2's vulnerable involvement encountered the mediocre hired staff, the animosity of other detached *pe'ilim* and the autocratic coerciveness of Yatzek, who practiced CCMI-Im-C, seeking a "jump" to a more prestigious job and little interested in better ginning. This barred both a high-trust shop-floor culture and nurturing a knowledgeable staff; brain drain continued, and L-TM-2's sincere efforts at enhancing efficiency and effectiveness achieved only minor improvements. His frustration explains his late shift to support of Yatzek's autocracy.

As against the drawbacks of *rotatzia* and "parachutings," the lack of any succession system was no better, as proved by the cases of Avraham, L-TM-1, and their correlates, V-TM and Moav. However, the Board was another culprit: seemingly for political reasons the three Regional Council heads and private farmer representatives allowed Avraham's absentee management, ignoring its drawbacks and its worsening after a few years as L-TM-1 commenced dysfunctioning, all the more so when old Avraham as full PM allowed L-TM-1's dysfunction to become lawlessness, coming to work only in the afternoon and traveling abroad for weeks with no competent replacement. The co-ownership by kibbutzim, moshavim, and private farmers caused conflicts of interest that often paralyzed the Board, and Avraham used this to hold double jobs. The Board did not prevent this, nor did it prevent L-TM-1's lawlessness, reconciled with staff turnover, brain drain, and other causes of ineffectiveness under Avraham's prolonged detached immoral rule.

The second era of the plant's ownership by the I-KRC changed the situation only little as the CEO was a detached veteran *pa'il* in a dysfunction phase who promoted Deputy PM Yatzek to PM due to loyalty and seemingly capability proved in the erection of second processing unit. He did not interfere with Yatzek's autocratic ignorant mismanagement, as Yatzek created an image of success, which was not so hard considering the mismanagement by Avraham and L-TM-1: vulnerably involved L-TM-2 failed to create a high-trust culture and did not prevent brain drain, but his sincere efforts directed by frequent consultation with TM Yunus of Southern Gin achieved some learning and somewhat improved functioning. Yatzek used this positive image, in addition to proving loyalty to a new, also detached CEO, to advance to the more prestigious job of PM of the larger plant.

Lowland's case further proves the merits of explaining managerial stupidity by a cultural theory of contrary processes caused by executives' choices of either CCMI-Im-C or the opposite. PM Avraham's absenteeism left him ignorant and detached even in his late years despite his physical presence, in accordance with the hypothesis whereby the vicious distrust and ignorance cycle tends to entrench. Vulnerably involved L-TM-2 failed to create a high-trust culture and to become fully knowledgeable, but improved plant's functioning accords the theory of vulnerable involvement's positive impact. However, his case shows that learning is considerably hampered without a supporting group work culture (Fine 2013), which enabled both Thomas's success and that of Northern's ginners. He suffered Yatzek's ignorant involved autocracy, helped by loyalist *pe'ilim*, which led to secrecy and brain drain. Lacking the PM's support, bums, fools, and impostors were not replaced by capable employees and he failed to overcome the resistance of incompetent Jewish workers to promoting talented and potentially competent Arab workers.

Last but not least, the Lowland case corroborates the futility of I-KRCs' democracy of kibbutz "representatives" analyzed with regard to Merkaz's Boards of Directors (p. 54). Lowland's Board was supposed to prevent continued plant mismanagement but it did not. Only in the seventh year did the new Regional Council head nominate kibbutz manager Yatzek to the Board because "kibbutzim cotton growers are deeply indignant of Avraham"; "there was mistrust and a rift between the kibbutzim and the plant because of him," said Yatzek. This rift and Yatzek's four years as a Board member before becoming Deputy PM were discussed at length in Yatzek's interview but nothing was said about the mismanagement that caused Avraham's indignation, pointing to Yatzek's ignorance of ginning despite 13.5 years of Board and plant offices. Yatzek's lengthy discussion of his eight years as PM mentioned kibbutz representatives on the Board only once, their concern that ginning-ignorant "parachuted" TM-2 would fail in his job, but not a word about his own major mistaken decisions such as deferring introduction of the Movers for seven years despite cotton growers' interest. Lowland's Board democracy was clearly futile, much as that of Merkaz.

Valley Gin Plant

The plant was established in 1956 by The Jewish Agency[6] as part of a regional development project. In 1959 the Pima (long fiber cotton) ginning unit was added, and in 1965 it was turned into a regular ginning unit, as farmers stopped growing Pima. An experienced locksmith from the plant's erection team was hired as TM, though lacking both mechanical and ginning expertise, which he learned "the hard way through work," citing the American supervising engineer who coached the plant's erection and trial running. This veteran TM (27 years on the job when interviewed) clearly failed professionally; his major technical failures that continued for years caused losses that encouraged the Jewish Agency to grant the plant at no charge to the Valley I-KRC in the early 1960s as its kibbutzim constituted most of the cotton growers. Valley TM (V-TM for short) described this failure:

> "The lint cleaner was a disaster since it did not fit the air blast as its condenser was too small and we did not know this and became incensed at

it. We summoned all the experts and major figures in the US manufacturer but they could not find the reason and for three years we produced low-quality fibers. Today it makes me laugh, I know that a 24-inch condenser cannot separate 8000–9000 CFM[7] of air blast, but at that time all these Americans could not find the cause; [then] most farmers left us, from 13,000 bales [per season] we plummeted to 5,000 bales until we replaced the lint cleaner with one used in other plants and fiber quality returned to normal."

The I-KRC's CEO replaced PM-1, who had allowed continued failures, with PM-2 David, who had a convincing managerial record although he was not a *pa'il*, unlike all other studied PMs; rather he previously had a usual kibbutz managerial career until leaving the kibbutz: first managing an agricultural branch, then managing the kibbutz economy, then a *pa'il* in an I-KO's economic unit and then leaving the kibbutz to manage an NGO-owned processing plant for two years. He left this job due to ethical conflicts with the NGO's CEO about fulfilling the promise of a salary rise he had given to a hard-working bookkeeper, deemed unauthorized by the CEO. David thought that it was unethical to go back on his promise and he resigned. Soon he was called to the rescue of Valley Gin. The nominating I-KRC's CEO authorized any necessary changes but demanded minimal investments, as the I-KRC was much shorter of money than other I-KRCs.
As a high-moral, successful and experienced manager, David was not concerned about ignorance-exposing vulnerable involvement and he learned the technology almost like Yaakov, without delving into technical questions such as the fit of the lint cleaner's air blast to its condenser, described above, and he came to Valley only after V-TM solved this problem. Nor did he note that V-TM also failed to solve problems with an S&GH-like machine for two years, succeeding only when David took charge. "Parachuted" David did not know about these failures, probably because the CEO avoided mentioning them in order to gain David's acceptance of the job. David did not suspect V-TM's incompetence and left all technical problems to him, not only because he did not know the latter's failures and believed him to function reasonably, but seemingly also to defend his own authority and status as he lacked technical qualifications:

"I did not want to descend to the level of shift foreman and to take care of technical problems, since it was not my domain."

David was a trusted high-moral and job-committed manager praised by both I-KRC's two consecutive CEOs and Valley's interviewees, despite Valley Gin's deficient fiber quality for several years, sometimes even the worst of all gin plants. His only inside critics were veterans who bemoaned the recent plant's moving 15 kilometers from its former location on the outskirts of town, where they had been able to come and go by foot. The move was aimed at building a higher-capacity plant. All other TMs interviewed harshly criticized V-TM as incompetent, pointing to Valley's lagging fiber quality and productivity. David explained these faults during the pre-move years by postponing equipment renewal until the plant was moved to the greenhorn site. However, after Valley moved and was completely renewed with state-of-the-art equipment both fiber quality and productivity still lagged considerably versus other plants: in the last study season Southern Gin processed 32,000 tons of raw cotton in 11 weeks, Merkaz processed 30,000 tons in 13 weeks, while Valley processed only 25,000 tons in 16 weeks. Southern's highly expert veteran Yunus (below) bluntly offered a negative professional assessment of V-TM:

> "V-TM? What can one say [about him]? Just see how [bad] the brand new Valley Gin is looking after just two years; this is V-TM."

Indeed, touring the renewed plant it looked old, shabby, and neglected, more than other plants. Its productivity was much lower than expected *inter alia* because of S&GH problems, similar to those of Merkaz. This was a year after these problems were solved in Merkaz, and it seemed strange that Valley did not emulate Merkaz's solutions. I asked the new PM Shlomo, who replaced David a year before, about this and he answered:

> "V-TM is my technical man who is the most veteran of [Israeli] TMs. I can't replace him right now although he is extremely lazy and I have an excellent foreman with technical experience [as replacement]; I can't myself take all the responsibility."

"Parachuted" Shlomo suspected that V-TM's laziness was causing the low productivity and deficient fiber quality, but the fact that V-TM did not consult with Merkaz's experts on solving the S&GH problems, in addition to all the other findings (below) suggests that, like Avi, V-TM as well avoided consulting due to CCMI. At first glance it seems implausible that V-TM with all his experience avoided learning Merkaz's solution due to defensive immoral CCMI, as Avi did with the sampler, but I learned to suspect managers' explanations of subordinates' motives such as laziness. I returned to V-TM's description of the 1960s failures with the lint cleaner condenser and the S&GH-like machine; at the time he mentioned only "experts and major figures in the US manufacturer" called to solve these multiyear problems, and did not mention any Israelis although, for instance, TM Arbiv at Northern Gin was just 20 minutes' drive away; he could have been consulted and had no reason to avoid helping V-TM. While it would have been reasonable to first consult with the American manufacturer of the lint cleaner, as other Israeli lint cleaners were produced by different manufacturers, continuing this for three years while the Americans repeatedly failed was unreasonable; all lint cleaners used similar operation principles so why not consult with other TMs? Even more unreasonable was not seeking such help for the S&GH-like machine, since in other plants similar machines worked smoothly. As a veteran ginner, V-TM knew other TMs personally, while Israeli gin plants did not compete with each other the in market, and hence it was common to help colleagues with their problems (p. 129 and below). David, for instance, mentioned other TMs, while V-TM mentioned no one throughout the seven-page interview. Other TMs never mentioned V-TM, aside from the cited negative mention by Southern's top expert, Yunus. V-TM clearly avoided Israeli TMs, consulted only with Americans, especially his Californian consultant, friend, and supplier, unlike other Israelis:

> John Smith helped us very much, gave us advice [on buying secondhand machines], sold us some machines and promptly answered my letters of inquiry. He remains the number one ginning expert and supplier of machines. I travel to the US every year and I always visit him, whether at Valley's expense or on my own. David also values him; he is our winning card."

No other TM mentioned this "winning card"; all Americans they mentioned were non-Californians, while the consulting of this "card" did not gain Valley any success as cited. Valley's secondhand, cheap machinery, with which David followed the I-KRC CEO's demand for minimal investments in plant renovation and enlargement, could partially explain Valley's ineffectiveness except for the last two years, but not the prolonged failures of early years in which V-TM avoided consulting Israeli TMs, a clear authority- and job-defending strategy of concealing meager competence from others in the industry, reminiscent of Blau's (1955) senior law enforcers consulting only lesser ones. V-TM defended his expert image by consulting only distant Americans with whom no other Israeli consulted; hence no negative information could reach his boss from Israeli ginners. He himself confessed both to his mediocrity as a ginner and to his lack of concern for owner kibbutzim's interest in the gin plant's effectiveness, saying: "this is off-the-record" (hence it was written later from memory):

> "I have no blue blood [of a *pa'il*]; I left the kibbutz at an early stage and I am an ordinary man, a hired employee who does not care much for the interests of the kibbutzim. I have a deputy *pa'il* who is a certified engineer; for him all that I have learned through hard work, all those 27 years, is only the tip of his fingernail."[8]

V-TM was clearly jealous of his deputy's superior expertise as the latter, for instance, recently easily solved the S&GH problem, versus V-TM's failure at solving a similar problem for two years in the early 1960s. However, V-TM proved improvization capacities in his early days, which suited David's mission of saving the failing plant with minimal investments: due to farmers replacing Pima cotton with Acala cotton, the Pima ginning unit had to be changed to Acala fiber ginning; V-TM bought two old gin machines discarded by another plant for pennies and turned the unit into a provisional Acala unit. The next year John Smith helped him complete the furnishing of this unit with Californian secondhand equipment and soon this unit's ginning results almost equaled that of the other unit. This successful improvisation saved the I-KRC a lot of money and boosted V-TM's image as a ginning expert.

V-TM's concealment of his incompetence contrasted with David's openness, of which, for instance, I became aware in his new job as PM of another I-KRC plant: employees of all ranks would drop into his office and he dealt with everyone patiently, repeatedly distracting our interview until he decided it was intolerable and ordered his secretary to stop it and schedule seekers for later dealings. Highly trusted in Valley, he knew all the employees I have mentioned, and he described his considerable efforts to keep them informed and to advance their ginning know-how. He also modeled commitment by deeds such as replacing a line worker for a lunch break, initiating a profit-sharing scheme, and caring for various employees' needs and wants—for instance allowing those who lived close to the plant to go home for lunch during the off season, although it took a quarter of an hour longer than lunching at the plant. His relationships with the union committee were positive, preventing any industrial action, and Valley culture during his era resembled the "indulgency pattern" (Gouldner 1954), i.e., employee cooperation elicited through paternalistic leniency. He insisted that this was the pattern only between seasons and that strict iron discipline prevailed during the cotton season, but it seemed that some employees who were accustomed to leniency nine months a year did not change their habits during the season, which may be another explanation for the low productivity, one that I could not confirm conclusively without conducting observations during the season.

Further explanations for the mediocre results were David's avoidance of ginners' technical deliberations, his minimal learning of ginning, leaving this domain to mediocre V-TM, and missing his incompetence and indifference to the prime goal of best serving the cotton growers. David also did not notice that V-TM rejected innovations, except those offered by his Californian friend. David missed that V-TM's conservatism spared him the need to consult other plants' TMs about innovations, which concealed his incompetence. Without engaging in major deliberations and with his minimal learning of ginning, David missed V-TM's use of CCMI, his strategic avoidance of others' solutions and other plants' innovations such as Movers. By allowing V-TM's CCMI, David's leadership did not model full commitment to best ginning and to plant effectiveness; his restricted involvement somewhat resembled Danton's, which caused ginning ignorance that led to a destructive conflict with Thomas, defining his rejection of fiber cleaners as "a caprice" (p. 31). Thus, David's restricted involvement caused the fatal mistake that profoundly shaped Valley history, maintaining for another 17 years a mediocre TM who failed for years prior to David's taking charge, and who was uncommitted to the plant's prime goal, a blunder that only immersion in ginners' deliberations and acquiring interactional expertise could expose and subsequently lead to replacement.

Discussion and Summary of the Valley Gin Case

After the eight years of the first PM, who was not studied, came "parachuted" David, who became a high-moral, trusted leader for 15 years but nevertheless achieved mediocre results; he received a failing plant and aimed to achieve a turnaround, "[b]ut change only really comes about when those involved actively engage in the work of change, and are part of the cognitive shift often necessary to start turning the organization around" (Grint and Holt 2011: 92); and this he avoided, missing V-TM's incompetence (e.g., Collins and Weinel 2011) and letting him continue. His trustful relations spared conflicts and strikes but forsook efficiency and effectiveness by retaining V-TM in his pivotal mid-level job, as he spared delving into ginning secrets. Unlike Northern's three high-moral, trusted PMs, David's open trustful relations did not "teach others to seek the highest ideals of public service, and thereby . . . a legacy of trust, integrity, and responsibility, as well as high-quality service delivery and accountability" (Fairholm 2004: 587) as they did not lead to wise technical decisions and enabled V-TM's camouflaging and concealing of incompetence and mismanagement. David's trust in him, with no effort to gain interactional expertise and no ability to assess his intentions and actions due to minimal engagement of technical deliberations, invited V-TM's concealment of mediocrity by avoidance of other TMs who could expose it and by exclusive consulting of a foreign expert. David's high-moral aim should have motivated him to learn ginning enough to discern and replace mediocre V-TM, preventing him from using the discretion granted him to self-servingly defend his unjustified authority and job.

Valley's findings suggest that a high-trust culture by itself is not a panacea for the problem of CCMI of essential know-how and *phronesis*; a high-moral executive aiming for such a culture must be vulnerably involved in subordinates' deliberations in order to create virtuous trust and learning cycles, acquiring interactional expertise for major domains until able to discern mid-levelers' (in)competence, (un)trustworthiness, and possible use of CCMI. Restricted learning, such as that of David, invites CCMI by incompetent mid-levelers who avoid true experts to conceal incompetence (Blau 1955). Had David been involved in major technical deliberations and had he become sufficiently knowledgeable to ask intelligent questions about V-TM's solutions, sooner or later he would have encountered a problem solved by another plant, which V-TM failed to solve, but he avoided going there to learn. Then he would have discerned V-TM's other concealed subterfuges and his CCMI and would have replaced him.

David's restricted involvement that invited V-TM's CCMI was a cardinal mistake, while the case also suggests a questionable CEO detachment, similar to that of others. The Valley I-KRC had two CEOs during the 17 years it owned the gin plant; the first CEO needed no involvement to know the plant's failure and replace its PM, but then the two CEOs were concerned only about investment costs, urged minimizing them, and there was no sign in the interviews and in observations of any other involvement, such as questioning Valley Gin's deficient results. Valley I-KRC received a failing plant; aside from replacing the failing PM, a responsible CEO would have mandated that the new PM review the staff's expertise to achieve successful functioning. Had David reviewed this by delving into past failures he might have untangled V-TM's prior three years of failed coping with dysfunctioning machines, suspected his expertise, allowed him less discretion, exposed his incompetence and replaced him. The second CEO seemingly accepted as inevitable the old plant's poor productivity and deficient fiber results, but faced with the same results of the costly state-of-the-art new facility, he should have asked David's successor serious questions and urged immediate replacement of V-TM rather than allowing him more years. The detachment of the two CEOs helped V-TM's entrenchment, to Valley's detriment.

Valley's case corroborates the decisiveness of the trust and learning cycle due to vulnerable involvement, warning against the danger of trust created by an "indulgency pattern" (Gouldner 1954) with *laissez-faire* mismanagement. David's high-moral practices aroused employees' trust, which helped the plant's functioning by keeping industrial peace, but they caused the major mistake of trusting V-TM. A newcomer who limits his learning by partial detachment is bound to arrive at other negative results as well: mid-levelers who follow his modeling make mistakes and fail due to ignorance; employees' trust in the leader diminishes due to suffering mid-levelers' use of CCMI, abuses, and subterfuges aimed at concealing/camouflaging mistakes and failures; managers' negative modeling discourages commitment to plant goals and employees do not inform/screen information provided to superiors about mistakes and failures. Valley's consistently mediocre results suggest that such negative processes furthered David's and V-TM's mismanagement.

Southern Gin Plant

In contrast to Valley, in which V-TM was a prime factor in its mediocre results, in Southern Gin for 17 years out of the 21 studied, vulnerably involved, highly trusted expert TM Yunus mostly achieved both high productivity and fiber quality mentioned by other plants' experts and corroborated by national fiber quality statistics. However, his achievements were not consistent as were Northern's in Gabi's era because of negative interference by most of the six short-term "parachuted" PMs who opted for CCMI-Im-C. Thus, the Southern case also corroborates the negative impact of "parachuting" and *rotatzia* practices.

Throughout its 21 years, Southern had six PMs, of whom four served 4–5 years, one served a little more than a year, and the incumbent had been occupying his job for 1.5 years when interviewed. PM 1 resembled Yaakov and Aharon, became knowledgeable enough by involvement to discern the incompetence of the hired TM-1, and replaced him with his kibbutz member who was formerly the TM of another processing plant. TM-2 Yunus left this job because of conflicts over salary and a company car, which he was denied although he consented to receive the most modest car on the market, a Citroën De-Chevau, and although the TM job required many unconventional working hours, including night calls. He was ignorant of ginning at first but had taken technical courses, enjoyed many years of experience in mechanics at his kibbutz agricultural machinery garage and practical engineering in his previous TM job. Similar to Thomas and other successful TMs, he learned ginning and the job the hard way, through vulnerable involvement. The first season was "very bad," with both low productivity and low fiber quality; mid-season a pivotal machine broke, and Yunus worked with technicians to repair it for three days and nights until they managed to do so, although some of them repeatedly told him it would fail. Then he radically changed a major practice: instead of hitherto overhauling only problematic machines between seasons, despite workers' resistance all machines were overhauled and the next season passed smoothly with better ginning results.

One reason for his radical problem-solving was his positive experience with changes and innovations contrary to the manufacturers' recommendations, while making sure to obtain the boss's backing. For instance, one reason for low-quality fibers during the first season was the failure of 16D cleaners, which were bypassed as they caused burnings. Yunus found that the problem could be solved by minor changes but PM-1 demanded a manufacturer's approval. Many telex massages were exchanged with the US maker to no avail. Only toward the season's end did the PM give his consent, and from that time on the machines worked smoothly. Yunus explained this:

"What was wrong with the 16D was simply that the saws rolled too slowly and instead of disintegrating the 'quilt' that came from the condenser, they took large chunks that blocked the machine. Without much understanding I watched it happening more than once and decided to speed up the saws and then the blockings stopped. One simply had to take a risk, to dare and try."

Soon PM-1 was succeeded by PM-2, who remained detached but unlike Moav and Shavit he encouraged innovation; when Yunus asked for his view concerning a major proposed innovation he answered: "Do as you please, I understand nothing about it in any case." One explanation for his readiness to take innovation risks was his psychological safety (e.g., Nienaber et al. 2015), as his older brother and mentor was a most powerful leader in the kibbutz field, serving as the CEO of a large commercial I-KC with thousands of employees (Arad 1995). It did not take Yunus long to use the discretion given him by PM-2 and he implemented many innovations depicted in the 12 pages of the 3.5-hour home interview transcript. He, for instance, also faced the problem of a condenser that was too small to separate the fibers of the large air blast, as described above by V-TM (p. 130), but Yunus solved this problem by changing the rotation direction of the condenser screen cylinder such that a larger part of it was used to separate air blast from fibers; this he did after finding that the original direction used too small a part of the cylinder for the separation, hence it was insufficient. Soon this solution was "stolen" by the manufacturer's visiting engineer:

"We were visited by an American engineer invited to solve the 16D problem in other plants such as Valley. He subsequently offered my solution to all Israeli plants as his own at a price of US$500 and all TMs bought it from him though I offered them to come and learn it free of charge. But at that time I was still unknown and they had no trust in me."

After other similar successes, some TMs came to trust Yunus and consulted with him frequently, for instance Lowland's TM-2. Southern's second PM remained on the job for five years and was succeeded by PM-3 who was an ex-treasurer of his kibbutz and similar to Moav was a stingy detached CCMI-Im-C conservative. However, Yunus was empowered by his successes and extracted from this third boss support for almost all changes needed for further success. Like Moav's "riding" on Yaakov and Aharon's successes, PM-3 "rode" on Yunus's successes and after four years was promoted to treasurer of the Southern I-KRC (e.g., Armstrong 1987). Yunus's practices resembled those of Thomas: when faced with an unsolved problem involving a recalcitrant machine he remained by it as long as required to identify the fault. He never concealed his ignorance, always sought effectiveness through vulnerable involvement and openness that generated virtuous trust and learning cycles, and built a high-trust shop-floor culture similar to that of Thomas-Danton. He often consulted with another plant's veteran TM "who is a better ginner than me," achieved high productivity by minimizing downtime to 3–5%, and for several years fiber quality results approached those of Northern and Merkaz during Thomas's late era. However, unlike Thomas's five-year tenure, Yunus continued for 17 years under six bosses, five of them ignorant *rotational* "parachutists." In addition to successes that strengthened his position, he endured them by using several strategies that often compromised required changes and promising innovations:

1   Unlike Thomas, he did not fight to introduce radical new equipment against the opinion of reluctant bosses. For instance, he proposed importing Movers and an automatic feeder not when his US tour convinced

him of the effectiveness of this technology, but only some years later when his boss returned enthusiastic from such a tour.

2   He did spread information about his successes in the industry, hence other TMs came to consult with him and their visits enhanced his prestige and power vis-á-vis PMs.

3   When introducing a radical change or innovation he always kept a retreat route to the previous solution; he was never caught without a working solution.

4   Conscious of the fact that some other TMs were better educated and knew more about machines than he did, he prevented mistakes by consulting with them when unsure of a solution.

5   He reviewed a proposed new machine by comparing its solutions to common problems to those of proven older machines. For instance, the propulsion system of Southern's S&GH never failed because when ordering the machine he demanded that the manufacturer equip it with the propulsion system of the good old LST machine.

Yunus was one of the experts with whom Merkaz managers consulted concerning the dysfunctioning S&GH. He strongly criticized Avi's ineptitude, and said:

> "It was really a cataclysm; facing such a mechanical failure one must simply go and change it. You say that Avi wanted confirmation from the US? It reminds me of an American who offered me a new machine, saying 'And if does not work I'll replace it.' I asked him: 'And then who will do the work for the [ginning] season [while waiting for replacement]? Who will gin my region's cotton during that lost season?' "

Unfortunately, Yunus's leadership of Southern's staff suffered from his limited education and drawbacks that prevented him from achieving lasting top performance. One was that he wasted a great deal of time and attention on the politics involved in promoting changes without confrontations with ignorant bosses to retain his own discretion and prevent their foolish intervention. As he did with the 16D and with the introduction of the Mover-automatic feeder, he postponed other promising innovations until he saw a chance for their eager acceptance by ignorant PMs. As a result, Southern often lagged behind technologically and Yunus's expertise suffered from not experiencing the problems caused by innovations and from wasting much energy and time on politics rather than advancing ginning. Expert employees' trust in his leadership also suffered, as they felt that professional decisions were dictated by politics rather than by performance requirements and a brain drain ensued.

Another reason for the distrust was the lack of care for the well-being of employees. For Yunus this task was the job of PMs who could not contribute to ginning due to practicing CCMI, but like most other PMs studied

Southern's PMs cared little for these needs. As a result, the union committee was peopled by "brambles" and "worst trouble-makers" (McGregor 1960) who demanded more and more remuneration and, like Atad, led "Italian strikes" ahead of the season. Yunus scorned these militants but left the trouble they caused to his bosses, and they often failed to contend with them due to ignorant detachment and their short time horizon due to *rotatzia*, which prevented them from seeking creative and lasting solutions (Jaques 1990). Yunus's neutrality concerning employees' demands enhanced their distrust and damaged motivation and plant functioning. Two years before the study a major wage dispute erupted with disgruntled hired staff and the coercively involved *pa'il* PM-5 boldly fired them all, replacing them with kibbutz mechanics and youngsters. For Yunus, the ignorance of the latter of ginning was a major headache but at the relatively young age of 48 he resumed his early days of much involvement, working from 5:00 AM to midnight, achieving results that retained his professional authority and job:

> "The fact was that we managed without the permanent staff, with only temporaries we remained at the top [of gin plants] with an unequaled daily processing of 730 tons. It was a big bet to enter a season only with temporaries who had never seen a cotton gin plant from within . . . but a good guy with an open mind and motivation is sometimes much better than an experienced but unmotivated skilled fellow."

Yunus maintained Southern's high productivity due to his own expertise and high commitment and thanks to motivated kibbutz members who came from cotton branches or cotton machinery garages to rescue their "white gold"; unfortunately, their ginning ignorance caused deficient fiber quality. Yunus de-emphasized this negative outcome, as he previously tended to ignore such faults stemming from disgruntled hired staff. For him, the prime achievement was maintaining the high level of productivity while enduring mistakes by ignorant "parachuted" bosses, much as Thomas and Danton related to Shavit. However, unlike top experts Arbiv and Thomas, whom WLGEP invited to its R&D unit, Yunus was not invited. This explains: 1) his lack of a practical engineering certificate, 2) Southern's mediocre fiber quality in many seasons, 3) lagging adoption of innovations, and 4) having no major original invention.

Yunus's cautious innovation strategy was also explicable by means of detached I-KRC CEOs who did not encourage innovation and provided no opportunity to overcome a PM's conservatism by seeking the CEO's support. CEOs' detachment is evident from their complete absence from the 12-page interview with Yunus except for the first CEO's support of the replacement of incapable TM-1 with Yunus by PM-1.

Discussion and Summary of the Southern Gin Case

The Southern case focused on Yunus and his achievement of top productivity. PMs were only briefly mentioned as they mostly resembled other "parachuted" detached PMs who practiced CCMI-Im-C, aside from PM-1 whose limited involvement and learning resembled those of Merkaz's Yaa-kov and Aharon; he learned enough to discern the ineptness of TM-1 and replaced him with Yunus. Highly involved Yunus gradually raised South-ern's productivity to the top of the list, with detached PM-2 backing his innovativeness. Then other PMs (3, 4, and 6) were detached conservatives; only PM-5 was coercively involved, boldly fired all hired staff and succeeded due to committed Yunus, whose exceptional efforts and top expertise pre-vented failure of the ginning-ignorant kibbutz member replacements who were better educated than fired hired staff and highly motivated to rescue their "white gold."

Yunus's case corroborates explanations of Thomas, Gabi, and other vul-nerably involved managers' successes, but it adds the lesson that politics enabled a mid-leveler empowered by success to overcome the obstacles of *rotatzia* + "parachuting" by taking care to avoid threatening bosses' con-servative authority by compromising required changes and innovation. The price was laggard technology and failing to prolong the high-trust shop-floor culture, but by job continuity Yunus became a top expert and achieved high productivity despite lesser technical education than some less success-ful TMs and despite ignorant bosses. As in other cases, the detachment of PMs and CEOs diminished trust relations, caused bitter conflicts with hired staff, brain drain, and the rise of Atad-like "brambles" to its leadership. The latter incited militant remuneration demands so that an ignorant-of-ginning-complexity PM fired all hired staff; he trusted that the expertise of successful Yunus would be enough to cope with the exceptional situation, taking a huge gamble: Yunus could have either quitted or limited work to normal working days rather than the 19 hours a day by which he achieved plant's functioning, and this could have left PM-5 in a shambles. It was not PM-5's authority that explained Yunus's avoiding this, rather other factors over which PM-5 had no control:

1   Defending his image as one of Israel's best ginners by achieving top productivity;
2   Dutiful membership of a collective commune for which cotton was the prime source of income;
3   Witnessing enthusiastic kibbutz members coming to rescue their kib-butzim's "white gold" while knowing that only his own expertise could lead them to success.

PM-5's bold move was exceptional, but so was Yunus's prolonged tenure under six ignorant PMs, of whom only two, PMs 1 and 2, backed him; no other TM endured CCMI-Im-C using bosses for so long. One clue to Yunus's exception is his compromising changes and innovation, while another is his indifference to hired subordinates, some of whom he had worked with for 15 years and some of them surely helped his success; not even one word was said throughout the lengthy interview about their firing. Contrary to

Northern's involved PMs, he did not care about these people nor did he develop social ties with them; he let his superiors care for their personal and social needs and succeeded by investing all his efforts in the technical-operational domain. Southern Gin gained years of effectiveness and efficiency but also disgruntled staff, unending remuneration demands, and destructive conflicts that led to strikes (e.g., Parkinson et al. 1973).

For Yunus, his technical and operational achievements morally justified his job survival strategy; opting for Thomas-like confrontations with ignorant bosses would probably not have resulted in a better outcome, as exemplified by Shavit and Zelikovich's deferring Thomas's automatic feeder long enough to constrain this invention to Merkaz, to Thomas's frustration. A more determined and politically astute Yunus did not quit as Thomas did, but he probably paid other intangible prices for his compromising that Thomas did not. However, his job survival strategy reacted to a situation created neither by him nor by his PMs, but rather by higher-ups, detached CEOs, and the context of the kibbutz field (Shapira 2015; see Ch. 6).

Summary and Discussion of Northern Gin versus Four Mismanaged Plants

The findings concerning the four plants corroborate those regarding Merkaz: "parachuted" executives' practicing CCMI-Im-C is the prime explanation of immoral mismanagement; of the 32 executives studied only seven were high-moral, vulnerably involved executives who acquired interactional expertise and became job-competent, five from Northern Gin and I-KRC and two from Southern Gin and I-KRC. Northern's success explains its unique high-trust innovation-prone culture during 13 of its first 15 years due to three ignorance-exposing, vulnerably involved, high-moral competent PMs and the backing of two high-moral CEOs, while immoral mismanagement by three subsequent Northern PMs resembled that of other plants. Effective high-trust cultures were nadir in all other plants, short-lived, or limited to TMs and their subordinates on the shop floor, as in Merkaz's Thomas-Danton era. High-moral PMs who restricted their engaging ginners' deliberations and minimally learned their trade, such as Valley's David, achieved trustful relations but not effective and efficient innovation-prone, high-trust cultures as achieved by fully vulnerably involved PMs and TMs through virtuous trust and learning cycles. Restricted involved, high-moral PMs and Deputy PMs had positive effects by enhancing trust and cooperation and preventing industrial conflicts (Danton, David) and by discerning and weeding out inept mid-levelers (e.g., Southern TM-1), but there were also negative effects such as David's missing V-TM's incompetence, which enabled his entrenchment for decades. The other 15 distrusted immoral PMs mostly shaped inefficient and ineffective conservative-prone cultures and some also failed TMs' efforts to do otherwise (Lowland's Yatzek). This majority of self-serving conservative PMs explains why the adoption of Movers and automatic feeders was deferred for almost a decade while investing heavily in a technologically obsolete system.

As in the case of Merkaz and in accordance with the discussion in Chapter 3, prime factors that impacted managerial practice choices of either CCMI-Im-C or the contrary were:

1 How much pertinent knowledge, competencies, and referred expertise managers have of those that ensured successful learning and functioning;
2 Their degree of mutual trust with employees based on past relationships or the lack thereof, which promised that employees would use ignorance exposure to their detriment;
3 Their degree of psychological safety due to pertinent expertises and past successes;
4 Their habitus of either detachment/seductive-coercive involvement or vulnerable involvement;
5 Superiors' moral modeling: managers practiced CCMI-Im-C following superiors' Im-C and other immoral practices ("the fish stinks from the head"; Liu et al. 2012).[9]

The sixth contextual factor, discussed in Chapter 6, is the kibbutz field's prevalent sponsored mobility that encouraged practicing CCMI-Im-C by promising career advancement through patronage. In this field Northern's CEO Dan and his following by two PMs and their TMs were exceptions that emphasized the negative impact of detached, conservative, immoral CEOs on PMs' choice of CCMI-Im-C. While Dan allowed Gabi a second four-year term in view of his success, other CEOs allowed immoral PMs extra tenure due to loyalty rather than job success. CEOs also modeled Im-C by delaying the firing of failing managers in order to defend their own image, as did Zelikovich with Shavit and Avi. Merkaz CEOs modeled either nepotism or preference for other types of self-serving social ties, while amoral modeling was also Zelikovich's disregard of Yuval's vicious affair, known to everyone, for months during the high season. PMs mostly used CCMI not only because "parachuting" and *rotatzia* denied them incentives for ignorance exposure, but also because CEOs' Im-C encouraged it through modeling that encouraged CCMI, resulting in vicious distrust and ignorance cycles and ineffective, conservative, low-trust mismanagement, as well as encouragement for Im-C.

Both PMs and TMs practiced CCMI-Im-C and maintained detached ignorant superiors' trust, retaining their jobs despite mediocre functioning and/or irresponsible laziness (Lowland TM-1, V-TM). The dark secret of CCMI-Im-C constituted common knowledge among subordinates, many of whom emulated superiors' Im-C, distrusted them and their abuses and bluffs, and avoided communicating with them, as explained for instance by Lowland's proficient garage manager. PMs' CCMI-Im-C explained the prevalence of low-trust, conservative-prone cultures in a processing industry that was more innovative than Burns and Stalker's (1961) rayon industry and less than the electronic industry, while much more dependent on specialized know-how and *phronesis* than Crozier's (1964) tobacco industry. These findings warn against organizational literature's disregard of CCMI-Im-C, indicating that processing industries dependent on much specialized know-how and *phronesis* of operators, foremen, and technicians may suffer heavily from the ineffectiveness of "jumper" executives who practice CCMI and Im-C rather than risking their authority by vulnerable involvement aimed at learning and effective job functioning. As Collins and Weinel (2011) found, only socially learned know-how and *phronesis* enable one to discern experts from smart bluffers, impostors, and inexpert employees who talk experts' language and use local knowledge advantages to fool job-ignorant managers self-servingly.

The etiology of the successes of the few non-careerist, high-moral, vulnerably involved PMs and TMs resemble cases of exceptional successes by similarly behaving outsiders.[10] Among these few were prominent TMs such as Thomas and Yunus, who led plants to success despite the negative influence of ignorant "parachuted" bosses. The latter "rode" on the successes of vulnerably involved deputies and TMs, using the dark secrets of CCMI and Im-C for gaining power, prestige, and self-perpetuation. Job survival of these PMs often pruned out effective deputies and TMs or made them docile, keeping their jobs by deferring and forsaking reasonable innovations (e.g., Yunus). The secrecy of CCMI-Im-C helps explain how organizational research missed the negative impact of *rotatzia* and "parachuting" on executives' job functioning and morality, indicated by cited US and Israeli armed forces' critical studies and cited Wilson's (2011) assertion that Im-C executives "are so prevalent because bureaucracies are in effect designed by and for [immoral] careerists." Chapter 6 will explain that the studied executives did not design *rotatzia* and "parachutings," but many of them believed in their positive effect, advanced careers with their help, and did not try to change them as support for these practices was voiced/written by all Israeli researchers but two (Vald [1987] and myself).

A prominent case supporting my theory was the failure of Valley's PM David to create an effective goal-oriented, high-trust culture despite leading by trust and consent. Leaving all technical problems to V-TM and technicians spared him the effort of learning ginning up to achieving interactional expertise. Lacking such expertise, he trusted veteran V-TM, who used his discretion to defend his job rather than advance plant goals, concealing/camouflaging his incompetence by avoiding Israeli TMs and most American experts aside from a Californian unknown to other TMs. With partial learning, the PM's benevolence led to mismanagement, a warning against trusting assumedly competent mid-levelers without the superior's acquiring interactional expertise and seeking their real competence by involvement (see "The Emperor's New Clothes" syndrome below).

A contrary case was Southern's PM-1, who discerned TM-1's dysfunction and replaced him with Yunus who succeeded due to PM-2's encouragement and overcoming of four successive *rotational* "parachuted" ignorant PMs by compromising innovation and confining himself to technical and operational problems. Mistrust crept into his effective local high-trust culture as ignorant, detached *rotational* bosses engendered a low-trust plant culture, turnover, brain drain, and the rise to power of militant "brambles." These grasped Yunus as affiliated with untrustworthy *pe'ilim* bosses, as he did not care about hired employees' well-being, disrupting his nurturing of trustful relations by immoral means and industrial action, culminating in their firing.

Northern PM 4 Emanuel exemplified the failure to renovate the high-trust culture ruined by his predecessor. Emanuel's efforts to restore Gabi's trustful culture failed despite trustful relations with senior employees; as an absent PM similar to Lowland's Avraham, Emanuel's annual six-month absence and his substitution by a "parachuted" CCMI user *pa'il* did not restore the trustful culture. Quite similar to friendship relations, trust relations are personal and not so transitive (McCall et al. 2010); Emanuel could not convey trust in him to a deputy user of distrustful practice of detached CCMI, resulting in conflicts and "Italian strikes." But as staff mostly consisted of veteran expert ginners united behind their leader TM-3, distrust did not cause brain drain, turnover, and docility as at Lowland; detached, ignorant, distrusted *pe'ilim* PM 5 and PM 6 faced staff demoralized by conflicts but united and proud of ginning expertise, backed by the powerful Histadrut General Union; hence they did not try to carry out wholesale dismissals as done by Southern's PM-5.

High-trust cultures proved elusive and dependent on high-moral leaders committed to plant goals (Shapira 2012) who created a "we" feeling with employees (Haslam et al. 2011) and managers who followed their modeling knowledge acquired through vulnerable involvement. Such cultures were nadir for the additional reason that many of PMs' functions did not relate to problems discussed in staff deliberations, helping the majority of PMs defend their authority and jobs without knowing the trade. TMs' functions invited the opposite behavior of involvement as an immediate way of solving problems, indwelling in ginners' coping and learning-by-doing, being taught their language and gaining interactional expertise for communicating and effectively managing them; hence TMs mostly succeeded in creating high-trust shop-floor cultures and created a "we" feeling with ginner staff. This process was easier for hired TMs who were socially closer to hired staff (Wilson et al. 2008), but this was a minor factor; the major one was TMs' high-moral signaling practices: venerably involved *pe'ilim* TMs created a "we" feeling just as hired TMs did, proving that the manager's practices were the decisive factor for creating trust. This way all vulnerably engaged TMs succeeded, while TMs who practiced CCMI-Im-C retained their jobs by detachment (Avi) or by guarded involvement, exposing incompetence only to a far-away Californian not connected to other Israelis (V-TM).

Vulnerably involved TMs succeeded even when ignorant PMs limited their learning by barring participation in professional meetings and in business tours abroad, which concealed their own ignorance, spared its exposure by meetings and tours. This measure did not stop *pe'ilim* TMs who overruled their PMs' objections through the legitimization provided by their task needs and supported by fellow *pe'ilim* TMs of other gin plants, while such *pe'ilim* also used the advantage of having company cars to travel to meetings on plant expense. Hired TMs such as Northern's TM-3 could not overrule their *pe'ilim* bosses as they jeopardized jobs; this TM accused the boss of not striving for optimal ginning, but the ginning-ignorant PM showed little interest in optimal ginning, much as expert ginner Nekhas said about Shavit:

> "Every morning Shavit would drop into [the control room], just to ask how many bales we produced that night, never asking the more important questions: what fiber quality did we produce or how much cotton did we burn."

Northern's involved and trusted PMs 1, 2, and 4 behaved otherwise, modeled prime concern for fiber quality and for minimal cotton losses during processing; their modeling was a prime reason for Northern's high-trust, innovation-prone culture for its first 12 years, which was partially resumed during Emanuel's years and engendered managerial competence. Hence Northern was effectively managed for some 14 of the 21 years studied, i.e., some 67% of its studied history. Other plants show the following bleak picture:

1   Merkaz enjoyed effective management during four of its first six years, from the third year of Yaakov's and Aharon's learning gining basics until Aharon left, and some two to three years of Thomas's five, only when he became a knowledgeable ginner—that is some 8.5 of the 19 years studied, i.e. some 37% of its history.

2   Lowland enjoyed effective management only during TM-1's first three to four years and during the last three to four years of L-TM-2, when he learned and enjoyed much discretion since Yatzek was busy lobbying his jump to the larger plant, and when PM-4 replaced him—that is seven of the 20 years studied, i.e. some 35% of its history.

3   Valley is harder to measure; for all its 27 years mediocre V-TM caused ineffectiveness, while for 15 years of them David's restricted involvement generated trust relations which made him effective at most for some three to five years, after an initial learning period and before entering a dysfunction phase of complying with V-TM's mediocrity; hence only three to five years of effective management, i.e., some 15% of its history.

4   Southern is also hard to measure; effective PM periods were PM-1's last year with TM Yunus after his initial learning, four years of encouraging PM-2, and only a few intermittent years during the time of PMs 3–6, when Yunus circumvented PMs' negative impact. Thus, the estimation is that Southern's effective management consisted of seven to eight years out of 20, i.e., some 37% of its history.

In conclusion, versus Northern's effective management about 67% of the time, the four other plants enjoyed such management only 32% of the time on average.

The four plants were not that exceptional, compared to studies cited on p. 23 which found 50–95% of managers incompetent, i.e., 72% on average versus the four gin plants that were mismanaged 68% of the time on average. However, unlike previous studies that explained managerial incompetence psychologically by stupidity (Wagner 2002), by being oligarchic fools and impostors (Kets De Vries 1993), by psychopathy (Boddy et al. 2010), and by hubris, narcissism and other bad traits (Judge et al. 2009), my findings explain it processually and relationally, by the impact of careers and relationships managers create throughout the different phases of their tenure (Hambrick 2007). Psychological and other personal characteristics impact these processes and relationships, while my findings emphasize the indirect but decisive impact of managers' choice of either trust and learning-generating vulnerable involvement or detachment/seductive-coercive involvement that generates contrasting cycles. The latter two choices by the majority kept them job-incompetent and passively or actively engendered mismanagement, in accord with the pessimistic views of the two cotton industry experts cited on p. 9.

Detached PMs did less damage to plant functioning than seduction-coercion PMs, since they often granted discretion to vulnerably involved deputies and TMs who were mostly effective competents. Only one PM of 22, Gabi, became truly competent by such a choice, and four other PMs who had no mechanical education and experience acquired interactional expertise (Collins and Evans 2007) by vulnerable involvement and learned enough to enhance plants' efficiency and effectiveness by high-trust innovation-prone cultures. Sixteen of the 17 job-ignorant PMs successfully used CCMI-Im-C to remain for a full term or even longer, particularly those who granted discretion to vulnerably involved deputies and TMs while these PMs "rode" on TMs' successes and presented an image of success to detached ignorant CEOs, who missed their mismanagement or ignored it for immoral reasons. The opposite proportion was found among TMs: seven of 10 became competent and job-effective as they chose vulnerable involvement due to the above cited reasons and since the features of the TM job encouraged this, contrary to PMs' jobs. Although TMs could survive in jobs as detached or seductive-coercive CCMI users, these required abuses and subterfuges which were bound to cause mistakes and failures that jeopardized their job and authority (e.g., Avi); hence TMs mostly chose otherwise.

These findings emphasize the negative impact of concomitant *rotatzia* and "parachuting" of job-ignorant outsiders, which encourage CCMI-Im-C. Only a few *pe'ilim* were effective, as *rotatzia* encouraged such "parachutings" and such "parachutings" plus prospects of *rotatzia* within a few years encouraged CCMI-Im-C, which was especially detrimental for CEOs' leadership: their detached CCMI deprived PMs and TMs of any trusted, effective supreme authority and its positive modeling; CEOs rarely interfered to prevent/stop debacles such as the S&GH in Merkaz or the lint cleaner in Valley, nor did they have any discernible effect on negative processes such as brain drain, turnover, and the rise of troublemaker "brambles" due to mismanagement (also next chapter); when a CEO replaced a PM after conspicuous failure he did it only late (Zelikovich). *Pe'ilim*'s "parachutings" were legitimized by kibbutzim's interest in having I-KRC managers care for their interests, but this care rarely materialized due to prevalent immoral mismanagement enhanced by detached CEOs: Yuval's mismanagement stretched on for four years until conspicuous moral failure caused his late firing; the detached CCMI of Merkaz's Moav, and Lowland's Avraham were rewarded by overruling *rotatzia* for 10 and 12 years, respectively, prolonging their mismanagement beyond retirement age; Lowland's Yatzek's eight years of mismanaged, ignorant autocracy was rewarded by promotion to lead a much larger I-KRC plant.

However, the CCMI-Im-C complex engendered other negative processes that worsened mismanagement by "parachuted" *rotational pe'ilim*. These processes contributed meaningfully to maintaining and deepening vicious distrust and ignorance cycles while they were mostly unknown to plants' owner kibbutzim and detached CEOs, and new "jumpers" mostly repeated the negative CCMI-Im-C practices and continued mismanagement. This is the subject of the next chapter that is based mostly on Merkaz's findings.

Notes

1 Interviews mostly took place at interviewees' homes. The few most knowledgeable were interviewed twice or for three to four hours. Plants' annuals summarized both regional cotton crops and ginning results.
2 The 1960s tractor-pulled cages limited the storage capacity of picked raw cotton much more than the 1970s stretches; in the 1970s cotton was also stored in compressed heaps on the ground, over metal nets that enabled cranes to subsequently lift them onto stretches or lorries.
3 Arbiv was interviewed twice on visits to Israel.
4 Moshavin were village cooperatives of individual farmers.
5 Regional Councils are rural municipal statutory governments, each in charge of a region's settlements. The Lowland Council is in charge of seven settlements with some 3,000 residents.
6 The Jewish Agency was and still is the operational organ of the World Zionist Organization.
7 Cubic feet per minute.
8 Many considered kibbutz members "blue blood" as they were mostly Ashkenzis, like higher Israeli strata.

9 Liu et al. (2012); Piff et al. (2012); Trevino et al. (2003).
10 See: Bennis (1989); Guest (1962); Semler (1993); Useem et al. (2011); Washburn (2011).

References

Arad, Nurit. 1995. More secret than the nuclear reactor, larger than the Electric Corporation. *Yedi'ot Achronot*, September 15 (Hebrew).

Armstrong, Peter. 1987. Engineers, management and trust. *Work, Employment and Society* 1(4): 421–440.

Bennis, Warren. 1989. *Why Leaders Can't Lead*. San Francisco: Jossey-Bass.

Blau, Peter M. 1955. *The Dynamics of Bureaucracy*. Chicago: University of Chicago Press.

Boddy, Clive R. P., R. Ladyshewsky, and P. Galvin. 2010. Leaders without ethics in global business: Corporate psychopaths. *Journal of Public Affairs* 10(1): 121–138.

Burns, Tom, and Gerald M. Stalker. 1961. *The Management of Innovation*. London: Tavistock.

Chan, Simon C. H. 2014. Paternalistic leadership and employee voice: Does information sharing matter? *Human Relations* 67(6): 667–693.

Collins, Harry M., and Robert Evans. 2007. *Rethinking Expertise*. Chicago: University of Chicago Press.

Collins, Harry M., and Martin Weinel. 2011. Transmuted expertise: How technical non-experts can assess experts and expertise. *Argumentation* 25: 401–415.

Collinson, David. 2005. Questions of distance. *Leadership* 1(2): 235–250.

Crozier, Michel. 1964. *The Bureaucratic Phenomenon*. Chicago: University of Chicago Press.

Cunha, Miguel P. E. 2002. 'The best place to be': Managing control and employee loyalty in a knowledge-intensive company. *Journal of Applied Behavioural Science* 38(4): 481–495.

Deutsch, Morton. 1969. Conflicts: Productive and destructive. *Journal of Social Issues* 25(1): 7–42.

Dineen, Brian R., R. J. Lewicki, and E. C. Tomlinson. 2006. Supervisory guidance and behavioural integrity: Relationships with employee citizenship and deviant behaviour. *Journal of Applied Psychology* 91(3): 622–633.

Fairholm, Matthew R. 2004. A new sciences outline for leadership development. *The Leadership and Organization Development Journal* 25(4): 369–383.

Fast, Nathanel J., Ethan R. Burris, and Caroline A. Bartel. 2014. Managing to stay in the dark: Managerial self-efficacy, ego-defensiveness, and the aversion to employee voice. *Academy of Management Journal* 57(4): 1013–1034.

Fine, Garry A. 2012. *Tiny Publics: Idiocultures and the Power of the Local*. New York: Russell Sage.

Flyvbjerg, Bent. 2001. *Making Social Science Matter*. Cambridge: Cambridge University Press.

Fox, Alan. 1974. *Beyond Contract*. London: Faber.

Geneen, Herold. 1984. *Managing*. New York: Avon.

Goldratt, Eliyahu M., and Jeff Cox. 1992. *The Goal*. Great Barrington (MA): North River.

Gouldner, Alvin W. 1954. *Patterns of Industrial Bureaucracy*. New York: Free Press.

Grint, Keith, and Clare Holt. 2011. Leading questions: If 'Total Place', 'Big Society' and local leadership are then answers: What's the question? *Leadership* 7(1): 85–98.

Guest, Robert H. 1962. *Organizational Change*. London: Tavistock.

Hambrick, Donald C. 2007. Upper echelons theory: An update. *Academy of Management Review* 32(2): 334–343.

Haslam, S. Alexander, S. D. Reicher and M. J. Platow. 2011. *The New Psychology of Leadership*. New York: Psychology Press.

Hosmer, Larue T. 1995. Trust: The connecting link between organizational theory and philosophical ethics. *Academy of Management Review* 20(3): 379–403.

Ingvaldsen, Jonas A., Helvor Holtskog, and Geir Ringen. 2013. Unlocking work standards through systematic work observation: Implications for team supervision. *Team Performance Management* 19(5/6): 279–291.

Jaques, Elliot. 1990. *Creativity and Work*. Madison (CN): International Universities.

Jonas, Hans. 1996. *The Creativity of Action*. Cambridge: Polity.

Judge, Timothy A., R. F. Piccolo, et al. 2009. The bright and dark sides of leader traits: A review and theoretical extension of the leader trait paradigm. *The Leadership Quarterly* 20(4): 855–875.

Kets De Vries, Manfred F. R. 1993. *Leaders, Fools, and Impostors*. San Francisco: Jossey-Bass.

Klein, Gary. 1998. *Sources of Power*. Cambridge (MA): MIT Press.

Kruger, Justin, and David Dunning. 1999. Unskilled and unaware of it: How difficulties in recognizing one's own incompetence lead to inflated self-assessments. *Journal of Personal and Social Psychology* 77(6): 1121–1134.

Liu, Dong, H. Liao, and R. Loi. 2012. The dark side of leadership: A three-level investigation of the cascading effect of abusive supervision on employee creativity. *Academy of Management Journal* 55(5): 1187–1212.

McCall, G. J., M. M. McCall, et al. (Eds.). 2010. *Friendship as a Social Institution*. New Brunswick: Transaction.

McGregor, Douglas. 1960. *The Human Side of Enterprise*. New York: McGraw-Hill.

Mehri, Darius. 2005. *Notes from Toyota-Land*. Ithaca (NY): ILR Press.

Michels, Robert. 1959[1915]. *Political Parties*. New York: Dover.

Milliken, Frances J., Elizabeth W. Morrison, and Patricia F. Hewlin. 2003. An exploratory study of employee silence: Issues that employees don't communicate upward and why. *Journal of Management Studies* 40(6): 1453–1476.

Moss, Sherry E., J. I. Sanchez, et al. 2009. The mediating role of feedback avoidance behavior in the LMX—performance relationship. *Group & Organization Management* 34(6): 645–664.

Nienaber, Ann-Marie, V. Holtorf, et al. 2015. A climate of psychological safety enhances the success of front end teams. *International Journal of Innovation Management* 19(2). DOI: 10.1142/S1363919615500279.

Norman, Steven M., Bruce J. Avolio, and Fred Luthans. 2010. The impact of positivity and transparency on trust in leaders and their perceived effectiveness. *The Leadership Quarterly* 21(3): 350–364.

Orlikowski, Wanda J. 2002. Knowing in practice: Enacting a collective capability in distributed organizing. *Organization Science* 13(3): 249–273.

O'Toole, James. 1999. *Leadership from A to Z*. San Francisco: Jossey-Bass.

Parker, Martin. 2000. *Organizational Culture and Identity*. London: Sage.

Parkinson, C. Nortcote, N. Selvin, et al. 1973. *Industrial Disruption*. London: Leviathan House.

Piff, Paul K., D. M. Stancato, et al. 2012. Higher social class predicts increased unethical behaviour. *Proceedings of the National Academy of Science*. Retrieved 8.8.2013: www.pnas.org./cgi/doi/10.1073/1118373109

Poulin, Bryan J., M. Z. Hackman, and C. Barbarasa-Mihai. 2007. Leadership and succession: The challenge to succeed and the vortex of failure. *Leadership* 3(3): 301–325.

Semler, Ricardo. 1993. *Maverick*. New York: Warner.

Shapira, Reuven. 2008. *Transforming Kibbutz Research*. Cleveland: New World Publishing.

Shapira, Reuven. 2012. High-trust culture, the decisive but elusive context of shared co-operative leaderships. In: J. Heiskanen et al. (Eds.), *New Opportunities for Co-Operatives: New Opportunities for People*. Mikkeli, Finland: University of Helsinki Press, 154–167. http://www.helsinki.fi/ruralia/julkaisut/pdf/Publica tions27.pdf

Shapira, Reuven. 2015. Prevalent concealed ignorance of low-moral careerist managers: Contextualization by a semi-native multi-site Strathernian ethnography. *Management Decision* 53(7): 1504–1526. http://dx.doi.org/10.1108/md-10–2014–0620

Shepher, Israel. 1983. *The Kibbutz: An Anthropological Study*. Norwood (PA): Norwood Editions.

Simons, Tony. 2002. Behavioural integrity: The perceived alignment between managers' words and deeds as a research focus. *Organization Science* 13(1): 18–35.

Soekijad, Maura, B., Van den Hooff, et al. 2011. Leading to learn in networks of practice: Two leadership strategies. *Organization Studies* 32(8): 1005–1028.

Trevino, Linda K., M. Brown, and L. P. Hartman. 2003. A qualitative investigation of perceived executive ethical leadership: Perceptions from inside and outside the executive suite. *Human Relations* 56(1): 5–37.

Useem, Michael, R. Jordan, and M. Koljatic. 2011. How to lead during a crisis: Lessons from the rescue of the Chilean miners. *Sloan Management Review* 53(1): 48–55.

Vald, Emanuel. 1987. *The Curse of the Broken Tools*. Jerusalem: Schocken (Hebrew).

Wagner, Richard K. 2002. Smart people doing dumb things: The case of managerial incompetence. In: R. K. Sternberg (Ed.), *Why Smart People Can Be So Stupid*. New Haven: Yale University Press, 42–63.

Washburn, Kevin K. 2011. Elena Kagan and the miracle at Harvard. *Journal of Legal Education* 61(1): 67–75.

Wilson, George C. 2011. Careerism. In: W. T. Wheeler (Ed.), *The Pentagon Labyrinth*. Washington (DC): Center for Defense Information, 43–59.

Wilson, Jeanne M., M. B. O'Leary et al. 2008. Perceived proximity in virtual work: Explaining the paradox of far-but-close. *Organization Studies* 29(7): 979–1002.

5   Other Negative Processes of Low-Trust "Jumping" Cultures that Furthered Mismanagement

The Rise to Power of the "Brambles" Syndrome

The Book of Judges in the Holy Bible explains the rise to power of Abimelech, Judge Jerubaal's son, by a parable brought by his other son, Jotham, on the bramble that became king of the trees: the olive tree, the fig tree, and the grapevine refused to assume kingship and to rule over the trees as this would stop them from furnishing beloved fruits; the bramble, which has no fruit of value, happily accepted power and, when crowned, warned that its fire would burn any non-abiding tree (Judges 9: 8–16). Shrewd, astute ineffective employees who seek power and promotion without performing are ubiquitous. *Rotatzia* and "parachutings" encouraged outsider managers to practice CCMI-Im-C, which was fertile ground for the ascendance of employees who became "bramble"-like rulers. Douglas McGregor warns in *The Human Side of the Enterprise* (1960) that managerial adherence to Theory X, to the belief that employees are lazy and unconcerned about their company, hence only seducing and coercing them by tight control could cause them to fulfill their duties, leaves employees no opportunity to fulfill higher needs, encouraging their self-serving behavior up to recalcitrance; such a policy elevates to power the worst troublemakers, wrote McGregor. Jotham's parable explains this elevation: tight control leaves no room for the talented, high-moral best "olives," "figs," and "grapevines" to lead employees' contributions to the common goals by which they can obtain respect, prestige, and social status, hence they forsake employees' leadership; the "brambles" who cannot achieve prestige and status by performing fill the vacuum, gain such advantages by power politics of servility and ingratiation to superiors as well as coercing and exploiting the weaker beneath them, as Atad did at Merkaz. CCMI-Im-C–practicing executives often covertly prefer "brambles" as employees' formal/informal leaders, as they are ready for immoral covert deals unacceptable by decent employees. "Brambles," for instance, thrive as "two-way funnels": they serve the autocrat's needs for spying on employees and for a speakerphone that notifies them of his demands and expectations (Dalton 1959: 232), as Atad served Shavit and as another "bramble" served Moav.

Management literature has long since stressed the danger of managers of limited capability surrounding themselves with like people or even incompetents whose views they often ignore (e.g., Fast et al. 2014). However, due to minimal research of managerial ignorance, another major reason for such actions was missed, i.e., ignorance and incompetence due to opting for CCMI-Im-C and engendering vicious distrust and ignorance cycles. "Parachuting" creates a combination that is especially convenient to the rise of "brambles" to power: "parachuted" managers are very much in need of allies with some experience in the plant who accept their authority and supply essential local knowledge. Knowledgeable employees wait for proof of the newcomer's trustworthiness before sharing information and knowledge, while even a "bramble's" meager inside knowledge is a treasure for CCMI-Im-C–practicing outsiders, for which they are ready to pay generously, particularly "jumpers" who know very little about a plant's know-how and *phronesis* and next to nothing about its staff's expertises. A CCMI using "jumper" is unable to discern the ignorance and incompetence of "brambles" and their cover-up by bluffs, scapegoating, "old wives' tales," and other subterfuges; he elevates the "brambles' " status in return for their help, which expert employees denies her/him without proving trustworthiness. This explains how the "bramble" Atad rose to the powerful position of de facto TM, which he held at Merkaz after Avi's authority collapsed, 11 years after Yaakov failed to dispose of him and after foremen objected to employing this lazy bum on their teams; but Moav retained him as a cheap worker.

Chapter 2 depicted Atad's behavior and the main stages of his rise to power; while each stage posed obstacles, he overcame them, assisted by "parachuting" defects. "Parachuted" deputy PM Yuval did not know that his predecessor Yaakov had failed to fire Atad, nor did he know of Atad's loafing, bluffing, and subterfuges; Atad created the image of an ordinary loyal worker by using ingratiation and a short-lived radical positive change of behavior, and Yuval kept him despite complaints by Levi and others as he was cheap. Then CCMI-user Avi took charge and sought insiders' help; Atad as a provisional worker offered to help in return for a permanent job that Avi granted him. Soon came professional Thomas and Atad was in real trouble; Thomas disqualified Atad's weldings time after time. Atad conscripted Avi, Yiftach, and two friends to side with him against Thomas, who was busy learning ginning and rescuing the plant, clashing with Amram and Levi on some technical decisions, some of which were mistaken. Atad troubled Thomas but was not fired, both due to his allies and due to the difficulty of finding a better replacement. Then Amram told Atad of his intention to leave as Thomas entrenched and became a successful TM. Atad was quick to discern this promotion opportunity and completely changed his behavior to take advantage of it by becoming Thomas's loyalist. After Amram left, Thomas sought a replacement from the outside but failed; then the high season began and a shift foreman was needed after Yiftach replaced

Amram as senior technician, and despite his reservations Thomas promoted the seemingly loyal Atad to shift foreman.

This was a mistake, as Thomas later admitted, but it was irreversible; soon Atad targeted and achieved another power position, head of the union committee instead of weak foreman Rabina. As mentioned, he agitated against the committee, accused it of allowing Yuval to demote and cut the salary of an experienced operator who was injured in a work accident. Rabina had only recently replaced the highly trusted prestigious Levi who left; Rabina was quite inept both due to inexperience and to his unwilling assumption of the job, only to please his fellow foremen friends. Acting on a popular demand for work injury compensation insurance which the Committee avoided demanding, Atad and his clique replaced Rabina and his supporters and obtained the insurance by an "Italian strike" ahead of the high season. Had Yuval not believed in Theory X, listened to employees' feelings, and avoided the above salary cut, he could have spared the insurance money, the costly "Italian strike", and above all Atad's empowerment.

Shavit replaced Yuval and his detached ignorance revived Moav's stinginess: he made small but very antagonizing expense cuts which oiled Atad's negative campaigns; for instance, he stopped the free supply of milk to ginners, aimed at helping them cope with the gin plant's dusty air during high season. Worse still, he declared that "the plant staff is sub-standard," meaning he would replace ginners with no technical secondary education certificate with younger certified graduates. This move was stupid on four counts:

1   Technical education is less crucial for becoming a good ginner than experience and talent, as proved by both Yunus and the uneducated best ginner, Nekhas (below);
2   It takes years to learn ginning, hence replacement can only be gradual; the threat of forthcoming dismissals at an unknown time demotivated ginners;
3   It encouraged the brain drain of talented ginners to alternative jobs, while few if any certified graduates applied for ginner jobs considered unattractive in the job market;
4   The staff's standard had already been degraded by the departure of Levi, Amram, and the expert electrician; by supporting Thomas's efforts at enhancing high-trust culture Shavit could create a more attractive workplace and improve staff's ginning know-how, but he did the opposite.

Shavit's stupidity played into Atad's hands: Shavit antagonized the hired staff and diminished their morality and motivation. This made the support of Atad and his union committee clique essential for Thomas's efforts to motivate hired staff, despite Shavit's demotivating policy. Atad was also empowered in another way: Shavit's moves had further antagonized *pe'ilim* Thomas, Danton, the electrician, and garage manager; this left him isolated and uninformed about most domains; Atad became his two-way funnel while formally visiting his office to discuss union matters. Thus, both the PM and the TM were dependent on Atad so any idea of firing this lazy, loafing, highly remunerated ignorant troublemaker became implausible. When another technician left, Atad was promoted to technician and no longer had to work shifts; every shift foreman who faced unsolved problems or hesitated concerning major decisions was supposed to call in Yiftach or Atad for help—another empowering change.

When Thomas left and Avi became the real TM rather than only in title, Avi's ignorance required help and Atad obtained it in return for de-facto promotion to Deputy TM, above Yiftach and above certified practical engineer Yehu, the new *pa'il* imported to serve as a Deputy TM. Avi's promotion let Atad usurp his authority when it collapsed with Shavit's acceptance or even secret backing. Until then Avi tried to limit Atad's power by curtailed discretion. For instance, Atad was sent to solve the automatic sampler's problems after Avi failed, but he was not allowed to travel to the other plant whose managers invited Merkaz technicians to learn about their smoothly working sampler. Failing Atad abandoned the sampler and left it blocked despite Avi's demands to continue attempts to make it operational, one of the first signs of the collapse of Avi's authority.

The Low-Trust Culture of CCMI-Im-C Was an Opportunity for the "Brambles"

Atad's rise to power was not simply the result of a series of incidental managerial errors of the kind that every manager makes when judging employees' capabilities and aspirations, but largely a result of a low-trust culture of secrecy, information abuse, scapegoating, bluffing, and other subterfuges by three consecutive "parachuted" CCMI-Im-C–practicing PMs who made inevitable mistakes. In Merkaz's low-trust culture, knowledge and information were used as means of controlling others rather than of serving common aims. Atad rose to power due to his astute use of advantageous insider knowledge to win over ignorant bosses whose mistaken decisions missed his dismal functioning record, misled by short-lived behavior changes that created a positive image. His career progression repeatedly profited from "jumper" ignorance that concealed the dangers of employing and promoting such a "bramble."

If Moav had not been detached and had known how much ginning ignorance could fail his decision-making, he would have chosen to learn ginners' basic language and expertise and gained interactional expertise like deputy Yaakov. Then he might have understood and accepted Yaakov's insistence on firing Atad, as he might have learned how easy it is to conceal incompetence by astute use of the automatic ginning system's complexities, as exemplified by Avi's misleading of Shavit for six weeks concerning the mistaken contour of the S&GH piping. Had Moav escorted Yaakov and Levi to the shop floor and understood why Levi said, "I would not rely on his [Atad's] welding if it had anything to do with carrying heavy weights," he might have approved Atad's dismissal. Unfortunately, in order to discern unreliable from reliable welding Moav would have had to expose his ignorance of welding and learn its basics to be able to communicate with welders and gain discerning capability, i.e., acquire interactional expertise. By such an acquiring Moav could discern Atad as "bramble" and rid of him before he entrenched while Moav would have proved his high-moral trustworthiness (Hosmer 1995), enhanced expert employees' trust, and become insider to their "we" group (Haslam et al. 2011). It would have enhanced open communication with experts (Thomas et al. 2009), invited complaints about other bluffer bums and their weeding out, to the plant's benefit, as proven by Gabi's weeding at Northern. But Moav kept Atad and he continued his loafing despite whistle blowing on his laziness and advanced by using immoral means as depicted.

However, Thomas's mistaken promotion of Atad proves that even a vulnerably involved "jumper" who is quite familiar with a subordinate's incompetence and loafing may be misled to believe in his faked good intentions due to timely ingratiation and provisional behavioral change. A major reason for Thomas's mistake was the common Achilles' heel of "parachutists," unfamiliarity with employees' past record and chance of repeating it. Thomas did not know how Atad had misled Yuval and Avi and received promotions through provisional behavioral changes; if he came from the inside he would probably have known about Atad's past camouflages and/ or noticed foremen's avoidance of Atad and would have paid attention to his abrupt behavioral change. A second reason for his mistake was also caused by "parachuting": his greenhorn clashing with Amram and Levi about his mistaken professional decisions prevented them from warning him about the dangers of Atad's promotion. In Gabi's Northern Gin or any other plant managed by trustworthy, vulnerably involved insiders, Atad would probably have been dismissed at an early stage unless he changed his behavior permanently. In such a high-trust culture promotion is slow (Dore 1973), hence he would have had to prove himself years before promotion.

Worse still, Atad exploited Thomas's deficient acquaintance with locals. Thomas became a top-level ginner but this only slightly helped him discern employees' intentions, proclivities, and goals, while Atad specialized in this task in order to keep job despite incompetence; he retained his neutrality when Thomas clashed with Amram and Levi, and when they left he became Thomas's loyalist. As mentioned, Thomas faced a demotivated, demoralized staff due to Avi's failed first season as TM and then Shavit's threat of firing uncertified employees. Ingratiating Atad seemed to offer valuable assistance in solving the staff's motivation problem as he led the union committee clique. In Jotham's parable, the bramble fire burns any non-abiding tree and, similarly, this clique subdued all senior veterans, misleading Thomas to believe that this promised him obedience. Danton discerned that the opposite was true, openly criticized Atad and called him "the biggest liar" in front of shop-floor staff meeting in the shade of the office building, but seemingly neither he nor Thomas actively objected to Atad's vicious leadership; maybe they did not notice how he helped their opponent Shavit as a "two-way funnel" or/and they apprehended Atad's power secretly backed by Shavit.

However, not only Atad misled CCMI-user "parachuted" managers—all his clique members did, concealing from managers mistakes and failures or scapegoating non-clique members for them (Dalton 1959: 57–68). When I was a participant observer, three years after this clique gained dominance, all its members were shift foremen whose support of Atad crowned him the de facto TM when Avi's authority collapsed. Throughout the previous seven years since Yaakov tried to fire Atad, ignorant "parachuted" managers missed clique members' mediocrity, negative character, and aims, which helped their ascendance. The managers missed these also due to screened and biased information; as much as managers used information to control employees, the reverse was also true. Even during the three years of Thomas-Danton's high-trust shop-floor culture (p. 64), the plant's dominant culture was low-trust and secrecy prevailed between most *pe'ilim* and hired employees, as well as between Atad's clique and rival veterans. The high-trust culture was limited to the jurisdictions of the four *pe'ilim*; elsewhere there was no open communication.

This resembled phenomena characteristic of other plants: "parachuted" PMs mostly practiced CCMI-Im-C and generated low-trust cultures although the majority of TMs chose to do otherwise in order to function effectively, trying to nurture high-trust shop-floor cultures but often failing due to PMs' contrary impact. This suggests that the "brambles" advance was less explained by the personalities involved than by structural and processual factors. The prime factor elevating "brambles" was "parachuted" PMs' opting for CCMI-Im-C by detachment or by seductive-coercive involvement, believing in "Theory X" and shaping low-trust cultures.

Merkaz's secrecy climate effected my study: throughout the season Atad stubbornly rejected my plea for an interview, but at the season's end on my last work day he came to the registrar's cabin, stood by me for almost five hours (with a few distractions), and dictated his views and assertions on 10 pages written in the 1/2–3/4-minute pauses I had between registering one bale to the next. Many of his assertions were answers to my critical comments in my journal pages held under the registration documents, exposing that his clique spied on me and informed him, although I had repeatedly promised that no one would be hurt by possible future publication of my findings.[1] The spying also testified to the low-trust culture in which Atad, the astute politician, thrived by keeping his cards close to his chest.

One month later I interviewed Atad for two hours; the 20 pages of the two interviews further explain how he and other "brambles" managed to ascend due to immoral mismanagement. He explained proficient ginner Amram's departure as not only a result of Avi's "parachuting," which prevented him from succeeding TM Muli, but also of the many clashes with Yuval's ignorant, amateurish autocracy that pushed out expert ginners, coercing Amram to repeatedly teach greenhorns, suffer their mistakes, and see them leave after acquiring expertise because of hating Yuval's ignorant interfering and stupid orders. Atad depicted Yuval's arbitrariness thus:

> "In Yuval's time there was no Board [control] above him—he did what he wished or to be precise what his lover secretary wished."

Amram was particularly annoyed by the dismissal of a very talented ginner whom even Yuval liked, simply because the ginner dared to have a cup of coffee with Yuval's lover secretary when driving her home one evening. Even if another reason caused his firing, Atad's belief in this arbitrariness, which other employees similarly uttered, further explains the distrust of Yuval, which encouraged brain drain—the opportunity of the "brambles."

Outsiderness and "The Emperor's New Clothes" Syndrome

The "brambles" thrived in Merkaz and in other "jumper"-managed gin plants also because specialized knowledge is a wonderful resource, enabling us to do things we had never dreamed of, but it is a fluid resource that requires suitable training and experience. One lesson learned from Andersen's "The Emperor's New Clothes" is that in order to effectively impact experts' behavior a superior needs more than intuition and general knowledge; he needs minimal knowledge of experts' concepts and their meanings (Collins 2011) and interactional expertise that allows one to judge the degree of truthfulness and validity of their assertions (Collins and Evans 2007). Anyone who claims that the manager does not need to know everything because he has experts who specialize in the problems he is facing and can offer solutions must answer how the manager decides who the experts are. The fact that Avi was a certified practical engineer and that he was called "TM" does not prove TM expertise; CCMI-user Shavit, who missed his own ignorance, presumed that Avi had learned enough throughout his 5.5 years at Merkaz and could serve as TM. He soon fell victim to TM Avi's bluff or ignorance that the contour of the S&GH piping was "a marginal problem," as the emperor fell victim to the bluffs of his ministers trapped by the swindlers in a trap that the emperor tried to avoid by sending his ministers before going himself.

Fear of exposing their own ignorance and incompetence is a strong covert motivator of many power-holders, one missed by management research. This is particularly true of non-owner executives whose legitimization for office is supposedly having the pertinent knowledge and competence to manage and lead, hence they seek a knowledgeable and competent image. A basic feature of knowledge and competence tempts them to fake such an image: the ultimate test of having these resources is successful use that achieves results plus the capability to explain failure to achieve them and the competence to overcome it. One can firmly judge others' expertise only by witnessing its use, but in the case of a trade that one has never practiced, judging their explanations for specific outcomes requires learning by vulnerable involvement in their deliberations because "practical wisdom and judgment . . . emerging developmentally within an unceasing flow of activities in which practitioners are . . . immersed" (Shotter and Tsoukas 2014b: 377). Promoted insiders are no different than outsiders, with a lack of "practical wisdom and judgment" of many expertises in their new/enlarged jurisdictions which they never experienced; but if they advance by proved performance achieved through trustful learning cycles they differ radically from outsiders with regard to knowing and understanding basic trade concepts and *phronesis* that even a vulnerably involved outsider may learn only after years on the job because these concepts and *phronesis* can often only be learned from specific events.

One basic *phronesis* of ginning is that the flow of cotton through the large serpentine pipes is complex, intricate, and unforeseeable, such that even experts are often unsure how cotton will flow in the piping they designed, and in order to solve a flow problem they often require several trials until finding a solution. Experienced ginners know this basic *phronesis* as they have witnessed experts using trial-and-error to find the right piping. Finding it may require considerable effort: to correct Avi's mistaken design of the S&GH feeding pipe, 10 meters of serpentine, 30-inch-diameter pipe had to be added (p. 60). The same is true for finding the proper air blast and condenser: Valley's V-TM worked three years with "all the big names of the lint cleaner's US manufacturer" until he managed to fit the condenser to the air blast (p. 130). An insider, even a non-ginner such as a store manager, could learn such *phronesis* in the S&GH debacle when his work schedule changed due to a 10-hour production stoppage to repair piping. An outsider manager, and especially a "parachuted" industry-outsider as were *pe'ilim*, could not know this *phronesis*, as he never witnessed it. Without this *phronesis* Shavit did not suspect Avi's bluff/ignorant view when he said that piping contour was "a marginal problem," did not listen to Nekhas and others' contrary assertion, nor did he try to check it himself though it was simple. Likewise, Valley's "parachuted" PM David missed V-TM's mediocrity by keeping a distance from technical problems and not knowing V-TM's prior years of failure to solve two major technical problems.

Use of CCMI ensured such oversights since it barred "jumpers" from learning the necessary basics of the trade, to discern CCMI users. At the time of the S&GH debacle Shavit had been on the job for four years; I assessed him as more intelligent and as experienced in lengthier managerial jobs than most of the other 21 PMs studied, but he nevertheless missed Avi's bluff/ignorance. An experienced insider, knowing the *phronesis* that piping mistakes could cause major dysfunction, would have suspected Avi's assertion, and if used to learning by vulnerable involvement he would have climbed the blocked S&GH and probably discerned Avi's bluff. Unfortunately, outsider Shavit had enjoyed four successful years of detached CCMI with TM Thomas; why should he change his successful strategy and become involved in checking Avi's assertion? Shavit lacked referred expertise (Collins and Sanders 2007) for assessing the assertion and did not trust ginners who called the bluff. Checking Avi's assertion would have been quite simple even for inexperienced Shavit, provided he forsook the detached CCMI strategy, climbed up to see the S&GH blockings, and consulted expert employees—but for this he would have to know which experts it was worth listening to. Deputy Danton was not such a one; unreliable Atad and his clique supported Avi for political reasons including suppressing Nekhas; and others seemed similarly politically motivated. Shavit did not suffer hubris like Andersen's emperor, but due to detached CCMI he knew very little of the plant's know-how and *phronesis* and about others' expertise, suspected them all, and even the prolongation of the debacle did not convince him to call outside experts to review the S&GH problem until Avi's authority collapsed. Thus, he was paralyzed and accepted "soothing sessions" as a substitute for real action; similar to the emperor who sent one minister after the other, Shavit summoned Avi and Danton for one session after another despite their futility.

The "Emperor's New Clothes" syndrome was implausible in Gabi's Northern Gin because:

1   Secrecy was minimal; openness of information and timely, exact, reliable and valid communication among hierarchical ranks exposed abuses and subterfuges, and enabled leaders to discern inevitable signs of bluffs and to identify swindlers.
2   Vulnerably involved, knowledgeable executives discerned, suppressed, and ousted immoral managers bound to bluff if having to admit ignorance.
3   Prospective swindlers, knowing that well-informed, knowledgeable executives would check the truth of problematic assertions on-the-spot and would probably discern and harshly punish swindling and abuses, avoided such immoral means.
4   Executives failed subordinates' bluffing and other immoral means, exposed their users, and replaced them with high-moral, learning employees whose expertise would expose swindlers.
5   Swindlers were deterred from swindling by knowing that even a superior who could not decide on-the-spot whether they were bluffing or not would soon find out the truth due to trustworthy reliable expert employees informing him.
6   Trustful relationships ensured that swindlers would not find the support of employees.
7   Swindlers could not find "brambles" in power positions to support their bluffs.

However, Northern was unique; "parachuted" executives mostly practiced CCMI-Im-C, and even high-moral Valley PM David did not enjoy an open and trustful relationship with V-TM as he avoided technical deliberations, missed his CCMI and incompetence that pruned talents, generating a fertile ground for swindlers.

The Pruning of Top Experts by CCMI-Im-C–Practicing "Jumpers"

Gin plants' low-trust culture also engendered mismanagement through the pruning of top experts, another reason for the rise of "brambles." In a contemporary automated processing plant, success is determined in the long run to a large degree by the skills and competences of specializing staff members, acquired through lengthy expert careers that differ from managerial careers; the difference causes major misunderstandings and tends to result in the pruning of best experts by CCMI-Im-C–practicing managers despite their contrary intentions.

The motivations and career intentions of Shavit, Danton, and Avi differed radically from those of Thomas due to career differences that commenced when Thomas became a mechanic helper for three hours a day at the age of 14 and continued specializing in mechanics for 21 years before becoming TM. The managerial careers of the three commenced later in life and included a variety of authority jobs without such continuity in one action domain and often with little specialization. Thomas advanced his mechanic career by performance achieved through vulnerable immersion and trust and learning cycles, resulting in his excelling with the automatic feeder invention. Managerial non-continuous careers of *rotatzia* and "prachutings" encouraged practicing CCMI-Im-C and often caused misunderstanding of the motivations, aims, and intentions of top experts such as Thomas. As mentioned, Thomas's departure surprised Shavit: why would one leave just as his three-year struggle for the automatic feeder succeeded? In Shavit's managerial worldview, successes were means of obtaining extrinsic rewards: prestige, authority, and power. These were also resources for furthering a managerial career, "jumping" to head a larger and more powerful organization and gain more such rewards. Thomas's worldview differed radically: though he did not disparage managerial rewards, he valued them primarily as resources for professional achievement, for solving most complex mechanical problems such as those posed by the automatic gin plant. Thomas sought the intrinsic rewards of achieving a higher level of expertise, proven for instance by inventing an original automatic feeder that could have competed with world-class feeders if it had not been deferred for three years; after that he proved he could seek other challenges. He did not imagine that Shavit, who obstructed the feeder for three years, would be so immoral as to appropriate the innovation's prestige, not invite him to the inauguration ceremony, and not mention his name as its inventor (e.g., Mehri 2005).

This fundamental difference was augmented by "parachutings," which encouraged Im-C and diminished executives' organizational commitment. The contrasting aims were reflected in company car differences: Thomas's seeking of intrinsic rewards needed no prestigious shiny automatic "executive car" like Shavit's; the old scruffy station wagon better served his aim of minimizing the plant's downtime (p. 51). Likewise was the difference in clothing: Shavit wore typical clean kibbutz Sabbath (Saturday) clean clothes, including shorts and sandals unsuited for the hazardous shop floor, which was often oily and greasy, versus Thomas's dirty work clothes and boots with their anti-skid sole for the greasy floor. While Shavit was a fluent and easy talker, Thomas's speech was heavy, less fluent, and slower, often demonstrating his intentions with his hands and mechanics' tools rather than talking. A committed workaholic, Thomas never left a task uncompleted, nor did he leave a stalled ginning unit until processing was resumed, while if Shavit visited such a unit at all he soon left without waiting for work to resume. His deferring of Thomas's automatic feeder also delayed the adoption of Movers, signified conservatism uncommitted to the success of the cotton industry, preferring to wait for others to try it, defending his own power and career prospects. Beneath the overt conflicts between Shavit and Thomas lie these deeper contrasts, which further explain Thomas's frustration and departure. "Parachuted" CCMI-Im-C–practicing PMs often pruned top experts with contrary inclinations; such *pe'ilim* shaped low-trust cultures that obstructed experts' goals by placing all kinds of obstacles to reliable knowledge sharing, learning, and innovating, which encouraged them to leave. Only few did not leave and compromised their professionalism by deferring promising changes and innovations to keep the job they liked, as did Southern's TM Yunus.

The background for the immanent conflict between managers and experts was the complexity and limited understanding and control of many ginning process factors. Similar to the unforeseeable cotton flaw in the huge serpentine pipes, forecasting the effect of various machines on ginning results was problematic as well, explaining for instance the bitter conflict over adding fiber cleaners versus adding S&GH (p. 31). Often a change intended to solve a major problem turned out to be very partial, requiring further solutions. There was often little understanding of cause/effect links, and even prolonged experience did not enable conclusive explanations of many operational problems. The more expert and experienced a ginner was, the more complexities he saw with numerous and unclear causal links and variables over which control was difficult. According to the ex-head of the national cotton fiber grading laboratory, "until one learns the subject [of ginning] . . . [he] needs at least 5–6 years," while the American engineer who erected Valley Gin in 1956 said to V-TM: "I have been in the trade for 25 years but I am still learning ginning" (p. 125) and then mentioned names of well-known top experts who had been seeking answers to important professional puzzles for 40 years. Top expert Arbiv asserted:

"One always has to try out and seek solutions for every concrete ginning problem; there are so many possibilities, so many surprises, that until you operate the gin plant you never know what will happen and which problems you'll have to solve."

For the genuine ginning professional these problems are a challenge of overcoming the limitations of existing know-how, furthering their own professionalism, and an opportunity for self-actualization. For the manager these problems imply uncertainty, which makes it more difficult to take well-founded decisions and create recurrent situations that captivate the manager in the hands of the experts, while he knows that they too lack conclusive solutions to many of the problems. Allowing them discretion to try out solutions does not ensure the manager that problems will indeed be solved and, worse still, that his prestige will not suffer in case of failure as he assumed authorized experts' action. Moreover, superiors were also concerned with experts' possible outstanding successes, as Shavit was concerned by Thomas's plausible empowerment due to the possible success of his innovative feeder.

Furthermore, even "parachutings" of *pe'ilim* who avoided CCMI-Im-C caused pruning of top experts, as with the departure of Amram and Levi following Thomas's "parachuting." Besides frustrating Amram's anticipated promotion to TM, he and Levi were annoyed by Thomas's mistaken greenhorn decisions. Thomas admitted these mistakes later on but at the time, when he took charge and had to prove his superior expertise to legitimize his nomination (Watkins 2003), he found it hard to admit that Amram and Levi's contrary assertions were correct even when he himself discerned this, as he overruled them but failed to solve problems. When insiders are promoted with many around them knowing and appreciating their professionalism, they can more easily admit mistakes as they enjoy the credit ensuing from trust in their success, credit which the unknown "jumper" lacks and thus finds it harder to admit mistakes. Worse still, the superiors of vulnerably involved TMs were mostly ignorant Im-C-practicing PMs; it was futile to try and make them grasp the challenges of complex technical problems, and such attempts invited, at best, amateurish shallow appraisal of TMs' efforts.

Aside from experts' frustration by PMs' ignorance, mistaken decisions and lack of esteem for their efforts, TMs were negatively affected by PMs' little interest in enhancing their expertise or even worse, their concern for TMs' empowerment by professional achievements. Shavit's distrust of Thomas signaled efforts to limit his discretion, which further pushed him out because Shavit's distrust meant no discretion, which was essential for expertise advancement, and minimal opportunities to learn by trial and error, as Shavit deferred the US$15,000 experiment for the feeder development for two years. Minimal discretion also meant less learning from others and less nurturing staffs' professionalism as, for instance, all PMs except that of Northern did not take senior hired staff members to professional meetings of Israeli ginners, nor did they let these staff members travel abroad to learn. PMs' distrust of TMs also meant consulting top outside experts over their heads, excluding them from meetings on topics crucial for their functioning, informing them selectively, asking them to overcome problems caused by PMs' mistaken decisions, and causing their failure by misinterpreting outside experts' suggestions and recommendations.

However, an even more fundamental reason for pruning top experts were destructive conflicts often won by ignorant PMs and their loyalists.

The Destructive Conflicts at the Top: "Jumpers" versus Top Experts

At the height of the Vietnam War social psychologist Morton Deutsch delivered a highly instructive address entitled "Conflicts: Creative and Destructive" (1969). He analyzed the process that leads a conflict onto a destructive rather than a constructive course. In this process, the two sides forego any attempt at mutual persuasion or seeking consent by compromise with the other and turn towards power tactics ranging from threats, abuses, and deception to various coercive strategies. A destructive conflict then develops more easily between sides who share no common culture or social background and who have no shared past experiences which could enable communication in the direction of a more positive interpretation of the other's intentions. Very different backgrounds prevent each side from understanding many of the other's behaviors and cause them to interpret these behaviors negatively, less legitimately, and less benevolently than intended. Conflictual pressures and tensions lead to a tendency to negatively interpret the other's behavior and to narrow down the perspectives of plausible solutions to the only one, of destroying the rival. In an organizational context destroying usually meant ousting the rival or his voluntary departure after a defeat. When prospects of ousting rivals are high, the parties are less deterred from using immoral means against each other, since a rival who leaves cannot take revenge against the winner.

"Parachuted" *pe'ilim* PMs and TMs mostly opted for CCMI, which led to defense of their authority, jobs, and career prospects by immoral means. Beside these means, PMs concealed their ignorance by "parachuting" loyalist *pe'ilim* or prospective loyalists to deputy jobs to create defensive cliques (Dalton 1959). This frustrated successful insiders, who witnessed how ignorant outsiders received the jobs they had hoped for, and their distrust was enhanced by outsiders' choice of CCMI and consequent stupid deeds. Distrust was furthered by communication short-circuits, due to a lack of prior familiarity that led to misinterpretation of the other's intentions, grasping his action as threatening one's status and authority. Secrecy furthered misunderstandings and mutual suspicion by limiting one's information about rivals. Thomas, for instance, often interpreted Amram's arguments with him as aimed at his failure, while if he had been acquainted with Amram as a colleague and not as a boss he would have known that, as testified to by everyone, Amram's meticulousness and thoroughness in seeking solutions to technical problems did not allow such a motive to enter his professional considerations. If Thomas had been an insider some conflicts would have been avoided, as local know-how and *phronesis* would have spared his greenhorn mistakes, and when he erred insiders trusted by both him and Amram would probably have helped find an agreed-upon solution. Moreover, insiders who know each other for years and do not expect the other side to leave even if he loses a conflict have an incentive to minimize personal injury in order to enable future working relationships.

Frequent "parachutings" and the availability of potential *pe'ilim* as replacements from kibbutzim encouraged PMs to perceive mid-levelers as expendable: when Avi failed, Karmi brought Thomas to the rescue rather than promoting Amram; ignorant Yuval did not understand that it would take two years and many greenhorn mistakes for Thomas to reach Amram's level of expertise. Grasping such experts as expendable helped make the conflicts between them and *pe'ilim* destructive, until becoming covert wars of organizational annihilation; each side tried to get rid of opponents by whatever immoral means available, as sociologist Simmel asserted, citing philosopher Kant:

"In every war in which the belligerents do not impose some restrictions in the use of possible means . . . becomes a war of extermination. For where the parties do not abstain at least from assassination, breach of word, and instigation of treason, they destroy that confidence . . . which alone permits the materialization of a peace treaty following the end of the war"

(Simmel 1971: 81).

Machiavelli had already advised the prince to kill his dangerous rivals rather than just punish them, which would have made them more bitterly dangerous enemies. "Parachuted" *pe'ilim* executives who habituated the importing of *pe'ilim* from prior I-KO jobs (see Chapter 6) frustrated inside experts by "parachuting" *pe'ilim* to the jobs for which the former were suited and hoped for. Ignorant Yuval replaced Yaakov as Deputy PM and frustrated Muli; he behaved autocratically as an elephant in a porcelain shop, furthering expert ginners' distrust of *pe'ilim*, originally created by detached Moav. Distrust was furthered by the "parachutings" of Avi and Karmi instead of promoting Amram and Levi, and distrust mounted as Avi replaced Muli and failed and Thomas was "parachuted" to the rescue. Thus conflicts with him became destructive despite his replicating Amram's readiness for hard mechanics' work and seeking professional excellence, as previous "parachutings" had built up distrust of *pe'ilim*. All Merkaz hired employees detested ignorant mismanagement by *pe'ilim*, their mistakes, and failures, while barring promotion of proven capable insiders, occupying jobs that better suited insiders. Thomas's initial trusting behavior did not gain experts' trust as he often insisted on his greenhorn mistakes; as frustrated as Amram and Levi were, conflicts with him became destructive until the two's repeated defeats pushed them out.

Similar were findings of destructive conflicts and brain drain at other plants except for Northern in PM 1 and Gabi's years. In its high-trust culture, the two nurtured employee expertises, got rid of troublemakers, and trust relations together with the optimal ginning-oriented culture prevented conflicts from becoming destructive. Mikha's "parachuting" changed this radically but his destructive conflicts with hired expert employees did not prune the latter; expert TM-3 and his veteran ginners, who suffered CCMI-Im-C Mikha's suppression, did not leave; TM-3's highly trusted leadership united them against *pe'ilim* (e.g., Haslam et al. 2011) and later efforts by PMs 5 and 6 to break this unity by firing veterans failed as the shop steward was TM-3's loyalist; he recruited outside support against these PMs and many of the region's cotton growers also objected to the dismissals; they were personally familiar with veterans' expertise and optimal treatment of the cotton, as they had worked together when replacing religious ginners on Sabbaths during the high season.[2] Conflicts with PMs caused "Italian strikes" and demoralization, which negatively impacted ginning but TM-3 and most experts remained.

Valley Gin, on the other hand, avoided major destructive conflicts as it had neither *rotatzia* nor "parachutings" of *pe'ilim* or frustrated top experts; talents were pruned early before or just as their growing expertise became a menace to the superiority of mediocre V-TM. PM David granted discretion to V-TM by which he pruned prospective successors and ruled with no challengers with regard to ginning and the technical domain decisions. Employees accepted his authority, as they trusted David, who backed him and cared for their personal and social problems. David's involvement prevented escalation of conflicts into destructive ones. Valley employees enjoyed a culture of leniency and working close to home, while CEOs and cotton growers trusted David despite his mediocre performance due to his modesty and abstemious management, which spared them money, contrary to the lavish PMs of the other I-KRC's plants. Moreover, he spared them "Italian strikes" ahead of the high season, which were common at other gin plants.

In both Lowland Gin and Southern Gin, PMs initially granted discretion to vulnerably involved TMs who shaped high-trust cultures that minimized destructive conflicts, but later on such a culture disappeared in Lowland and in Southern it was confined to the shop floor. In Lowland PM-1's absence permitted L-TM-1's autocracy, which caused turnover, brain drain, and employee division and conflicts, sometimes destructive between Jews and Arabs but not with *pe'ilim*. PM Yatzek's ignorant autocracy generated similar results. Continued turnover and brain drain left only a mediocre, divided work force that did not mobilize for industrial action to achieve decent wages (e.g., Nichols and Armstrong 1976).

In Southern Gin, destructive conflicts appeared in the eighth to ninth years soon after the "parachuting" of CCMI user PM 3, who caused TM Yunus to annoy the staff he had initially skillfully nurtured. Trust in him diminished as he shelved innovative ideas, obeyed stupid decisions by ignorant Pms, and ignored staff members' social and personal needs, leaving these for the uncaring, distrusted, detached PMs. He managed to conserve some trustful relations on the shop floor, which mitigated some conflicts with hired staff, but other conflicts became destructive due to distrust that militated frustrated hired staff and caused "Italian strikes" until PM 5 fired all hired staff members.

As "parachuted" *pe'ilim* mostly practiced CCMI-Im-C and shaped low-trust cultures, they often caused destructive conflicts with hired top experts as well as their pruning. Only where and when *pe'ilim* shaped high-trust cultures, nurtured hired staff, recognized its members' capabilities and trustworthiness, and cared for their social and personal needs did no such conflicts erupt. "Parachutings" and *rotatzia* enflamed destructive conflicts through the ruinous impact of turnover on trust and cooperation (Axelrod 1984), and through the distrust caused by *pe'ilim*'s CCMI-Im-C, through "parachutings" that frustrated top experts' promotion expectations, and through putting them under the rule of ignoramuses who were not aware of their ignorance. However, experts' animosity towards this rule led to destructive conflicts and industrial action only in some cases; some conflicts pruned top experts, caused turnover, and no organized industrial action, but in other cases the pruning of experts elevated militant "brambles" to staff leadership and engendered industrial action. *Rotatzia* and "parachutings" were not integral to destructive conflicts and brain drain; entrenched immoral autocratic insiders caused them as well. Moreover, *rotatzia* did not prevent the immoral entrenchment of some executives (Moav, Yatzek), which caused distrust and invited destructive conflicts.

One implication of these findings is the decisive role of high-trust cultures shaped by vulnerably involved executives in preserving and nurturing expertise by prevention or at least mitigation of the negative impact of destructive conflicts between executives, managers, and experts. Northern excelled not just because its high-trust culture enhanced knowledgeable decision-making and innovation, but it also prevented ruinous conflicts that could prune precious expertise, top experts with the "ability to be guided . . . by contingent sensing" of the "unique contours of the circumstances" (Shotter and Tsoukas 2014a: 240), experts with "[p]ractical wisdom . . . emerging developmentally within an unceasing flow of activities, in which practitioners are . . . immersed" (Shotter and Tsoukas 2014b: 377).

The second implication is the significance of preventing destructive conflicts and covert wars between "jumpers" and local experts by vulnerable immersion of "jumpers" in practitioner deliberations, acquainting "parachuted" PMs with experts' personal and social problems, and encouraging solving them to prevent brain drain. Ethnographers who depicted covert wars between "jumpers" and insiders (e.g., Gouldner 1954) did not study the resulting brain drain, nor did most other cited works on "jumpers" allude to it, although the loss of top brains appeared in many press stories on imported CEO successions. A rare case was an Austrian "parachuted" to manage a Norwegian subsidiary: initially he resembled Gouldner's "jumper" but soon he forsook autocracy, which contradicted local democratic culture and the requirement of rapid decision-making in the tailoring of auto parts produced for automakers according to their frequently changing demands. By trusting these decisions to design team leaders, he enhanced effectiveness and barred brain drain (Holtskog 2014: 162).

However, the pruning of top experts did not merely cause destructive conflicts between a boss and an expert; often such conflicts were clique events. Dalton (1959) depicted struggles of inside cliques, while "parachuted" *rotational* managers' cliques are unique for the outsiderness of their participants, which deprived them of insiders' knowledge and trustful ties with insiders who could supply such knowledge. These deprivations added negative effects to "jumper" cliques.

The Uniqueness of "Jumper" Cliques and the Pruning of Top Experts

Managerial cliques are ubiquitous phenomena amply criticized in the literature for their negative effects, as they protect and advance particularistic interests of their members at the expense of organizational interests.[3] Such a negative clique was that of Atad and his union committee foremen, while a less cohesive clique was that of Zelikovich, Shavit, Avi, and a few supporting *pe'ilim*, which enhanced Shavit's rule over the clique of Thomas, Danton, and two other mid-level *pe'ilim*. This rule stood in contrast to the plant's and cotton growers' interests in effective ginning, to which only the latter clique aimed. However, both cliques differed from Atad's in their shorter duration, as they dissolved when their leaders left.

Dalton depicted "Cliques as Fountainheads of Action" (1959: 52), finding that only executives supported by strong cohesive managerial cliques introduced major changes and innovations; executives without such cliques were powerless, as found by others.[4] An effective positive clique was that of Yaakov, Aharon, Muli and Levi; it survived for eight years: after six years it weakened as Aharon left; a year later Muli weakened it further by using his energies to organize the settling of the occupied territories, and after another year it dissolved when Yaakov left. Cohesive, powerful cliques depicted in the literature, such as that of Atad, consisted of insiders who created ties while working and hobnobbing, while cliques of I-KRC "jumpers" were often created in previous jobs elsewhere and were often short-lived due to *rotatzia* and "parachuting" used by higher-ups to bolster power. These two practices encouraged clique moves by legitimizing the early replacement of subordinate *pe'ilim* by one's "parachuting" own loyalists or prospective loyalists in their stead; their "parachuting" encouraged CCMI and Im-C and made the defense of one's authority and job by the clique's ties essential (Gouldner 1954).

"Jumper" cliques of CCMI users are often weak: the season-long S&GH debacle indicated the ineptness of the CEO's clique; the detached ignorance that defended the authority and jobs of Zelikovich, Shavit, and Avi, kept them paralyzed and incompetent. For five weeks after Nekhas pointed out the mistaken S&GH piping, the clique did nothing to check it. One reason was that inviting an expert to check it could have exposed Shavit's stupid believing of Avi's bluff/ignorance, while another reason was Shavit's and non-clique member Danton's missing that Avi's detachment from the troubled S&GH was part of an unchangeable job-survival strategy; the two did not suspect the strategic importance of the bluff/ignorant assertion for Avi until an outside expert's intervention overcame it. "Jumper" cliques are often formed in previous work group cultures (Fine 2013), such as the collaboration of Shavit and Zelikovich in the Regional Council. Unfortunately, when members face the different problems of a new organization and use CCMI, they often create a mistaken consensus of ignorance that leads to stupid decisions and actions like the S&GH debacle, a major omission of stupidity research.

Worse still, such a consensus is formed also due to clique members' animosity toward knowledgeable insiders, especially lower-status best performers such as Nekhas; his low status was the prime reason that his view was not followed and that the piping contour was not reviewed by experts for six weeks. My participant observation journal leaves no question that illiterate Nekhas was Merkaz's best ginner (aside from Thomas); I often witnessed him solving operational problems faster and better than others. He could resume plant operation after a stoppage within 10–12 minutes, something that required 25–30 minutes of others. At a height of 190 centimeters, he was also very strong; for instance he lifted and mounted a hoop plotter weighing 60–70 kilos with no assistance. His agility was astonishing, both when using wrenches and other mechanic's tools to repair broken machines and when swiftly climbing tall, faulty machines like a monkey in the woods. He was often the first to identify a machine failure causing damage to the cotton and to stop and repair it; when watching damaged cotton with others he was many times the first to identify the reason. He was often the first to smell and identify cotton burning in the pipes and to stop operations; hence on his shifts burnings did not cause many hours of firefighting and up to a shift and a half of halted production, as happened to a shift foreman from Atad's clique.

One explanation for his excelling was 19 years of experience, as he left primary school after four years and started helping his father clean the shop floor at the age of 11. Yaakov made him operator when he was 17 years old and eight years later Thomas promoted him to shift foreman, despite Shavit's objection. His lengthy experience taught him a lot about fiber quality and which machines cause each type of damage; hence he could identify a machine's dysfunction simply by reviewing the outcoming fibers. A second explanation was seemingly the lack of education, which made him extra-sensitive to sensory cues such as unusual noises and smells that signaled machine dysfunction. A third explanation was his high motivation to prove he was a better ginner than all the educated foremen, especially hating Atad and his clique, as well as to prove to Shavit that his intention to replace less educated employees with more educated ones was wrong: the best ginner was the least educated.

Many of the above facts were unknown to ginning-detached Shavit and Danton, helping explain why neither was moved by Nekhas's assertion that Avi's mistaken S&GH piping was a prime reason for its blocking. Could it be that such an illiterate Arab was the first to identify a major source of such a troubling problem? Danton could believe it as he knew Nekhas better than Shavit from ginners' meetings in the shade of the office building (p. 64), but even he did not witness the supremacy of Nekhas's expertise as I did since he was detached from the processing halls. Acting upon Nekhas's assertion contrary to Avi's antagonized Shavit, disproving his policy of "raising the standard of workers" by replacing less educated with more educated ones.[5] This was a seemingly unbearable admission for intelligent, educated Shavit; hence he did not act upon Nekhas's assertion until Avi's authority collapsed.

As cited, the consultant came and offered a solution to the piping problem, which he had learned by a prior visit at Nekhas's village, and it was implemented and succeeded (p. 28), but no one mentioned Nekhas's primacy in identifying the problem and offering its solution. Likewise, his supreme expertise was ignored in many other cases; only Thomas granted him recognition, while neither Avi nor Yehu did so. In a home interview after the season he was pessimistic about his future at Merkaz; later on I was told that he became demotivated, avoided ginners' deliberations, was frequently absent, and eventually Shavit's successor fired him. Thus the loss of one best ginner, Thomas, was followed by the loss of another.

Opposite Cases of Vertical Positive Cliques

An opposite case of a vertical positive clique of "jumpers" and hired managers that was a "Fountainhead of Action" was Northern's clique consisting of CEO Dan, PM Gabi, TM Arbiv, and his deputy and successor TM-3. Clique members were unified by a high-trust culture that gave them the tools (Swidler 1986) to cope successfully with plant problems, primarily the free sharing of information, know-how, and *phronesis*, helpful for solving work problems and innovating. This culture enabled "expertise of every kind to be drawn into the decision without any difficulties being imposed by the lines of authority . . . [D]uring the process of formulation suggestions and recommendations flowed freely . . . the appropriate experts [we]re consulted, [and] their exact location in the hierarchy of authority [did] not much affect the decision[s]" (Simon 1957: 230). The plant's vulnerably involved leaders created a "we" feeling (Haslam et al. 2011) by never concealing ignorance in unending efforts to enhance ginning, much as V-TM's American tutor continued doing for 25 years (p. 125). Managers solved problems and advanced plant goals by modeling commitment, which mostly employees could not do but followed. Common goals united them in viewing differences of opinion concerning solutions to various problems as benevolent and subject to collaborative seeking of solutions and maintaining trustful relationships, as Fox (1974: Ch. 2) explained.

Merkaz's positive clique, consisting of Thomas, Danton, and two other *pe'ilim*, created for a few years a high-trust shop-floor culture with quite similar results; *pe'ilim*'s authority and power overcame the negative impact of Atad's self-serving clique. Like this one and Gabi's clique at Northern, all other such cliques that shaped local high-trust cultures were led by a performance-oriented, high-moral "parachuted" *pa'il* or *pe'ilim*. Thus, not "parachuting" by itself prevented positive cliques and effective, high-trust cultures, but "parachuting" + *rotatzia* + career advancement prospects by patrons' auspices (also Chapter 6) led *pe'ilim* to choose CCMI and to unite in negative cliques that pruned top inside experts, either taking their jobs and/or suppressing them. However, the pruning of Amram and Levi by Thomas's "parachuting" showed that even a "jumper" who eventually led a positive clique and shaped a high-trust effective culture may cause brain drain and negative results until he learns local know-how and *phronesis* and can appreciate and nurture locals' expertise.

This pruning was not incidental: Thomas was called to rescue a failing plant; he did not know ginning, hence he did not discern expert ginners from ignorants. Ingratiating "bramble" Atad supported Thomas's belief in his mistaken views, contrary to the knowledgeable views of Amram and Levi. Without prior acquaintance, trust, common cultural background, or shared past experiences to enhance communication, conflicts became destructive (Deutsch 1969). However, if Thomas had been an expert ginner, would it have ensured that the conflicts would be productive? Would it have led to creating a positive clique with top expert insiders who largely shared his values and habituses?

Unfortunately, even in such a case destructive conflicts are plausible. A knowledgeable, self-confident "jumper" often chooses seductive-coercive autocratic involvement, missing the uniqueness of some local problems unknown in previous quite similar jobs and her/his mistakes prevent the creation of trust and cooperation.[6] An expert "jumper" often habituated a different work group culture than insiders (Holtskog 2014: 162). A group work culture is a tool that every community of practitioners develops while coping with work problems,[7] and each group work culture differs as it is a product of different circumstances, exigencies, traditions, and histories.[8] For instance, both sides of the controversy on adding S&GH as against adding final cleaners were supported by top experts, each with his own reasons.

Their different experiences could explain contrary views because many variables impacted the effectiveness of the two machine types and control of these variables differed among plants, for instance humidity: drying cotton to the proper humidity made the S&GH effective but if the operator did not know the raw cotton's humidity in advance, as was the case in all plants except Northern, he could only adjust the boilers to achieve the correct humidity after a considerable amount of cotton had already passed the S&GH and was often treated less than optimally. Experts who experienced plants without measuring humidity may have grasped the S&GH as ineffective, while a Northern expert would conclude the opposite since his S&GH was provided with cotton of the correct humidity.

Professional controversies often continue due to different experts' experiences and learnings. A "parachuted" executive can build a positive goal-oriented clique only if well acquainted with insiders' work culture through trustful involvement and if they are convinced that s/he learned the uniqueness of the local work culture before trying to change it. As cited, this is how "jumper" Gerstner succeeded at IBM. Karaevli (2007: 691) is right in saying that his initial two years of learning gave him knowledge and a power base, but it appears that they also gave him a more potent resource, the confidence that his decisions considered the peculiarities and *phronesis* of IBM's work culture, a consideration that no one can learn in 90 days (e.g., Watkins 2003). As mentioned, Covey's (2006) *The Swift of Trust* creates a mistaken image of common swift trust building, although trust building by an incomer is a slow mutual process: locals have to reciprocate the incomer's trust-signaling acts for the latter to add such acts; her/his adding takes time to be reciprocated, and so on and so forth, until building full trust (Fox 1974). This process is slow since it is fraught with opportunities for missing partners' trust-signaling acts. Thus, although pertinent expertise helps create trust and cooperation, it is no guarantee that it shortens time for incomers' proving competencies that justify trusting.

The Pitfalls of Relying on Outside Expertise

One of the grave illusions with which many managers delude themselves is the illusion that one can always compensate for loss of know-how and *phronesis* due to the pruning of top experts and the rise of "brambles" by means of outside expertise. Unfortunately, outside expertise is helpful in many cases but it can barely compensate for such losses due to the use of CCMI by educated, intelligent "parachuted" executives. Chapter 1 depicted the 3.5-month long faulty solving of the S&GH problem with the help of both top-level Israeli ginning experts and WLGEP experts' advice. A prime reason was executives' dysfunction due to practicing CCMI, which generated vicious distrust and ignorance cycles. Outside experts did not change the negative cycles and consequent mistaken decisions and indecision of executives that prevented solving the problem.

The first occasion in which outside experts failed to help insiders was WLGEP experts' advice to rebuild the propulsion system, which would have required three days of stoppage with no ensuring of its success. WLGEP offered to pay for the costly renewal only partially another reason the offer was rejected. Worse still, Avi's mistaken piping contour was the easier part of the problem, but WLGEP experts did not know this as no one informed them; hence they could not advise about it. Shavit knew that ginners blamed Avi's mistaken piping, but ignorant of his own ignorance he did not suspect Avi's assertion that this was "a marginal problem"; hence he did not call any outside expert to consult about it. Suspecting Avi's bluff/ignorance and inviting outsiders to check Nekhas's and others' contrary assertions required both trust in them and minimal ginning expertise, which Shavit lacked and worse still, it required some involvement in experts' debate, contrary to using detached CCMI. Thus, outside experts cannot help an executive whose choice of CCMI prevents suspecting and trying to probe a mid-leveler's false assertion criticized by distrusted subordinates.

Second, in order to offer a solution of which the proposing expert was assured or that had at least more than a 50% chance of succeeding, one had to thoroughly check both the blocked machine and its piping or at least receive reliable detailed information about all relevant factors and variables; without these one lacked the "unshakeable facts" required for sound decision-making (Geneen 1984: 101). Unfortunately, Avi was not interested in informing outsiders about his mistaken piping in order to conceal his mistake, and detached, ignorant Shavit could not do it both due to ignorance of which details were relevant for problem-solving and because he believed Avi's assertion and saw no reason to inform outsiders about it. It seems that WLGEP experts and managers felt they were not fully informed and did not offer a better deal; Merkaz management stuck to rejection of their costly proposal, demanding that all costs be covered, as they interpreted the machine's purchase warranty, and both stalemate and arguments continued for months. Outside expertise proved futile when locals kept their cards close to their chest and/or were unable to fully inform outside experts.

Outside expertise proved futile at a later phase as well, when major shafts broke due to overload, twice stopping work for 24 and 30 hours, respectively. Since the proposed renewal required 48–72 hours, it could have been done on one of these occasions, making renewal more economical by using this enforced downtime. It did not happen both because of the above stalemate and because ignorant Shavit and Danton believed Avi would solve the S&GH problem and prevent such paralyzing events with a little more "soothing"; the two's detached ignorance of ginning prevented discerning Avi's sampler failure due to the job-defending strategy of avoiding consultations with outside experts offered free of charge as it could have exposed his ignorance; without discerning Avi's CCMI strategy, "soothing sessions" continued to no avail. A similar fateful omission due to the PM's detachment from a TM's job functioning, though with much worse results, occurred when Valley's David missed V-TM's concealed incompetence by avoiding any outside expert's help, both in Israel and abroad, with the exception of V-TM's Californian friend.

Outside expertise did not help Merkaz later as well when the defective propulsion system continued unchanged. Outside experts came and offered solutions for it but Avi's failure with the sampler reminded him of his ignorance; he rightly assumed that deferring renewal of the propulsion system would protect his job; he simply did not forecast the humiliation of Atad and Yehu's de facto replacing him in mid-season with Shavit's covert backing. These two ginning ignorants might not have feared exposing their ignorance as no one suspected them of much expertise, but they were even more reluctant to cope with the costly-to-solve propulsion system; its repair was of a different magnitude than the piping problem: WLGEP's proposed solution was seven times costlier in downtime terms and some 10 times more expensive than the piping repair. Worse still, it was more hazardous: the danger involved in a failed piping change was minor and an additional repair was relatively cheap, versus the up to 50% probability of failure of a renewed propulsion system and a costly further repair; only close trustful cooperation between local experts and outside experts could have ensured the probability of success, but except for Nekhas there were no real local experts.

Outside expertise proved a futile substitute to insiders' expertise. Outside experts could not bring about the replacement of inept Avi, but Shavit could; his detached CCMI deferred for six weeks the exposure and repair of the piping mistake, but why did he not replace Avi when the repair exposed his bluff? Did he miss that such a detached bluffer/incompetent would never endanger his job by the more hazardous and costly coping with the propulsion system?

The answer is definitely "yes"; Shavit's detachment caused him to miss Avi's systematic CCMI practice of avoiding faulty machines after initial coping with them failed, as was with the sampler, pointing to a zero chance of his sincere cooperating with outsiders on solving the S&GH problem. As a result of this omission Avi's job was formally retained, while allowing Atad, whom Danton called "the biggest liar," to usurp his authority. An outside expert could not help Avi without his making a turnaround of strategy from detached CCMI to ignorance-admitting vulnerable involvement. Such a change required sincerity, but Avi did not even admit his piping mistake after it was repaired, as proved by the better-functioning S&GH. Any outside expert invited who realized Avi's detached CCMI and concluded that only his replacement would enable problem-solving could not ask Shavit to do it. Outside experts were called in for their ginning expertise, not for advice on personnel reshuffles, especially not to Shavit, who aimed at concealing the debacle. A formal reshuffle would have publicized the S&GH failure, while an outsider needed insiders' acceptance to achieve results; even after Avi lost his authority his formal status let him interfere with decisions concerning outside experts' assistance, thus outsiders had to maintain a good working relationship with him.

The assistance of outside experts is limited in many ways. In mismanaged, low-trust firms with CCMI-Im-C–practicing managers, such experts face obstacles formed by insiders' defensive secrecy, abuses, and subterfuges that often frustrate their help. Outside expertise may be a substitute to inside expertise in simple plants but not in complex, sophisticated automated plants; in these experts can help high-moral, ignorance-admitting managers through open, sincere assistance with problem-solving, as in the example of university professors who rescued DEC's competitiveness after the De Castro team's exit (Rifkin and Harrar 1988: Ch. 11). Outside experts can barely substitute for the expertise deficiency of managers practicing CCMI-Im-C because:

1 The belief in outside experts filling in for expertise deficiencies encourages bypassing local uncertified experts, and consequently their frustration, non-cooperation, and/or leaving (e.g., Nekhas);

2 Using CCMI detracts from the identification of suitable outside experts and/or from openly and trustfully consulting with them (e.g., V-TM);

3 Using CCMI or even just limiting involvement in mid-leveler deliberations may bar managers from consulting truly expert outsiders (e.g., Valley's David);

4 Implementation of outside experts' recommendations often requires overcoming mid-levelers' objections; detached superiors fail or even don't try it;

5 Guarded relations with outside experts due to CCMI diminish the effectiveness of consulting with them as they lack full information (e.g., WLGEP experts);

6 The effectiveness of outsiders' help is limited by CCMI users' selective acceptance of their help according to CCMI needs (e.g., Avi and the sampler);

7 CCMI users pose mistaken questions to outside experts and/or supply them with unhelpful information, which prolongs or even ruins their problem-solving efforts;

8 Use of defensive CCMI limits/prevents managers' learning from outside experts' problem-solving; outsiders minimize teaching them without open, sincere communication;

9 Outside experts cannot help if a detached CCMI-user PM misses mid-levelers' failing to implement outsiders' solutions due to their CCMI and/or to prove the inferiority of outsiders' expertise.

Unfortunately, gin plants' "parachuted" *pe'ilim* executives and managers mostly practiced CCMI-Im-C. Contextualizing this finding by analyzing the kibbutz field, of which the I-KRCs were a part, further explains this prevalent choice of *pe'ilim*.

Notes

1 To the best of my knowledge I fulfilled this promise.
2 The Jewish faith forbids working on the Sabbath, hence replacement by atheist cotton growers enabled ginning.
3 Dalton (1959: Ch. 3); Fine (2013); Jackall (1988); Levenson (1961); Martin and Strauss (1959); Mehri (2005).
4 Brass and Krackhardt (1999); Fine (2013); Lally (1974).
5 See Clark (1979) for a similar foolishness.
6 Bennis (1989); Geertz (1983); Hargadon and Bechky (2006); Wagner (2002).
7 Fine (2013); Orr (1996); Swidler (1986).
8 Fine (2012), (2013); Hedgecoe (2012); Parker (2000); Roy (1959–60); Yanow (2000).

References

Axelrod, Robert. 1984. *The Evolution of Cooperation*. New York: Basic Books.

Bennis, Warren. 1989. *Why Leaders Can't Lead*. San Francisco: Jossey-Bass.

Brass, Daniel, and David Krackhardt. 1999. Social capital for the twenty-first century leaders. In: J. G. Hunt and R. L. Phillips (Eds.), *Out-of-the Box Leadership Challenges for the 21st Century Army*. Amsterdam: Elsevier, 179–194.

Clark, Rodney. 1979. *The Japanese Company*. New Haven: Yale University Press.

Collins, Harry M. 2011. Language and practice. *Social Studies of Science* 41(3): 271–300.

Collins, Harry M., and Robert Evans. 2007. *Rethinking Expertise*. Chicago: University of Chicago Press.

Collins, Harry M., and Garry Sanders. 2007. They give you the keys and say 'drive it!'. Managers, referred expertise, and other expertises. *Studies in History and Philosophy of Science* 38(4): 621–641.

Covey, Stephen M. R. 2006. *The Speed of Trust*. New York: Simon and Schuster.

Dalton, Melville. 1959. *Man Who Manage*. New York: Wiley.

Deutsch, Morton. 1969. Conflicts: Productive and destructive. *Journal of Social Issues* 25(1): 7–42.

Dore, Ronald. 1973. *British Factory—Japanese Factory*. Berkeley (CA): University of California Press.

Fast, Nathanel J., Ethan R. Burris, and Caroline A. Bartel. 2014. Managing to stay in the dark: Managerial self-efficacy, ego-defensiveness, and the aversion to employee voice. *Academy of Management Journal* 57(4): 1013–1034.

Fine, Gary A. 2012. *Tiny Publics: Idiocultures and the Power of the Local*. New York: Russell Sage.

Fine, Gary A. 2013. Group cultures as arenas of action: Inhabited institutions as social worlds. Keynote address at the 8th Organization Studies Summer Workshop, Mykonos, Greece, May.

Fox, Alan. 1974. *Beyond Contract*. London: Faber.

Geertz, Clifford. 1983. *Local Knowledge*. New York: Basic Books.

Geneen, Herold. 1984. *Managing*. New York: Avon.

Gouldner, Alvin W. 1954. *Patterns of Industrial Bureaucracy*. New York: Free Press.

Hargadon, Andrew B., and Beth A. Bechky. 2006. When collections of creatives become creative collectives: A field study of problem solving at work. *Organization Science* 17(4): 484–500.

Haslam, S. Alexander, S. D. Reicher, and M. J. Platow. 2011. *The New Psychology of Leadership*. New York: Psychology Press.

Hedgecoe, Adam M. 2012. Trust and regulatory organisations: The role of local knowledge and facework in research ethics review. *Social Studies of Science* 42(3): 662–683.

Holtskog, Halvor. 2014. *How Industry Makes Knowledge*. PhD Thesis, Norwegian University of Science and Technology, Trondheim.

Hosmer, Larue T. 1995. Trust: The connecting link between organizational theory and philosophical ethics. *Academy of Management Review* 20(3): 379–403.

Jackall, Robert. 1988. *Moral Mazes*. New York: Oxford University Press.

Karaevli, Ayse. 2007. Performance consequences of new CEO 'outsiderness': Moderating effects of pre-and post-succession contexts. *Strategic Management Journal* 28(4): 681–706.

Lally, Jim. 1974. Staff cliques, 'Peter' Principal, and parochialism. *Journal of Educational Administration* 12(1): 76–83.

Levenson, Bernard. 1961. Bureaucratic succession. In: A. Etzioni (Ed.), *Complex Organizations*. New York: Holt, 362–375.

Martin, Norman H., and Anselm L. Strauss. 1959. Patterns of mobility in industrial organizations. In: W. L. Warner and N. H. Martin (Eds.), *Industrial Man*. New York: Harper, 85–101.

McGregor, Douglas. 1960. *The Human Side of Enterprise*. New York: McGraw-Hill.

Mehri, Darius. 2005. *Notes from Toyota-Land*. Ithaca (NY): ILR Press.

Nichols, Theo, and Peter Armstrong. 1976. *Workers Divided*. London: Fontana.

Orr, Julian. 1996. *Talking about Machines*. Ithaca (NY): Cornell University Press.

Parker, Martin. 2000. *Organizational Culture and Identity*. London: Sage.

Rifkin, Glenn, and George Harrar. 1988. *The Ultimate Entrepreneur*. Chicago: Contemporary Books.

Roy, Donald F. 1959–1960. "Banana Time," job satisfaction and informal interaction. *Human Organization* 18(2): 158–168.

Shotter, John, and Haridimos Tsoukas. 2014a. In search of phronesis: Leadership and the art of judgment. *Academy of Management Learning & Education* 13(2): 224–243.

Shotter, John, and Haridimos Tsoukas. 2014b. Performing phronesis: On the way to engaged judgment. *Management Learning* 45(4): 377–396.

Simmel, George. 1971. *On Individuality and Social Forms*. D. Levine (Ed.). Chicago: University of Chicago Press.

Simon, Herbert. 1957. *Administrative Behaviour*. New York: Free Press.

Swidler, Ann. 1986. Culture in action: Symbols and strategies. *American Sociological Review* 51(2): 273–286.

Thomas, Gail F., R. Zolin, and J. L. Hartmen. 2009. The central role of communication in developing trust and its effect on employee involvement. *Journal of Business Communications* 46(3): 287–310.

Wagner, Richard K. 2002. Smart people doing dumb things: The case of managerial incompetence. In: R. J. Sternberg (Ed.), *Why Smart People Can Be So Stupid*. New Haven: Yale University Press, 42–63.

Watkins, Michael. 2003. *The First Ninety Days*. Boston: Harvard Business School.

Yanow, Dvora. 2000. Seeing organizational learning: A 'cultural' view. *Organization* 7(2): 247–268.

6 Contextualizing Gin Plants' Mismanagement in the Kibbutz and Israeli Fields

Explaining the prevalence of I-KRCs' executives' CCMI-Im-C requires a Strathernian contextualization that discerns impacting contexts and their interrelations combined with historical effects.[1] The findings suggest that it was dysfunctional executives that mostly ruled I-KRCs and their gin plants by practicing CCMI-Im-C, shielded by "cost-plus" systems, castrated democracy, "parachuting" loyalists or prospective ones to deputy jobs, and intermittently using knowledgeable mid-levelers to prevent anticipated failures or to rescue failing plants, only to be suppressed when empowered by successes until leaving; a few remained by employing politics of obedience, deferring essential changes and innovations (e.g., Southern's Yunus). *Pe'ilim* were mostly imported to replace those who left, often opted for ignorance concealment, failed, and were replaced by rescuer *pe'ilim* who succeeded as depicted, were empowered, suppressed, and so on; this seesaw prolonged the rule of dysfunctional, ignorant CEOs and PMs. The exception of vulnerably involved Northern I-KRC CEO Dan, his high-moral but less involved predecessor, and four PMs of the 32 studied only served to reinforce this bleak picture in which the large majority of executives violated the high-moral democratic and egalitarian kibbutz ethos and the high-trust cultures of many innovative and successful kibbutz work units with vulnerably involved managers who led to the success of many kibbutzim.[2] Explaining the prevalence of CCMI-Im-C and this contradiction enables Strathernian contextualizing that uses my ethnographying of the kibbutz field; its comprehensive exposition is found in my referred works and is here only briefly sketched, enough to analyze its role in engendering the prevalence of negative I-KRC practices, which explain gin plants' immoral mismanagement.

Biased Study of the Kibbutz Field Concealed Mismanagement of I-KOs

Though Lewin (1951) and Bourdieu (1977) advanced the field theory in the social sciences, both anthropological and leadership research rarely contextualized findings, often missing the impact of social fields.[3] Likewise, kibbutz social scientists, except for Landshut (2000[1944]), Kressel (1974), and myself, missed major impacts of I-KO leaderships on kibbutzim and *pe'ilim* and never contextualized their findings, although critical novels ever since the 1930s (Keshet 1995) and subsequently other non-research literature such as biographies and autobiographies exposed much of these leaderships' impacts. "The kibbutz field" is a term unknown in kibbutz canonical research literature, which in accord with leaders' wishes evades I-KOs including I-KRCs in order to conceal their use of capitalist practices (Shapira 2016b). Students ignored the fact that the kibbutz became the most successful of all communal societies by being a radical social movement, societally involved by a large and complex system, which included, besides collectivist, egalitarian, democratic kibbutzim, hundreds of bureaucratic, hierarchic, and autocratic I-KOs. Other communal societies hoped to influence surrounding society by modeling collectivist egalitarianism; they avoided national problems such as wars and their cultures blossomed at the price of marginalization.[4]

The kibbutz was the opposite: intensive societal involvement through I-KOs was integral to its spearheading of the Zionist movement (Buber 1958[1947]). I-KOs were integral to the success of kibbutz society[5] but canonic research evaded their study because it would have exposed a conservative conformist sector of a radical society whose practices violated its principles.[6] Such exposure of anti-kibbutz practices would have ruined the radical kibbutz image and members' trust in leaders who headed I-KOs; hence, leaders opposed it and researchers acquiesced: while hundreds studied kibbutzim and produced over 5,000 publications, only five studied I-KOs rather recently, all without such exposure except for me.[7] "The kibbutz movement" was a common phrase in Israeli discourse, but its students never studied kibbutzim and I-KOs as organs of a social movement that had created a unique field, ignoring Lewin's (1951) and Bourdieu's (1977) field theory. I-KOs were presented as auxiliaries that did not affect kibbutz cultures, ignoring the hegemony of oligarchic tenured I-KO heads and power elites who achieved this hegemony largely by violation of radical kibbutz principles.[8] Rank-and-file members knew a little about these violations, but could not grasp their full scale and how they ensured continued hegemony of I-KO heads and their loyalists, nor knew how I-KO heads concealed and camouflaged this undemocratic hegemony, helped by co-opted social scientists.[9]

I-KOs were kibbutzim's prime context, and kibbutz society was inexplicable without their study (Shapira 2008). In 1985, the peak of the kibbutz field's growth as a communal society,[10] it consisted of 269 kibbutzim with 129,000 inhabitants and 250–300 I-KOs with 15,000–18,000 hired employees and 4,000–4,500 *pe'ilim* managers and administrators.[11] Kibbutz canonic research ignored the field perspective to defend the kibbutz image of a high-moral, progressive society. This was untangled by my 30 years of ethnographying I-KOs, kibbutzim, and their plants, but as the findings disproved canonic research, kibbutz researchers' dominant coalition (e.g., Collins 1975: Ch. 9) ignored them to protect dominance (Shapira 2016b). A prime finding was that the two more radical leaders, Tabenkin and Yaari, who founded the two largest kibbutz federations in 1927 consisting of some 80% of kibbutzim and members, exemplified at first Fairholm's (2004: 587) leadership ideal of "public service as an opportunity to engage in leadership . . . [that] supports . . . continual efforts to teach others to seek the highest ideals of public service, and thereby to leave to citizens a legacy of trust, integrity, and responsibility." But after 12–15-year tenures they entered a dysfunction phase, in accord with LLCT (Leadership Life Cycle Theory) and oligarchy theory, became conservative self-perpetuators, castrated democracy, centralized control, and turned in 1937 and 1939 (respectively) to reverence of Stalinism, which they had previously criticized, to legitimize these changes and the censorship of publications, remaining oligarchic rulers until the 1970s.[12] They had immense visible and invisible power (e.g., Ahonen et al. 2014):

1   Stalinist indoctrination legitimized the above oligarchic centralized autocracy like mini-Stalins; *rotatzia* legitimized the demotion of critical *pe'ilim*, returning them to kibbutzim much as Stalin used Siberia;
2   Their federations called The Movements grew up to some 60 kibbutzim and some 25,000 inhabitants each already in the 1950s and their two political parties became major forces in national politics;
3   Each led hundreds of *pe'ilim*, seven to ten Knesset (parliament) members (of 120), two-three cabinet ministers (of 15–18), and other loyal *pe'ilim* as senior government officials ever since 1955;
4   Senior *pe'ilim*, who either overruled *rotatzia* by tenure or moved from office to office, became powerful under leaders' or deputies' auspices, enjoyed prestige and privileges by which they dominated their kibbutzim, and secured support for prime leaders by castrating local democracies and suppressing innovators (Shapira 2008);
5   Tangible privileges of leaders were modest to retain the egalitarian image, but they enjoyed status symbols and social and cultural capital, by which they suppressed critics and innovators.[13]

Similarly oligarchic though not Stalinist and less autocratic were the leaders of the third, smaller Movement of Hever Hakvutzot (henceforth: Hever) with some 15% of kibbutzim, which aligned with the Mapay Party and were part of its leadership.[14] Four leaders dominated Hever as senior tenured officials of Mapay, the Histadrut, and/or the Zionist Movement (Ben-Avram 1976). Mapay dominated the Histadrut, the General Union of Labour, and the umbrella organization of all socialist movements and cooperatives. The Histadrut became bureaucratic and oligarchic as early as the 1930s, and largely conformed to capitalist norms including tenured privileged officials (Shapira 1993). Mapay leader Ben-Gurion led the Histadrut from 1920, the

Zionist Movement's Jewish Agency and the Jewish Palestinian community from 1935, and the Government of Israel from 1948 to 1963, with a two-year respite in 1954–1955 (while remaining the major power behind the scenes).

The kibbutz Movements established hundreds of I-KOs, which largely followed Histadrut capitalist conformity aside from the kibbutz norms of *rotatzia* and uniform *pe'ilim* salaries paid to their kibbutzim. However, powerful CEOs and senior *pe'ilim* violated *rotatzia*, continued in their jobs for decades, or circulated from one high office to another.[15] Unlike evasion of I-KOs by kibbutz social scientists, historians who wrote leaders' biographies could not evade leader-headed Movements and other I-KOs, but they missed their mismanagement as they followed the hegemonic functionalist kibbutz research, which like Israeli sociology followed functionalist American sociology and ignored non-functionalist sociologists.[16] Some historians exposed functionalists' mistakes, but without sociological theories of trust, leaders' morality, power elites, bureaucracy, oligarchy, LLCT, and social fields (Chapter 3), they missed functionalists' major mistakes, sparing the latter the need to admit them. Later on, the co-optation of some conflict sociologists and some historians by the dominant scientific coalition enlarged it and ensured its continued hegemony into the 21st century as well as its avoidance of studying I-KOs as major parts of the kibbutz field (Shapira 2012b, 2016b).

Contextualizing I-KRCs in the Kibbutz Field

The first national I-KOs were established in the mid-1920s and the first I-KRCs in 1940 as regional purchasing cooperatives. From the late 1950s industrialization enlarged each I-KRC to hundreds or over a thousand employees. Conformity to veteran I-KO capitalist norms enhanced oligarchization: many mid- and low-level *pe'ilim* were *rotated*, in contrast to CEOs who mostly continued, for up to three decades; some PMs remained up to 10–15 years (Moav, David) while deputy PMs and TMs mostly had shorter terms unless PMs retained them (V-TM, Yunus). *Pe'ilim* were publicly stratified by company car models from the best ones for CEOs down to the humblest ones for lesser *pe'ilim* (p. 51). Ranking by company cars clearly signaled status and encouraged *pe'ilim* struggles to obtain cars or for car betterment; many of those who lost these battles left their jobs. *Pe'ilim*'s career ladders explain these struggles rather than simply justifying them by the pleasure of driving better cars: as a prestigious car signaled one's high status and power, it helped deter one's replacement by a new "jumper" PM; alternatively, ahead of a plausible *rotatzia* a *pa'il* sought another managerial job by visiting other I-KOs as plausible outlets. On such a visit one's nice company car created the image of a successful manager, essential for impressing potential future employers (Shapira 2008: Ch. 8).

The impact of the oligarchic kibbutz field context on *pe'ilim* also explained the prevalence of Im-C and CCMI in I-KRCs. Institutionalization of practices in an organizational field may cause outside impacts combined with "internal circuits" (Gherardi and Perrotta 2011). In this field, during the 1960s–1970s, old-guard leaders and their successors preached *rotatzia* under the pretext of preventing oligarchy but negated their own preaching by oligarchic practices: they held their jobs for life and their supporting clique members moved from one high office to another with no democratic election or re-election, contrary to the democracy and egalitarianism they preached; they appropriated privileges and accumulated intangible capital by which they ruled the field. The leaders and I-KO CEOs used immoral practices common in the surrounding society and loyalist deputies defended their rule, which violated kibbutz principles (Shapira 2001, 2008). Immoral prime leaders Tabenkin and Yaari never admitted that their reverence of Stalinism was wrong, not even after the 1956 exposure of Stalin's brutal dictatorship and the bloody suppression of Hungarian democracy, since admission would have opened a Pandora's box leading to their succession by critical younger leaders.[17]

In this oligarchic context often *pe'ilim* were promoted due to loyalty to entrenched higher-ups rather than due to effectiveness, critical thinking, and innovation. Their "parachuting" was legitimized by the pretext of sparing agency problems (Arthurs and Busenitz 2003): they supposedly cared for the interests of kibbutzim better than hired managers. Unfortunately, both practices curbed *pe'ilim*'s readiness to risk their authority and jobs by ignorance-exposing vulnerable involvement. In firms without these practices, a manager's taking ignorance exposure risks to enhance her/his performance might be rewarded by job continuity and career advancement, while acquired know-how and *phronesis* together with trustful relationships with locals minimizes the chance of major mistakes, failures, and demotion. With kibbutz field practices, demotion by "parachuting" a boss's loyalist to one's job was presented as normal *rotatzia*, while the "jumper's" lack of pertinent competences for the job encouraged playing safe by CCMI-Im-C and other immoral job-survival strategies and tactics, as depicted in the organizational literature. Thus, the institutionalization of *rotatzia* and "parachuting" in the kibbutz field encouraged negative and vicious distrust and ignorance cycles, low-trust cultures, and immoral mismanagement.

Rotatzia and "parachuting" weakened *pe'ilim* managers and encouraged Im-C, as found in the US armed forces (p. 48). *Rotatzia* discouraged critical thinking and innovation: managers' short terms prevented productive use of experience-acquired job know-how, *phronesis*, and power to introduce changes and innovations; it encouraged seeking advancement to privileged high-level I-KO and I-KRC jobs and accumulating power and capital to obviate *rotatzia* or to move from one I-KO high office to another by use of patronage rather than performance. *Rotatzia*'s shortening of kibbutz managers' tenures deterred those of them who were "kibbutz delegates" to I-KRC Boards from criticizing *pe'ilim*: after occupying short-term kibbutz managerial jobs they needed *pe'ilim*'s auspices to themselves become *pe'ilim*. The threat of demotion by *rotatzia* encouraged I-KRC managers to entrench by importing them as loyal lieutenants, nurturing yea-sayers by conservatism, while self-empowering by excessive growth of OPM and technological virtuosity (Galbraith 1971) rather than seeking efficiency and effectiveness. Worse still, *rotatzia* helped suppress innovative, successful *pe'ilim* like Gabi and Thomas: the pretext of *rotatzia* legitimized their replacing when their empowerment threatened bosses' superiority. Thus, Thomas left not just due to his fatigue of the conflicts with Shavit but also because he expected dismissal on the pretext of *rotatzia*. This pretext also defended CEOs' prestige: the dismissal of failed nominees was camouflaged as *rotatzia* and enabled nominees to advance further managerial careers elsewhere, as did both Shavit and Avi.

The practice of "parachuting" encouraged *rotatzia* by offering plausible successors for any *rotated* manager, while retaining I-KRCs' managerial jobs exclusively for *pe'ilim*. Exclusiveness commenced in the 1940s, after the first I-KOs began to succeed; urban employees were hired, and some of them might have advanced to management based on merit but this rarely happened. Exclusiveness was formally aimed at defending owner kibbutzim's interests by sparing agency problems, but it enhanced immoral mismanagement. The kibbutz field context further explained the logic of the seemingly illogical practices (Bourdieu 1990) of *rotatzia* and "parachuting": these practices enabled the successful careers of *pe'ilim* by proving loyalty to higher-ups versus the lesser career prospects of those who sought performance; their empowerment by successes threatened the supremacy of ignorant bosses and disturbed relationships with them, culminating in dismissal or resignation (e.g., Thomas). Facing the dilemma of either risking their authority by ignorance-exposing vulnerable involvement or defending authority by CCMI, *pe'ilim* mostly avoided the risks in view of the field's domination by self-perpetuating conservative oligarchs who promoted according to loyalty rather than performance, as in surrounding Histadrut bureaucracies.[18] The kibbutz field encouraged this: when a CCMI user "jumper" failed, kibbutzim would hurry to provide a Thomas-like rescuer who succeeded, and was then empowered, suppressed, and ousted by ignorant superiors. Then "parachuting" new outsiders repeated this cycle, which retained the rule and advanced careers of immoral CEOs presiding over mismanaged plants and I-KOs.[19]

Why did *Rotatzia* and "Parachuting" Become Institutionalized in the Field?

The contextual impact of the kibbutz field in which veteran I-KO heads institutionalized *rotatzia* and "parachutings" largely explains the prevalence of these two negative practices in the I-KRCs studied. But why were these practices institutionalized by veteran I-KO heads?

From the 1940s Movements' tenured leaders entered dysfunction phases and became oligarchic in accord with oligarchy theory and LLCT and from the early 1950s *pe'ilim* were no longer motivated by servant transformational leadership and the challenges it offered (Chapter 3). In the 1920s–1940s, *pe'ilim* led the establishment of kibbutzim in hostile, arid, and hard-to-settle lands, as well as struggles with the Arabs and with British rulers, organized illegal Jewish immigration, and established the quasi-IKO underground Palmach army; their exhilarating efforts led to establishment of the State of Israel in 1948. Then these challenges mostly disappeared; the new state took over both old and new tasks by disbanding the sectorial society (Yatziv 1999), while Stalin's anti-Semitic campaign damaged belief in Tabenkin and Yaari's preaching of USSR reverence. Major problems of the kibbutzim also did not motivate *pe'ilim*'s creative action as the old guard suppressed innovation.[20] In accord with oligarchy theory, self-perpetuating leaders conscripted and motivated *pe'ilim* by using privileges, but these were weak controls as they were mostly granted according to one's status and left little to leaders' manipulation. *Rotatzia* enhanced control, made the status of *pe'ilim* and their symbolic privileges such as company cars dependent on I-KO heads' whims, and legitimized early replacement of critics and successful innovators, preventing their accumulation of prestige, empowerment, and entrenchment in pivotal jobs.

Rotatzia followed extant practices: since the 1920s *pe'ilim* emissaries to the Jewish diaspora served two-to-three-year terms, and in some problematic kibbutz offices such as that of work coordinator (*sadran avoda*) *rotatzia* had been institutionalized in the 1940s. *Rotatzia* of *pe'ilim* seemed a legitimate egalitarian practice, while both members and researchers missed its enhancement of oligarchy, as higher-ups entrenched by their power and intangible capital and became tenured patrons who controlled the careers of short-term *pe'ilim* and kibbutz managers. Patron CEOs and PMs sent critics back to their kibbutzim seemingly as normal *rotatzia*, and suppressed empowered innovative *pe'ilim* who then left also as seemingly *rotatzia* (Thomas), while *rotatzia* believers waiting their turn (Yaakov, Aharon) were frustrated by the retention of the CEO's loyalist (e.g., Moav). *Rotatzia* camouflaged the dismissal of failing PMs (Shavit), while enhancing the egalitarian progressive image of the kibbutz; for instance, *pe'ilim*'s privileges were presented as provisional. Only late did critical students expose that many *pe'ilim* were afforded privileges for life by circulation ("jumping") between I-KO and kibbutz managerial jobs (Helman 1987; Shapira 1987).

Rotatzia also helped institutionalize "parachutings" by encouraging *rotated* kibbutz officers to maintain their managerial status by accepting I-KO jobs in action domains unknown to them, due to familiarity with their bosses: Moav's first CEO was his relative; Yuval's CEO was a member of his kibbutz; likewise Shavit who also helped Zelikovich manage the Regional Council; and so on. However, lack of pertinent expertise made the status of these managers fragile and encouraged loyalty to patrons while using

CCMI. CCMI caused failures and successions by "parachuted" rescuers, while the short tenures of Thomas-like rescuers furthered *rotatzia's* institutionalization. The brain drain of the 1950s crises also explained many failures and successions: following this brain drain the kibbutz managerial job market exploded in the prosperous 1960s–1970s (below), thus many mediocre members became kibbutz managers and then *pe'ilim*. Facing unknown domains with limited talent and few job-relevant competences, mediocre *pe'ilim* mostly opted to CCMI and failed functioning; these failures and resulting successions furthered institutionalized *rotatzia* and "parachutings."

Contextual Impacts of Kibbutzim and I-KOs' 1960s–1970s Successes

Due to the Brum Club invention (below) and many local and I-KO innovators (e.g., Northern Gin), the kibbutz field succeeded in the 1960s–1970s: I-KRCs became industrialized, with more than 110 new plants and some 11,000 employees; the kibbutz population doubled to some 120,000 and factories inside kibbutzim tripled to some 300 with some 11,500 employees (Shapira 2008: 102). A full exposition of this change is found in my other works; here I deal only with those aspects that help explain the mismanagement of the gin plants.

Kibbutzim had previously prospered also in the 1930s–1940s: within two decades their population grew from 1,453 to 49,140, while their numbers grew from 17 to 177.[21] During the 1948 war many kibbutzim suffered heavily, both many casualties and destruction as outposts of Jewish settlement. Then a huge wave of immigrants arrived in Israel, requiring ample means for their absorption and for the establishment of many new kibbutzim in areas inhospitable to agriculture such as the Negev Desert and the mountainous Galilee. At that time kibbutzim also suffered a series of political crises and mass attrition; only absorption of immigrants and growing fertility achieved some growth. However, in the late 1950s kibbutzim efficient, innovative agriculture, whose innovations diffused to moshavim (semi-co-operative agricultural settlements), created surpluses of products in local markets and falling prices, leading to losses. Kibbutzim then turned to export crops such as cotton and avocado, industrialized by establishing factories, and industrialized agriculture by establishing regional processing plants that enhanced efficiency by economies of scale.[22]

The local entrepreneurs who led these major changes were often backed by new-generation kibbutz economic managers and treasurers who succeeded older officers, who became *pe'ilim*. Innovators faced major obstacles for the above restructuring:

1   Resistance by local conservative veteran informal leaders who dominated decision-making because of their old-guard status and I-KO

prestigious offices or other outside high offices on Movements' behalf (Shapira 2008: Chs. 12–15).

2   Conservative oligarchic I-KO leaders and power elites already in their dysfunction phases (Hambrick 2007), who were patrons of the informal local leaders and who ignored the need for restructuring and its financing (Shapira 2008: Chs. 10–11).

3   Conservative banks, skeptical of kibbutz innovations, avoided financing and unwilling Movement Funds (below), both because of old-guard conservatism and limited means (Sack 1996; Shalem 2000).

"The Brum Club" Solution: Cooperation of Kibbutzim and Funding Institutions

The most severe obstacle to restructuring was the lack of financing. Movement Funds were small financing I-KOs established in 1933–1935, collecting small fees from kibbutzim and giving both kibbutzim and I-KOs loans and guaranties for bank loans. One reason for not seeking a more comprehensive solution for financing growth was that main financing for the establishment and development of kibbutzim came from Zionist organs, and Kibbutz Fund loans and guaranties answered special needs not financed by these organs (Sack 1999). This financing was sufficient in eras of moderate growth and a prosperous economy, but not when large sums of money were required to finance restructuring in turbulent periods; innovators could barely find proper financing for investment in innovations. Kibbutzim's dependency on agriculture that became unprofitable in the late 1950s and their minimal realizable assets deterred banks from financing their innovations, using the desperate need of kibbutzim for credit and giving it against promissory notes (IOUs) at a very high interest rate (Shalem 2000: 88). As early as 1952, kibbutzim paid 11.2% of their revenues as interest on loans to banks and this continued for a decade (Brum 1986: 78). A major reason, besides the unwilling banks, was the effort by the Bank of Israel, the governmental issuing bank, to stop inflation by severe credit limitations.

However, the three kibbutz Movements gained considerable political power since 1955, as the parties affiliated with the two radical Movements, Tabenkin's Kibbutz Me'ukhad (KM) and Yaari's Kibbutz Artzi (KA), joined the Mapay coalition government and together with Ikhud Movement leaders[23] the kibbutzim held a third of all cabinet ministers. Why did their leaders not use their political power to alter this severe financial situation?

A prime reason was old-guard leaders' dysfunction ever since the 1940s. They were mostly involved in national politics in Tel Aviv or Jerusalem, and they were detached from day-to-day kibbutz life and the hardships caused by financial distress while enjoying perks unknown to ordinary members; as cabinet ministers and MKs (=MPs, Members of Knesset [parliament]) they remained indifferent to the financing problem (Shapira 2008: Ch. 10). Ikhud's leader Kadish Luz, who was nominated Agriculture Minister in

1955, tried to help by employing a common bureaucratic medication: in 1957 he nominated the Horowitz Committee to deal with the problem. But when it concluded some 30 months of discussions (a slowness that also signaled indifference to the plight of kibbutzim), Ex-General Moshe Dayan replaced Luz and shelved committee recommendations although its head, Horowitz, was the Governor of the Bank of Israel. Other signs of indifference were the year it took to organize a convention of kibbutz treasurers to discuss their plight and object to Dayan's shelving (Sack 1999: 122–124), as well as the fact that up to 1962 none of the Movement secretariats dealt with the problem and then only one discussed it (Shalem 2000: 92). Worse still, kibbutz leaders could have pointed out to government officials that solving kibbutz financial problems by implementing the Horowitz Committee's recommendations would have enhanced restructuring according to government policy that favored exports and industrialization. At that time, the government wasted much money on bogus industrialists who had promised to export much of their production but rarely did so, while kibbutz industry proved to be the opposite (Shapira 2008).

Some kibbutz treasurers financed investments by short-term loans, but as the fruits of investments came much later, this often caused a snowball of mounting debts. A more creative solution was "check rolling," by which a treasurer could create fake money up to the equivalent of US$50,000 (Gelb 2001: 98–99). However, even this fake money solved treasurers' adversity only for a limited time; a genuine solution that enabled the renewed prosperity of the kibbutzim for some two decades was the creation of cooperation between Movement Funds, the banks, the Jewish Agency, and the government by mid-level transformative leaders led by KM *pa'il* Avraham Brum, head of the Ministry of Agriculture's credit department. The new scheme called "The Brum Club" (a "Club" because a kibbutz was free to join) created cooperation by all funding institutions in answering a kibbutz's credit needs according to an agreed-upon yearly development plan. Then the Jewish Agency and/or the government gave their share of the required money to one bank to which the kibbutz was "clatched" and only through which it performed all financial transactions. The bank added an equivalent sum of its own money and the kibbutz treasurer got all the credit needed from this bank as long-term loans at reasonable interest rates. Brum followed bankers and Jewish Agency officials who found that such a solution rescued US farmers in the 1930s crisis. The "Club" was a major success that enlarged fast: from nine kibbutzim in 1964, to 57 in 1967, and up to 185 kibbutzim (some 75%) in 1972 (Shalem 2000: 113–114). The results of the "Club" solution were a diminishing burden of loan interest, from 9% of revenues in 1963 to 3% in 1978, and due to profitable investments kibbutzim-owned capital grew from 8.6% of total fixed assets, to 46% (Brum 1986: 78). By 1970 the kibbutzim financed 48% of their investments from their own profits versus the 13% financed by the "Club" (Brum 1986: 122–123), while its success encouraged other institutions to follow suit. For instance, experts of the World Bank were enthusiastic about it, and in 1973 the bank enlarged its loans to Israeli agriculture by US$35 million (Brum 1986: 77).

The Kibbutz Field Prosperity in the 1960s–1970s Helped Explain Mismanagement

> "But Jeshurun waxen fat, thou art kicked . . . thou art grown thick, . . . covered with fatness; then he forsook God which made him, and lightly esteemed the Rock of his salvation"
> (Deuteronomy Ch. 32, para. 15).

The context of the prosperous kibbutz field in the 1960s–1970s encouraged dysfunctional, immoral leadership. Kibbutz leaders were not as corrupt as some Mapay leaders, but self-serving actions and decisions were common; for instance, prime leaders Tabenkin and Yaari defended their dominance by avoiding admitting mistaken Stalinism even after the 1956 exposure of its horrors and the bloody suppression of Hungarian democracy (Shapira 2016a). Political leaders also minimally cared about kibbutzim's financial distress, allowed 30 months of Horowitz Committee discussions, and then allowed Dayan to shelve its recommendations. They modeled detached CCMI-Im-C: as solving financial problems was not simple, required ignorance-exposing delving into their complexities that promised little prestige and power and much toil and frustration before arriving at an agreed-upon solution, they avoided it.

Leaders' CCMI-Im-C legitimized that of fodder mix plant's *pe'ilim*, Im-C of Board members representing kibbutzim in this enlargement case (p. 51), and CCMI-Im-C of many I-KRC CEOs and PMs. The prosperous kibbutz field encouraged *pe'ilim* to risk "parachuting" into unknown jobs with minimal pertinent know-how and *phronesis*, promising career advancement as many detached/seductive-coercive PMs advanced to CEO posts and then to high government and Histadrut positions; their situation encouraged the use of CCMI as did habituses created through repeated "parachutings" into a variety of I-KO jobs, job survivals, and advancing careers without ignorance exposure; the field's prosperity encouraged the belief in career advancement with minimal job-pertinent competence (Shapira 2008). Accordingly, none of the successful TMs advanced to be PMs, similar to British engineers' failure to advance to management positions (Armstrong 1987).

Another contextual effect of the 1960s prosperity was the conservation of dysfunctional Movement leaderships and loyalist conservative power elites. The kibbutz crises of the early 1950s led in both KM and KA to the emergence of groups of new-generation young leaders whose critique of prime leaders Tabenkin and Yaari (respectively) encouraged the latter to enhance power by joining the government in 1955. Both leaders maintained Movement hegemony with conservative loyalists' help and Stalinist reverence of the USSR until the early 1970s, barred open and democratic elections, which could have elevated successors and renewed Movements' secretariats and councils.[24] However, a prime reason for their success in maintaining a conservative hegemony was the field's prosperity and co-optation and/or suppression of younger leaders, whose critique did not gain momentum as economic I-KOs and emerging kibbutz industry offered talented critically thinking innovators alternative careers to those of Movements' political careers.[25]

The conservative dominance of the Ikhud Movement's old-guard leadership that barred its succession was different but had the same outcome: as part of the oligarchic Mapay Party these leaders did not need centralization and autocracy to retain supremacy; as cabinet ministers, MKs, and high-level Mapay officials, they dominated their kibbutzim and the Ikhud, conforming to Histadrut conformist practices, while the decentralized structure of Ikhud encouraged young radicals to opt for a variety of local innovations; thus, unlike KM and KA no group of young leaders challenged the old guard's conservative hegemony.[26]

The contextual impact of all three Movements was conservative, while the field prospered due to innovations by new-generation innovators both locally and in I-KOs encouraged by Brum's Club. But leaders' conservative impact discouraged reconsidering the deleterious effects of *rotatzia* and "parachutings" and no Movement leader questioned I-KRCs' violations of kibbutz principles, their excessive OPM growth, their inefficiency, and ineffectiveness. Neither did any such leader visit I-KRCs to learn their unique problems, nor did they encourage innovators like Dan, Gabi, and their like to restructure I-KRCs to overcome their faults. Prime leaders' detachment supported the Im-C of I-KRC executives by never criticizing their oligarchic practices that they themselves used to control the Movements. While KM and KA leaders criticized the Im-C of many Israeli officials, they ignored the Im-C of I-KRCs' officials. Ever since Landshut's 1944 book they pressed researchers and authors to ignore I-KOs quasi-capitalist cultures and evade them as supposedly auxiliary organs that served kibbutz needs without affecting its progressive culture (Shapira 2008, 2012b). Without any public critique of I-KRCs' violations of kibbutz principles up to the mid-1970s due to leaders' censorship, immoral careerist executives paid no price in terms of prestige for practicing Im-C and using CCMI, much like business "superstars" until recently (Ailon 2015).

The prosperity of the kibbutz field encouraged CCMI and Im-C in other ways as well. A major reason for using CCMI by many *pe'ilim* was, seemingly, mediocrity due to the brain drain suffered by kibbutzim in the 1950s crises. A major reason was the dysfunctional conservative Stalinism of KM and KA leaders that suppressed critical, innovative, talented young leaders who objected to USSR reverence, failed, and left. These leaders' policies were grossly mistaken (Near 2008: 467) and one outcome was the 1950s financial devastation of kibbutzim. Ben-Gurion attacked the kibbutzim, dismantled the sectorial structure of society favorable to kibbutzim (Yatziv

1999), and the new state bureaucracies took over some of kibbutzim's pre-state tasks, depriving them of prestige and status (Near 2008: 433–439). As a result, throughout the 1950s thousands of educated young talents left the kibbutzim (Near 2008: 502) to study at universities and to take ample jobs offered by the new state and municipal organs. In the prosperous 1960s–1970s, the kibbutz managerial job market exploded with hundreds of new plants that required thousands of managers. This facilitated the "parachuting" of mediocre *pe'ilim*, whose lack of pertinent job know-how encouraged opting for CCMI-Im-C. Many failed and were replaced, and the considerable replacements helped institutionalize *rotatzia* and "parachutings," which empowered and entrenched CEOs, enhanced their control of *pe'ilim*'s sponsored mobility (Turner 1960), and furthered *pe'ilim*'s tendency to practice CCMI-Im-C.

Wherever a new *pa'il* would have looked in I-KOs, s/he would see *pe'ilim* who advanced by "jumping" from one short managerial job to another, often a better one, until entrenching as a CEO or other high I-KO official in a powerful position. Minimal probing untangled that *pe'ilim* mostly advanced due to the auspices of powerful patrons (Shapira 2008: Ch. 6). This discouraged risky ignorance exposure and performance-seeking involvement, preferring to opt for CCMI-Im-C and seek patrons' auspices. Only a few, such as PMs Yuval and Lowland's Yatzek, opted for seductive/coercive autocratic CCMI and empowerment by "parachuting" loyalists, while mostly detachment was preferred. The field's growth, with new plants frequently inaugurated on kibbutzim, I-KRCs, and other I-KOs, demanded more managers; it encouraged the managerial belief that one's mediocre success as a PM with no authority-risking vulnerable involvement would be enough to find another job in case of *rotatzia*. The career successes of mediocre managers (e.g., Valley Gin's David and V-TM) supported belief in this strategy.

Last but not least, *pe'ilim* faced leaders' suppression of the critique of I-KO managerial practices; critical public probing of these practices commenced in Movements' weeklies and other kibbutz publications only in the late 1970s, years after prime leaders had perished or retired;[27] even then researchers mostly continued to support their policy, which vindicated I-KRC oligarchic practices. Kibbutz canonical research ignored this critique, as did the four other students who studied I-KOs beside myself (Shapira 2012b). It was likewise ignored by old guards' successors, conservative loyalists who lacked critical thinking and continued old guards' outdated policies but implemented them even worse due to this lacuna (Hirschman 1970). Only in the wake of the major kibbutz debt crisis in the late 1980s, to which I-KRCs' and I-KOs' debts contributed meaningfully, did public interest in their mismanagement emerge. Similar to Enron and other scandalous firms, many I-KRC plants went bankrupt or were sold, since the economic crisis of kibbutzim barred them from further paying for their inefficiencies. Those left mostly became marginal in the kibbutz economy and in managerial careers *inter alia*, because agriculture became marginal in most kibbutzim due to industrialization. Cotton growing shrunk to some 20% of its 1980s scale, with only two gin plants left.

Notes

1 On contextualization see: Huen (2009); Morita (2014); Strathern (2004); on hegemonic plants' contexts see: Holtskog (2014); on historical analysis see: Bunzl (2004); Wallerstein (2004).
2 Barkai (1977); Near (1992–1997); Ringel-Hofman (1988); Shalem (2000); Shapira (2008, 2011); Spiro (1983).
3 In anthropology: Huen (2009); Marx (1985): 147; Morita (2014); in leadership research: Peus et al. (2013).
4 Brumann (2000); Oved (1988); Pitzer (1997).
5 Brum (1986); Niv and Bar-On (1992); Rosolio (1975); Sack (1996); Shalem (2000); Shapira (2008).
6 Adar (1975); Atar (1982); Barak (1992); Ginat (1981); Ilana and Avner (1977); Ron (1978); Shapira (1979, 1987, 2005).
7 See: http://research.haifa.ac.il. The 4: Avrahami (1993); Niv and Bar-On (1992); Rosolio (1975, 1999).
8 Footnote 6 and: Fadida (1972); Helman (1987); Shapira (2001, 2008); Topel (1979).
9 Previous footnote, footnote 6 and: Shapira (1990, 1992, 1995a, 2012b, 2016b).
10 Today's field (2016) includes some 165,000 inhabitants, but it is mostly inegalitarian and non-communal.
11 Due to a lack of research, numbers are estimated, reached through use of many sources, too numerous to cite; see: Brum (1986); Gilboa (1991); Lifshitz (1990); Near (1997); Niv and Bar-On (1992); Shapira (2008); Yadlin (1989).
12 Aharoni (2000); Beilin (1984); Cohen (2000); Gilboa (2000); Kafkafi (1992); Kynan (1989); Shapira (2016a); Shure (2001).
13 See previous footnote; e.g., Brumann (2000); Hirschman (1970); Michels (1959[1915]); Stryjan (1989).
14 Leadership in the fourth tiny Movement of *Kibbutz Dati* (religious kibbutzim) was not studied.
15 Only one quasi-I-KO, the Palmach underground army which Tabenkin and KM established in 1942, was egalitarian and democratic; it was cancelled in 1948 by Ben-Gurion to boost his dominance (Yatziv 1999).
16 Ram (1995); Shapira (2012a, 2016b).
17 Beilin (1984); Shapira (2008: Ch.10–11, 2016a); Shure (2001).
18 In large I-KOs: Aharoni (2000); Cohen (2000); Shure (2001); in the Histadrut: Shapira (1984).
19 In the case of I-KO air-spraying co-op 'Chimavir' the rescue failed and it went bankrupt (Arnon 1982).
20 Beilin (1984); Cohen (1978); Kafkafi (1992); Kynan (1989); Near (1997, 2008); Ron (1978); Shapira (2008, 2016b).
21 Landshut (1944: 61); Near (1997: 364).
22 Kibbutz factories: Barkai (1977); Rosner et al. (1980); Shapira (1978/9, 1979, 1980, 2008); Regional industry: Brum (1986), Rosolio (1975); Shapira (2008)
23 In 1951 one-third of Kibbutz Meukhad kibbuzim left this Movement and joined the Hever, which changed name to Ikhud Hakibbutzim Vehakvutzot Movement.
24 Tabenkin died in 1971 and Yaari relinquished offices due to poor health.
25 Aharoni (2000); Gilboa (2000); Halamish (2013); Shapira (2008: Ch. 11); Shure (2001); personal experience as a supporter of critical young leaders.

26 Inbari (2009); Kressel (1974); Shapira (1980, 2008: Chaps. 14–15); Warhurst (1996).
27 Cohen (1978); Ginat (1979a, 1979b); Ilana and Avner (1977); Ron (1978); Shapira (1979).

References

Adar, Banko. 1975. Company car: Needs and passions. *Hashavua Bakibbutz Haartzi*, January 3 and 10 (Hebrew).

Aharoni, Arie. 2000. *From the Diary of a Candidate for Treason*. Tel Aviv: Sifriat Poalim (Hebrew).

Ahonen, Pasi, J. Tienari, et al. 2014. Hidden contexts and invisible power relations: A Foucauldian reading of diversity research. *Human Relations* 67(3): 263–286.

Ailon, Galit. 2015. From superstars to devils: The ethical discourse on managerial figures involved in a corporate scandal. *Organization* 22(1): 78–99.

Armstrong, Peter. 1987. Engineers, management and trust. *Work, Employment and Society* 1(4): 421–440.

Arnon, Ofra. 1982. *The Collapse of Chimavir*. Final Thesis, Ruppin College (Hebrew).

Arthurs, Jonathan D., and Lowell W. Busenitz. 2003. The boundaries and limitations of agency theory and stewardship theory in the venture capitalist/entrepreneur relationship. *Entrepreneurship Theory and Practice* 28(2): 145–162.

Atar, Asaf. 1982. Nothing is new in the regional enterprises. *Yahad*, November 19 (Hebrew).

Avrahami, Eli. 1993. *The Functioning of the TKM—Dilemmas and Directions for Change*. Ramat Efal: Yad Tabenkin (Hebrew).

Barak, Moshe. 1992. Leave equality [aside]. *Kibbutz*, November 24 (Hebrew).

Barkai, Haim. 1977. *Growth Patterns of the Kibbutz Economy*. Amsterdam: North-Holland.

Beilin, Yosi. 1984. *Sons in the Shade of Fathers*. Tel Aviv: Revivim (Hebrew).

Ben-Avram, Baruch. 1976. *Hever Hakvutzot*. Ramat Efal: Yad Tabenkin (Hebrew).

Bourdieu, Pierre. 1977. *Outline of a Theory of Practice*. Cambridge: Cambridge University Press.

Bourdieu, Pierre. 1990. *The Logic of Practice*. Cambridge: Polity.

Brum, Avraham. 1986. *Always Controversial*. Ramat Efal: Yad Tabenkin (Hebrew).

Brumann, Christoph. 2000. The dominance of one and its perils: Charismatic leadership and branch structures in utopian communes. *Journal of Anthropological Research* 56(4): 425–451.

Buber, Martin. 1958[1947]. *Paths in Utopia*. Boston: Beacon Press.

Bunzl, Matti. 2004. Boas, Foucault, and the "Native Anthropologist": Notes toward a Neo-Boasian Anthropology. *American Anthropologist* 106(3): 435–442.

Cohen, Mulla. 2000. *To Give and to Receive*. Tel Aviv: Hakibbutz Hameukhad (Hebrew).

Cohen, Reuven. 1978. *The Singles Society*. Final Thesis, KM's Seminar Center Efal (Hebrew).

Collins, Randall. 1975. *Conflict Sociology*. New York: Academic.

Fadida, Michael. 1972. *The Dynamics of Career Patterns among Political Activists in a Kibbutz*. M.A. thesis, Sociology and Anthropology Department, Tel Aviv University (Hebrew).

Fairholm, Matthew R. 2004. A new sciences outline for leadership development. *The Leadership and Organization Development Journal* 25(4): 369–383.

Galbraith, John K. 1971. *The New Industrial State*. Boston: Houghton Mifflin.

Gelb, Saadia. 2001. *The Chase is the Game*. Englewood Cliffs (NJ): Dworkin.

Gherardi, Silvia, and Manuela Perrotta. 2011. Egg dates sperm: A tale of a practice change and its institutionalization. *Organization* 18(5): 595–614.

Gilboa, Nachman. 1991. Much downsizing. *Hadaf Hayarok*, May 14 (Hebrew).

Gilboa, Nachman. 2000. Still afraid of Yaari and Hazan. *Hadaf Hayarok*, April 18 (Hebrew).

Ginat, Avshalom. 1979a. The second blow of botulism. *Hashavua Bakibbutz Haartzi*, November 2 (Hebrew).

Ginat, Avshalom. 1979b. All for silencing [of the fiasco], and who profits from it. *Hashavua Bakibbutz Haartzi*, December 14 (Hebrew).

Ginat, Avshalom. 1981. Will the cars of *pe'ilim* be at the car manager's disposal? *Hadaf Hayarok*, December 7 (Hebrew).

Halamish, Aviva. 2009–2013. *Meir Yaari* (Two volumes). Tel Aviv: Am Oved (Hebrew).

Hambrick, Donald C. 2007. Upper echelons theory: An update. *Academy of Management Review* 32(2): 334–343.

Helman, Amir. 1987. The development of professional managers in the kibbutz. *Economic Quarterly* 33: 1031–1038 (Hebrew).

Hirschman, Albert O. 1970. *Exit, Voice and Loyalty*. Cambridge (MA): Harvard University Press.

Holtskog, Halvor. 2014. *How Industry Makes Knowledge*. PhD thesis, Norwegian University of Science and Technology, Trondheim.

Huen, Chi W. 2009. What is context? An ethnophilosophical account. *Anthropological Theory* 9(2): 149–169.

Ilana and Avner. 1977. The desired. *Bakibbutz*, February 14 (Hebrew).

Inbari, Assaf. 2009. *Going Home*. Tel Aviv: Yediot Ahronot (Hebrew).

Kafkafi, Eayl. 1992. *Truth or Faith*. Yad Izhak Ben-Zvi (Hebrew).

Keshet, Shulamit. 1995. *Spiritual Underground: The Beginning of the Kibbutz Novel*. Tel Aviv: Hakibbutz Hame'uchad (Hebrew).

Kressel, Gideon M. 1974. *Stratification Versus Equality in the Kibbutz*. Tel Aviv: Cherikover (Hebrew).

Kynan, Ofra. 1989. *In Our Own Image: Hashomer Hatzair and the Mass Immigration*. M.A. thesis, Jewish History Department, Tel Aviv University (Hebrew).

Landshut, Zigfried. 2000[1944]. *The Kvutza*. Ramat Efal: Yad Tabenkin (Hebrew).

Lewin, Kurt. 1951. *The Field Theory in Social Science*. New York: Harper.

Lifshitz, Oded. 1990. Thin is nice. *Al Hamishmar*, March 11 (Hebrew).

Marx, Emanuel. 1985. Social-anthropological research and knowing Arab society. In: Aluf Har'even (Ed.), *To Know Neighboring People*. Jerusalem: Van Lear, 137–152 (Hebrew).

Michels, Robert. 1959[1915]. *Political Parties*. New York: Dover.

Morita, Atsuro. 2014. The ethnographic machine: Experimenting with context and comparison in Strathernian Ethnography. *Science, Technology & Human Values* 39(2): 214–235.

Near, Henry. 1992–1997. *The Kibbutz Movement: A History*. Vol. I—New York: Oxford University Press; Vol. II—London: Littman Library.

Near, Henry. 2008. *Only a Track My Feet Made*. Jerusalem: Bialik Institute (Hebrew).

Niv, Amitai, and Dan Bar-On. 1992. *The Dilemma of Size from a System Learning Perspective: The Case of the Kibbutz.* Greenwich (CN): JAI.

Oved, Yaakov. 1988. *Two Hundred Years of American Communes.* New Brunswick (NJ): Transaction.

Peus, Claudia, S. Braun, and D. Frey. 2013. Situation-based measurement of the full range of leadership model: Development and validation of a situational judgment test. *The Leadership Quarterly* 24(4): 777–795.

Pitzer, Donald E. (Ed.). 1997. *America's Communal Utopias.* Chapel Hill (NC): University of North Carolina Press.

Ram, Uri. 1995. *The Changing Agenda of Israeli Sociology.* Albany (NY): SUNY Press.

Ringel-Hofman, Ariela. 1988. 28 years of singular rule, 390 million Shekels debt. *Yedi'ot Achronot,* July 29 (Hebrew).

Ron, Yaakov. 1978. The kibbutz ideology—theory and reality. *Hedim* 43(108): 170–189 (Hebrew).

Rosner, Menachem, Uri Leviatan, et al. 1980. *Self-Management and Hired Labor in Kibbutz Industry.* Tel Aviv: KIA (Hebrew).

Rosolio, Daniel. 1975. *The Regional Structure in the Kibbutz Movement: Sociological Aspects.* Tel Aviv: Am Oved (Hebrew).

Rosolio, Daniel. 1999. *System and Crisis.* Tel Aviv: Am Oved (Hebrew).

Sack, Yaakov. 1999. *Idea and Money—Spirit and Material.* Ramat Efal: Yad Tabenkin (Hebrew).

Shalem, Eldad. 2000. *Public Funding of Collective Organizations.* Ramat Efal: Yad Tabenkin (Hebrew).

Shapira, Reuven. 1978/9. Autonomy of technostructure: An inter-kibbutz regional organization case study. *The Kibbutz* 6/7: 276–303 (Hebrew).

Shapira, Reuven. 1979. Who hold the steering? The Regional Enterprises: A portrait. *Shdemot.* 69(Autumn): 9–23 (Hebrew).

Shapira, Reuven. 1980. *The Absorption of Academicians in Kibbutz Industry.* Tel Aviv: KIA (Hebrew).

Shapira, Reuven. 1987. *Anatomy of Mismanagement.* Tel Aviv: Am Oved (Hebrew).

Shapira, Reuven. 1990. Leadership, rotation and the kibbutz crisis. *Journal of Rural Cooperation* 18(1): 55–66.

Shapira, Reuven. 1992. Non-leadership in Israel: The paradox of *rotatzia,* fast promotion and 'parachuting'. *International Problems, Society and State* 31(1): 56–77 (Hebrew).

Shapira, Reuven. 1995. The voluntary resignation of outsider managers: Interkibbutz rotation and Michels's 'Iron Law'. *Israel Social Science Research* 10(1): 59–84.

Shapira, Reuven. 2001. Communal decline: The vanishing of high-moral leaders and the decay of democratic, high-trust kibbutz cultures. *Sociological Inquiry* 71(1): 13–38.

Shapira, Reuven. 2005. Academic capital or scientific progress? A critique of the studies of kibbutz stratification. *Journal of Anthropological Research* 61(3): 357–380.

Shapira, Reuven. 2008. *Transforming Kibbutz Research.* Cleveland: New World Publishing.

Shapira, Reuven. 2011. Institutional combination for cooperative development: How trustful cultures and transformational mid-levelers overcame old guard conservatism. In: J. Blanc and D. Colongo (Eds.), *Co-Operatives Contributions to a Plural Economy*. Paris: L'Harmattan, 75–90.

Shapira, Reuven. 2012a. High-trust culture, the decisive but elusive context of shared co-operative leaderships. In: J. Heiskanen et al. (Eds.), *New Opportunities for Co-Operatives: New Opportunities for People*. Mikkeli, Finland: University of Helsinki Press, 154–167. http://www.helsinki.fi/ruralia/julkaisut/pdf/Publica tions27.pdf

Shapira, Reuven. 2012b. Becoming a triple stranger: Autoethnography of a kibbutznik's long journey to discoveries of researchers' faults." In: H. Hazan and E. Hertzog (Eds.), *Serendipity in Anthropological Research: The Nomadic Turn*. Farnham (UK): Ashgate Press, 93–108.

Shapira, Reuven. 2016a. Rethinking the reverence of Stalinism in the two major kibbutz movements. *Israel Affairs* 22(1): 20–44. http://dx.doi.org/10.1080/135 37121.2015.1111640

Shapira, Reuven. 2016b. Co-opted biased social science: 64 years of telling half truths about the kibbutz. *Open Journal of Social Sciences* 4(1): 17–32. http:// dx.doi.org/10.4236/jss.2016.46003

Shapira, Yonatan. 1984. *An Elite without Successors*. Tel Aviv: Sifriat Poalim (Hebrew).

Shapira, Yonatan. 1993. The historical sources of Israeli democracy: Mapay as a dominant party. In: U. Ram (Ed.), *The Israeli Society: Critical Aspects*. Tel Aviv: Brerot, 40–53 (Hebrew).

Shure, Khaim. 2001. *I Bring Him Down From Heaven*. Tel Aviv: Ministry of Defense (Hebrew).

Spiro, Melford E. 1983. Introduction: Thirty years of kibbutz research. In: E. Krausz (Ed.), *The Sociology of Kibbutz*. New Brunswick (NJ): Transaction, 1–6.

Strathern, Marilyn. 2004. *Partial Connections*. Savage (MD): Rowman & Littlefield.

Stryjan, Yohanan. 1989. *Impossible Organizations*. New York: Greenwood.

Topel, Menachem. 1979. *To Build and Be Built: Power Elite in an Egalitarian Community*. M.A. thesis, Sociology and Anthropology Department, Tel Aviv University (Hebrew).

Turner, Ralph H. 1960. Sponsored and contest mobility and the school system. *American Sociological Review* 25(6): 855–867.

Wallerstein, Immanuel. 2004. *The Uncertainties of Knowledge*. Philadelphia: Temple University.

Warhurst, Christopher. 1996. High society in a workers' society: Work, community and kibbutz. *Sociology* 30(1): 1–19.

Yadlin, Aharon. 1989. The budget of the movement for 1989. *Kibbutz*, January 4 (Hebrew).

Yatziv, Gadi. 1999. *The Sectorial Society*. Jerusalem: Bialic Institute (Hebrew).

7 Conclusions, Discussion, and Plausible Solutions

The findings of prevalent immoral mismanagement in "jumper"-managed I-KRCs offer a plausible explanation for the many corporate scandals: the common practice of managerial career advancement by "jumping" among firms, often with minimal job-pertinent know-how and *phronesis*, encouraged practicing CCMI and Im-C; habituating immoral practices on the way to top positions socialized some executives to the corrupt use of scandalous practices of the kinds recently exposed. Although the kibbutz field differed much from the corporate world and none of the 32 executives studied was publicly accused of unethical behaviors, nevertheless at least 22 of them used Im-C practices resembling those commonly found in this world. Albeit, immoral mismanagement was less common among mid-levelers, only a minority of some 25% opted for CCMI; the majority opted for contrary high-moral trust, creating ignorance-exposing vulnerable involvement but some of them did so only in their jurisdictions (e.g., deputy PM Danton). Considering this finding as against 72% of PMs and 80% of CEOs who avoided such involvement suggests that the higher one advances through "jumping"/"parachuting" the more one tends to practice CCMI-Im-C, in accord with Piff et al.'s (2012) findings that the higher one's status, the lower her/his morality; this further suggests that the common practice of career advancement by "jumping" and CCMI-Im-C was fertile soil that bred scandalous executives.

Answers to the research questions are mostly in the affirmative: use of CCMI was a common dark secret that defended managers' authority, jobs, and careers; normative *rotatzia* and "parachuting" encouraged career advancement by "jumping," which mostly engendered CCMI, Im-C, and mismanagement, while the mid-levelers who opted for trust-creating vulnerable involvement enabled ignorant bosses to practice CCMI and Im-C by "riding" on their successes that furthered bosses immoral mismanagement. The context of the oligarchic kibbutz field encouraged CCMI and Im-C by offering better prospects of career advancement by patrons' auspices rather than by performance; hence PMs mostly followed the 80% of detached CEOs. Only two CEOs, a few PMs, but most TMs were high morally vulnerably involved, opted for virtuous trust and learning cycles and high-trust local cultures that enabled sound management. Other mid-levelers mostly remained ginning-ignorant due to detachment from ginning problem-solving, and as members of management committees impacted their functioning negatively similar to ignorant PMs. On plants' early days ex-cotton growers who became mid-levelers impacted management positively by learning ginning through vulnerable involvement until acquiring interactional expertise. Their highly committed socialized leadership (Poulin et al. 2007) is explained by seeking advancement through performance while overcoming the 1950s kibbutzim devastation by advancing the new export crop of cotton. However, ignorant conservative PMs "rode" on these mid-levelers' successes, appropriating the resulting prestige, and prolonging their own dysfunctional tenures.

Organizational research missed the inevitable managerial ignorance that comes with promotion and especially "parachuting," the requirement that it be exposed to learn local tacit know-how and *phronesis*, and the common use of CCMI, which explains mismanagement with no need for behaviorist psychological dysfunction explanations. Such a dysfunction is less amenable to change after the choice of CCMI, which is affected by social, cultural, and other factors of which leaders have more control than on psychological dysfunction. Unfortunately, books encourage CCMI, telling managers they cannot and need not acquire much local expertise as they have expert employees for solving specialized problems. But mostly these books do not answer how a newcomer can acquire the local expertise needed to discern experts from smart bluffers, fools, impostors, and ingratiatory "brambles" who talk experts' language and use local knowledge advantages to fool incoming managers for their own ends; it was missed that without trust-creating, ignorance-exposing vulnerable indwelling in practitioner deliberations one cannot create virtuous trust and learning cycles that teach the local language, interactional expertise, premises of local decision-making, sensitivity to the unique contours of circumstances, and the know-how and *phronesis* of "what to do and how to do it, at the right time and with the right people, . . . the crucial knowledge for leading is knowing which facts and theories matter, when to use which skills, and who should perform the actions needed" (Schweigert 2007: 339–340) as well as who should not, despite competence image.

Management books are right in saying that only results indicate expertise for certain, but they missed that an industry-outsider "jumper" cannot discern achievers of results from others unless/until s/he learns local expertises up to having socially learned interactional expertise by ignorance exposure, gaining locals' trust and will to share know-how and *phronesis* (Collins and Evans 2007; Collins and Weinel 2011). Worse still, in a team-operated complex automatic processing plant that combines tens of connected machines, it is hard to pinpoint one's personal impact on results. Also, feedback from analyzing results often comes late, interfering with the discernment of personal impact, and furthermore, interpretation of results requires expertise while proven experts often interpreted the same results contrarily. A manager cannot decide who is right and who is not without local expertise and without knowing the premises on which interpretations are based (Simon 1957: 227). Informed decisions "draw systematically on all those whose information is relevant" and "[t]here must . . . be a mechanism for testing each person's contribution for its relevance and reliability" (Galbraith 1971: 70), but the prime test mechanism is a *phronesis*-equipped knowledgeable superior who discerns experts' relevant and reliable contributions from the opposite ones of others, one who unlike PM Shavit would discern that educated certified Avi called TM is an impostor, often bluffing, and job-ignorant, while the true expert is the illiterate and trustworthy veteran foreman Nekhas who calls the bluff and exposes Avi's ignorance.

A major reason that most "jumpers" chose CCMI was facing low-trust cultures, with bosses and fellow *pe'ilim* practicing CCMI-Im-C. Swidler (2001) pointed out that a culture shapes human action by repertoires, codes, and institutions it provides to actors. In accord with the maxim that low morality begins at the top (in Hebrew we say, "The fish stinks from the head"; e.g., Kets De Vries 1993) and the finding that higher social class predicts lower morality (Piff et al. 2012), I-KRC bosses' CCMI and covert Im-C taught most "jumpers" an immoral repertoire through codes of conduct involving abuses, bluffs, scapegoating, and other prestige-enhancing and job-defending subterfuges. Previously, as kibbutz managers, *pe'ilim* encountered less use of such immoral means than in I-KRCs; facing vast use of such means by role-partners encouraged use of CCMI and use of information and knowledge as a means of control that shuttered learning and open communication with experts. Remaining ignorant of their own ignorance, *pe'ilim* missed how ignorance and locals' distrust failed them by using similar means, screened information, and other local knowledge advantages.

The institutionalized *rotatzia* norm encouraged the practice of "parachuting" by vacating jobs and encouraging the import of ex-kibbutz officers while making disservice to many of them, failing them despite talent, education, and managerial experience by offering the seemingly less risky alternative of CCMI. An additional explanation for this choice, contrary to the kibbutz ethos and culture, was the common complete ignorance of one's action domain that deterred ignorance exposure. *Rotatzia* also deterred it, as learning local know-how and *phronesis* was bound to become worthless in one's next job elsewhere in the field within a few years. Mostly CEOs and PMs were uncommitted to *rotatzia*, often prolonged their tenures by "riding" on mid-levelers' successes and using patrons' auspices. The combination of *rotatzia* + "parachuting" was found harmful in US and Israeli armed forces, in Imperial China, and *rotatzia* failed ancient Athenians, Latin American states, and Japan in the 1970s–1980s (p. 14). The lack of a general theory of *rotatzia* + "parachuting," with each study focusing on a specific case, explains the continuous belief in their positive effect despite the many negative findings and despite findings indicating the positive effect on management of a long time horizon (p. 79). *Rotatzia* invited immoral "improving" resumes and concealing/scapegoating previous failures as in the corporate world, often causing managerial circulation, which caused vast loss of tacit know-how and *phronesis* acquired by vulnerably involved managers, many of whom could have remained effective even beyond LLCT studies' limit of 12 years, as proven by some cases cited.

Rotatzia + "parachuting" served the rule of the kibbutz field by immoral conservative old-guard leaders and oligarchic elites and then by loyalist successors who lacked critical thinking and continued outdated policies but implemented them even worse due to this lack (e.g., Hirschman 1970) and by seemingly loyal but destructive ignorant autocrats (Thoroughgood et al. 2012). A Strathernian contextualization (Morita 2014) of the plants studied in the kibbutz field further explains *rotatzia* + "parachuting": when plants failed, the kibbutz context supplied rescuers, who habituated vulnerable involvement in egalitarian and democratic kibbutz work units. Aiming at performance-based career advancement, they created virtuous trust and learning cycles and local high-trust successful innovative-prone cultures. These continued only until suppressed by supremacy-defending ignorant Im-C-practicing superiors, PMs, and CEOs. Like a classic Greek tragedy, rescuers could not avoid empowering themselves by their successes, for which they had come, while careerist superiors who lost power suppressed and replaced them by imported loyalists or prospective ones; they often failed and once more rescuing non-careerists were called in, and so on. This seesaw retained ignorant careerist executives' rule over mediocre-functioning I-KRCs and plants.

Contextualization also explains the relative scarcity of rescuers. The officially democratic and egalitarian kibbutz field became autocratic and oligarchic in the 1940s, dominated by conservative, immoral, self-perpetuating leaders who used their immense power to conceal/camouflage their own low morality. These leaders ignored the violation of kibbutz principles by I-KRCs, as they practiced such violation in I-KOs they headed, contrary to the democracy and egalitarianism they preached. This immoral hypocrisy cascaded to I-KRCs' CEOs and PMs (e.g., Liu et al. 2012), encouraging immoral job survival abuses and subterfuges by many. Though *pe'ilim* mostly commenced managerial careers inside kibbutzim as high-moral, performance-seeking careerists, the field context impacted I-KRCs' inner circuits (Gherardi and Perrotta 2011), encouraging CCMI and vicious distrust and ignorance cycles. Learning local knowledge became riskier by secrecy, abuses, and subterfuges common in low-trust plant cultures; only a few *pe'ilim* who brought considerable job-pertinent knowledge and were confident of successful learning chose trustful, vulnerable involvement. Their successes empowered ignorant superiors to add status-symbolizing privileges and to use OPM plant enlargements and technological virtuosity for obviating *rotatzia*. Efficient economies of kibbutzim (Barkai 1977), with many high-trust, innovative-prone production units led by true socialized leaders, paid the price of I-KRCs' inefficiency, while I-KRCs' thriving encouraged the "parachuting" of job-ignorant loyalist *pe'ilim*: executives could assume they would not fail due to such "parachutings," as no I-KRC went bankrupt until the late 1980s crisis and no literature familiar to them rejected this practice,[1] which served their rule and was common in the Israeli context: mostly ex-generals and ex-colonels were "parachuted" to head civilian organizations (Maman 1989). Had the field not obtained Thomas-like rescuers, total failures might have encouraged promotions of competent insiders and prevented institutionalization of "parachuting." The same pertains to the institutionalization of *rotatzia*: the Israeli armed forces use *rotatzia* and Israeli students consider it helpful despite the critical literature cited.

Last but not least, *rotatzia* + "parachuting" pruned the best experts by destructive conflicts (Deutsch 1969) with unacquainted, distrusted CCMI and Im-C-practicing "jumpers." Such conflicts served the worst insiders, who used "jumpers'" ignorance selfishly, for instance by supporting their bluffs (e.g., Atad) contrary to the opinions of expert insiders who were suppressed and often exited. Positive cliques nurtured by the few trusted knowledgeable leaders defended such experts, but their succession by CCMI-user "jumpers" due to *rotatzia* inflamed conflicts, as for instance such ones tried to get rid of "costly" experts (Northern's PM-5). However, even the "parachuting" of expert managers who avoided CCMI and Im-C sometimes caused conflicts that pruned experts until the newcomers learned the uniqueness of local problems and solutions and could discern experts from impostors.

Organizational research missed the lessons of studies of *rotatzia* + "parachuting" in the cases of Imperial China and US and Israeli armed forces, as well as the lessons of *rotatzia* historical cases, without combining their case studies with social science (Bunzl 2004; Wallerstein 2004). These lessons were missed also by half a century of succession studies that remained inconclusive as to whether insiders or outsiders are preferable, as they missed the point that the decisive variable is not outsiders/insiders but rather newcomers' choice between ignorance-exposing, trust-creating vulnerable involvement and CCMI and Im-C. My study has exposed this decisiveness, because it was phronetic, and it sought a concrete, practical, and ethical answer to a troubling question concerning the "jumpers" rule of major organizations in my kibbutz society, much as the Aalborg Project did for Flyvbjerg (2001, 2006). He persevered, studying the project for years (Flyvbjerg 2001: Ch. 10), and so did I, and as he first published in Danish to help his society (Flyvbjerg 2001: 159), so did I (Shapira 1987).

Beyond the Uniqueness of the Kibbutz Field

Much organizational research was found to be superficial; both knowledge and learning studies and stupidity research ignored the impact of the inevitable ignorance that comes with managerial promotion, missing the

CCMI-Im-C complex, and not explaining how institutionalization of the "jumping"/"parachuting" practice with its specialized institution, the head-hunting firm, made its mark on firms' management and leadership. Practicing CCMI and Im-C explains the common phenomena of ineffective but career-successful managers and corporate-scandalous executives: they practiced CCMI and Im-C along their way to top-level positions and, reaching these, lacked the moral codes that inhibit scandalous use of power; research missed that the outsiderness of "jumpers" encouraged practicing CCMI and Im-C:

1   Large job-pertinent knowledge gaps deprived outsiders of psychological safety required to risk authority and job by ignorance exposure, suspecting that it would damage authority due to failed learning;
2   A lack of mutual trust with locals minimized the chance of locals sharing their know-how and *phronesis*, rather using incomers' ignorance against them;
3   Good prospects of career advancement by CCMI and Im-C due to sponsored mobility in oligarchic autocratic fields/firms;
4   Succeeding by and habituating of Im-C and/or CCMI in previous jobs encouraged repetition;
5   Emulating CCMI and Im-C by superiors and/or by the field/corporate leaders ("the fish stinks from the head"; Liu et al. 2012) and/or by fellow executives/managers;
6   Prospects of expeditious *rotatzia* and "parachuting" to another job with different know-how and *phronesis* discouraged ignorance exposure in order to learn local ones.

Using CCMI was a dark secret unheard of in management books despite Blau's (1955) and Shapira's (1987, 1995) exposure. Mostly incomers missed how its use caused failed job functioning and could not tell students about it, nor did they allude to its stickiness and missed how the larger knowledge gaps they suffered made their dilemma concerning ignorance exposure all the more difficult (Shapira 1995). CCMI signals distrust of locals; they retaliate by keeping their cards close to their chest, keeping managers "out of touch" with local realities while detecting discrepancies between their policies, discourses, and practices, and become cynical about their efforts to establish trust (Collinson 2005: 1428; O'Mahoney 2005).

For Wang and Clegg (2007: 150), it "remains ambiguous . . . how leaders develop trust in . . . followers," as much research missed that incomers' signaling trust of locals from inception is essential for causing virtuous trust and learning cycles, as did Merkaz's Yaakov and Thomas, Northern's Gabi, Southern's Yunus, and other servant transformational leaders.[2] They sought "the highest ideals of public service, and thereby to leave to citizens [=employees] a legacy of trust, integrity, and responsibility, as well as high-quality service delivery and accountability" (Fairholm 2004: 587; also:

Chen and Hsieh 2015). Their vulnerable involvement created a "complex moral relationship between people, based on trust, obligation, commitment, emotion, and a shared vision of the good" (Ciulla 2004: xv). Their successes took years to achieve; contrary to some authors (e.g., Watkins 2003) they did not prove managerial prowess by early major moves; at first they made only urgent essential changes, built up trust by ignorance-exposing immersion in locals' deliberations, learned while helping problem-solving, and "actively engaged in the work of change" (Grint and Holt 2011: 92). They effected major changes after becoming trusted and knowledgeable, enjoyed locals' sharing of know-how and *phronesis*, discerned experts from others, listened to them, and succeeded with the latter's cooperation (Bennis 1989: 17; Karaevli 2007).

Unlike the pessimistic conclusion of managerial stupidity studies whereby smart managers are inevitably bound to do dumb things (Wagner 2002), vulnerably involved managers who exposed their ignorance and created trust and learning cycles managed effectively with others' help, doing very few "dumb things." Stupid major mistakes, failures, and wrongs, were effected by "jumpers" who opted for CCMI-Im-C, for instance the near-decade of Israeli gin plants not adopting Movers-automatic feeder innovative technology and investing heavily in an obsolete one, disregarding such proposal by ex-cotton branch manager Deputy PM Danton. My optimistic conclusion is that ubiquitous managerial stupidity is largely preventable by vulnerably involved socialized leaders aimed at career success by performance, who suppress CCMI and Im-C users through high-trust, innovation-prone cultures of openness that encourage learning local know-how and *phronesis*, and discerning and discarding of CCMI users, incompetents, bluffers, "brambles," etc. Such cultures often shape high-moral mid-levelers, and executives can make them all-organizational by following their lead and following other high-trust firms while adopting truly anti-oligarchic norms of leaders' succession proposed below.

This conclusion supports considerable literature on such cultures, shaped by high-moral leaders who became transformational whenever transformation was required. But as the review in Chapter 3 untangled, leadership research rarely discerned the mutual trust with such leaders that led to virtuous learning cycles from the unilateral trust called for by charismatic leaders who distrust followers, avoid vulnerable involvement, manage autocratically, and do dumb things due to CCMI. Burns (1978) and some others alluded to transformational leaders' succeeding by mutual trust (p. 79), a point missed by many who also missed that virtuous trust and learning cycles are essential for effective management and servant transformational leadership. The literature on managerial knowledge and learning and on managerial stupidity revealed the indispensability of tacit know-how and *phronesis*, learned by practicing jobs and participating in practitioner communities, but missed the common CCMI and managers' use of their powers and immoral means to keep CCMI a dark secret. Also missed was that the higher one's position, the easier it is to conceal CCMI by detachment, as did most of the CEOs and PMs studied. Mostly managerial knowledge and learning studies missed five prime insights:

1   Managers' detachment/seductive-coercive involvement explains ignorance of job-essential know-how and *phronesis* held and developed by practitioners;
2   CCMI by both practices defended authority and jobs and advanced the careers of job-incompetent managers who used immoral means to conceal incompetence;
3   Im-C accompanied CCMI, which shuttered performance-based, high-moral career advancement;
4   Practicing Im-C was kept a dark secret by concealing/camouflaging use of CCMI by immoral means and scapegoating others for managers' own mismanagement;
5   The CCMI-Im-C complex was a vicious and stubborn personal strategy rarely amenable to change by those who embraced it when taking charge (below).

This omission emphasized 66 years of repeated findings of negative effects of managers' Im-C (Riesman 1950), which only recently led to a few studies of managerial ignorance and incompetence, while stupidity studies missed the dark secret of how CCMI use leads to stupidity independent of psychological dysfunction. Findings showing that autocracy kept managers ignorant (e.g., Gittell 2000; Gouldner 1954) did not penetrate this dark secret; its untangling here indicates that practicing CCMI-Im-C often undermined one's authority, job, and career, encouraging additional defenses:

1   Conservatism minimized the necessary expertise for sound decision-making and helped suppress innovative, knowledgeable subordinates empowered by successes;
2   Avoiding innovations, especially locally proposed ones, spared the need to assess and consider proposers' expertise, proposals' feasibility, and their success prospects, bound to expose managers' ignorance and incompetence;
3   Minimizing the consulting of outside experts and barring employees from consulting with them, even if this left problems unsolved, sometimes faking solutions instead;
4   CCMI was enhanced by avoiding experts' controversies and deferring/abusing/canceling controversial decisions that required expertise;
5   Adopting experts' views according to their prestige, status, and power rather than their appropriately solving problems, which one's ignorance and lack of open and trustful communication with them prevented evaluating;

6 Bolstering one's own views by political means: recruiting patrons' and fellow managers' support and "parachuting"/promoting according to loyalty or prospective loyalty rather than proven capability;

7 Accepting the mistaken decisions of CCMI-user patron(s) to retain her/his (their) auspices;

8 Modeling CCMI and Im-C to incomers encouraged their taking this example, leaving them ignorant and dependent on bosses' backing that ensured unquestioned loyalty;

9 Never admitting one's own mistakes, wrongs, and failures even after it was clearly proven to defend CCMI;

10 Appropriating to oneself subordinates' successes, which presumably proved one's job-expertise, bolstering one's authority and power.

My findings support Ficarrotta's (1988) proposal of the violation of moral principles as a prime criterion of negative Im-C, better than Feldman and Weitz's (1991) advancement by non-performance-based means. Some such means are morally benign as is loyalty to superiors that is fair and just; they become a repugnant sin when using bluffs, subterfuges, and other immoral means to defend authority and job and to gain promotion. Arendt (1963) asserted that few vices were more vicious than Im-C, but research did not explain this viciousness as do my findings: opting for CCMI led to Im-C by vicious distrust and ignorance cycles which were hard to reverse because using defensive, immoral means and secrecy ruined trust; building it anew required of a manager to actively engage in getting rid of immoral practices:

1 Exposing one's own ignorance and incompetence by vulnerable involvement;

2 Admitting one's own vicious use of immoral defensive means;

3 Taking responsibility for mistakes and failures engendered by this vicious use;

4 Apologizing about these and promising to use only high-moral means;

5 Proving trustworthiness by: 1) exposing other dark managerial secrets, 2) granting discretion to employees, 3) proving integrity by deeds matching one's words, 4) caring sincerely, benevolently, and consistently for employees' vital interests.

These requirements help make CCMI and Im-C sticky practices; their users, especially "jumpers," don't know how ignorant they are, nor what ignorance exposure will look like. They learn by hearing contrasting expert views that problems are often incorrectly formulated and/or ill-defined, lacking essential information, and have no single correct answers. They may presume that knowledgeable locals can help generate correct formulations and solutions, but gaining their help requires trust that necessitates taking unknown risks of ignorance exposure, and without taking them from inception one faces the above quintuple hard tasks; no wonder no CCMI-user *pa'il* ceased its use. This stickiness was exemplified by the three Merkaz managers who "soothed" one another for months rather than coping with the plant's master debacle that paralyzed it for some 25% of the time and considerably degraded its fiber quality. As cited, only one "parachutist," an Austrian expatriate CEO in Norway, was known to change from initial detachment to vulnerable involvement (Holtskog 2014: 161–162).

The immoral mismanagement revealed conclusively proves the need to discard *rotatzia* + "parachuting": *rotatzia* is a sodom bed; equal tenures are rationed to CCMI users and other incompetents who should have been replaced early and to successful leaders who are capable of remaining effective, trusted and high-moral, even transformational, for 10–12 years or more. Worse still, as explained, *rotatzia* helps entrench dysfunctioning oligarchic higher-ups by weakening mid-levelers, the latter mostly accept *rotatzia* as they find patrons whose auspices enable circulation among privileged managerial positions rather than descending back to the ranks (Shapira 2005). Circulation means "jumping," hence discarding of *rotatzia* is necessary in order to stop "jumping"/"parachuting." However, the alternative of no succession norm is even worse, as proven by oligarchy theory studies and LLCT research. Thus, part 1 of the solution consists of finding an alternative to *rotatzia*, while parts 2 and 3, which complement part 1, consist of nurturing trustworthy successor executives and democratic participative management who fairly care for all stakeholder interests.

Solution, Part 1: Executives' Succession upon Entering the Dysfunction Phase

A proper succession system should replace successful leaders by a democratic process before they become irreplaceable due to accumulated power, prestige, and intangible capital. A good example is the fourth election of F. D. Roosevelt after he violated in 1940 the 131-year informal norm of two-term-only tenure by his third election. Roosevelt's effectiveness diminished during the last year of his third term due to deteriorating health, which he concealed by using wartime censorship of the press; his re-election furthered this dysfunction for five months until his death.[3] Thus, a prime unsolved leadership problem is the timely succession of effective successful leaders as they reach the final dysfunction phase, before entrenching through accumulated advantages. A succession system aimed at obtaining high-moral, trusted and trusting effective leaders would have to replace early ineffective ones and allow full effectiveness periods to others who are replaced only when they begin dysfunctioning.

1 Current Moderately Successful Alternatives to Rotatzia

The half a century of succession research did not solve the problem of leaders' timely succession to prevent oligarchic entrenchment. LLCT research ignored this problem,[4] maybe because a few wise leaders who were aware of the dangers of oligarchic entrenchment without succession norms introduced two moderately successful norms that considerably reduced the number of entrenched dysfunctional leaders.

Large corporations obviate leaders' entrenchment tendency by rewarding early retirement of CEOs with generous severance benefits known as "golden parachutes" (p. 91). Vancil (1987: 83) found this a success, as only 13% of CEOs stayed longer than the maximum anticipated tenure of 12 years (1987: 79). This expensive instrument, however, has considerable negative effects: like *rotatzia* it is formally unrelated to a leader's degree of job success; hence it allows dysfunctioning CEOs who wish to do so unlimited self-perpetuating immoral mismanagement; one who continued was Enron's 15-year CEO and chairman Lay, who used these years for multi-billion-dollar fraud. Secondly, due to its egotistical nature, self-serving deeds are encouraged, such as adding outsiders who have granted generous "parachutes" elsewhere to the Board of Directors (Davis 1994: 220). The huge "golden parachute" of US$28 million awarded to ex-HP CEO Fiorina, plus some US$80 million she was paid for six years of failure that took her successor years to correct (Johnson 2008) exemplifies the faults of this solution, which does not encourage true socialized high-moral effective leadership with which employees could identify (Haslam et al. 2011).

Two centuries ago a more democratic and much more economical solution was created by two US presidents: both successful Washington in 1797 and Jefferson in 1809 declined seeking a third term in office, creating a norm that let public trust decide who would continue for a second four-year term, while limiting the presidency to a maximum of two terms. This norm survived without legislation until F. D. Roosevelt's violation, and was reinstated in 1951 as the 22nd amendment to the constitution (Sobel 1975).

Both Roosevelt's violation of the Washington-Jefferson norm and violations of *rotatzia* by kibbutz leaders prove the vulnerability of a normative limit, thus, a more robust solution is required. Roosevelt's violation was not just an outcome of voters' trust in him; probably no less significant were the power and capital he accumulated during eight years in office that gained him the support of influential figures, of many loyalists that he promoted to his administration, etc. Hence, the 55% of the votes that he received in 1940 included a significant part of the constituency that might not have really trusted him and would not have voted for him without the power and intangible capital that he accumulated during eight years on the job. Thus, the intruding effect of this power and capital should be neutralized if trust in a leader is to be the factor deciding office continuity, enabling longer periods only to socialized, high-moral trusted leaders who are still in their effectiveness phase. Neutralization can be a threshold of higher trust, for instance, requiring a two-thirds majority for a third term rather than the simple majority required for the first two terms. For instance, in Israel's 1977 elections the Labour Party pruned out many old guards who already held Knesset (parliament) seats for two or more terms and intended to continue by making the minimal 60% support of its council a condition for candidacy for an additional term (Brichta 1986: 23).

2 A Trust-Based Escalating Majority Solution for Executive Succession

The idea of a higher majority threshold for political decisions of special importance is not new in democracies, and is common in deciding constitutional changes. The question of whether leaders should continue beyond eight years is of special importance, since history shows that an additional four years can often make a leader irreplaceable democratically. One example among many was Roosevelt's fourth term, obtained in November 1944 despite his deficient functioning for most of that year. As cited, US "golden parachutes" were aimed at a maximum of 12 years and this is compatible with the LLCT research finding that CEOs mostly reached their dysfunction phase within 12 years (p. 83). However, there are a few who remain effective beyond 12 years. For instance, Ben-Gurion's most praised deed, the establishment of the State of Israel, was effected after he had headed the Jewish community in Palestine for 13 years, and Tabenkin led the establishing of the underground Palmach army which made possible Israel's establishment after 15 years of KM leadership. Thus, allowing highly trusted leaders 12 years in office, and a few ultra-trusted ones even 16 years, seems preferable as it slows down promotion by allowing full use of their phase of effectiveness.[5] The findings of Karaevli and Zajac (2013) support a slow-down of CEO successions that enhances corporate stability: "parachutings" of outsider CEOs aimed at causing turnarounds met with more success in stable firms with long-tenured predecessors.

Following the idea of requiring a larger majority for re-election for a third term, I propose that re-election for a fourth term should require an even larger majority than 60–66%, such that only very few exceptional leaders who remain high-moral, trustworthy, effective, and creative for 12 years will gain it. This threshold should be high enough to shatter further continuity in accord with a targeted limit of 16 years; as far as is known no leader ever remained socialized, high-moral, effective, and avoided self-perpetuation through accumulated power and capital for more than 16 years. Successful leaders who retained their power longer performed horrible atrocities: Mao Zedong had been in power for 22 years when his Great Leap Forward cost the lives of 18–45 million people.[6] Thus, a fifth-term threshold on the same gradient should have to be above 100%, i.e., impossible.

How much higher does each threshold have to be in order to assure that? Must the gradient of threshold elevation be linear or is an exponential one more proper?

Goode (1978) found leaders' prestige tends to exponential growth with continuity; thus, in order to neutralize its growth, exponential growth of majority thresholds should be required. A first re-election contest is selective even with a simple majority threshold, as indicated, for instance, by only some half of US presidents being chosen to a second term. Hence, higher majority thresholds are required only from a second re-election onward, and they should be raised exponentially. Thus, if a re-election for a third term will require, let us say, a 66% majority, then for the fourth term, the threshold for re-election will have to be an 88% majority, and this creates a built-in mechanism that bars a fifth term since the same elevation gradient means over 122% majority, i.e. impossible. This limitation will be more robust than a formal limit of terms, if it will be applied not only to leaders but also to all executives, such as corporate division heads and PMs in multi-plant I-KRCs (Shapira 1987: Ch. 28).

Using the trust-based escalating majority succession norm offers many advantages over both "golden parachutes" and the US presidential norm, while it raises the major question of which constituency will decide a leader's succession? This will be discussed in the next section, but part of the answer seems clear: directors or even directors plus corporate executives often miss a CEO's change to job dysfunction versus mid-levelers involved in deliberations who discern a leader's dysfunction, including avoiding major deliberations, at an early stage; hence their inclusion in constituencies is desirable. As against "golden parachutes," the advantages of the proposed escalating majority succession norm are:

1   Frees the firm from heavy costs and impending low morality and corruption;
2   Spares adding a CEO's loyalists to the Board for a prospective generous "parachute" (Davis 1994: 220) and thus helps retain a qualified effective Board,
3   Encourages CEOs performance by connecting it causally to their tenures;
4   Discourages detached CCMI, encouraging a CEO's vulnerable involvement in trustful learning to know and consider the views and interests of non-Board constituency, facilitating a high-trust culture and effective leadership;
5   The involved CEO is familiar with uncertified best experts (e.g., Nekhas) and "Rudies" who know which knowledge is held by whom (Stewart 1997: 99); learning from them s/he can encourage contributions to the firm's know-how, *phronesis*, and innovation.
6   Involving the ranks in succession decisions minimizes the impact of instability in the markets and other external events on successions; an enhanced firm stability promises the success of an outsider-led turnaround when required (Karaevli and Zajac 2013).

As against the presidential succession norm of two four-year terms at most, the advantage of the proposed succession norm is quite obvious: by not replacing leaders who are still effective after eight or 12 years it spares nominations which cost the firm inevitable greenhorn mistakes or even worse—immoral mismanagement; it enables an incumbent major initiatives born from years of leadership, which an innovative successor may try but fail without the experience, know-how, *phronesis*, and accumulated power and capital of a trusted veteran leader (e.g., Ben-Gurion, Tabenkin). A leader's defined tenure will enhance the grooming of a successor: well-groomed successors were heir apparents for several previous years, e.g., presidents or COOs (Bigley and Wiersema 2002); by setting a timetable for impending succession the proposed norm creates a clear timeframe that encourages grooming. The leader is ensured of no abrupt succession and the heir apparent of a forthcoming chance for advancement. Such grooming without a succession norm cures the uncertainty of an unlimited grooming period; without it, heir apparents may use the visibility of such jobs to "jump" the competition or to elsewhere to escape the uncertainty.

3 Managerial Levels and Constituency: Knowledgeable Mid-Levelers and Stakeholders

Hitherto I did not problematize the succession of secondary executives such as PMs. Both the literature and my findings indicate that detached CEOs preferred to conserve seemingly effective loyalist PMs, unable to identify their dysfunction as Akerman missed it concerning Moav while all employees knew that plant's functioning had deteriorated since Yaakov left. To prevent such dysfunction and to make the succession norm more robust, it will be better to apply it to both CEOs and PMs, periodically deciding succession or continuity of the incumbent in each office. In each case a proper knowledgeable constituency will decide that includes mid-levelers who are the first to discern that a leader has reached the dysfunction phase. A different constituency size may be suitable, considering various pros and cons of different sizes. The literature on democratic participative management points to the advantages of a larger constituency of all managerial ranks, and many authors believe in a democracy that includes all employees (pp. 90–92) as in Semco (Semler 1993). However, whether more or less participatory alternatives are chosen, one limit is clearly required: voting succession must be limited to those with minimal seniority who have some perspective of the CEO's/PM's performance that informs their vote.

However, what about the participation of other stakeholders such as owners and users of the firm's services? Instrumental stakeholder theory studies propose a positive relationship between fairness toward stakeholders and firm performance (Bridoux and Stoelhorst 2014); disregard of such fairness engenders the dysfunctioning of a veteran leader, thus inclusion of stakeholders in the constituency that decides succession could have a positive effect provided they are involved and learn enough to assess a leader's functioning. Had kibbutz cotton branch managers who knew Merkaz through frequent visits had a say in Moav's succession, he might have been replaced after Yaakov left. The opposite case is minimally involved stakeholders, as for instance Lowland Gin's private farmers who complied with PM Avraham's detached mismanagement with dysfunctioning TM-1 (p. 123). Stakeholders' motivation is often merely financial, and unless managerial dysfunction engenders crises and losses, they may remain silent; hence their inclusion in a constituency requires escorting measures that enhance their involvement to keep them informed. Unfortunately, a CEO/PM who commences dysfunction uses his power to conceal this information; hence such measures must be instituted from inception as constitutional.

An enlarged constituency may be futile without provisions to prevent autocratic secrecy that results in a low-trust culture in which everyone keeps their cards close to their chest. Such a culture may emerge gradually through minor changes only towards the leader's dysfunction phase, and the gradual nature of this change may help it avoid notice. Also, a leader's technological choices can enhance autocracy and help conceal dysfunction (p. 91). One remedy is norms that enhance open information and make it easy to discern leaders' immoral efforts at concealment; these achieve high-trust relations in democratic organizational cultures. Such cultures flourish by preferring members' and community needs over immediate profits, though long-range profitability is also sought to retain competitiveness. This is exemplified by cooperatives such as some kibbutzim and the Basque Mondragon federation of cooperatives, high-trust Japanese firms, Brazilian democratically managed Semco, the British John Lewis Partnership, and many employee-owned democratic firms.[7]

4 Insider Successors

The next crucial question is: where do successors come from?

Succession studies failed for half a century to conclude whether insiders or outsiders were preferable while recent students found superiority of insiders.[8] Unlike I-KOs, the above-cited democratic firms mostly prefer insiders, and as cited, Jim Collins (2001) found that 95.2% of best firms' CEOs were insiders, versus only 69% of the second-best firms. My findings suggest that the prime reason for the superiority of insiders is their lesser dilemma concerning ignorance exposure, as they enjoy psychological safety due to much more local know-how, *phronesis*, and referred expertise than outsiders; by ignorance-exposing vulnerable involvement they create virtuous trust and learning cycles and function more effectively. Moreover, inside successors can be well-groomed for the job by years of learning the firm's working knowledge and culture in deputy jobs, while trust relations created with many role-partners during grooming also encourage vulnerable involvement and learning.

Moreover, insiders are integral to constituencies that include mid-levelers, because a truly democratic vote takes place when the choice is between known alternatives. A succession ballot truly measures trust only if an incumbent is equated with well-known candidates for succession, and not if voters equate him with prestigious outsiders for whom the true reasons for their successes are barely known, their mistakes and failures concealed or masked in order to "jump," and their competencies, beliefs, aims, trustworthiness, and commitments unknown. "The neighbor's grass is always greener" since, due to this lack of knowledge, an outsider's prestige is not contaminated by his real past as that of equally talented and competent insiders, while they possess precious local knowledge which he lacks. This knowledge is crucial for the vital decision of whether to expose ignorance; an insider's promotion to leadership by a local constituency expresses trust in her/him, granting initial credit that encourages coping with prime hard-to-solve problems by ignorance-exposing practitioner engagement, creating trust and learning cycles. Insiders' preference enhances effective high-trust cultures for another major reason: as in these cultures the main rewards are received in the long run (Fox 1974), and the major reward is promotion, "parachuting" outsiders curtail this reward for best-performing insiders. An insider successor also enhances employees' trust by her/his promotion, enabling promotions down the managerial line, rewarding other effective insiders for their efforts, versus "parachuting" that signals to prospective successors they would do better to seek "jumping" elsewhere.

All these point to the better prospects of insider successors to shape high-trust, innovation-prone cultures, provided they are not conformist loyalists of dysfunctioning predecessors who retain the outdated policies of the latter but implement them worse (Hirschman 1970). Periodic re-election by proper constituencies, as depicted above, can prevent leaders' dysfunction; mid-levelers are rarely fooled concerning leaders' functioning, as leaders can mislead Board members. Mid-levelers also know much of the work and management records of potential inside successors and their trustworthiness; if the best successors are inside-outsiders, i.e., insiders who grasp the firm as do outsiders but due to inside knowledge spot the roots of its weakness (Bower 2007), then mid-levelers who are familiar with the records of potential successors can choose the inside-outsider capable of overcoming these weaknesses as CEO.

5 Slow Promotion

The trust-based escalating majority solution will slow down managerial promotion, as against other succession systems, by allowing leaders a full effectiveness period. While it will replace successful leaders as they enter the dysfunction phase, Kets De Vries's (1993) findings point to power's negative effects often commencing earlier, after a number of major successes, some loyalist promotions, and cementing a ruling clique. Both Ansell and Fish (1999) and my kibbutz research found that a leader may become indispensable by tripping up critical ascenders through their suppression and pushing out. However, a strong incentive against such low morality can be a succession system that, as Dore (1973: Ch. 9) explains, allows highly trusted leaders 12 years in office, and a few ultra-trusted ones even 16 years, immunizes leaders against an early loss of standing.

Slowing down promotion requires a reward provision, which will encourage talented executives, heads of divisions, and PMs to prefer remaining in office over seeking promotion elsewhere by "jumping." A proper reward could formally symbolize extra trust of better leaders: third and fourth terms decided by re-election by a much higher majority would symbolize extra trust, publicly proving the extra esteem enjoyed by an executive. S/he will be known as an excellent leader since only a few are re-elected for a third term due to support by a majority of more than 66%, and even fewer to a fourth term by a majority of over 88%. This extra esteem may become a prime yardstick for choosing CEOs, while creating a strong incentive for executives to remain for more terms, preferring to seek re-election rather than promotion elsewhere by "jumping."

Solution, Part 2: Nurturing Trustworthy Successor Executives

According to Swidler (1995), the most economical way to change a culture is by changing its codes, which in the case of I-KRCs meant eradicating immoral practices that contradicted the high morality of leaders of successful kibbutzim (Shapira 2008: Chs. 15–16). The prime immoral practice, which all CEOs practiced except for Northern's first CEO and second one Dan, was detachment from practitioner deliberations; one reason the S&GH debacle continued throughout an entire season was Zelikovich's defense of his authority and job by detachment; this emphasizes the simplicity and effectiveness of this immoral strategy in an oligarchic field ruled by dysfunctional conservative old guards. Their rule explains the prevalence of immoral autocracy in I-KRCs and other I-KOs. The proposed succession system would have discouraged such detachment and would have elevated trustworthy and trusting effective insiders. However, elevation of such insiders required proper yardsticks to nurture managers who seem to be prospective high-moral competent executives. Four yardsticks seem best for forecasting which insiders will be such executives if promoted:

1   Habituating vulnerable involvement aimed at learning and problem-solving;
2   Having proved commitment to tasks and seeking advance by performance;
3   Having referred and interactional expertises that fit a firm's major problems;
4   Having a record of socialized, effective, high-moral trusted leadership aimed at creative coping with the most challenging managerial tasks.

These yardsticks can be useful both for choosing among inside candidates and for comparing them to outsiders, if a majority of the constituency prefers considering outsider successors as well, in view of the need of a major strategic change. However, as the relative importance of each yardstick in forecasting who among insiders and outsiders will avoid CCMI and Im-C may differ, further study of this question is suggested.

Second, vulnerable involvement has multiple effects (Shapira 2013); thus, further study is required to ascertain their relative importance in various situations, to help executives use their limited time and efforts effectively. For example, expertise in some domains of a newly promoted insider means "outsiderness" in others, in which only vulnerable involvement will engender virtuous trust and learning cycles; however, can s/he devote all the time required for this involvement and still retain updated proficiency in other domains, in addition to fulfilling all her/his major tasks? This requires research.

Solution, Part 3: Democratic Participation in Small Federated Units

The third essential part of the solution is workplace democracy in other decisions beside leaders' continuity or succession. Subordinates are the first to discern bosses' use of CCMI, thus no further study is needed in order to know that their democratic participation in other major decisions is also required to suppress the tendency to CCMI and Im-C. However, research on such participation in kibbutzim (Chapter 6) and in other types of democratic work organizations pointed to the negative impact of oligarchic change with success and growth on democratic participation in decision-making. One explanation was mutual distrust between members and dysfunctioning oligarchic old guards blocking the knowledge sharing required for the creativity necessary to retain the viability of participative democracy amid success and growth, as crippled democracy deterred participation and minimal participation furthered degeneration of democracy (Argaman 1997).

Stryjan's (1989) study of cooperatives and kibbutzim pointed to this omission: he found that with success and growth cooperatives used many non-participating hired workers and became bureaucratic, hierarchic, autocratic, and conservative, while participative democracy vanished with no creative solutions for its problems caused by growth and success. He studied kibbutzim at the height of their success, before the crisis of the late 1980s, and explained this success by their remaining small, democratic, and creative, eagerly sharing knowledge of successful innovations which were subsequently adopted by other kibbutzim, while I-KOs performed functions that required economies of scale.[9] However, my studies found that, like all kibbutz students, Stryjan missed the negative impact of oligarchic processes in I-KOs and leaders' dysfunction that caused immoral mismanagement, which destroyed trust, democracy, participation, and creativity in both I-KOs and kibbutzim (Chapter 6). But although old guards' dysfunction phase commenced in the 1940s, kibbutzim continued to flourish for three decades despite leaderships' negative impact, since in many work units or their segments in both I-KOs and kibbutzim creativity continued until the end of the 1970s, for instance Thomas's automatic feeder. This clearly proves the essential role of a federative structure that keeps units small, enabling democratic participation and creativity; this is part 3 of the solution, besides leaders' timely succession and the nurturing of trustworthy, knowledgeable inside successors. Brumann's (2000) study of all known successful communal societies corroborated this: only communes with a federative structure continued to succeed beyond the life span of their founders, since this structure gave individual communes autonomy that prevented suppression of local creativity by a leader of the whole communal society who had become an autocratic oligarchic conservative ruler. A federative structure is found in the successful Brazilian Semco group of democratic firms, with over 3,000 employees and sales of over US$240 million; business units are kept smaller than 150 employees by splitting off part of an overly large unit and establishing it as a new unit.[10] More proof is found in the history of the Basque Mondragon group of cooperatives: a major reason for their 1974 crisis was the lack of a federative structure in their larger cooperative which numbered thousands; such a structure was subsequently created and resulted in success (Whyte and Whyte 1988: 91–102; 159–165).

Similar to kibbutzim, federative Semco firms also adopted managerial rotation, but unlike the *rotatzia* norm this was flexible and democratic: unit managers must be replaced within two to five years by their own or members' choice, so that 20–25% of them changed jobs every year (Nayak 2013: 9). However, Semco enhanced trust and creativity by profound participative democracy that empowers employees and enables much discretion, making them true partners (e.g., Fox 1974): they control managers more than in most cooperatives and, like early-day kibbutzim, deciding every major decision, not only choosing and replacing managers but also their salaries, as well as their own salaries and many other decisions, while in order to reach wise decisions they are informed of firms' finances and their union organizes courses on reading financial balance sheets. Semco firms also encourage employees to constantly learn additional jobs, which enables the agile reaction of a firm to market changes with no need to seek new hires; hence turnover is less than 1% annually. With such a low turnover the investment in creating a knowledgeable workforce is clearly worthwhile and enhances democracy.[11]

Some Open Questions Concerning the Proposed Solution

A federative structure can enable success and growth well beyond Semco's 3,000 people, up to more than 70,000 people, as was true of the kibbutz movement and the John Lewis Partnership, while the Mondragon group of cooperatives even exceeded 80,000 employees, but they mostly were not members and could not vote (Basterretxea and Albizu 2011; Errasti 2013). Emery (1995) calls for a "participative design: effective, flexible and successful, now!"; but in all three large federations, unlike Semco, democracy is problematic and far from truly participative, thus one returns to Stryjan's (1989) problem: how to ensure creativity that would maintain democracy with success and growth?

Periodic democratic leader elections and impending succession in case of insufficient trust is one provision for participation and against leaders' CCMI and Im-C that may encourage committed creative problem-solving in the service of common aims. Democracies use many additional provisions to achieve such encouragement, such as constitutions, legislatures, courts, and legitimate sanctions, and likewise do some democratic firms, sometimes quite successfully. For instance, the John Lewis Partnership has a constitution decreed by its founder, John Spaden Lewis, in 1930 when turning his firm into a trust according to British trust law, with which it grew throughout 86 years to the above scale (Storey et al. 2014: 629). But as everyone knows, legal provisions do not prevent many tenured leaders from becoming self-serving self-perpetuators, as for instance the Israeli Cooperative Association Law did not prevent it in I-KOs. This does not mean that these provisions are superfluous, rather the opposite is true, but it calls for research on the effect of various provisions and norms on democracy in work organizations.

For instance, is cooperatives' ownership equality norm necessary to maintain a lively democracy which timely and effectively reacts against leaders' self-serving deeds? In the literature, a growing number and percentage of hired workers in cooperatives signals democracy degeneration, but Darr and Lewin (2001) found that this was not true of Israeli taxi cooperatives: cooperatives with a majority of hired drivers were more democratic than those with only a minority of such drivers. This is compatible with Fox (1974: Ch. 2), who pointed out that high-trust relations require that everyone is considered an equal partner in decision-making concerning his/her work, and not an employee whose fate and the fate of his/her work unit is decided by superiors chosen by others. As cited in Brazilian Semco, in which the Semler family holds 50% of equity, effective high-trust democracy seemingly prevails, as business information is available to every employee and there are more provisions that enlighten everyone's participation in decision-making. Thus, ownership differences must not hamper trustful democracy if everyone with minimal seniority and proven trustworthiness becomes an equal partner. Unfortunately, the study of cooperative democracy degeneration missed the problem of information openness and members' acquiring business knowledge, much as kibbutz research missed it, as well as how leaders' holding many cards close to their chest and censoring publications had a negative impact on democracy (Shapira 2016). The exception was KA Movement leader Hazan, who regularly discussed with members of his Kibbutz Mishmar Ha'emek unpublicized national political information (Tzachor 1997: 180), one explanation for the exceptionally lively democracy of this successful kibbutz (Argaman 1997). But historians of kibbutzim and cooperatives and biographers of their leaders missed leaders' and managers' aversion of followers' contributions to decision-making (e.g., Fast et al. 2014) much as management students missed CCMI, thus the study of both and concomitant Im-C awaits cooperative management and leadership scholars.

Another question awaiting them, concerning the choice between managerial openness through vulnerable involvement and CCMI, is managers' and employees' mutual impacts on choice continuity. While CCMI and Im-C are sticky practices, an outsider who chooses involvement and trusting locals who in turn try to teach him may fail to do so if he is too ignorant of local working knowledge premises and/or is foolish and/or for other reasons, and his failure induces them to stop trying. It is plausible that he will then regress to CCMI and Im-C, but this is open to further study.

Further study is also suggested of the five prime factors that impact the choice between vulnerable involvement and detachment/seductive-coercive control:

1) The extent of pertinent know-how, *phronesis*, and interactional and referred expertises;
2) The extent of trust relations with locals;
3) The extent of having a habitus of vulnerable involvement aimed at learning;
4) Career prospects with either vulnerable involvement or detached/coercive CCMI;
5) Organizational contexts that encourage one choice or the other.

The relative weight of each of these factors has yet to be studied and explained. It seems that a lack of trust relations due to "parachuting" encouraged the use of CCMI equally in all managerial ranks, while the first and third factors mostly impacted the choices of mid-levelers, and the fourth and fifth factors impacted more executives, but further research is required in order to reach firm conclusions. Further research is also needed to identify other factors that may be decisive in other contexts than that studied, such as salaries, which were uniform for *pe'ilim* and hence ignored here.

Can the Proposed Solution Ensure High-Trust, Innovation-Prone Cultures?

The last question to be answered is whether the proposed solution ensures the high-trust, innovation-prone cultures required for today's large sophisticated work organizations?

Critics may be right in pointing to my own analysis of kibbutzim and I-KOs, which proves that problems of retaining genuine democracy and high-trust cultures in a large and complex modern organizational field cannot be solved by just a few new measures for succession of leaders and executives (Shapira 2008). However, they have to put the proposals in context. These will not only enhance executives' morality, engender high-trust cultures, and encourage innovation by itself, but one can presume that the executives who adopt the proposals will also cope creatively with derivative problems of sustaining such cultures. Their actions will surely use kibbutz and other democratic work organizations' lessons to enhance creativity in the service of advancing high-moral management and trustful cultures, as their etiology is much clearer now. Every history of a viable democracy has witnessed constitutional amendments, and the same will be true of large firms once they adopt the decisive succession system changes.

This is also plausible because once the principle of a higher majority among a relevant constituency decides executives' continuity, an executive will have a stronger incentive to promote what Yankelovich (1991) called high-quality public judgment among constituency, since, when such judgment fully appreciates his/her achievements, it will enhance trust in her/him and career success. This incentive was lacking in I-KRCs mostly because loyalty to oligarchic patrons and cliques gained promotion. High-quality public judgment is feasible where information and knowledge flow freely and sincerely, which is more plausible in high-trust cultures led by high-moral, vulnerably involved servant inside leaders who are transformational whenever a transformation is required. Such cultures have their own self-enhancing tendencies. For instance, they breed cultural creativity, which enhances value consensus that enhances trust and critical journalism, which, in turn, diffuses information and knowledge for high-quality public judgment (Shapira 2008: Ch. 16). When the proposal will change basic succession laws, these self-enhancing tendencies will emerge and ascending trust spirals due to competent, high-moral, and creative leaders will expedite the suppression, side-tracking, and exiting of self-servers and power mongers, as has occurred in creative kibbutzim in their creative periods. These exits will curb opposition to radical innovations and will enable high-trust firms to defeat low-trust rivals in markets.

The proposal can also make major change because it prefers trusted, effective managers who prove themselves for long periods in mid-echelons, over "high fliers," "meteoric" amoral careerists who advance due to seemingly outstanding performance, achieved by brilliant solutions which are often proven to be spurious after the "high fliers" are off the scene and take no responsibility for bad long-term effects. "High fliers" are part and parcel of low-trust bureaucracies where only superiors decide on promotion, causing a negative correlation between career advancement and officers' effectiveness (Luthans 1988). The proposed solution will curb this tendency by preferring trusted servant leaders, because the main yardstick for promotion will not be an officer's few recent successes, but years of effective, creative leadership with a long time horizon (Jaques 1990) and continued high performance achieved by mustering participants' intangible resources for optimal solutions.

With all due modesty required of a proposal which stems from the work of a single student, I do not think the decisiveness of the change I propose is very different from that provided by Washington's and Jefferson's succession norm which spared the US many perils that have troubled Latin America's *rotational* presidents who were ruled by entrenched oligarchs behind the throne. Moreover, the great difference between US democracy and that of Latin America emerged despite the partial nature of the US solution: on the one hand, it has caused premature replacement of some presidents while still in their phase of effectiveness, while on the other, it did not bar oligarchization of senators (Drury 1959) and powerful lifetime officials like J. Edgar Hoover.

Notes

1 Classics critical of "parachuting" such as Gouldner's (1954, 1955) were not translated to Hebrew.
2 DePree (1990); Graham (1991); Guest (1962); Hasle and Møller (2007); Karaevli (2007); Semler (1993); Useem et al. (2011); Washburn (2011); Whitener et al. (1998).
3 Sweeny (2001: 183–185); https://en.wikipedia.org/wiki/Franklin_D._Roosevelt
4 Even Ocasio (1994), who mentions Michels, does not deal with oligarchic entrenchment.
5 In addition to Ben-Gurion and Tabenkin I know personally some such leaders; my father was one of them.
6 See: https://en.wikipedia.org./wiki/Mao_Zedong
7 See respectively: Shapira (2008); Morrison (1991); Dore (1973); Semler (1993); Storey et al. (2014); Erdal (2011).
8 On succession studies: Karaevli (2007). On advantageous insiders: Bower (2007); Collins, J. (2001); Heskett (2011); Santora (2004); Shapira (1987, 2008, 2013).
9 See support in: Geherardi and Masiero (1990); Niv and Bar-On (1992); Russell (1995).
10 Nayak (2013); Peterson and Spängs (2006); Semler (1993).
11 See previous footnote and: http://blog.howistheanswer.com/2014/02/19/the-key-to-semco-groups-culture.

References

Ansell, Christopher K., and M. Steven Fish. 1999. The art of being indispensable. *Comparative Political Studies* 32(3): 283–312.
Arendt, Hanna. 1963. *Eichmann in Jerusalem*. New York: Viking Press.
Argaman, David. 1997. *The Kibbutz Will Discuss and Decide*. Ramat Efal: Yad Tabenkin (Hebrew).
Barkai, Haim. 1977. *Growth Patterns of the Kibbutz Economy*. Amsterdam: North-Holland.

Basterretxea, Imanol, and Eneka Albizu. 2011. Management training as a source of perceived competitive advantage: The Mondragon Cooperative Group case. *Economic and Industrial Democracy* 23(2): 199–222.

Bennis, Warren. 1989. *Why Leaders Can't Lead*. San Francisco: Jossey-Bass.

Bigley, Gregory A., and Margarethe F. Wiersema. 2002. New CEOs and corporate strategic refocusing: How experience as heir apparent influences the use of power. *Administrative Science Quarterly* 47(4): 707–727.

Blau, Peter M. 1955. *The Dynamics of Bureaucracy*. Chicago: University of Chicago Press.

Bower, Joseph L. 2007. *The CEO Within*. Boston: Harvard Business School Press.

Brichta, Avraham. 1986. Selection of candidates to the Tenth Knesset. In: Howard R. Penniman and D. J. Elazar (Eds.), *Israel at the Polls 1981*. Bloomington: Indiana University Press.

Bridoux, Flore, and J. W. Stoelhorst. 2014. Microfoundations for stakeholder theory: Managing stakeholders with heterogeneous motives. *Strategic Management Journal* 35(1): 107–125.

Brumann, Christoph. 2000. The dominance of one and its perils: Charismatic leadership and branch structures in utopian communes. *Journal of Anthropological Research* 56(4): 425–451.

Bunzl, Matti. 2004. Boas, Foucault, and the "Native Anthropologist": Notes toward a Neo-Boasian anthropology. *American Anthropologist* 106(3): 435–442.

Burns, James M. 1978. *Leadership*. New York: Harper.

Chen, C. A., and C. W. Hsieh. 2015. Knowledge sharing motivation in the public service sector: The role of public service motivation. *International Review of Administrative Sciences* 81(4): 812–832.

Ciulla, Joanne B. (Ed.). 2004. *Ethics, the Heart of Leadership*, 2nd edition. Westport (CT): Praeger.

Collins, Harry M., and Robert Evans. 2007. *Rethinking Expertise*. Chicago: University of Chicago Press.

Collins, Harry M., and Martin Weinel. 2011. Transmuted expertise: How technical non-experts can assess experts and expertise. *Argumentation* 25: 401–415.

Collins, Jim. 2001. *Good to Great*. New York: HarperCollins.

Collinson, David. 2005. Questions of distance. *Leadership* 1(2): 235–250.

Darr, Asaf, and Alisa Lewin. 2001. Democratic justice regimes in work organizations: The case of Israeli taxi cooperatives. *Economic and Industrial Democracy* 22(3): 383–405.

Davis, Gerald F. 1994. Corporate elite and the politics of corporate control. *Current Perspectives in Social Theory, Supplement* 1: 215–238.

DePree, Max. 1990. *Leadership is an Art*. New York: Dell.

Deutsch, Morton. 1969. Conflicts: Productive and destructive. *Journal of Social Issues* 25(1): 7–42.

Dore, Ronald. 1973. *British Factory—Japanese Factory*. Berkeley (CA): University of California Press.

Drury, Allen. 1959. *Advise and Consent*. New York: Doubleday.

Emery, Fred E. 1995. Participative design: Effective, flexible and successful, now! *Journal for Quality and Participation* 18(1): 6–9.

Erdal, David. 2011. *Beyond the Corporation*. London: Bodley Head.

Errasti, Aniel. 2013. Mondragon's Chinese subsidiaries: Capitalist multinationals in practice. *Economic and Industrial Democracy* 36(3): 479–499.

Fairholm, Matthew R. 2004. A new sciences outline for leadership development. *The Leadership and Organization Development Journal* 25(4): 369–383.

Fast, Nathanel J., Ethan R. Burris, and Caroline A. Bartel. 2014. Managing to stay in the dark: Managerial self-efficacy, ego-defensiveness, and the aversion to employee voice. *Academy of Management Journal* 57(4): 1013–1034.

Feldman, Daniel C., and Barton A. Weitz. 1991. From the invisible hand to the gladhand: Understanding the careerist orientation to work. *Human Resource Management* 30(2): 237–257.

Ficarrotta, Joseph C. 1988. Careerism: A moral analysis of its nature, types, and contributing causes in the military services. Retrieved 14.2.2013: www.isme. tamu.eduJSCOPE88Ficarrotta88

Fox, Alan. 1974. *Beyond Contract*. London: Faber.

Flyvbjerg, Bent. 2001. *Making Social Science Matter*. Cambridge: Cambridge University Press.

Flyvbjerg, Bent. 2006. Making organization research matter: Power, values and *phronesis*. In: S. R. Clegg et al. (Eds.), *Sage Handbook of Organization Studies*. Thousand Oaks (CA): Sage, 357–381.

Galbraith, John K. 1971. *The New Industrial State*. Boston: Houghton Mifflin.

Gherardi, Silvia, and Attilio Masiero. 1990. Solidarity as a networking skill and a trust relation: Its implications for cooperative development. *Economic and Industrial Democracy* 11(5): 553–574.

Gherardi, Silvia, and Manuela Perrotta. 2011. Egg dates sperm: A tale of a practice change and its institutionalization. *Organization* 18(5): 595–614.

Gittell, Judy H. 2000. Paradox of coordination and control. *California Management Review* 42(3): 101–117.

Goode, William J. 1978. *The Celebration of Heroes*. Berkeley (CA): University of California Press.

Gouldner, Alvin W. 1954. *Patterns of Industrial Bureaucracy*. New York: Free Press.

Gouldner, Alvin W. 1955. *Wildcat Strike*. New York: Harper & Row.

Graham, Jill W. 1991. Servant-leadership in organizations: Inspirational and moral. *Leadership Quarterly* 2(2): 105–119.

Grint, Keith, and Clare Holt. 2011. Leading questions: If 'Total Place', 'Big Society' and local leadership are then answers: What's the question? *Leadership* 7(1): 85–98.

Guest, Robert H. 1962. *Organizational Change*. London: Tavistock.

Haslam, S. Alexander, S. D. Reicher, and M. J. Platow. 2011. *The New Psychology of Leadership*. New York: Psychology Press.

Hasle, Peter and Niels Møller. 2007. From conflict to shared development: Social capital in a Tayloristic environment. *Economic and Industrial Democracy* 28(3): 401–429.

Heskett, John. 2011. *The Culture Cycle*. Upper Saddle River (NJ): FT Press.

Hirschman, Albert O. 1970. *Exit, Voice and Loyalty*. Cambridge (MA): Harvard University Press.

Holtskog, Halvor. 2014. *How Industry Makes Knowledge*. PhD thesis, Norwegian University of Science and Technology, Trondheim.

Jaques, Elliot. 1990. *Creativity and Work*. Madison (CN): International Universities.

Johnson, Craig E. 2008. The rise and fall of Carly Fiorina. *Journal of Leadership & Organizational Studies* 15(2): 188–196.

Karaevli, Ayse. 2007. Performance consequences of new CEO 'outsiderness': Moderating effects of pre-and post-succession contexts. *Strategic Management Journal* 28(4): 681–706.

Karaevli, Ayse, and Edward J. Zajac. 2013. When do outsider CEOs generate strategic change? The enabling role of corporate stability. *Journal of Management Studies* 50(7): 1267–1294.

Kets De Vries, Manfred F. R. 1993. *Leaders, Fools, and Impostors*. San Francisco: Jossey-Bass.

Liu, Dong, H. Liao, and R. Loi. 2012. The dark side of leadership: A three-level investigation of the cascading effect of abusive supervision on employee creativity. *Academy of Management Journal* 55(5): 1187–1212.

Luthans, Fred. 1988. Successful versus effective managers. *Academy of Management Executive* 2: 127–132.

Maman, Daniel. 1989. *The Second Career of Top Military Officers and the Civilian Elites 1974–1984*. Jerusalem: Academon (Hebrew).

Morita, Atsuro. 2014. The ethnographic machine: Experimenting with context and comparison in Strathernian Ethnography. *Science, Technology & Human Values* 39(2): 214–235.

Morrison, Roy. 1991. *We Build the Road as We Travel*. Philadelphia: New Society.

Nayak, Amar Kjr. 2013/14. Case study of Semco Partners. *3Continent Master of Global Management*. Retrieved: 24.5.2016: http://threeconitinentcourseforthewick edandbrave.files.wordpress.com

Niv, Amitai, and Dan Bar-On. 1992. *The Dilemma of Size from a System Learning Perspective: The Case of the Kibbutz*. Greenwich (CN): JAI.

Ocasio, William. 1994. Political dynamics and the circulation of power: CEO succession in U.S. industrial corporations 1960–1990. *Administrative Science Quarterly* 39(2): 285–312.

O'Mahoney, Joseph K. 2005. Trust, distrust and anxiety: The new manufacturing philosophy at Gearco. Retrieved 17.8.2008: http://joeomahoney.googlepages. com/JOM_FinalPaper.doc

Peterson, Mary, and Anna Spängs. 2006. *Semco & Freys: A Multiple-Case Study of Workplace Democracy*. M. A. thesis, Södertörns högskola, Stockholm.

Piff, Paul K., D. M. Stancato, et al. 2012. Higher social class predicts increased unethical behaviour. *Proceedings of the National Academy of Science*. Retrieved 8.8.2013: www.pnas.org./cgi/doi/10.1073/1118373109

Poulin, Bryan J., M. Z. Hackman, and C. Barbarasa-Mihai. 2007. Leadership and succession: The challenge to succeed and the vortex of failure. *Leadership* 3(3): 301–325.

Riesman, D. 1950. *The Lonely Crowd*. New Haven: Yale University Press.

Russell, Raymond. 1995. *Utopia in Zion*. Albany (NY): SUNY Press.

Santora, Joseph C. 2004. Passing the baton. *Academy of Management Executive* 18(2): 157–159.

Schweigert, Francis J. 2007. Learning to lead: Strengthening the practice of community leadership. *Leadership* 3(3): 325–342.

Semler, Ricardo. 1993. *Maverick*. New York: Warner.

Shapira, Reuven. 1987. *Anatomy of Mismanagement*. Tel Aviv: Am Oved (Hebrew).

Shapira, Reuven. 1995. 'Fresh blood' innovation and the dilemma of personal involvement. *Creativity and Innovation Management* 4(2): 86–99.

Shapira, Reuven. 2005. Academic capital or scientific progress? A critique of the studies of kibbutz stratification. *Journal of Anthropological Research* 61(3): 357–380.

Shapira, Reuven. 2008. *Transforming Kibbutz Research*. Cleveland: New World Publishing.

Shapira, Reuven. 2013. Leaders' vulnerable involvement: Essential for trust, learning, effectiveness and innovation in inter-co-operatives. *Journal of Co-operative Organization and Management* 1(1): 15–26. http://dx.doi.org/10.1016/j.jcom.2013.06.003

Shapira, Reuven. 2016. Rethinking the reverence of Stalinism in the two major kibbutz movements. *Israel Affairs* 22(1): 20–44. http://dx.doi.org/10.1080/13537121.2015.1111640

Simon, Herbert. 1957. *Administrative Behaviour.* New York: Free Press.

Sobel, Lester A. (Ed.). 1975. *Presidential Succession.* New York: Facts on File.

Stewart, Thomas A. 1997. *Intellectual Capital.* New York: Doubleday.

Storey, John, I. Basterretxea, and G. Salaman. 2014. Managing and resisting 'degeneration' in employee-owned businesses: A comparative study of two large retailers in Spain and the United Kingdom. *Organization* 21(5): 626–644.

Stryjan, Yohanan. 1989. *Impossible Organizations.* New York: Greenwood.

Sweeney, Michael S. 2001. *Secrets of Victory: The Office of Censorship and the American Press and Radio in World War II.* Chapel Hill (NC): University of North Carolina Press.

Swidler, Ann. 1995. Cultural power and social movements. In: H. Johnston and B. Klandermans (Eds.), *Social Movements and Culture.* Minneapolis: University of Minnesota Press, 25–42.

Swidler, Ann. 2001. *Talk of Love.* Chicago: University of Chicago Press.

Thoroughgood, Christian N., W. T. Brian, et al. 2012. Bad to the bone: Empirically defining and measuring destructive leader behaviour. *Journal of Management and Organizational Studies* 19(2): 230–255.

Tzachor, Ze'ev. 1997. *Hazan—A Life Movement.* Jerusalem: Yad Izhak Ben-Zvi (Hebrew).

Useem, Michael, R. Jordan, and M. Koljatic. 2011. How to lead during a crisis: Lessons from the rescue of the Chilean miners. *Sloan Management Review* 53(1): 48–55.

Vancil, Richard F. 1987. *Passing the Baton.* Boston: Harvard Business School Press.

Wagner, Richard K. 2002. Smart people doing dumb things: The case of managerial incompetence. In: R. J. Sternberg (Ed.), *Why Smart People Can Be So Stupid.* New Haven: Yale University Press, 42–63.

Wallerstein, Immanuel. 2004. *The Uncertainties of Knowledge.* Philadelphia: Temple University.

Wang, Karen Y., and Stewart Clegg. 2007. Managing to lead in private enterprise in China: Work values, demography and the development of trust. *Leadership* 3(2): 149–172.

Washburn, Kevin K. 2011. Elena Kagan and the miracle at Harvard. *Journal of Legal Education* 61(1): 67–75.

Watkins, Michael. 2003. *The First Ninety Days.* Boston: Harvard Business School.

Whitener, Ellen M., S. E. Brodt, et al. 1998. Managers as initiators of trust: Exchange relationships framework for understanding managerial trustworthy behaviour. *Academy of Management Review* 23(3): 513–530.

Whyte, William F., and Kathleen K. Whyte. 1988. *Making Mondragon.* Ithaca (NY): ILR Press.

Yankelovich, Daniel. 1991. *Coming to Public Judgement.* Syracuse (NY): Syracuse University Press.

Index

For Product Safety Concerns and Information please contact our EU
representative GPSR@taylorandfrancis.com
Taylor & Francis Verlag GmbH, Kaufingerstraße 24, 80331 München, Germany